Rethinking the Vietnam War

D1454197

WITHDRAWN

Rethinking World Politics
Series Editor: Professor Michael Cox

In an age of increased academic specialization where more and more books about smaller and smaller topics are becoming the norm, this major new series is designed to provide a forum and stimulus for leading scholars to address big issues in world politics in an accessible but original manner. A key aim is to transcend the intellectual and disciplinary boundaries which have so often served to limit rather than enhance our understanding of the modern world. In the best tradition of engaged scholarship, it aims to provide clear new perspectives to help make sense of a world in flux.

Each book addresses a major issue or event that has had a formative influence on the twentieth-century or the twenty-first-century world which is now emerging. Each makes its own distinctive contribution as well as providing an original but accessible guide to competing lines of interpretation.

Taken as a whole, the series will rethink contemporary international politics in ways that are lively, informed and – above all – provocative.

Rethinking the Vietnam War

John Dumbrell

palgrave
macmillan

First published 2012 by
PALGRAVE MACMILLAN

Palgrave Macmillan in the UK is an imprint of Macmillan Publishers
Limited, registered in England, company number 785998, of Houndmills,
Basingstoke, Hampshire RG21 6XS.

Palgrave Macmillan in the US is a division of St Martin's Press LLC,
175 Fifth Avenue, New York, NY 10010.

Palgrave Macmillan is the global academic imprint of the above
companies and has companies and representatives throughout the
world.

Palgrave® and Macmillan® are registered trademarks in the United
States, the United Kingdom, Europe and other countries

ISBN 978–0–333–98490–1   hardback
ISBN 978–0–333–98491–8   paperback

This book is printed on paper suitable for recycling and made from fully
managed and sustained forest sources. Logging, pulping and manufactur-
ing processes are expected to conform to the environmental regulations
of the country of origin.

A catalogue record for this book is available from the British Library.

A catalog record for this book is available from the Library of Congress.

10   9   8   7   6   5   4   3   2   1
21 20 19 18 17 16 15 14   13 12

Printed and bound in China

Contents

Foreword

Reading John Dumbrell's wonderfully balanced study of the Vietnam War brought back memories of many events in my own life – some distant, some of more recent vintage. The distant events begin with me marching, along with many others, in London in the late 1960s in solidarity with Vietnam, then being bombed back into the proverbial 'Stone Age' by someone who many of us then regarded as that 'madman' Richard Nixon, supported by his 'warmongering' adviser, Henry Kissinger. To my generation, then, it all seemed pretty straightforward: America was the enemy. Internationalism was our preferred moral position. Distant strangers like the Vietnamese needed to be helped.

History also seemed to be on our side. Indeed, for a while, it really did look as if it were moving in the right direction. In 1975, Vietnam finally achieved its long-awaited unification. As the decade wore on, the Third World revolt against imperialism scored one striking victory after another. Then, in 1979, Iran finally threw out the hated Shah. The revolt of the oppressed – largely inspired by the example originally set by the brave Vietnamese – still had wind in its sails.

But then it all began to go very badly wrong. In fact, in many ways, it had been going wrong for some time, except we rebels – even the most anti-Stalinist amongst us – just didn't seem to understand it at the time. First, we learned that the Khmer Rouge in Cambodia were doing their level best to wipe out most of their own people: meanwhile, in Vietnam, thousands seemed to be fleeing the country in double-quick time. So much for liberation. This was followed in 1978 and 1979 by two wars between former comrades: first, Vietnam went into Cambodia and then, a year later, China attacked Vietnam. So much for internationalism. And finally, in December 1979, the USSR took it upon itself to invade Afghanistan, murdering the leaders of the communist factions it did not like, before going on to destroy the country in a war of rare savagery whose terrible, tragic consequences we are still living with today.

The rest, as they say, is history. But the drama did not begin in the United States, where the newly-elected Ronald Reagan promised to lay the ghost of the Vietnam War by revitalizing American power. Rather, it began in the USSR – where Gorbachev promised to rethink the whole socialist experience, but ended up unintentially engineering its total collapse by 1991. And the ideological rout did not end there. In the 'Third World', a combination of debt, corruption and sheer economic incompetence saw its end as a progressive project: meanwhile the Chinese, after having slaughtered their own youth in Tiananmen Square, began to embrace the very global capitalism they once claimed to be against. It was all very sobering. It became more sobering still for those of us left standing when we found out that even the Vietnamese – having been abandoned by the Russians – were beginning to experiment with the market, too. Is that what they had been fighting for, many now wondered? Was this what we had been making solidarity for back in the 1960s? Had it, in fact, all been for nothing?

Well, perhaps – and perhaps not. But, as Dumbrell shows in this fine book, whatever else might be said about the Vietnam War, it formed a central part of the experience of a whole generation in the west, and not only for those who made up that diverse band known as the 'New Left'. Indeed, one could easily argue that it was not so much the left but more the American foreign establishment who drew the soberest 'lessons' of all from Vietnam – ones they applied with ruthless, realist conviction during the first Gulf War of 1991, but then seemed to forget entirely when it came to the second Gulf War of 2003.

The debate meantime goes on: not only, as Dumbrell reveals so superbly, amongst American strategists and historians, but also amongst those in the old socialist camp, as well. However, this new discussion – which is throwing up all sorts of intellectual surprises – is now taking place in a totally new world, where Vietnam seems to have embraced globalization with enthusiasm; where its old ally China (now rising fast) is seen in Hanoi as being more enemy than friend; and where its old enemy – the United States of America – is now regarded as a useful stabilizing factor in a region where it was once seen by many as the source of all woes. How fast the changing tides of history makes fools of us all. Important, therefore, today to rethink the 'real' history of the Vietnam War: in part, because it is a fascinating story, but more obviously because we need to be reminded why this most brutal of racist wars waged by the west against a backward country (claiming nearly two million Vietnamese lives) had the impact it did on the international history of the late twentieth century. No doubt many of us suffered from our own kind of utopian thinking back in the 1960s and 1970s, when we chanted those slogans in solidarity with the Vietnamese. But better, I will always feel, to be counted amongst the utopians than amongst those who insisted then, and continue to insist today, that the war was not only necessary but the more desirable option.

MICHAEL COX
IDEAS, London School of Economics

Acknowledgements

I would like to thank Mick Cox, the series editor, as well as Helen Caunce and Steven Kennedy at Palgrave Macmillan. Steven, in particular, has shown saintly patience as this project has developed. I also wish to thank the following people who have shared their thoughts about the war over the years: David Adams, Bobby Garson, Donna Jackson, David Fitzgerald, David Ryan, David Milne, Andrew Preston and David Barrett.

JOHN DUMBRELL
School of Government and International Affairs
Durham University

List of Abbreviations

ARVN	Army of the Republic of South Vietnam (South Vietnamese Army)
ASEAN	Association of South-East Asian Nations
CALCAV	Clergy and Laymen Concerned about Vietnam
CAPs	Combined Action Platoons (of US Marine Corps)
CBS	Columbia Broadcasting System
CIA	Central Intelligence Agency
CMEA	(Soviet-led) Council of Mutual Economic Assistance
CORDS	Civil Operations and Revolutionary Development Support
COSVN	Central Office for South Vietnam (communist forward command)
CWIHP	Cold War International History Project
DMZ	Demilitarized zone
DRV	Democratic Republic of Vietnam (North Vietnam)
FBI	Federal Bureau of Investigation
FRUS	Foreign Relations of the United States (document collection)
GI	Government Issue (US serviceman)
INR	Bureau of Intelligence and Research (US State Department)
IPC	Indochina Peace Campaign
JCS	Joint Chiefs of Staff
KGB	Soviet security and intelligence service
MACV	Military Assistance Command, Vietnam
MIA	missing in action
NATO	North Atlantic Treaty Organization
NBC	National Broadcasting Company
NLF	National Liberation Front
NSA	National Security Agency (also National Security Archive)

NSAM	National Security Action Memorandum
NSC	National Security Council
NVA	North Vietnamese Army (otherwise PAVN)
OH	Office of the Historian (US State Department)
OSS	Office of Strategic Services
PAVN	People's Army of Vietnam (North Vietnamese Army)
PLAF	People's Liberation Armed Forces (in South Vietnam)
PP	Pentagon Papers
PPPUS	Public Papers of the Presidents of the United States
PRG	Provisional Revolutionary Government
SAM	surface-to-air missile
SANE	National Committee for a Sane Nuclear Policy
SDS	Students for a Democratic Society
SEATO	South East Asia Treaty Organisation
SMC	Student Mobilization Committee
TTU	Texas Tech University
UN	United Nations
USSR	Union of Socialist Soviet Republics
VC	Viet Cong ('communist Vietnamese' fighters in South Vietnam)
VCI	Viet Cong infrastructure
VV	Victory in Vietnam
VVAW	Vietnam Veterans Against the War

Sobriquets

FDR	Franklin Delano Roosevelt
'Ike'	Dwight David Eisenhower
JFK/'Jack'	John Fitzgerald Kennedy
LBJ	Lyndon Baines Johnson
RFK/'Bobby'	Robert Francis Kennedy

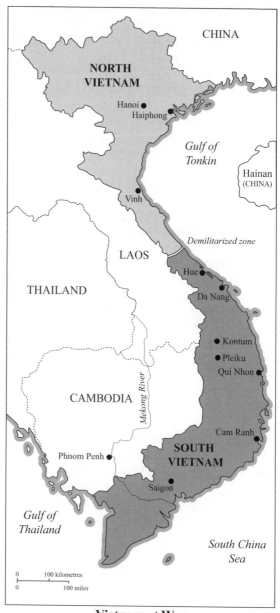

Vietnam at War

1

Rethinking the Vietnam War

Western popular memory of the Vietnam War is dominated by persist-ent myths and stereotypes. Some of the more familiar stereotypes include the morale-shattered 'grunt' or American infantryman, turning eventually into the traumatized veteran; the female Viet Cong fighter with a pistol at her hip; and the far-sighted and relentlessly determined North Vietnamese Politburo. Among the more prominent myths of the conflict are that of an American public which turned against war when 'body bags' began to arrive home from the battlefield; a South Vietnamese population which was united in its yearning for the reuni-fication of their country under the leadership of Ho Chi Minh; and a war that was, from the American point of view, 'unwinnable'.

Not all popular memories of the war are inaccurate. The conflict is often lazily described as having defined a generation, but such an assertion has a ring of truth. The war had repercussions far beyond those countries which were directly involved in combat. For the young Christopher Hitchens, growing up in the Britain of the 1960s, the exotic name 'Vietnam' encapsulated all the horrors of war: 'To all appearances, it seemed as if a military-industrial superpower was employing a terrifying aerial bombardment of steel and explosives and chemicals to subdue a defiant agrarian society' (Hitchens 2010: 81). The war is accurately remembered as, by some distance, the most controversial fought by the United States since the American Civil War. It divided American society at every level. The conduct and result of the war called into question received truths about pres-idential authority, about America's role in the world, about the entire national purpose.

American veterans returning to Vietnam were sometimes surprised to find the conflict described there as 'the American War', an episode – important, but not uniquely so – in the story of the gaining of Vietnamese independence. Possibly between 1.5 and 2 million Vietnamese, northern and southern, were killed in the war, compared with just over 58,000 Americans. Significant fatalities occurred among forces, including those from South Korea and Australia, which assisted the United States. The neighbouring countries of Laos and Cambodia were inextricably bound up in the conflict and sustained huge losses in the era of the war. Some facts about the conflict still have the power to shock. For example, during 1973, the year which began with the exit of US forces from the country, the South Vietnamese army suffered over 25,000 battle deaths. The Vietnam War (or, more correctly, the Second Indochina War) represented a qualitative shift in Asian anti-colonialism. It shaped the history of the global Cold War in complex ways.

Rethinking the Vietnam War: **Purpose and Structure**

Scholarship on the war has not collapsed into anything approaching a consensus. Understandings of the war – especially regarding the purpose and moral defensibility of American involvement – have developed in tandem with the unfolding preoccupations of international politics: through the years of superpower détente, reinvigorated Cold War in the early 1980s, the ending of the Cold War, the US military interventions of the 1990s, and the era of the War on Terror. Some basic questions about the Vietnam War remain unanswered. When did it begin, and when did it end? How and why did the US become so deeply immersed in so unlikely a place as Vietnam? Why did America lose? *Did* America lose? What exactly was the relationship between communism and nationalism within Vietnamese politics? Was America always doomed to fail, or might different political decisions and/or different military strategies have produced a radically different result? Who precisely was the US fighting in Vietnam? How exactly did the communist takeover of the whole of Vietnam in 1975 affect the wider history of the Cold War? A host of more specific controversies still generate unresolved debate. Were chances for peace, and for avoiding war, squandered in the early years? Would President John Kennedy have disengaged from Vietnam if he had not been killed in 1963? Was the Tet Offensive of 1968 a success or a failure for North Vietnam? Did President Nixon have a coherent strategy for extricating America from Vietnam?

Rethinking the Vietnam War will provide a developing historical analysis of the conflict – here primarily identified with 'the American War' – along with an evaluation of the major schools of Vietnam War interpretation. The analysis is primarily political rather than military, though major controversies about military strategy will be considered. The book looks to set discussion of the war in an international context. If the war divided America, it also divided the world. The Vietnam War has increasingly come to be seen as an event in international, rather than primarily American and Vietnamese, history. Discussion in the ensuing chapters will take every opportunity to emphasize the global context of the conflict, especially in relation to the support given to North Vietnam by China and the Soviet Union. Scholarship on the war has also been refreshed in recent years by the use of non-American, and especially Vietnamese, sources. *Rethinking the Vietnam War* makes reference to this new scholarship, and discusses Vietnamese policies and perspectives.

Rethinking the Vietnam War engages directly with popular memory of the conflict and with various schools of specialized scholarship. It tackles and tries to integrate the various levels of the conflict: from domestic electoral politics in the USA to internal faction-fighting within the communist leadership in Hanoi; from global Cold War dynamics (especially in the context of the Sino–Soviet rivalry) to White House decision-making; from antiwar protest to arguments about the efficacy of bombing and counter-insurgency. It seeks to bring clarity to complex political, historiographical and military debates, questioning common assumptions and offering some answers to nagging questions. The book rests on primary sources, recent scholarship, and post-Cold War understandings of the most divisive 'hot' conflict of the era of the Cold War. While the United States remains at the hub of attention, non-American dimensions of the war frequently take centre stage.

This opening chapter offers a summary account of the war between France and the Viet Minh; of political developments in post-partition Vietnam; and, in outline form, of the American involvement. This brief discussion of the war's early development and outline history will provide a factual basis for the more analytic content of subsequent chapters. Chapter 1 introduces the central historiographical dispute between 'orthodox' and 'revisionist' interpretations of the war, principally by discussing some key interpretative texts. After this introductory chapter, the book proceeds with four broadly chronological chapters. These cover the growing American engagement and, from 1968, efforts to extricate the US from Vietnam. They discuss political and policy developments in both Saigon and Hanoi, setting such developments in the context of the roles played by Moscow and Beijing. Chapter 2 deals with the history of Vietnam from the Second World War to 1963, tracing the origins of American involvement. Chapter 3 considers the period from 1963 to 1967, emphasizing the growing internationalization of the conflict and the key decisions made in Washington in the mid-1960s. Chapter 4 focuses on the swing year of 1968: the year of the Tet Offensive; of bitter twists in the Sino–Soviet rivalry; and of major war-related political upheavals in the United States. Chapter 5 considers the years between the Tet Offensive and the American military withdrawal of January 1973. This was the era of even more intense internationalization, of circuitous peace negotiations, and of some of the most controversial military action. Having reached 1973, the book provides three thematic chapters. Chapter 6 considers the emergence, development and significance of the antiwar movement – primarily in the United States, but also internationally. Chapter 7 evaluates arguments about military strategy, primarily in relation to various critiques of the American military understanding of the war. Chapter 8 switches attention to the ongoing revolution in Vietnam. Drawing on the 'new' Vietnamese scholarship referred to above, this chapter will assess political developments and political leadership in both North and South Vietnam. Chapter 9 begins with an account of the final, post-1973 era of warfare. It continues with a survey of the war's repercussions – both on the structures of the Cold War and on subsequent international history and politics. That chapter's final section offers some succinct answers to the many questions of war interpretation raised in earlier discussion.

Along the way, we shall pause to discuss how particular individuals related to the war, and how they shaped it. These discussions will be used to further the chronological analysis and to broaden the thematic discussion in the later chapters. Chapter 2 contains individual portraits of Edward Lansdale, the personification of Cold War derring-do in Vietnam in the early years, and of South Vietnamese leader Ngo Dinh Diem. Subsequent chapters will assess a range of other figures who contributed to the history of the war, and whose lives and careers were affected by it: American war manager, Walt Rostow; Eugene McCarthy, antiwar presidential candidate for the Democratic Party nomination in 1968; Frank Church, effective leader of the Senate 'doves' after 1968; radical American antiwar figure Tom Hayden; General William Westmoreland, head of the US Military Assistance Command Vietnam (MACV) between 1964 and 1968; and North Vietnamese leaders Ho Chi Minh and Le Duan.

The ultimate purpose of *Rethinking the Vietnam War* is to provide enhanced understanding of the conflict in Indochina, drawing on a range of scholarship and adopting a twenty-first-century perspective.

The Vietnam War: Origins and Outline History

French colonialism in Vietnam involved an alliance between missionary zeal and politico-economic aggrandizement. By the later nineteenth century, Saigon had emerged as a cosmopolitan financial centre and rice exporting centre. French policy rested on exploitation of Vietnam's ethnic, dynastic, religious, and geographical divisions. The country was divided into three administrative units: Tonkin in the north, Annam in the centre, and Cochinchina in the south. The French colonists were backed by elements from the Vietnamese mandarin class and from the largely Chinese commercial sector. The cause of Vietnamese independence was promoted by a generation of scholar-leaders, as well as by the Indochina Communist Party, founded in 1930.

Between 1940 and 1945, Japanese forces controlled Vietnam, with the Annamese Emperor Bao Dai retained as a puppet authority. The US Office of Strategic Services, predecessor to the Central Intelligence Agency (CIA), worked with anti-Japanese communist guerrillas during this period. Franklin Roosevelt (US president, 1933–45) put forward a vague plan for a postwar Indochinese 'trusteeship' as a route to eventual independence. However, the historic opportunity for Vietnamese independence came not in connection with the 'trusteeship' proposal, but after Roosevelt's death, with the 'August Revolution' of 1945. The nationalist/ communist Viet Minh, led by Ho Chi Minh, came to power in

Vietnam as Japan's control receded. The independent Democratic Republic of Vietnam (DRV) was pronounced in Hanoi on 2 September 1945. The short period of independence was derailed by the intrusion of the major war powers. In line with decisions taken at the Potsdam conference (held between the US, Britain and the Soviet Union in July 1945), British forces occupied the south of Vietnam, the area where Viet Minh control was weakest, in September 1945.

Restoration of French authority was made possible by the British occupation and by the support of Washington, by complex compromises between the French and the Chinese, and by pragmatic concessions from the Viet Minh. President Harry Truman (US president, 1945–53) failed to respond to overtures made to him by Ho Chi Minh, and reassured France that the US did not intend to recognize the Viet Minh as the legitimate government of Vietnam. For his part, Ho Chi Minh negotiated the French return to the north in 1946, as the price of the exit of Chinese Nationalist forces. France, in the Ho–Sainteny agreement, undertook to recognize 'Vietnam' as a 'free state' within a new 'French Union', though keeping Cochinchina under direct French control.

War between France and the Viet Minh began in December 1946, with France attempting somehow to turn back the anti-colonialist tide. In 1947, the French installed Bao Dai as head of the Associated State Government of Vietnam. The Franco-Vietnamese conflict drew in China and the United States, following Mao Zedong's revolution and the communist accession to power in Beijing in 1949. The First Indochina War thus became part of the Cold War battlefield. The Truman administration had no faith in the 'Bao Dai solution' and attempted to pressure Paris into developing a more serious commitment to negotiated independence. France's response was to play up the Cold War context, with Henri Buonet of the French Foreign Ministry reminding Washington that France was on the 'hot' front line against communism (Statler 2007: 19).

In April 1950, National Security Council (NSC) Resolution 68, largely composed by Paul Nitze, was forwarded to Truman. It outlined a policy of global, militarized 'containment' of communism, 'a policy of calculated and gradual coercion'. Against this background, the North Korean invasion of South Korea seemed to confirm Washington's fears; and Buonet's line about France holding the line in Vietnam gained acceptance within the Truman administration. US military assistance to France in Vietnam jumped, from the

$10 million announced in May 1950, to $107 million (for the fiscal year 1951) after the outbreak of the Korean conflict. By the middle of 1951, the United States was underwriting almost half of the French war effort. In March 1953, John Foster Dulles, Secretary of State in the incoming administration of Dwight Eisenhower (US president, 1953–61), declared that holding the line in Indochina was even more important than Korea, 'because the consequences of loss there could not be localized, but would spread throughout Asia and Europe' (Anderson 1991: 17).

As the Korean War drew to a stalemated conclusion, Beijing began to pressure the Viet Minh to consider a negotiated settlement. In September 1953, the Soviet leadership proposed that France, the US, Britain and China join Moscow in a conference to try to bring the conflict to a conclusion. By this time, French public opinion was also increasingly calling into question the possibility of an outright victory. Henri Navarre, the French military commander, himself harboured doubts about the possibility of victory, even as he identified himself with a US-backed plan to introduce new troops and to strengthen the anti-communist Vietnamese National Army. Events in early 1954 were thus played out against the background of possible impending settlement, with both sides – France and the Viet Minh – seeking to maximize their negotiating leverage by quick military progress. French forces were parachuted into Dien Bien Phu, near the Laotian border, in an effort to draw the Viet Minh into a conventional, set-piece confrontation. The French deployments were a reaction to a new Viet Minh push – itself the product of Chinese pressure – to conduct a campaign in the northwest of Vietnam. The ensuing siege of Dien Bien Phu, and subsequent French collapse, marked the beginning of the end of French influence in Vietnam.

International discussions on the future of Indochina, co-chaired by the USSR and Britain, began on 8 May, the day following the French defeat. The Geneva Accords of July 1954 divided Vietnam in two, setting the stage for the Second Indochina War. Communist China, taking part in its first international conference, sent over 200 delegates to Geneva. The Accords duly reflected Beijing's desire to establish a buffer-state on its southern border without provoking direct US intervention. Pham Van Dong, the lead Viet Minh negotiator, made a series of momentous compromises. Following the agreement, communist forces were to move north from positions below the 17th parallel, where they controlled about half of the emerging country of South Vietnam. Partition, to be monitored by an International Control Commission, was to be temporary, pending a general election in 1956. Apart from Chinese and Soviet pressure, the Viet Minh leaders were reconciled to the Accords by the prospect of national reunification as a result of elections in 1956, as well as by the likelihood of a complete French abandonment of Indochina. The Accords satisfied the immediate needs of the Viet Minh, who actually suffered more casualties than the French at Dien Bien Phu, and welcomed the chance to regroup (Harrison 1989: 126–7; Zhang 2000; Lawrence 2008b: 50; Asselin 2011).

Following partition, the two governments – the northern communist Democratic Republic of Vietnam, led by Ho Chi Minh, and the southern anti-communist State of Vietnam, led uncertainly by the frequently absent Bao Dai – turned to the business of power consolidation. In North Vietnam, this took the form of repression of dissent and radical land reform. Large numbers of Catholics, urban professionals and the landlord class travelled south, thereby removing significant sources of opposition. Consolidation in the south proved a more complex task, as various candidates emerged to threaten the precarious stability. One of these – the French army, which had moved south after the Geneva Agreement – departed fairly rapidly. Other groups included criminal gangs in Saigon; armed religious sects, such as the religiously eclectic Cao Dai organization, which controlled areas northwest of Saigon; Buddhist monks; and those former Viet Minh activists who looked to Hanoi for leadership.

Both governments relied on outside support. Saigon became increasingly absorbed into Washington-led global anti-communist Cold War structures. Hanoi began to be pulled in different directions by its great-power sponsors. Moscow, whose aid levels to the DRV exceeded those of China by 1958, saw the possibility of building 'socialism in half a country' and counselled against militarized efforts to promote reunification. In 1956, Premier Nikita Khrushchev delivered his 'secret speech', rejecting the legacy of Stalin and raising the possibility of North and South Vietnam being admitted to the United Nations as separate countries. Beijing recommended to Hanoi a combination of political and military struggle, yet was still very wary of US intervention at a time when China was trying to recover from the economic disaster of its Great Leap Forward policies. Neither Beijing nor Moscow showed enthusiasm for elections as provided for under the Geneva Accords, with Beijing advising that the forces of imperialism were never going to accept the verdict of 'the people' (Thayer 1989: 160–2; Duiker 1995: 100; Zhai 2000b: 77; Westad 2007: 181).

Between 1954 and 1963, the politics of South Vietnam were dominated by the anti-communist nationalist leader, Ngo Dinh Diem. Originally appointed Prime Minister by Bao Dai in 1954, Diem effectively ousted the tired Emperor via a rigged referendum in 1955, and proclaimed a new Republic of Vietnam. Diem initially achieved significant success in asserting his power over the sects. He managed to finesse away any prospect of meaningful elections being held in 1956. Diem, increasingly seen by Washington as the man of the future, built up the South Vietnamese military, and achieved success in the late 1950s in advancing the anti-communist cause in rural South Vietnam. Over 20,000 people were detained under his 'Denounce the Communists' campaign, begun in 1955, with many killed. Diem's rule became increasingly authoritarian, with the setting up in 1959 of local machinery for the arrest, summary trial and execution of suspected communists. Some 2,000 opponents of Diem were killed in Kien Hoa (also known as Ben Tre province in South Vietnam's Mekong Delta) in the late 1950s. Though Diem's repression was more than a little random, most of these activists would have been communist supporters whose loyalty went back to the days when the Viet Minh were fighting the French. Diem's 1959 crackdown, however, marked the beginning of a new insurgency. To quote James Harrison (1989: 172), 'after rapid growth in 1959, the Communists were able to take over parts of Ben Tre province, January 17–24, 1960, in an action that many mark as the real beginning of the Second Indochina War'.

Hanoi reacted to Diem's rural purges, first by supporting local efforts to coordinate anti-Saigon military action in South Vietnam; and then by launching the National Liberation Front (NLF). Firmly under communist direction though operating in South Vietnam, the Front undertook to 'unite all sections of the people, all social classes, nationalities, political parties, organizations, religious communities and patriotic personalities' to achieve 'the peaceful reunification of the fatherland' (Hunt 2010: 41). The NLF, in its various incarnations – many decidedly warlike rather than 'peaceful' – provided the focus for Hanoi's sponsorship of the cause of reunification until the early 1970s. NLF fighters (the PLAF, or People's Liberation Armed Forces) were dubbed 'Viet Cong' or 'communist Vietnamese' by the

Americans. From the early 1960s, the communist military effort in the South was coordinated by a mobile forward command post, known to American intelligence as COSVN (Central Office for South Vietnam) and most frequently located in Tay Ninh province, close to the Cambodian border. The launch of the NLF reflected increased Chinese influence in Hanoi, with Beijing now taking over from Moscow as leading external sponsor of the DRV. Soviet concerns about Chinese rivalry surfaced in Khrushchev's January 1961 public commitment to support 'wars of national liberation'. Infiltration into the South of armed fighters from North Vietnam began in the late 1950s, and was stepped up from 1960. In this period also, Hanoi commenced construction of the complex network of infiltration routes, via Laos and Cambodia, which would soon become familiar as the 'Ho Chi Minh Trail'.

The upsurge in the villages put Diem on the back foot. His main response, other than securing increasing amounts of American aid, was the Strategic Hamlets programme, begun in 1962 and drawing on models from Malaya and from the earlier Vietnamese 'agroville' initiative. The hamlets were fortified settlements, designed to afford peasants a degree of security from communist intimidation and influence. Saigon suffered some spectacular reversals, notably at the battle of Ap Bac (near My Tho in the Mekong Delta) in January 1963. By this time, Diem was under intense pressure from the administration of John Kennedy ('JFK': US president, 1961–63) to undertake some degree of political and land reform. Buddhist monks demanded freedom from persecution. In June 1963, harrowing pictures of a self-immolating Buddhist monk appeared in the American media. Ever mindful of the danger of tying his future entirely to decisions made in Washington, Diem began (mainly via his brother Ngo Dinh Nhu) to make tentative contact with Hanoi. In November 1963, shortly before John Kennedy's own death, Diem was murdered by senior members of his own military.

The death of Diem set the stage for Americanization of the war against communism in the South. Between 1963 and 1965, South Vietnam had five different governments. A coup in June 1965 led to military leadership under Nguyen Van Thieu and Nguyen Cao Ky. The ensuing directorate experienced numerous reconfigurations, linked to intra-military and military–civilian rivalries (influenced in their turn by the US Embassy in Saigon). However, General Thieu emerged as principal South Vietnamese political leader between

1967 and 1975. Considered in detail in subsequent chapters, the American involvement deepened following the factually disputed Gulf of Tonkin attacks on American vessels in August 1964. The following year saw decisions on major escalation, with the sustained air campaign of Operation Rolling Thunder beginning in March. Also in February–March 1965, parts of the 9th Marine Expeditionary Brigade were despatched to protect Danang airbase, in the coastal zone of the northern provinces of South Vietnam, from guerrilla attacks. From a commitment of 16,300 military personnel by the end of 1963, American involvement grew to 23,300 by the end of 1964 and over 184,000 by the end of 1965. November 1965 saw the first major direct battle between the US and the North Vietnamese armies at Ia Drang, in the Central Highlands. The battle, which the US won with significant losses, was the major conventional military clash in the war's early phase.

The year 1966 saw the development of large-scale 'search-and-destroy' American sweeps to flush out main enemy units. The conflict developed into a war of attrition, distinguished far more by small engagements, usually instigated by communist forces, rather than actual battles. In February 1966, President Lyndon Johnson ('LBJ': US president, 1963–69) announced a new commitment to what became known as 'the other war', the war of counter-insurgency – techniques developed to win the 'hearts and minds' of local populations, including what the US Army manual described as the creation of 'an environment of order and stability' and encompassing economic development. By early 1968, with over 500,000 US military personnel in-country, the war was transformed by the Tet Offensive. Coinciding with the Vietnamese New Year 'Tet' holiday, the Offensive involved concerted communist-force action in South Vietnamese urban centres and against US bases. It was a military failure for the communists and would-be Vietnamese reunifiers, but had a major impact on American perceptions of prospects of success. From 1968, the war changed from a mainly guerrilla conflict to a more conventional engagement between the US and South Vietnamese military on the one hand, and North Vietnamese forces (assisted by the PLAF) on the other. Peace talks commenced in Paris in May 1968. They continued under Richard Nixon (US president, 1969–74), with numerous interruptions, until the signing of an agreement in January 1973. In the early 1970s, American priorities switched to 'Vietnamization' (handing security and other responsibilities over to the South Vietnamese); and to 'pacification' activity, primarily designed to eradicate the grass-roots communist organization, or 'Viet Cong infrastructure', in the South. Saigon eventually accepted the need for widespread land reform, beginning with the 1970 Land-to-the-Tiller Law. By 1972, nearly 500,000 South Vietnamese peasants had gained title to land plots. In April 1970, US forces invaded Cambodia. The year 1972 saw a major communist assault, the so-called Easter Offensive, launched in March, and the most intense American bombing of North Vietnam, notably the 'Linebacker II' air campaign of December. Following the exit of US forces in early 1973, Vietnam was finally reunified by communist forces in April 1975, less than one year after Richard Nixon's resignation as a result of the Watergate scandal.

The war frequently spilled over into the rest of Indochina, and a few words about Vietnam's neighbours may help clarify future discussion. Land-locked Laos, once described by a US official as 'the end of nowhere', was what later generations would identify as a 'failed state'. The country witnessed complex conflicts between government (Royal Lao), communist guerrilla (Pathet Lao), North Vietnamese, CIA-directed, and South Vietnamese military forces – despite having its neutrality internationally recognized in 1962 (Taylor 1998: 73). From the early 1960s, in northern Laos, the CIA organized a clandestine force of tribal groups, numbering typically around 30,000. Otherwise known as the Meo, these Hmong tribal peoples played an increasingly controversial role in the war, especially in light of allegations of CIA assistance with the transportation of Meo-grown opium. US action was linked to the prospect of Laos coming entirely under the control of Hanoi, and to the presence of the communist infiltration routes in the centre and east of the country. Laos was invaded by South Vietnamese forces in February 1971. The Ho Chi Minh Trail extended into Cambodia, whose leader in the 1960s, Prince Norodom Sihanouk, attempted to maintain a plausible neutrality. Conflict was, again, associated with the presence in parts of the country of the North Vietnamese military. Sihanouk's overthrow in March 1970 precipitated the American invasion. Both Laos and Cambodia experienced intense US bombing. In April 1975, the extreme leftist (and by this time increasingly anti-Vietnamese) Khmer Rouge took the Cambodian capital of Phnom Penh, while four months later the Laotian capital, Vientiane, fell to the Pathet Lao.

Perspectives on the War: Orthodox and Revisionist Interpretations

It says much about the controversial nature of the Vietnam War that the received western interpretation of the conflict is essentially anti-war. This 'orthodox' view emerged from the writings of early journalistic, academic and other critics, who opposed America's conduct of the war and/or the very presence of US soldiers in Vietnam. From its earliest days, the orthodox interpretation veered between realism, the view that the commitment to Vietnam far outweighed any importance which the fate of that country had for objective American interests; and moralism, the view that this was an immoral war, pursued for purposes far removed from the stated American desire to promote 'freedom' for the Vietnamese people. Orthodox interpretations of the war have gained in subtlety and complexity as new evidence has become available to scholars and as war-related passions have cooled, however slightly.

According to Vietnam War interpretative orthodoxy, the precepts of globalized anti-communist containment, adopted by Washington after the Chinese revolution, were excessively rigid and unsuited to any sophisticated understanding of the Vietnamese nationalism, of which Ho Chi Minh was the authentic embodiment. American involvement in Vietnam was rooted in hubristic power-projection and severe underestimation of the associated difficulties. Most orthodox writers stop short of attributing villainy to the key American policy-makers. They do hold, however, that the war was in no sense 'necessary' – either in terms of US national security interests, or in terms of the expansionist dynamic of American capitalism. Orthodoxy should be distinguished from Marxist explanations of American conduct in Vietnam, of which the pre-eminent example is Gabriel Kolko's *Anatomy of a War* (1987). For most orthodox commentators, US presidents miscalculated and misunderstood: the 'domino theory' – the idea that the 'loss', even of a small country, to communism would inevitably lead to other countries also toppling – was plain wrong, and shown to be wrong by events after 1975. According to one important strand within orthodoxy, President Lyndon Johnson was especially blameworthy, but his successor, Richard Nixon, disastrously and mendaciously prolonged the agony. In Vietnam itself, US strategy and tactics were poor but, even if battlefield practice had been improved, the war was never really 'winnable'. American bombing in Vietnam is roundly condemned within the orthodox position as cruel and counter-productive. In order further to comprehend the variety of orthodoxy, and to trace its development, we will consider three important orthodox texts.

Our first book is one of the most influential and widely-read of all books on the war: David Halberstam's *The Best and the Brightest*, published in 1972. Halberstam, born in 1934, reported on the war for the *New York Times* from 1960. He was a major critic of the South Vietnamese regime of Ngo Dinh Diem. Along with fellow journalist Neil Sheehan, he covered the battle of Ap Bac, directly bringing to worldwide attention the precarious hold on power of Diem's government. In *The Best and the Brightest,* Halberstam argued that the Chinese revolution and the outbreak of the Korean War were, indeed, the framing events for American involvement in Vietnam. He added hysterical domestic US anti-communism, especially in the early 1950s, as a framing factor. Among other things, McCarthyism pushed out of prominent public service diplomatic 'Asia hands' such as John Paton Service, leaving Indochina policy to the regionally ignorant and the over-confident. Halberstam's fire was directed at the 'Cold War liberals' who advised President Kennedy and went on to serve Lyndon Johnson. The Vietnam War advisers were obsessed with what they saw as the lesson of the 1930s: one should not appease dictators – 'one had to stand up, to be stern, to be tough'. Reading the book some forty years after publication, one is struck by the incisiveness of some of the character sketches. McGeorge Bundy (national security adviser to Kennedy and Johnson) was 'the finest example of a special elite, a certain breed of men whose continuity is with themselves. They are linked to one another rather than to the country; in their minds they became responsible for the country but not responsive to it'. Robert McNamara (Defence Secretary, 1961–67) was 'marvelous with charts and statistics' but, in Vietnam, was 'the quantifier trying to quantify the unquantifiable'. As for the South Vietnamese ally, Diem was 'isolated, rigidly moral, unable to come to terms with a world which had passed him by'. There was no place for Kennedy-worship in Halberstam's attack on the war. JFK understood much about nationalism, communism and the Sino–Soviet split, but acted out of hubris rather than intellectual understanding. He committed the US to a 'quagmire'. As for Johnson, 'the more he tried to hide his warts, the more he revealed them'. The US military failed to realize that this was a guerrilla conflict, not a war where 'you searched out your enemy, killed him and went home'. General William Westmoreland, US military commander in Vietnam, was a 'supremely conventional man in a supremely unconventional war'. From the Kennedy years onwards, America's political and military leaders were committed to the lie that progress was being made in Vietnam. The 'truth of the war never entered the upper-level American calculations: that this was a revolutionary war, and that the other side held title to the revolution because of the colonial war that had just ended' (Halberstam 1972: 7, 60, 147, 185, 217, 247, 301, 430, 463, 552).

Our second orthodox text is Lloyd Gardner's *Pay Any Price: Lyndon Johnson and the Wars for Vietnam* (1995). Gardner's title, a reference to JFK's Inaugural Address of 1961, indicated the asserted continuity between Kennedy and Johnson. For Gardner, Kennedy was not about to withdraw from Vietnam when he was killed in November 1963. Rather, JFK left Vietnam on 'the edge of chaos', while Lyndon Johnson determined not to lose Vietnam – avoiding (as press secretary Bill Moyers reported LBJ as saying) becoming 'the President who saw Southeast Asia go the way China went'. For Gardner, early American involvement in Vietnam was also driven by economic motives, notably the project of establishing a Far Eastern capitalist system centred on a resurgent Japan. By the early 1960s, 'the original causes of American involvement in Vietnam were transformed into more abstract questions'. Japan was now prosperous. 'The perspective of American policymakers shifted from the tasks of creation to those of sustaining the Pax Americana'. Economic motives were mediated through the experiences and assumptions of Lyndon Johnson. LBJ's April 1965 speech at Johns Hopkins University, wherein North Vietnam was promised development aid if its government refrained from military aggression and infiltration prior to negotiation, was (for Gardner) Johnson's 'answer' to the riddles of Vietnam. It was part of Johnson's middle-way between right- and left-wing critics of his war leadership. He would undercut the appeal of communism by moving Vietnam towards state-directed developmental capitalism; holding the line in Vietnam would rob American conservatives of the chance to destroy the LBJ reforms at home. Johnson compared the Vietnamese communist leader to an American labour boss: 'My God, I've offered Ho Chi Minh $100 million to build a Mekong Valley. If that had been George Meany, he'd have snapped at it!' The orthodox theme, of Americans seeing

Vietnam through home-made lenses, could hardly be illustrated more graphically than in this quotation. Johnson's efforts to take the Great Society to Vietnam were rooted in self-deceiving, wishful thinking. They made scarcely a dent in the destructive dynamics of the war, even as they exacerbated America's domestic disarray (Gardner 1995: xiii–xiv, 87, 197, 536).

Jeffrey Kimball's *Nixon's Vietnam War* (1998) offered a scholarly account of how Richard Nixon and Henry Kissinger (Nixon's national security adviser, 1969–74, and also Secretary of State from 1973–77) led US policy in Vietnam. Kimball was much less preoccupied with economics than Lloyd Gardner, though he saw Nixon's foreign policy as having 'economic principles' – 'solidly capitalist and internationalist'. *Nixon's Vietnam War* signalled some changes in American scholarship on the war. It was the most comprehensive account to date of the American direction of the war's final phase. Kimball utilized a range of 'new' sources, including material released under US Freedom of Information legislation and Vietnamese sources. He interviewed some former members of the North Vietnamese leadership, eliciting some pearls. Nguyen Co Thach, former member of the Hanoi Politburo, told Kimball that the communist leadership had not been impressed by Nixon's combination of bombing and troop withdrawals: 'The question for us was not bombing or any kind of force. We should have been able to survive ... But for the Americans ... they must leave. That was their problem.' Kimball also gave significant attention to the wider, great-power and international context of the war – something which nearly all future commentators would deem necessary, and something which had been lacking in the work of writers such as Halberstam. *Nixon's Vietnam War* emphasized the inconsistencies and false understandings which underpinned the Nixon–Kissinger manner of extricating America from the war. President Nixon was seen as having miscalculated the extent and nature of Soviet and Chinese influence over Hanoi. Though at pains to stress that *Nixon's Vietnam War* should not be seen as psychobiography, Kimball gave considerable explanatory weight to the President's 'peculiar psychology and the odd relationship he had with Henry Kissinger'. As described by Kimball, Nixon's behaviour immediately before he decided to order intervention into Cambodia in 1970 was simply bizarre. The massive, Christmas 1972 'Linebacker II' bombing of North Vietnam helped 'fulfil the promise Nixon had made to himself that he would not go out of Vietnam whimpering'. Nixon's 'madman' theory of leadership – the projection of the view that the US president might unleash irrational force in Vietnam – was (for Kimball) more central to American strategy than either Soviet–Chinese diplomacy or the handing over of security responsibilities to the South Vietnamese. Nixon and Kissinger built their worldview on a realistic assessment of the limits of American power, but failed to adapt their Vietnam policy to such an understanding. Many of Nixon's 'madman' threats were simply not credible. For Kimball, Nixon's peace negotiations were conducted in bad faith; diplomacy merely prolonged a pointless and unwinnable war. Nixon initially did seek to win the war but, partly because of the influence of 'the antiwar movement writ large' in the US Congress and public, gave up this ambition. The Nixon–Kissinger goal became one merely of securing a 'decent interval' between US withdrawal from and communist takeover of South Vietnam (Kimball 1998: xii, xiii, 36, 65, 78, 113, 364, 240).

Sustained academic rebuttal of the orthodox case against the war is a fairly recent phenomenon. For many years, 'revisionism' – in the sense of defending US motives and conduct in Vietnam, and even arguing for some degree of American success – was largely confined to figures such as Lyndon Johnson and General William Westmoreland, not to mention Richard Nixon and Henry Kissinger. The orthodox consensus first came under a degree of concerted attack in the early 1980s. President Ronald Reagan, representing a new conservative upsurge, described the Vietnam War as a 'noble cause' in his 1980 election campaign. Neo-conservatives such as Norman Podhoretz (1982) argued that the war had triggered a dangerous and unnecessary mood of guilt and self-doubt among American elites. Revisionist scholarship, tending to see the war in wide geopolitical terms with the US acting as global defender against communism, also advanced the view that the war should be analyzed primarily in its international historical context (Smith 1985). The fall of the Berlin Wall in 1989 marked another new departure for Vietnam War revisionism: now rooted in the argument that the war, though it involved misjudgements and mistakes by Washington, was still part of the story of the eventual defeat of Soviet-style communism. Subsequent revisionist writing has focused particularly on questioning the orthodox assumption of 'unwinnability'. According to various revisionist writers, communism in South Vietnam actually *was* beaten at various points – whether in the early 1960s or the early

1970s – only for political Washington to betray the victory. We will look now at three major revisionist texts, beginning with Guenter Lewy's *America in Vietnam* (1978).

Lewy addressed himself directly to what was, in 1978, an overwhelmingly orthodox consensus on the recent war. What strikes the reader in the second decade of the twenty-first century is the extent to which Lewy was prepared to concede much of the orthodox case: 'American policy-makers ... exaggerated the geopolitical importance of Vietnam and Southeast Asia, thus making the consequences of failure far more critical than the facts warranted'. Lewy identified 'a failure to understand the political and social dynamics of a revolutionary war'. However, Lewy strongly anticipated a point which was to become central to later revisionist writing: Vietnam was important not just in some intrinsic geopolitical sense, but because several American presidents said it was important. The war was about credibility, the very currency of superpower politics: 'Protecting the nation's prestige in such a situation meant not the enhancement of national glory or grandeur but the preservation of the nation's ability to influence events and pursue American interests without the use of force'. President Johnson failed to appreciate the importance of the cause, foolishly neglecting to secure a formal declaration of war. Lewy also opened up, in a revisionist academic context, the long-running debate about the role of counter-insurgency in Vietnam. For Lewy, not enough attention was given to South Vietnamese 'hearts and minds': the peasantry needed to be won over to the view that the Saigon government could and would provide security, as well as opportunities for social and economic improvement. For Lewy, meaningful progress in winning the loyalty of the South Vietnamese population for the cause of democracy was made only during the Nixon years. Nixon's Linebacker bombing 'helped bring about a cease-fire, but it failed to achieve a settlement that could be considered a victory for either South Vietnam or the US'. Lewy saw the war as winnable by the United States. He even strayed into counterfactual history, speculating on the possibility of Nixon somehow dodging resignation and/or impeachment over Watergate and successfully reintroducing American power into Vietnam in 1975 to ward off communist aggression. Lewy emphasized the role of the US media and the antiwar movement in draining public support for the war. Nevertheless, for Lewy, Vietnam was certainly not an American victory, not even a 'lost' one. Lewy's book contained important arguments, though its use of war statistics – particularly to argue against the commission of war atrocities by US forces – was unreliable (Lewy 1978: vi, 63, 137, 222, 420, 425, 433, 436; DeGroot 2000: 16; Greiner 2010: 14).

In contrast to the diffidence of *America in Vietnam*, the tone of our second revisionist text – Michael Lind's *Vietnam: The Necessary War* (1999) – was pugnacious and confident. Lind introduced his book in the context of the end of the Cold War and the 'demise of the radical left'. *Vietnam: The Necessary War* was an attempted vindication of Halberstam's best and brightest – the Cold War liberals. Escalation in the mid-1960s, according to Lind, 'was necessary in order to defend the credibility of the United States'. 'Domino' thinking was seen by Lind as far from simplistic. While there was, according to Lind, a regional 'domino effect', the 'domino' strategic thinking of Washington in the 1960s extended to realistic evaluations of the importance of protecting American credibility on a global scale. However, as Lind said in a later interview, the book was never intended as 'a simple defence of the war'. In fact, it was necessary to 'forfeit the war after 1968, in order to preserve the American domestic consensus' for Cold War containment of communism on other fronts. Lind followed Lewy's line on the missed opportunities of counter-insurgency, leaving open the question of 'winnability'. Nixon's 'prolonged strategy of extrication' was, for Lind, too prolonged and insensitive to the needs of the Cold War consensus. As it was, America's exit from Indochina led, as Norman Podhoretz had argued in 1982, to a dangerous era of 'neo-isolationism' and Cold War defeatism. US leaders failed to devise or deliver a strategy for doing enough in Vietnam to protect credibility, without destroying domestic peace and consensus. Much of Lind's book was taken up with an attack on those strategic realists (like George Kennan) who concluded that the protection of Vietnam lacked compelling strategic value. For Lind, as for Lewy, credibility *was* the key value. The Soviet Union had only to humiliate the US in Vietnam in order to attract 'bandwagoning' support, as weaker nations fell into line behind the apparent top dog. With some relish, Lind attempted to demolish a number of liberal myths. Thus, Halberstam's 'Asia hands' in the executive bureaucracy were not victims of a McCarthyite witch-hunt, but were often 'dupes of Chinese communist propaganda'. Ho Chi Minh was a dedicated communist admirer of Chinese communism, not a leader who was suspicious of the giant country to the north. The US was not to blame for the genocide which followed the destabilization of Cambodia after the American invasion of 1970. American veterans of the Vietnam War were not especially psychologically disturbed. Hanoi never negotiated in good faith, and would never have honoured an acceptance of a coalition government in the South; and so on. Lind reserved special scorn for the recantations of the chastened former defence secretary Robert McNamara. The Vietnam War was, for Lind, a legal and justified conflict, properly authorized by the 1964 Gulf of Tonkin Resolution (McNamara 1995; Lind 1999: xiii–iv, 39, 51, 77, 102, 144, 165, 179–80; Toal 2008: 178).

Our final revisionist study, Mark Moyar's *Triumph Forsaken*, originally published in 2006, was even more confident and pugnacious than *Vietnam: The Necessary War*. Moyar consciously located himself in a revisionist tradition, beginning with Lewy, but also including Norman Hannah (1987), former CIA station chief in Saigon William Colby (1989), and C. Dale Walton (2002). Moyar's preface attacked the assertion of orthodox historian Frederik Logevall that most scholars now considered it 'axiomatic' that the US should not have gone to war in Vietnam. A consistent side-theme in the book was an attack on the distorted reports coming from South Vietnam in the early 1960s from David Halberstam and Neil Sheehan. Moyar also severely criticized John Paul Vann, maverick military adviser to the South Vietnamese military, and hero of Sheehan's 1988 study, *A Bright Shining Lie*. The defeat at Ap Bac was, in Moyar's view, largely due to Vann's incompetence. Moyar's sources reflected the huge expansion of primary material which had become available since Lewy's day. Prominent among these were North Vietnamese sources. After partition in 1954, communist leader Pham Van Dong was asked who would win the elections which had been mandated by the Geneva Accords. He replied: 'You know as well as I do that there won't be any elections'. Some of Moyar's arguments were familiar from the pages of Lewy and Lind. Credibility was central to American strength in the Cold War era, and neither could nor should have been surrendered in Vietnam. Ho Chi Minh was a doctrinaire communist; he was neither a closet liberal nor even a China-hating nationalist. America's Cold War understanding of the threat of communism, despite the erupting tensions between China and the Soviet Union, was also – according to Moyar – essentially correct. The domino theory was also broadly correct, especially if understood in wider terms than the simple vulnerability of Vietnam's neighbours. Moyar argued that many regional 'dominoes' would have fallen had the US abandoned South Vietnam in 1965. He quoted Asian regional leaders to the effect that US support for South Vietnam was very important to their own survival. Where Moyar went far beyond either Lewy or Lind was in regard to the concept of 'winnability'. Not only could the US and South Vietnam have won the war, they actually *were* winning in the period before Diem's assassination in 1963. Diem, for Moyar, was an authentic Vietnamese nationalist, whose autocratic behaviour was contextually appropriate. Buddhist opponents of Diem were often little more than communists in disguise, and, in any case, had scant impact on mass South Vietnamese opinion. Moyar assigned significant responsibility for Diem's killing to the US ambassador in Saigon, Henry Cabot Lodge. Political turmoil followed Diem's murder. However, for Moyar, there was still a chance to win the war in 1964 or 1965. Johnson's irresolution emboldened Hanoi. What was needed was 'hard action': invasion of North Vietnam in 1964 and incursions into Laos to interrupt the line of communist infiltration from North to South. *Triumph Forsaken* delighted in outraging liberal opinion, and its author cannot have been disappointed with the reaction to his book. Particularly controversial was Moyar's depiction of Vietnamese political culture: 'The peasants expected authoritarianism, and welcomed benevolent authoritarianism'. Reviewing *Triumph Forsaken* for *Diplomatic History*, Kathryn Statler compared the book to science fiction writer Philip K. Dick's *The Man in the High Castle*, a fantasy about the Axis powers winning the Second World War (Statler 2008: 153; Moyar 2009: xii–xiii, 94, 205, 273–4, 348–9, 378–9, 430).

2
The Developing War

We now consider the developing conflict in Vietnam, which was increasingly influenced by Washington's understanding of the place of Indochina within its scheme of global anti-communist containment. The first section of this chapter briefly discusses the development of Cold War understandings of the conflict during the presidency of Harry Truman, touching on some of many Vietnam War 'what-ifs'. We then concentrate on the period between partition and the 1963 assassinations of presidents Diem and Kennedy, raising some key questions of war interpretation. The chapter proceeds with an account of the career of Edward Lansdale. This, the first of our sketches of individuals at war, develops the chronologically-based analysis, while illustrating the impact of bureaucratic rivalries in Washington on developing politics in South Vietnam. Lansdale's career also provokes questions, discussed further in subsequent chapters, about the possible impact of counter-insurgency strategies in Vietnam. Other key questions considered in this chapter include: why, when and how did America become so deeply involved in a conflict so far from home? How defensible were both the Eisenhower and Kennedy policies in Vietnam? How far was the US implicated in the murder of Ngo Dinh Diem? Did President Kennedy miss opportunities for peace? Was JFK about to withdraw from Vietnam before he himself was killed? Building on the outline narrative given in Chapter 1, we finally consider recent interpretations of the role of President Ngo Dinh Diem.

1943–53: What If?

Franklin Roosevelt's (FDR) 'trusteeship' idea is often seen as one of the lost opportunities of the story of America and Vietnam. FDR told the Pacific War Council in July 1943 that 'Indo-China should not be given back to the French Empire after the war'. During their time in the region, declared FDR, the French had 'done nothing to improve the lot of the people'. Roosevelt proposed a postwar trusteeship, administered internationally and with a significant role for China. The vague 'trusteeship' would have stopped well short of immediate independence, for which Roosevelt did not see the Indochinese as properly prepared. Yet, the proposal set alarm bells ringing in the US State Department, while official London considered FDR's idea 'half-baked'. Roosevelt did not abandon the plan, though he did reassure the British about their imperial future. The Indochinese trusteeship died with Roosevelt in 1945. Vice President Truman was not even properly briefed about the idea, and – on entering the White House – was entirely preoccupied with achieving victory over Japan. Vietnamese nationalism was, for the Truman administration, a force to be managed in the context of relations with the European imperial powers (Hess 1987: 370; Bradley 2000: 76, 80; Gardner 2003: 345; Smith 2007: 5; Tonnesson 2007; Lawrence 2008a: 27).

The doctrine of anti-communist containment, adopted by the administration in 1947, was initially conceptualized in primarily European terms, with important elements of the Washington foreign policy bureaucracy retaining sympathy for the cause of Asian anti-colonialism. Some American diplomats saw Ho Chi Minh as a potential 'Asian Tito' – a possible eastern equivalent of the communist regime in Yugoslavia, which seemed, from 1948, to be following a path of at least quasi-independence from Moscow. Such opinions, however, were increasingly overwhelmed by the landmark events of 1949–50: the coming to power of the communists in Beijing, the consequent upsurge of partisan congressional criticism of the Truman administration, the promulgation of NSC 68 (with its substitution of global for European anti-communist containment), and the outbreak of the Korean War in June 1950. In May 1949, Secretary of State Dean Acheson stated a bald view which the events of the next few years would make it very difficult for official Washington to resist: 'All Stalinists in colonial areas are nationalists' (*PP*, I, 1971: 51). The international events of 1949–50, along with the rise of hysterical congressional anti-communism in the US, seemed to settle the fate of any US-backed neutralist or 'eastern Yugoslavian' solution in Vietnam. Besides these many factors, Truman was also receptive to the view that a non-communist Vietnam could be an important partner to a resurgent, capitalist Japan and, indeed, to the argument that Britain's economic recovery was linked to its access to the natural resources of Southeast Asia (Lawrence 2008: 31).

Washington watched the French war with a mixture of hope and frustration. The American administration was torn between the desire to pressure Paris towards sharing more power with the Vietnamese, and the fear that pushing too hard in this direction would cause France to give up the fight. David Bruce (US Ambassador in Paris) led the drive to establish an anti-communist Vietnamese National Army, which was eventually formed in July 1949. With US troops stretched in Korea, Truman was not prepared to use American ground forces in Vietnam, though he told London in 1952 that he would consider such a course in the event of direct Chinese intervention in Indochina.

The story of the decade following 1943 is dominated by 'what-ifs'. What if US foreign policy elites had somehow managed to avoid a conceptual division of world politics into warring armies of 'communism' and 'freedom'? What if chances for superpower conciliation after Stalin's death in 1953 had been taken? More directly related to events in Vietnam are the 'what-ifs' associated with Ho Chi Minh's overtures to the Truman administration. It is tempting to argue that any 'Asian Tito' settlement in Vietnam – any Washington-supported agreement which left the Viet Minh in a position of power – became literally inconceivable after 1949. Yet, such an argument is not entirely convincing. A Central Intelligence Agency survey, entitled 'Consequences to the United States of Communist Domination of Southeast Asia', in October 1950, concluded that the US *could* tolerate the 'loss' of Indochina. The CIA, of course, did not reflect the weight of bureaucratic opinion in Washington; neither did it take account of the domestic political pressure on Truman. However, the report illustrated that a communist or 'Titoist' communist Vietnam was not literally *unthinkable* (Leffler 1992: 382). Was there ever a possibility of 'Titofying' Ho Chi Minh, or, at least, taking seriously his offer of pragmatic cooperation with the United States?

The turning point here was Mao's revolution in China. By the early 1950s, Washington was giving large amounts of aid to the French. In January 1952, Ho condemned 'US interventionists' who 'have nurtured the French aggressors', invoking the 'People's China' as a 'brilliant example' to the Vietnamese (Hunt 2010: 25). In early

1946, however, Ho had tried to obtain American recognition, promising a capitalist future for his country. Hanoi's perspective, of course, changed dramatically with the revolution in China. Yet, surely, opportunities were missed in the pre-revolutionary years? One way of understanding this period involves an appreciation of the tension between 'field' or in-country perceptions of what might be possible, and the view from Washington itself. Archimedes Patti, head of the Office of Strategic Services (OSS) delegation to Hanoi at the close of the Second World War, argued that Americans in Vietnam saw the possibility – indeed, the necessity – of working with communist nationalists, but found their views ignored by Washington (Patti 1980). State Department diplomats, such as Kenneth Landon, sent to Vietnam in 1946, tended to report on the genuine popularity of the Viet Minh, only to find official Washington either unsympathetic or distracted by more pressing concerns.

This in-country *versus* Washington understanding of US policy has been challenged by historians who emphasize the racism which continued to affect even 'field' analyses of prospects in Vietnam. In May 1945, James R. Withrow of the OSS denied that there was such a thing as Vietnamese nationalism, since an 'Annamite's services are at the disposal of him who pays the best' (Bradley 2000: 135). The prior question persists: was there ever any possibility of Washington working with Ho's movement, a movement which did contain non-communists, and whose leader (at least prior to Mao's revolution) promised an independent Indochina as a fertile field for American capital? The answer must be that any serious effort to 'Titofy' the Viet Minh would have needed far more energetic bureaucratic entrepreneurship in support of that cause than ever existed in Washington, even before 1949. Ho Chi Minh represented the pragmatic wing of Vietnamese communism; convincing his colleagues of the practical wisdom of cooperating with America would have been extremely problematic. Even Ho's pragmatic type of Leninism would have made links with Washington very difficult. To have any prospect of success, any 'Titofying' agenda for Vietnam would have required a solution to the conundrum of how to unscramble nationalism and communism – something which was to elude US policy-makers for generations. Nevertheless, all this does not destroy the argument that the Truman administration failed even to explore an avenue which might have yielded results, and might even have spared much future agony.

The Eisenhower Administration

President Eisenhower inherited a view of the strategic importance of Vietnam which put Indochina firmly in the forefront of the Cold War contest against China and the Soviet Union. Like Franklin Roosevelt before him, and John Kennedy after, Eisenhower can be quoted in ways which seem to combine both a sensitivity to the complexities and dangers of US involvement in Indochina, and a neo-colonialist mind-set about the region. Indochina, for the Eisenhower administration, was a part of the wider Asian battle against communism: a battle which included the British war in Malaya and the US-sponsored anti-communist campaign in the Philippines. In April 1954, just before the French debacle at Dien Bien Phu, Eisenhower (often referred to by the sobriquet 'Ike') gave the definitive account of the 'domino theory': 'You have a row of dominoes set up, you knock over the first one, and what will happen to the last one is a certainty that it will go over very quickly' (*PPPUS* 1954: 382). In December 1954, Ike told his friend 'Swede' Hazlett: 'We can't get anywhere in Asia by just sitting here in Washington and doing nothing. My God, we must not lose Asia. We've got to look the thing in the face.' Yet, Eisenhower was also a member of the 'never again' club: someone who took from the Korean conflict the lesson that the US must not become bogged down in another Asian land war. He indicated to the National Security Council in January 1954 that 'he simply could not imagine the United States putting ground forces anywhere in Southeast Asia ... If we did so, the Vietnamese could be expected to transfer the hatred of the French to us'. During the debate in Washington about how to respond to the Dien Bien Phu crisis, Ike held that unilateral American intervention would 'lay us open to the charge of imperialism'. After partition, Eisenhower pondered long on the possibility of finding a nationalist leader in Vietnam with a degree of popular credibility. He explained to the French Prime Minister Edgar Faure in July 1955 that 'Mr Diem was sometimes difficult', but the US had been seeking 'for many years to find a figure who could be directly connected with popular aspirations'. Whatever Diem's faults, 'it would not be helpful to eliminate him as who else could be found' (*FRUS* 1955–57, 1: 492; Ambrose 1984: 182; Griffith 1984: 118; Boyle 2005: 51).

Though Ike's comments about Diem revealed an underlying attitude of colonialist patronage towards South Vietnam, they did at least reveal a president with a strong streak of pragmatic thoughtfulness. In our effort to understand developing US attitudes towards Vietnam, the underpinning Cold War philosophy of the Eisenhower administration deserves attention. This philosophy was the product of globalized containment and domino theories; but it also embodied an attempt to move beyond containment as practised by President Truman. Eisenhower sought to square the circle of anti-colonialist modernization and anti-communism in the doctrine of 'liberation', which had anti-imperialist as well as anti-communist overtones. His New Look policy was committed to cutting the defence budget – which, in the era of the Korean War, had risen precipitously. Ike was also keen to make American nuclear superiority count. Tactical nuclear weapons were used to intimidate Beijing during the 1958 communist shelling of Quemoy and Matsu, two islands off the Chinese coast under nationalist control. Eisenhower's Cold War policy in Asia was distinguished by a 'hard' version of the Sino–Soviet 'wedge strategy' inherited from the Truman years (Selverstone 2009: 172). The administration was well aware of the emerging Sino–Soviet split, with Dulles explaining in late 1953 that the 'best hope for intensifying the strain and difficulties between Communist China and Russia' was 'to keep the Chinese under maximum pressure rather than by relieving such pressure' (*FRUS* 1952–54, 5: Part 1, 1809). US policy in Vietnam reflected this perception that pressure on China would exacerbate the intercommunist split.

Eisenhower recalled the damage done to the previous administration by the 'loss' of China in 1949, and remained sensitive to congressional pressure for stout American resistance to Chinese expansion. Ike was keen not to upset the Republican right, represented particularly by Senator William Knowland of California, who became Senate Majority Leader in 1953. Ike's private view was that 'Knowland has no foreign policy except to develop high blood pressure whenever he mentions the words "Red China"'. Yet, Ike did take notice of Knowland (Boyle 2005: 48–9). Eisenhower's understanding of the requirements of New Look anti-communism had another important implication for his handling of Vietnam policy: his attraction to covert operations conducted by the CIA. These operations were putatively cheap, flexible and deniable.

The Eisenhower administration became increasingly committed to the French war effort in 1953–54. The impending crisis at Dien

Bien Phu set off a dramatic debate about appropriate American reactions. The hawks were led by Admiral Arthur Radford and Vice President Richard Nixon, who subsequently held that American inaction in 1954 set the stage for all future difficulties. Invasions of Laos and of North Vietnam were considered. The anti-escalation case was made by Army Chief of Staff General Matthew Ridgway, who argued in April 1954 that such action would 'commit our armed forces in a non-decisive theater to the attainment of non-decisive local objectives'. Despite his general openness to the possibility of using nuclear weapons, Eisenhower rejected the course of using 'new' weapons again in Asia. Eisenhower considered direct use of American air power but rejected unilateral (and, effectively, nondeniable) American action. All American intervention plans in early 1954 were predicated on the rather unrealistic assumption that the French would continue to fight. Ike plumped for a course of 'united action' between allies, including Britain. Eisenhower seems genuinely to have hoped for British support. London's refusal, in Anthony Short's phrase, to sign America's 'shotgun permit' ended any prospect of direct American intervention. However, with Moscow proposing a peace conference, and China pushing Hanoi in the same direction, America stood out as the major power most committed to a military solution in Vietnam in the period leading up to the French defeat (Short 1989: 148; Spector 1983: 208; Zhai 2000b: 46).

Secretary of State John Foster Dulles and his deputy, Walter Bedell Smith, were involved in the diplomacy that surrounded the Geneva Conference. Neither the US nor any representative of Vietnam below the 17th parallel actually signed the agreement. However, there was no escaping the fact that, with North Vietnam now – at least temporarily – clear communist territory, one Asian domino had fallen. For Dulles, the Accords had disturbing parallels with the Yalta agreement of 1945, with its recognition of a Soviet sphere of influence in Eastern Europe. Nevertheless, Eisenhower indicated on the record that the US would not disturb the Geneva arrangements for a partitioned Vietnam, even as Washington committed itself to the defence of South Vietnamese sovereignty.

Eisenhower's foreign policy had elements of deliberate ambiguity, and often gave the impression of relaxed control at the top. In general, Eisenhower's reputation as a foreign policy manager has grown over the years. On Vietnam, Ike was well-informed and closely involved in most key decisions. A partial exception occurred during 1955, yet another turning-point year for US policy in Indochina. At issue now was the future of US support for Diem. In November 1954, Ike sent an old military associate, General J. Lawton 'Lightning Joe' Collins to South Vietnam to report on the security and political situations. Collins, at times rather ambiguously, concluded that Diem was an unsuitable and unreliable leader, who did not deserve American support. Throughout late 1954 and into 1955, Collins and Dulles exchanged views on Diem. Dulles tended to follow the line of Asian experts in his own department: that the US really had little alternative but to back the current leader of South Vietnam. As we have seen, in the exchange between Ike and French Prime Minister Faure quoted above, Eisenhower backed Dulles and Diem. During 1955, remaining French forces left South Vietnam and the US effectively took over responsibility for the direction and survival of the new anti-communist government in Saigon.

After 1955, with South Vietnam now part of the South East Asia Treaty Organization (SEATO) – described by Dulles as an anti-communist 'no trespassing sign', Washington's policy was spelled out in a number of NSC documents. The US would work to develop the institutions of 'Free Viet Nam'. It would seek the 'eventual peaceful reunification of a free and independent Viet Nam under anti-Communist leadership', and encourage the formation of an effective 'indigenous' armed force in the South to deal with the threat of insurrection. The free elections promised for 1956 never took place, as each side looked nervously across to electoral prospects in the other half of the country. In truth, prospects for 'free' elections in either Vietnam were exceedingly poor. In theory, North Vietnam (with a population of about 14 million, compared with about 11 million in South Vietnam) might have been expected to welcome national elections, especially with many southerners – either will-ingly or under duress – likely to vote communist. The attitude of North Vietnam to the election issue is still a matter of some conjec-ture. It may have been influenced, as British Foreign Minister Harold Macmillan surmised, by the situation in Germany and Korea – two partitioned countries where the communist section was the smaller of the two (Eisenhower 1965: 449; Short 1989: 179; Anderson 1991: 71, 151; Schulzinger 1997: 89). In March 1956, Frederick Reinhardt (US Ambassador to Saigon) reported a conversation between Dulles and Diem. The Secretary of State stated that the 'time would come when it would be useful for Vietnam to take positive stand [*sic*] on principle of free elections. This would entail no danger to Vietnam since free elections could never take place in Communist-dominated territory' (*FRUS* 1955–57, 1: 660). Washington accepted that elections in the South would not be a good idea.

We continue with the first of our sketches of individuals in or at war. Edward Lansdale's career has attained near-mythological status, and has profoundly influenced popular memory of the war. For current purposes, Lansdale provides a convenient bridge between the Eisenhower and Kennedy years, while raising further interpretative 'what-ifs'.

Edward Lansdale: The Quiet American and Bureaucratic Politics

Eisenhower's eagerness to use 'quiet', covert activity as part of the war against communism was reflected in the career of Edward Lansdale. Sometime advertising executive, Army intelligence analyst, OSS and CIA officer, and major general in the US Air Force, Lansdale's is one of many ghosts which haunt collective memories of American involvement in Vietnam. Despite Greene's denials, Lansdale provided a model for Graham Greene's 1955 novel, *The Quiet American*. Greene's character, Alden Pyle, was an earnest promoter of the gospel of democracy and modernization, with a genuine interest in Vietnamese history and culture, and a determination to find a 'Third Force' of progressive Vietnamese nationalism between communism and colonialism (Greene 2004: 16–17). Lansdale also appeared as the less complex American abroad, Edwin Hillandale, in William Lederer and Eugene Burdick's 1957 novel, *The Ugly American*. John F. Kennedy, then representing Massachusetts in the US Senate, co-sponsored the distribution of copies of *The Ugly American* to fellow senators in 1959. Oliver Stone's 1991 film, *JFK*, about the Kennedy assassination, featured photographs of Lansdale, while the sinister figure of 'General Y' in the film reflected aspects of the Lansdale legend. Lansdale is sometimes portrayed as an authentic Cold War hero. His posthumous presence – Lansdale died in 1987 – informs the debate about whether counter-insurgency could have won the war for America. In *A Bright Shining Lie*, Neil Sheehan introduced Lansdale as a 64-year-old mourner at John Paul Vann's funeral in 1972. Lansdale was the man, according to Sheehan, who, in the mid-1950s, 'had denied the Vietnamese Communists the chaos that would have permitted them to take over Vietnam south of the 17th Parallel without another war' (Sheehan 1990: 9).

Lansdale was an exponent, probably the most celebrated of all exponents, of psychological warfare: efforts, drawing on Lansdale's advertising experience, to win over support – among the Vietnamese peasantry and, indeed, in the Washington bureaucracy – for the Diem regime in Saigon. Lansdale's great Cold War success was in the Philippines in the years 1950–53, where he orchestrated the anti-communist campaign of President Ramon Magsaysay. Lansdale was sent in 1954 to replicate the policy in Vietnam. Diem, with whom Lansdale rapidly developed a close relationship, was to be the new Magsaysay. Lansdale's constant refrain was that Washington should listen to the Vietnamese people as, indeed, should Diem. Washington should neither 'eliminate' Diem, nor encourage his tendencies towards authoritarianism. Diem, for Lansdale, was a 'city boy' who lacked understanding of the rural population, and whose efforts to centralize authority transgressed the ancient Vietnamese village code that 'the Emperor's rule ends at the village wall' (Lansdale 1972: 356). Yet Diem, like the Vietnamese people themselves, could be won over to the cause of capitalist democracy.

As chief of the Saigon Military Mission, Lansdale forcefully insinuated himself into the complex bureaucratic politics of the later Eisenhower years. He ran a freewheeling operation in parallel to the official CIA station in Saigon. Lansdale advised the State Department in April 1955 that 'nobody but the Viet Minh' would gain if the US failed to support Diem (*FRUS* 1955–57, 1: 305). He even made a positive case for Diem's brother, Ngo Dinh Nhu, regarded by most Americans as incautiously and excessively auto-cratic – though Lansdale did become more critical following the increase in Nhu's power after the failed coup of 1960. Lansdale clashed with Ambassador Reinhardt over the degree to which the CIA was encouraging Diem to develop the Can Lao – an authoritar-ian, repressive political organization, associated with various members of Diem's family and reflecting Nhu's authoritarian doctrine of 'personalism'. In 1956, John Foster Dulles and *his* brother, Allen (head of the CIA), sought, amid considerable bitter-ness, to educate Lansdale in the virtues of authoritarian government.

Rufus Phillips, who worked with Lansdale in Saigon, later summarized the Dulles brothers' attitude towards the Can Lao: 'If there were abuses, they could be corrected'. Lansdale's injunctions to listen to the people of Vietnam were, for the Dulleses, much too 'visionary and idealistic' (Phillips 2008: 83).

During the Eisenhower years, Lansdale was central to Diem's campaign against the non-communist political sects (in effect, private armies), including the formerly pro-French Binh Xuyen. The removal of French political and military presence from Vietnam was an important objective both of Lansdale and Diem. The Saigon Military Mission coordinated a 'psywar' effort to encourage Catholics in North Vietnam to move to the South. In one of many colourful episodes, the Saigon Military Mission paid North Vietnamese astrologers to compose doom-laden predictions for their regime; the predictions appeared in almanacs which were surreptitiously distributed in communist-held areas. Edward Lansdale was both protector and adviser to Diem. Lansdale also waged bureaucratic warfare on America's Diem-doubters, including 'Lightning Joe' Collins and Elbridge Durbrow (US Ambassador to Saigon, 1957–61). Durbrow opposed what he saw as Lansdale's cowboy approach, telling the State Department's Office of Southeast Asian Affairs in 1960: 'we have left the "Lansdale days" behind' (Anderson 1991: 187).

Contrary to Durbrow's expectations, 1960 was actually a year when Lansdale's star was rising. As David Halberstam put it in *The Best and the Brightest* (1972: 124), 'It was as if General Edward Lansdale had been invented with the Kennedy Administration in mind'. The young president who was inaugurated in 1961 embraced Lansdale as the counter-insurgency hot-gospeller, whose heroic and flexible approach to war would energize the American commitment to South Vietnam. Adoption of Lansdale's methods would obviate the need for American combat troops. Eisenhower had been a fan of 'psywar', but his successor had an even more expansive regard for unconventional and 'smart' techniques for fighting communism. Kennedy reacted positively to a 1961 report from Lansdale which argued that only counter-insurgency, combined with increased military and financial aid to Diem, could turn the tide against the renewed communist-backed rebellion in South Vietnam. Part of Lansdale's programme at this stage included various efforts, notably the arming of existing anti-communist groups – even ones which opposed Diem – to obviate the need for major and direct US military commitments. Such groups included the Cao Dai, which Lansdale had helped Diem suppress in the mid-1950s, and the tribal mountain-peoples (*montagnards*) of central Vietnam. Lansdale's analysis fed JFK's enthusiasm for Green Berets (US Army Special Forces) to be sent to Vietnam to train and assist the South Vietnamese military to fight a guerrilla war.

In the early part of the Kennedy administration, Lansdale had an important bureaucratic ally in Walt Rostow, especially during the period when Rostow served as deputy to McGeorge Bundy at the NSC. Lansdale had, however, something of a genius for making enemies, and his career under Kennedy and Johnson exemplified the frequently enervating and viciously fought bureaucratic politics which surrounded Vietnam decision-making. Kennedy toyed with the idea of sending Lansdale as Ambassador to Saigon in 1961. This proposal was effectively vetoed by Secretary of State Dean Rusk and by the Joint Chiefs of Staff (JCS). Rusk, with some justification, saw Lansdale as 'basically a CIA type of operator', rather than 'a disci-plined professional officer' (Nashel 2005: 71). The Joint Chiefs even wished to keep covert operations away from Lansdale. Lansdale made another enemy in the shape of Maxwell Taylor, who became Chairman of the JCS in 1962 and Ambassador to Saigon in 1964. Taylor later recalled Lansdale as turning out ideas 'faster than you could pick them up of [*sic*] the floor' (Rust 1985: 45).

Lansdale became a covert operations specialist at the Pentagon, working under Deputy Secretary of Defence Roswell Gilpatric. Robert McNamara, Gilpatric's boss at the Pentagon, accepted Maxwell Taylor's view of Lansdale. Asked to brief McNamara in early 1961, Lansdale constructed an exhibition of Vietnamese home-made weaponry, including spiked bamboo booby-traps. Designed to impress on McNamara the Vietnamese nexus of underdevelopment and nationalism, the exhibition simply angered the Defence Secretary. The bureaucratic out-flanking of Lansdale proceeded, with the Joint Chiefs setting up what was effectively a rival counter-insurgency unit at the Pentagon under Victor Krulak from the Marine Corps. Lansdale formed part of Maxwell Taylor's team which inves-tigated conditions in South Vietnam in 1961, but was shut out of Vietnam policy-making. What was needed, according to Lansdale, was for Americans in Saigon to establish a dialogue *with* Diem, rather than a constant stream of orders and imprecations *to* the South

Vietnamese leader. Lansdale, with justification, saw himself as the victim of complex bureaucratic conspiracies – not only to keep him away from policy decisions on Vietnam, but also to send him to Vietnam to eliminate Diem (Neese and O'Donnell 2001: 282; Frankum 2007: 132).

Kennedy seems to have concurred in the general view that Lansdale was unsuited to the complex politics of Saigon. In December 1961, the President asked Lansdale to take charge of Operation Mongoose, the failed effort, directed from the White House by Robert Kennedy, to extinguish Fidel Castro. This Cuban mission itself had implications for Lansdale's future involvement in Vietnam. CIA chief John McCone resented the near-exclusion of the Central Intelligence Agency from the anti-Castro operations, and joined the burgeoning ranks of Lansdale's Washington enemies. A surprising ally appeared in the person of Henry Cabot Lodge, appointed as US Ambassador to Saigon in June 1963.Though an enemy of Diem, in September Cabot Lodge asked that Lansdale be appointed head of the CIA station in Saigon. Lodge was partly concerned to see the back of the current station chief, John Richardson, whom Lodge regarded as insufficiently sceptical towards Diem. To request Richardson's replacement by Lansdale, Diem's protector for so many years, was rather extraordinary. Lodge was, in fact, looking for a plausible anti-Diem 'coup manager', and saw Lansdale as both willing and able to perform the role. Lansdale's case was presented to Lodge by Rufus Philips, who may have seen the Lansdale appointment as a way of eliminating Nhu, rather than Diem. In the event, the posting of Lansdale to Saigon was blocked by McCone. Lansdale had to stand aside and watch while the plot against Diem proceeded. There is some evidence that JFK himself wished Lansdale to travel to Saigon in early October 1963, in an effort to persuade Diem to break with Nhu. Lansdale apparently told Daniel Ellsberg (who worked on Vietnam policy at the Pentagon from 1964), during a Saigon drinking session in 1965, that JFK had asked about Lansdale's attitude towards actually getting rid of Diem. Lansdale replied that Diem was his friend (Moyar 2006: 251, 463; Phillips 2008: 193).

The murder of Diem in November 1963 did not mark the end of Lansdale's career in Vietnam. With the support of Vice President Hubert Humphrey, the quiet American was a contender for the Saigon ambassadorship in 1965, following the departure of Maxwell

Taylor. In the event, Lansdale returned to Saigon as special assistant to Henry Cabot Lodge, who began his second term as Ambassador in July 1965. Between 1965 and 1968, Lansdale devoted himself to the South Vietnamese pacification programme, and especially towards the setting up of peasant-dominated structures of local government: 'social and economic progress at a more rapid pace in the villages'. He urged Americans in the pacification programme to be 'revolutionaries without tearing up the social fabric'. Lansdale championed 'civic action' and opposed excessive and indiscriminate reliance on American military power. Lansdale's final bureaucratic campaigns involved an effort to bring together the various US military and civilian pacification agencies. He was rejected as formal coordinator of the pacification programme in early 1966. By 1968, the Lansdale team in Saigon had dwindled to a rump. Resigning in 1968, Lansdale exited Vietnam in protest at what he saw as the indiscriminate American military response to the Tet Offensive (Lansdale 1964: 84; Lansdale 1968; Currey 1998: 298).

Edward Lansdale's career takes its place among the Vietnam 'what-ifs'. What if Lansdale had been appointed Ambassador in 1961 or 1965? Could Ambassador (or even CIA station chief) Lansdale have saved Diem in 1963, perhaps by separating him from his brother? What if Washington had actually *listened* to Lansdale? The noisy 'quiet American' was often impossible to work alongside, frequently irresponsible, and prepared to use illiberal means to achieve liberal ends. As a leading in-country opponent of increasing Americanization and militarization of Vietnam policy, Lansdale did, however, deserve to be taken more seriously by the key decision-makers.

The New Frontier

John Kennedy's ambivalence towards the commitment to South Vietnam was evident in many apparently conflicting statements made during his Senate years, as well as in the White House. At times, America's first Roman Catholic president seemed to be proclaiming the centrality of a democratic Vietnam to the future of the free world; on other occasions, he seemed to be stating that successful defence of South Vietnam was impossible, and that the US should guard against open-ended promises. Complicating JFK's attitude to Vietnam was his concern about the domestic overspill of any decision either to intensify involvement, or, indeed, to cut loose from Indochina. Following the 1961 report on conditions in South Vietnam written by Walt Rostow and Maxwell Taylor, Kennedy expressed to close advisers his view that the threat to South Vietnam was 'more obscure and less flagrant' than the situation in Korea in 1950. Enhanced US support for Saigon would require the involvement of allies 'to avoid sharp partisan criticism as well as strong objections from other nations of the world'. JFK said he could make a strong case against 'intervening in an area 10,000 miles away against 16,000 guerrillas with a native army of 200,000 where millions have been spent for years with no success' (*FRUS* 1961–63, 1: 608). The presidential ambivalence intensified as Kennedy contemplated the Buddhist crisis two years later. JFK told journalist Charles Bartlett that the South Vietnamese people 'hate us', but 'I can't give up a piece of territory like that to the Communists and then get the American people to reelect me' (Thompson 1985: 16).

President Kennedy's early enthusiasm for the counter-insurgency policies being advanced by Edward Lansdale was genuine, but soon encountered stiff resistance from his generals. General Earle C. Wheeler, Army Chief of Staff, declared in 1962 that he disagreed with the 'fashionable' view that Vietnam's problems were primarily economic (Schlesinger 1978: 740). The US counter-insurgency effort in Vietnam in the Kennedy years was directed partly by Victor Krulak, and partly by the CIA. Krulak's upbeat assessments of the Strategic Hamlets initiative conflicted with evidence coming from central Vietnam in 1962 that, in the words of John Heble (US Consul in Hue), the 'program is mostly pure facade' (Kaiser 2000: 175). Roger Hilsman, working in the State Department, was strongly influenced by academic modernization theory and became a counter-insurgency advocate; he also came to view the hamlets programme as failing, and Diem as set against any realistic programme of reform.

In May 1961, Kennedy issued an order (NSAM 52) which required the CIA to pursue covert action: political and psychological warfare 'which would remain in force after any commitment of US forces to South Vietnam' (Ahern 2010: 42). The CIA and US Special Forces achieved successes during the Kennedy years in organizing self-defence operations at the village level. Organization of the *montagnards* in the Central Highlands proved a positive legacy of the period, though *montagnard* hostility to the centralizing policies from Saigon did continue, erupting into violence in 1964. Despite some Special Force successes, more general US Army resistance to counter-insurgency combined with the hollowness of the Strategic Hamlets programme to blunt and confuse Washington's strategy in these years. Following a brief outline of the key JFK decisions on Vietnam, especially those relating to Diem's killing, we will now directly consider two interpretative questions overhanging this phase of intensifying American engagement in Vietnam. Did Kennedy squander a chance of a peace deal with the North, along the lines of a 'neutralist' solution for Vietnam? Would Kennedy have further Americanized the conflict had he lived beyond November 1963?

Kennedy's decisions were affected by byzantine bureaucratic politics and by complex and confusing reports from Vietnam itself. Maxwell Taylor and Walt Rostow reported, in late 1961, that the situation in-country was deteriorating fast and that 8,000 US ground troops should be committed. Kennedy rejected the combat/ground troop option, instructing Ambassador Frederick Nolting to urge reform on Diem in exchange for increased American aid. The number of US military advisers increased from 700 – the figure Kennedy inherited from Eisenhower – to over 3,000 by the end of 1961, to 9,000 in 1962, and to over 16,000 by the time of Kennedy's death. From early 1962, General Paul Harkins (first chief of US Military Assistance Command Vietnam) was accorded equal status to Ambassador Nolting. At the time of the Taylor–Rostow recommendations, Secretary McNamara was urging significantly larger US troop commitments – 40,000 regular American military to be sent to Vietnam, with the possibility of further major escalation should the North Vietnamese and/or Chinese intervene directly. At the other end of the scale, dissenting voices about the whole Vietnamese commitment began to be heard in Kennedy's inner circle: most obviously in the shape of Undersecretary of State George Ball, who strongly argued against the Taylor–Rostow recommendations. Tending to follow the 'ambivalent soft hawk' line of national security adviser McGeorge Bundy, Kennedy threaded his way through competing positions, never committing to full Americanization of the conflict (Preston 2006: 141).

JFK became increasingly concerned about optimistic reports from the field. Even in the wake of the South Vietnamese defeat at Ap Bac in January 1963, Ambassador Nolting and General Harkins were offering upbeat assessments. Roger Hilsman, despatched with White House aide Michael Forrestal to investigate conditions in South Vietnam, swiftly concluded in January 1963 that 'things are going much much better than they were a year ago, but ... they are not going nearly as well as the people here in Saigon both military and civilian think they are'. In September 1963, Victor Krulak and diplomat Joseph Mendenhall reported on a recent joint visit. Krulak talked up the prospects of success, partly to deflect the case for supporting a coup against Diem, while Mendenhall reported that Diem was losing any semblance of national control. Kennedy asked if the two men had visited the same country (Kaiser 2000: 250–1; Preston 2006: 115).

The pre-1964 war involved, albeit in miniature, many of the more controversial features of the later, expanded conflict. The White House approved the use of defoliants, including Agent Orange, to destroy the cover of the guerrillas; while General Harkins promoted the use of napalm, used in flamethrowers and aerial bombs, to shock and destroy the enemy (Rabe 2010: 111). Most controversial of all, of course, was Kennedy's apparent complicity in the November 1963 coup against Diem.

JFK's decision to replace Ambassador Nolting with Henry Cabot Lodge, a possible Republican contender for the presidency in 1964, was designed to increase pressure on Diem, as well as to provide political cover for the Vietnam policy. Pressure on Diem was most obviously exerted via the aid budget. However, there was a consistent threat that Washington might support, or at least fail to oppose, an attempted coup. Apparently profoundly shocked by Diem's murder, Kennedy entrusted his private thoughts to a tape recorder three days after the coup of 1 November 1963. JFK enumerated the balance of forces in Washington for and against the coup. Opponents, according to the President, included Maxwell Taylor, Robert McNamara and, 'partly because of an old hostility to Lodge', CIA chief John McCone. Lodge's advocacy of the coup was supported by the State Department, primarily George Ball, Roger Hilsman and Averell Harriman, and by Michael Forrestal from the NSC staff. Kennedy acknowledged that 'we must bear a good deal of responsibility' for actually suggesting the coup, and then allowing the plot to proceed. Central to Kennedy's analysis was the cable, drafted by Hilsman, and sent to Lodge towards the end of August 1963. The cable indicated that Washington 'cannot tolerate situation [*sic*] in which power lies in Nhu's hands'. If Diem did not rid himself of his brother's influence, 'we must face the possibility that Diem himself cannot be protected'. On the 4 November tape, JFK regretted allowing the cable to leave Washington without obtaining the input of McNamara and Taylor (*FRUS* 1961–63, 3: 628–9; Kaiser 2000: 276–7).

The release of tape recordings, made originally in August 1963, of top-level Washington deliberations has shed important light on JFK's later comments and, indeed, has called some of them into question. The focus in the August discussions was on removing Nhu rather than Diem. Kennedy's role in the discussion was essentially a moderating one, very like his handling of discussion in the Executive Committee which dealt with the Cuban Missile Crisis the previous year. Kennedy was certainly pessimistic about the situation in Vietnam: 'We're up to our hips in mud out there'. However, JFK did not appear seriously to be considering withdrawal. Ever mindful of domestic pressures, Kennedy declared that Congress might get 'mad' at him if he were found to be supporting a coup, but also said that the legislature would be 'madder still if Vietnam goes down the drain'. All the high-level participants, including McNamara, accepted the necessity of removing Nhu. Still, on August 29, the Defence Secretary, backed by Ambassador Nolting, urged dissociation with the coup plans. However, there was little obvious dissent from the view that a coup might have to be supported if Diem refused to separate himself from his brother. The anxieties expressed in August 1963 concerned the timing of a coup, and the prospects of it succeeding, rather than any commitment to Diem. Kennedy and his advisers did not at this time directly contemplate murder of either or both of the Ngo Dinh brothers (Hammer 1987: 178; Jones 2003: 426; NSA 2009a).

Washington discussions immediately prior to the coup reveal a similar picture. Robert Kennedy was concerned about the likelihood of Washington becoming publicly implicated in any move against Diem: 'I mean, it's different from a coup in the Iraq or South American country; we are so intimately involved in this [*sic*]' (NSA 2003: 1). Some Kennedy advisers were clearly unimpressed by the coup plotters, and feared that anti-Diem forces in the South Vietnamese military would bungle the job, leaving Washington exposed to global criticism. To others, such as Michael Forrestal, the coup leader (General Duong Van Minh or 'Big' Minh) seemed more trustworthy and certainly more westernized than Diem. John McCone argued that a successful coup would harm the war against the NLF, and that a compromised or incompetent coup would be a disaster. Robert Kennedy, Maxwell Taylor and Robert McNamara were now opposed to the coup, and proposed the swift removal of Lodge from Vietnam. Secretary of State Rusk was concerned about a coup becoming just the opening to a new South Vietnamese civil war, but was also worried that failure to support the plotters would undermine the South Vietnamese military's commitment against the communists. The August and October discussions in Washington seemed far more preoccupied with Saigon faction-fighting than with either the war against the NLF, or the loyalty of the South Vietnamese peasantry. President Kennedy's main concern in the late October deliberations appeared to be whether or not the coup was likely to succeed. The Vietnam Executive Committee (as the elite advisers on the issue had now become) recognized the split between Lodge and General Harkins. (The latter wished to see the removal of Nhu, but opposed a coup against Diem.) Frenzied exchanges, including efforts to remove Lodge from the immediate vicinity of the likely coup, took place with the Saigon Embassy. On the morning of 1 November, Lucien Conein, CIA officer in Saigon, oversaw the delivery of $42,000 to the coup plotters. Asked by Diem, on the day of his death, to explain the American position on support for the plot, Lodge declined to provide any substantive answer (*FRUS* 1961–63, 3: 628; *FRUS* 1961–63, 4: 22, 379, 393; Ball 1982: 373; Kaiser 2000: 268–74; NSA 2003; Preston 2006: 104; Prados 2009a: 135).

Kennedy did not, as is sometimes alleged, 'order' the killing of Diem. JFK seems to have felt a combination of guilt and surprise in learning of the killing. What role in the coup decisions was played by the peace feelers put out by Diem and Nhu to Hanoi? Leslie Gelb, who worked in the Pentagon under JFK, wrote in 1992 that American support for the coup was directly linked to the fear that Saigon was conspiring with Hanoi to neutralize South Vietnam (Logevall 1998: 34). Seymour Hersh in *The Dark Side of Camelot* (1997) went even further, arguing that Diem was effectively removed by Washington in order to quash a peace deal. Such an allegation wildly exaggerates the malicious intent of Kennedy and his top associates. The Diem contacts with Hanoi exemplified the unpredictability and dangerously independent spirit of the Saigon regime, rather than any crude dash for peace in the teeth of White House opposition. US policy from August 1963 involved, in the words of William Bundy (then a Pentagon civilian) a decision 'to recognise, and to some extent help create, a situation where a military coup was entirely possible, and then to acquiesce in it'. By September–November 1963, the President seems to have accepted the view that the time for decisive change in Saigon had arrived. Political reform, designed to improve levels of support for the Saigon government in rural South Vietnam, would, so Kennedy hoped, complement and enhance military progress. JFK also did not wish to undermine Lodge, the most prominent and effective American encourager of the coup. Kennedy was an intelligent analyst of the complexities of Vietnam, but was not entirely immune to wishful thinking. 'The question now', the President confided to his tape recorder just over a fortnight before his own murder in Dallas, 'is whether the generals can stay together and build a stable government' (Thompson 1985: 261–2; Kaiser 2000: 277).

How seriously was Kennedy committed to finding a solution in Vietnam which did not involve intensified Americanization of the conflict? JFK in 1962 shelved an ambitious plan by Undersecretary of State Chester Bowles for the possible neutralization of Southeast Asia. It is going too far to conclude from the rejection of plans from people like Bowles and J. K. Galbraith that JFK had no intention ever of finding a way out. For one thing, Kennedy did approve tentative approaches to Hanoi and Beijing through Indian and Burmese channels (Porter 2005: 156–7). Another relevant consideration here is that of the uncertain status of any communist 'good faith' commitment to peace negotiations. By 1962, the promotion of a neutral South Vietnam had become a conscious strategy of Hanoi and the NLF. It was designed to win over international opinion against the Americans, as well as to put Washington in the invidious position of recognizing the NLF as an independent political force. There was, as JFK understood, a strong element of cynicism in Hanoi's embrace of neutralism for the South. A leader of the NLF, interviewed by Robert Brigham (1999: 31) later explained: 'We understood that the United States was not willing to accept our neutralist program, so we used it for propaganda value.' However, was progress along neutralist lines completely impossible? There was, after all, *some* overlap between American and North Vietnamese thinking on neutralization (Kahin 1986: 137). Who was to blame for the apparent failure to develop this into a genuine chance for peace?

Hardliners in both Washington and Hanoi should no doubt take a share of the blame. However, the nub of this story centres on the backwash from decisions made in relation to the neighbouring country of Laos. The problems in Laos, where the CIA was opposing both the Pathet Lao and neutralist forces, commanded Kennedy's attention throughout 1961 and 1962. Rejecting the Eisenhower legacy, JFK came to favour Laotian neutralization, achieving a deal at a Geneva Conference held in 1962. In General Maxwell Taylor's words, there emerged from Geneva a 'tacit understanding' that the fate of Laos, the backdoor to South Vietnam, would be 'resolved in Vietnam'. Averell Harriman, JFK's chief negotiator at Geneva in 1962, almost immediately began efforts to expand the neutralist 'solution' beyond Laos, raising the possibility of extending the Laotian deal at a private meeting in Geneva with North Vietnamese Foreign Minister Ung Van Kiem in July 1962. Both China and Russia, so Harriman felt, would breathe a sigh of relief if Vietnam could somehow be taken out of the Cold War (Taylor 1972: 218–19; McNamara *et al.* 1999: 110; Kaiser 2000: 143).

By the end of 1962, Laos officially had a neutral government, but ground-level reality was very different. Despite direct and indirect American incursions, the North Vietnamese were able to keep open the Laotian backdoor to South Vietnam. The Air America programme, operated by the CIA, had been providing support for Laotian anti-communists since 1959. JFK was actually in the course of approving plans for escalation of American involvement, including major air support for the Royal Lao regime in Vientiane (led by Souvanna Phouma), at the time of his death. President Diem warned before the 1962 Geneva agreement that neutralization of Laos was an illusion, and had attracted the hatred of Harriman in the process. American soldiers later delivered their verdict on the 1962 neutralization by nicknaming the Ho Chi Minh Trail, 'the Averell Harriman Freeway'. The failure of Laotian neutralization sealed the fate of any parallel American effort in Vietnam. Dean Rusk (1990: 434) later wrote that, with 'any semblance of North Vietnamese adherence to the (Laotian) accords, we could have entertained the idea of a neutralized South Vietnam'. Kennedy was not inclined to apply the Laotian formula to Vietnam.

Would John Kennedy have quit Vietnam in his second term? Until recently, there was a fairly strong scholarly consensus that JFK was irrevocably committed to South Vietnam. The text of the address that he was due to deliver in Dallas on the day of his assassination included the admonition that Vietnam policy was 'painful, risky and costly', but stressed that 'we dare not weary of the task'. Robert McNamara argued in October 1963 that progress in the war was possible, and that such progress should be accompanied by a handing over of responsibilities to the South Vietnamese. The Defence Secretary's recommendations underpinned JFK's order, kept from public dissemination, for one thousand US advisers to be withdrawn by the end of 1963. It has been suggested that tapes of discussions in October 1963 might indicate a degree of collusion between JFK and McNamara, with the two men subtly pushing the advisory consensus towards withdrawal. The threatened withdrawal of one thousand personnel, however, most sensibly appears part of an effort to exercise leverage on Saigon, rather than part of a 'plan' to withdraw. Kennedy certainly *hoped* to withdraw militarily by 1965, but only if conditions on the ground were improving (Logevall 1998: 25; Dallek 2003: 685–6; Blight *et al.* 2009: 125).

Yet, the argument – that Kennedy might *eventually* have withdrawn – has gained strength in recent years. The contention here is not that JFK had a withdrawal 'plan'. Various efforts to establish the existence of such a plan rest on extremely contestable readings of developing national security memoranda in late 1963 (Berman 1997; Logevall 1998; Newman 1992, 1997). A much stronger argument is that Kennedy – had he lived beyond November 1963 – would have reconsidered policy in the light of shifting circumstances, and might have ordered a withdrawal some time after a victory in the 1964 election. Second-term deviation from the foreign policy direction of a presidential first term is by no means unknown in American history – witness Ronald Reagan, or even George W. Bush. Second-term presidents do not have to worry about re-election. Kennedy did have private and not-so-private doubts about the war, and apparently told some associates that he would consider exiting from Vietnam when the domestic political context altered in the wake of an election victory. Roswell Gilpatric, a deputy to the Secretary of Defence, made this point in his 1970 Oral History, deposited in the JFK Presidential Library. Robert McNamara later gave his view that it was 'highly probable' that JFK would have pulled out. Roger Hilsman and McGeorge Bundy both later agreed that Kennedy would never have enlarged the war along the lines decided upon by Lyndon Johnson (O'Donnell 1970: 15; McNamara 1995: 96; Moise 2002: 171; Schlesinger 2008: 804; Blight *et al.* 2009: 240–1).

John Kennedy was, especially after the searing failure of the 1961 Bay of Pigs operation in Cuba, inclined to question 'gung ho' advice. He did not regard the prospect of withdrawal from Vietnam as unthinkable; the President indicated the need for a 'bottom to the top' review of Vietnam policy, including the option of withdrawal, in early November 1963. Despite periodic indulgence in wishful thinking, JFK had profound doubts about the possibility of clear victory in Vietnam, and about the reliability of optimistic reports coming from Saigon. He did not sanction the deployment of American combat troops during his lifetime, much less the kind of bombing campaign which Johnson approved in 1965. Both post-Truman presidents had their opportunities to cut loose from Vietnam. Eisenhower might have ended support for the French war effort before 1954, and could have used partition as an excuse to exit altogether in 1955 – probably, in both instances, without suffering impossible levels of domestic criticism. Ike's understanding of the responsibilities of the Cold War drew him into closer engagement. Similarly, Kennedy could have used the Buddhist crisis as a way out. JFK did not seriously consider such a course of action in 1963, partly because of his own ideological commitment, partly out of fear of the domestic consequences. It is difficult to imagine that such considerations would have led a second-term President Kennedy to escalate and Americanize the conflict in 1965.

We conclude this chapter with an assessment of recent efforts to resurrect the reputation of South Vietnam's anti-communist leader. Few commentators today would see Diem's assassination in 1963 as anything other than a disaster for the anti-communist cause. We now consider whether it makes any sense to go further and to install Diem as a plausible 'lost leader' of a viable non-communist South Vietnam.

Ngo Dinh Diem: Lost Leader?

Born in Annam in 1901, Ngo Dinh Diem inherited a family commitment to the imperial civil service. He held administrative positions in the 1930s, consistently advocating passive resistance to French rule. He declined Ho Chi Minh's offer to become Interior Minister in the government of 1945. His background was elite nationalist and Roman Catholic; he was resident for a time at a seminary in New

Jersey, while one of his brothers, Ngo Dinh Thuc, was the Roman Catholic Archbishop of Hue. By the mid-1950s, the 'Diem experiment' in authoritarian nation-building was being lauded by sections of American opinion as *the* way to defeat communism in the developing world. Diem cultivated the pro-Saigon Catholic lobby in the US, led by Francis Cardinal Spellman and supported by Senator John Kennedy. Diem welcomed to Saigon a string of American theorists of anti-communist modernization. One such, Wesley Fishel of Michigan State University, authored a 1959 piece in the journal *The New Leader* entitled by that magazine 'Vietnam's Democratic One-Man Rule'.

Constantly threatened by assassination and coup attempts, Diem was not someone to overvalue civil liberties. President Diem distrusted Washington, and assumed (with probable justification) that the CIA was cognizant of, and had done little to deflect, various pre-November 1963 plots against him. John Kenneth Galbraith, JFK's Ambassador to India, reported that Saigon was suffering 'total stasis' due to Diem's 'greater need to protect himself from a coup than to protect the country from the Vietcong' (Galbraith 1969: 267). Diem's keenest supporters cannot plausibly claim him as a democrat. Diem was an enthusiastic nepotist. Ngo Dinh Nhu, who had CIA connections going back to 1952, was effectively a junior co-ruler of South Vietnam, as was his wife ('Madame Nhu', formerly Tran Le Xuan). Combining great beauty with considerable menace, Madame Nhu was famously described as being inserted into her dress like a dagger into its sheath. Her reported condemnation of the 1963 Buddhist self-immolations as 'monk barbeques' is conventionally regarded as a major factor in influencing American opinion against Diem and his family clique.

What, then, is the case for Diem? At one level, the case is minimalist and commonsensical. Diem was an imperfect vehicle for the project of anti-communist modernization, much less for any transition to democracy; but he was the only credible nationalist and anti-communist leader of South Vietnam. We will see in the following chapter how the murder of Diem opened the door to radical Americanization of the war. As a result of the 1963 coup, Washington acquired a reputation for duplicity and for a propensity, as US commander General Paul Harkins put it in October 1963, to 'try to change horses too quickly' (*FRUS* 1961–63, 4: 484). It might be argued that Diem was always bound to fail. As Hanoi Politiburo member Pham Van Dong remarked: Diem 'is unpopular, and the more unpopular he is, the more American aid he receives, the more he will look like the puppet of the Americans, and the less likely he is to win popular support' (Baritz 1985: 88). The South Vietnamese leader acutely understood this dilemma. Indeed, Seth Jacobs (2006: 188) argues that part of Diem's unwillingness to democratize was traceable precisely to his need to avoid appearing as an American stooge. Nevertheless, bound to fail or not, Diem was the only credible show in this particular anti-communist town.

A more ambitious case for seeing Diem as the 'lost leader' is that advanced by Mark Moyar (2006), and discussed briefly in the previous chapter. In *Triumph Forsaken*, Moyar elaborated the view, held to his death by William Colby (head of the CIA's Far Eastern division, 1962–68), that the war could have been won for America if Diem had stayed in power. Colby clashed with Diem over many issues, including Strategic Hamlets, but ultimately saw Diem as a positive asset (Colby 1989; Prados 2009b: 70). Much of the 'triumph forsaken' thesis rests upon a positive evaluation of the progress made by Diem in rural South Vietnam in the early 1960s, as well as a reassessment of the 1963 Buddhist crisis. Let us consider these issues a little further.

As noted in the preceding chapter, Diem's anti-communist push of the late 1950s did enjoy positive results. Its success, after all, was the stimulus for Hanoi to form the NLF in 1960. However, even the success of the late 1950s push from Saigon can easily be exaggerated. CIA reports from the period reveal Diem as less an Asian miracle-worker, more a dilatory and inconsistent leader. A later CIA history held that 'the near-destruction of the Communist apparatus in the countryside between 1955 and 1959, resulted not in the consolidation of Saigon's control, but in the creation of a political no-man's land'. The post-1960 campaigns against the NLF were not entirely without success. General Le Quoc San, commander of a Mekong Delta communist force, later described setbacks in 1962, particularly in the face of new technology made available to Saigon by the Americans. However, there is little doubt that the push of the late 1950s was blunted in these years. The communist victory at Ap Bac was a highly significant straw in the Vietnamese wind. Frederick Nolting (US Ambassador to Saigon, 1961–63) later portrayed Ap Bac as 'a relatively small battle', which Washington 'blew up out of proportion'. Such a verdict is very unconvincing.

Any military success achieved by Saigon after 1960 was extremely brittle. Over 32,000 troops from the Army of the Republic of Vietnam (ARVN) deserted in 1963, far more than deserted from the communist forces in South Vietnam. Ngo Ngoc Tho, South Vietnamese prime minister, told US rural pacification officers shortly after Diem's death that the anti-communist war in the countryside was a shambles (Nolting 1988: 97; Hayslip 1989: xii; Grant 1991; Toczek 2001; Catton 2002: 188; Phillips 2008: 211–12; NSA 2009b: 7; Ahern 2010: 24–6).

Important, here, is the question of American doubts, reflected in the above-quoted remarks of J. K. Galbraith, about the depth of Diem's commitment to the anti-communist cause. Diem and Nhu, whose lives were constantly in danger, saw the virtues of keeping options open. Diem feared non-communist plots against him every bit as much as communist ones. Some Americans saw him as de-prioritizing the anti-NLF war on the grounds that too many victories would simply embolden his enemies within the ARVN (Brogan 1996: 192). Such arguments illustrate the extreme insecurity of the Diem regime and tell against the view that Saigon was on the brink of stability before November 1963. It is also worth emphasizing that Diem's many problems did not include too many victories over the NLF. Awareness of Diem's insecurities and inconsistencies does not in any way vindicate Henry Cabot Lodge's view that regime change would somehow lead to a more vigorous and effective anti-communist campaign in South Vietnam.

What of the argument that Diem was undermining support for the NLF in the villages, not least through the Strategic Hamlets programme? Diem revisionists suggest that such progress was occurring, and that the real tragedy was that Washington failed to recognize it (Neese and O'Donnell 2001: 283; Dommen 2002: 502). Again, any claim that Diem was popular in the villages does not stand up to much scrutiny. Efforts to depict Diem as a genuine land reformer, winning rural support as he proceeded, are absurd. The regime's social base was composed of large landowners, not tenant farmers. Significant amounts of land which had previously been redistributed by the Viet Minh were restored by Diem to the former owners. Diem sometimes responded to American pressure by giving the appearance of being a reformer. Such land redistributions as did take place largely involved the awarding of land to regime supporters who arrived from the North. Such land was usually expropriated from 'disloyal' *montagnards* and from the sects. Those tenant farmers who did obtain land under Diem did so after paying substantial sums of money (Jacobs 2004: 271; Jacobs 2006: 96; Prados 2009a: 58).

Revisionist efforts to rescue the reputation of the Strategic Hamlets programme are no more convincing than the argument that Diem was a champion of equitable land reform. Ngo Dinh Nhu convinced William Colby that the hamlets programme would embody a commitment to social justice. Nhu's assurances were empty. While provision of rural security was, indeed, a precondition of anti-communist progress in the countryside, the Strategic Hamlets programme proved just as coercive and counter-productive as the earlier 'agrovilles'. Viet Cong personnel controlled the fortified entrances and exits to many of the hamlets. Peasants who previously fled the settlements when the NLF entered at night, now found themselves incarcerated. Le Quoc San later described how the NLF smashed fortified hamlets in Long An 'like a rotten egg'. The communists were able to undermine the programme, exploiting anti-Diem resentments (Catton 2002: 191, 207; Prados 2009b: 87). The hamlets, depicted by war critics as concentration camps, also inflamed international criticism of Diem and of US policy in Vietnam.

Diem's handling of the 1963 Buddhist crisis is commonly interpreted as precipitating his demise, and as exemplifying the inhumanity of his regime, now increasingly dominated by the Nhus. Confrontation with the monks, traceable to the governmental ban on the flying of religious flags at the occasion of the Buddha's birthday, did indeed exemplify the regime's cavalierly unwise attitude towards mass opinion. Duong Van Mai Elliott (1999: 297) recalled: 'In attacking Buddhism, Diem and Nhu struck at what the Vietnamese viewed as the heart of their culture and tradition.' Attacks on the pagodas and the ensuing self-burnings reduced the regime's international reputation to new lows. Here, the case *for* Diem is not a strong one. It is true that the Nhus were more prominent in the repression than was President Diem himself. Diem did, to some extent, understand the place which Buddhism held in mass Vietnamese sympathies, and was consequently a less enthusiastic persecutor of the monks than many of his own officials. Before he left Saigon in August 1963, Ambassador Nolting reported that Diem was making concessions to the monks. Communist sources also confirm that the

NLF had penetrated the Buddhist pagodas. Nevertheless, the entire Buddhist crisis was itself symptomatic of internal chaos and domestic disquiet in South Vietnam – to a degree which calls the entire 'lost leader' thesis into severe question. Michael Forrestal was probably not far from the mark when he suggested to President Kennedy that the monks embodied popular aspirations far better than did Diem himself (Preston 2006: 120; Moyar 2006: 217, 231, 238; Thayer 1989: 154).

A more persuasive pro-Diem argument is that advanced by Ellie Hammer (1987: 317). The suggestion is that Diem, if he had remained in power, might have saved America from itself by refusing to admit a massive commitment of US soldiers to his country. Again, we return to the point about Diem being not so much a 'lost leader' but, rather, a credible nationalist who might have held the line against extreme Americanization of the war. A related line of argument concerns Saigon's nervous outreach to Hanoi in 1963. As indicated, the 1963 peace feelers should be understood in the context of Diem's desire to maximize his operational independence; they did not approach the status of a viable peace deal. Nevertheless, Diem did have some credibility in Hanoi. Pham Van Dong reportedly regarded Diem as 'a patriot in his way' and as, at least potentially, able to resist American threats (Maneli 1971: 125; Hatcher 1990: 148; Jacobs 2006: 128). It is tempting to argue that Diem, if he had lived, might have been able to secure some kind of negotiated peace, somehow navigating around the obvious obstacles to DRV acceptance of the legitimacy of a non-communist Saigon. The possible trajectory of a post-1963 Diem government is yet another of the Vietnam War what-ifs.

3

Lyndon Johnson's War

On a relatively quiet Sunday evening in March 1965, President Lyndon Johnson found time to have dinner with his wife. The couple discussed Vietnam. Lady Bird Johnson recorded her husband as saying: 'I can't get out, and I can't finish it with what I have got. And I don't know what the hell to do!' (Beschloss 2001: 316). The current chapter is preoccupied with Lyndon Johnson's agonies, his decisions and his mistakes. It focuses on the key Washington decisions of the mid-1960s: the train of events leading from the 1964 Gulf of Tonkin crisis to escalation of American involvement in 1965. We will give particular attention to the figure who, besides President Johnson, is most commonly identified with the hardening of American policy in Vietnam: national security adviser Walt Rostow. The chapter will consider key questions about the Americanization of the war. Why did LBJ decide to escalate? Did he consciously reject the ways of peace and choose war? What were the chances of achieving a negotiated solution in the mid-1960s? Before going along this track, however, we will – as in the first sections of Chapters 4 and 5 – consider political developments in South Vietnam, changing strategic choices in Hanoi, and the shifting role of the major communist powers.

Saigon, Hanoi, Moscow, and Beijing

Following the murder of Diem, the new 'military committee' in Saigon suspended the Strategic Hamlets programme in December 1963. Any prospect of the committee achieving a new unity of purpose was dispelled in late January 1964, when it was, in its turn, ousted in a bloodless coup by rival officers associated with General Nguyen Khanh. Attempting to consolidate his power, Khanh moved to accommodation with the Buddhist leadership. He organized a military push to the north of South Vietnam, while simultaneously opening contacts with Hanoi and the NLF.

The United States, in the wake of the anti-Diem coup, was almost universally assumed to be in charge of South Vietnamese politics. The US military commander in Vietnam, General Paul Harkins, had opposed the ouster of Diem and gave tacit support to the coup against the 'military committee'. The January 1964 coup swiftly became known as the 'Harkins coup'. Instability in Saigon was, in fact, the last thing that Washington craved and the complex cross-currents of South Vietnamese politics were not under American control. General Khanh's attempts to impose himself as a new strong man simply excited new rivalries within the South Vietnamese military; he finally relinquished power in February 1965. By this time, Khanh's contacts with the NLF had made him an object of suspicion in Washington. Maxwell Taylor, Ambassador to Saigon from mid-1964 to mid-1965, helped engineer Khanh's departure to exile in France. Following a short spell of civilian leadership under Dr. Phan Huy Quat, the military junta, led by Air Vice-Marshall Ky and General Thieu, took over in June 1965. Thieu was a graduate of Fort Leavenworth military staff college, and had led an attack on the presidential bodyguard during the 1963 coup against Diem. Elections held in 1967 confirmed Nguyen Van Thieu as president, with Nguyen Cao Ky as an increasingly insecure deputy. Throughout much of their period of shared power, Ky and Thieu were preoccupied with a new Buddhist rising, as well as a secessionist movement centred on Danang. Meanwhile, the Viet Cong continued its progress in the countryside.

Such developments were associated with the 'bigger war' strategies decided upon in Hanoi, reflecting a compromise between proponents of direct assault on the South, and the gradualist, 'protracted war' preferences of General Vo Nguyen Giap, who had led military strategy against the French. General Nguyen Chi Thanh, who ascended to a position of influence in 1964, looked to big-unit combat, rather than to the Maoist tradition of 'people's war'. The Ho Chi Minh Trail through Laos and Cambodia was consolidated in 1964 to permit large troop movements. Thanh managed to establish 'liberated base zones', particularly in the Central Highlands, from which to launch operations on areas under Saigon's control. South Vietnamese military losses were estimated at 3,000 per month by December 1964. In mid-1965, three North Vietnamese Army (PAVN, or NVA) regiments under General Chu Huy Man attempted to gain control of the Central Highlands, though the assault was diverted into action against the newly-deployed US First Cavalry Division at Plei Me, and culminated in the battle of Ia Drang. Even as PAVN incursions into South Vietnam increased, Hanoi continued its policy of keeping negotiations on the table. The possibility of neutralism and a coalition government for Saigon was, for example, communicated to United Nations and Canadian government officials on several occasions in 1964 (Moore 1992: 50–61; Duiker 1993: 30–6; Logevall 1999: 295–6; Bradley 2009: 108, 110).

Part of Hanoi's relative caution in late 1963 about directly committing its big military units south of the demilitarized zone (DMZ) – a five-mile-wide buffer between North and South, set up in 1954 – was linked to worries about upsetting Moscow. The rise of General Thanh, despite his flexible attitude towards Maoist military models, represented a perceptible shift towards China and away from the USSR. Moscow tended to see the North Vietnamese Communist Party as unorthodox in its degree of ideological commitment to the leading revolutionary role of Third World nationalism. Official Moscow criticized 'the Chinese splitters and those who support them'. Though the Soviets reacted to American escalation in Vietnam with apparent equanimity, Moscow did become more sensitive to the danger that it might appear increasingly irrelevant to the developing conflict in Indochina. From late 1964, Moscow both stepped up aid to Hanoi and increased its efforts to broker some kind of settlement (Gaiduk 1996: 8–9; 1998: 143).

On the surface at least, there was a significant contrast in the early to mid-1960s between relatively tepid support from Moscow and red-hot revolutionary enthusiasm from Beijing. In official Chinese pronouncements, China was the 'great rear' of the 'revolution in South-East Asia'. In June 1964, Mao Zedong promised Hanoi: 'Your business is my business and my business is your business' (Chen Jian 1998: 140). Mao viewed the US as an aggressive imperial power, but also saw the cause of fraternal aid to Hanoi as a rallying point to be used against revolutionary backsliders in China itself. A Beijing–Hanoi agreement of December 1964 provided for 300,000 Chinese troops to be stationed in North Vietnam, principally to deter a US invasion; between June 1965 and March 1968, around 320,000 Chinese forces were resident in North Vietnam. China contributed significantly to North Vietnam's air defences and general military capacity from 1965 to 1969. However, anxious to avoid direct confrontation with Washington, Beijing frequently declared that the anti-imperialist war in Vietnam would and could be won without actual participation from China's People's Liberation Army. In May 1965, Beijing signalled to Washington – via the British Chargé d'Affaires – that it did not intend to provoke war with America, even as it prepared to counter direct American provocation. Elements in the Chinese leadership continued to urge caution on Hanoi in the early to mid-1960s, though debates over Vietnam increasingly fed into bitter ideological rifts within Beijing's ruling elite (Garson 1997: 83; Hershberg and Chen Jian 2005; Lumbers 2008: 116; Mark 2012: 60–1).

Hanoi was keen both to keep its big communist friends, and to keep them apart. Even when it inclined to Beijing, Hanoi rejected an offer of Chinese aid which was conditional on North Vietnam refusing Soviet aid. John McCloy, one of LBJ's 'wise men' group of advisers, made a salient point in July 1965 when he referred to Hanoi's 'annealing' of the Sino–Soviet relationship, with 'the Soviets competing with the Chinese and acting on parallel lines, although with no necessary resolution of the policy differences between them' (*FRUS* 1964–68, 3: 140). The Sino–Soviet competition in Indochina was volatile. It reflected power distributions in all three capitals – Beijing, Moscow and Hanoi, as well as competing interpretations of how best to exploit the opportunity presented by America's difficult exposure in South Vietnam. Beijing's zeal for Indochinese revolution did not extend to enthusiasm for a pro-Soviet, unified Vietnam. Chinese leaders became preoccupied with the prospect of 'encirclement': by the Soviets to the North and by a US- or Soviet-dominated Vietnam to the South. Beijing rejected Soviet proposals for joint supportive action in respect of Vietnam, seeing such suggestions as a camouflage for Soviet military infiltration into China (Ang Cheng Guan 2000: 615; Radchenko 2009: 154).

By 1966, Hanoi was apparently benefiting from the Sino–Soviet split. Moscow was not prepared to see China taking over as the main sponsor of the Vietnamese revolution. It also interpreted events in Indonesia as a signal to increase its commitment to Hanoi, as a way of retaining credibility in the region. The ousting of the Sukarno regime in Jakarta led to the slaughter of communists by the Indonesian military. On 1 June 1966, President Johnson was advised by the CIA and by defence intelligence that Moscow was 'by far the major source of military equipment' for the DRV. Yet, in August 1967, Hanoi signed a new aid deal with Beijing. Thus was Hanoi able to achieve a degree of balancing between the communist great-powers, thereby enhancing its operational independence (*FRUS* 1964–68, 4: 432; Brigham 1999: 64; Nguyen 2008b; Simpson 2008).

Johnson's Dilemmas in 1964: The Gulf of Tonkin Resolution

President Lyndon Johnson constantly kept in mind the geopolitical competition which underpinned the worsening situation in Vietnam. LBJ was not simply the American president who was obsessed by, and prisoner of, domestic politics. In May 1964, he remarked to his old Senate friend Richard Russell that the US might be prepared to quit Vietnam if only Hanoi and its allies would refrain from making mischief: 'We tell them, every week, we tell Khrushchev, send China, Hanoi, and all of them word that we would get out of there if they just quit raiding their neighbors, and they just say, screw you' (*FRUS* 1964–68, 27: 130–1). Johnson was riddled with doubts: about his own abilities, about the wisdom of Americanizing the Vietnam War, and about the reliability of intelligence coming from Southeast Asia. McGeorge Bundy recalled that LBJ was simply 'worried about the unknown'. Johnson 'knew how many unknowns there were; he knew how complicated and uncertain life was'. However, insofar as Johnson was certain about anything, he was certain that appeasement should be avoided. He frequently circulated the view that if 'you let a bully come into your front yard, he'll be on your porch the next day and the day after that he'll rape your wife in your own bed' (Miller 1980: 386; Dallek 1991: 272). Johnson was not carried away by arrogance of power. Rather, he seemed to lack the confidence to question either the drift of Kennedy's policy in Vietnam, or contemporary elite notions of what constituted 'appeasement' in Indochina.

Johnson's stance towards the war is often linked to his desire to protect his domestic reform agenda from an attack from the right. LBJ correctly saw his legislative achievements – civil rights legislation and the Great Society spending programmes – as his best hope of being remembered as a great progressive American leader. He recalled the anti-communist panics which followed the 'loss' of China in 1948 and feared a possible parallel reaction to the 'loss' of South Vietnam. Yet, the view that Johnson somehow escalated in Vietnam to 'protect' the Great Society is not entirely persuasive. Mac Bundy later gave his view that, if Johnson had 'decided that the right thing to do was to cut our losses, he was quite sufficiently inventive to do that in a way that would not have destroyed the Great Society' (Logevall 1999: 391). Against this, former LBJ adviser Francis Bator (2008) has argued forcefully that LBJ did see a real connection between being seen to back Saigon and securing legislative support for the Great Society. Johnson's monumental complexity makes his motivations very difficult to read. Nevertheless, it is worth emphasizing that, though LBJ was a domestic policy-oriented president, he was also a leader with strong views on American global interests. Johnson saw containment of Soviet and Chinese power, in Asia as well as Europe, as the heart of Cold War policy.

Johnson had been involved tangentially with Vietnam as Vice President, visiting the country in 1961 and opposing the overthrow of Diem. He understood how important Vietnam had become to Kennedy's foreign policy, but was also aware of the doubts expressed by figures such as Senator Mike Mansfield. Johnson *could* have cut loose from Vietnam in 1963. Presidential assistant George Reedy (1982: 146) later opined that it would have been 'relatively simple' to disengage. Such a view, however, does underplay the force and nature of the circumstances attending LBJ's coming to power. For one thing, Johnson was deeply worried, as he told Doris Kearns (1976: 170), about being seen after the JFK assassination as 'an illegal usurper'. If disengagement from Vietnam was to come from the new president, the new line would have to wait at least until Johnson had secured his own electoral mandate. The key point here, however, is that LBJ set his face against disengagement, not so much because of political 'impossibility' (including the impact on the Great Society), but because of his own commitment to holding the line in Indochina. LBJ did not reject the idea of negotiating with communists. However, during his first year in office, Johnson was concerned not with preparing the way for quitting Vietnam, but with securing greater flexibility in the waging of war. Like JFK, Lyndon Johnson was aware of the neutralist option. The case for negotiated neutralism was stated clearly by distinguished journalist Walter Lippmann soon after the JFK assassination, and was taken up by key figures on Capitol Hill, including Mike Mansfield. However, Johnson was advised by the likes of McNamara and Rusk that neutralism simply equated to a communist takeover; the Laotian experiment must not be repeated. The President agreed with McNamara and Rusk (Logevall 1999: 90–3).

Lyndon Johnson's Vietnam decision-making in 1964–65 has been the subject of as much intense analysis as any comparable set of decisions in recent international history, with the exception of Kennedy's conduct of the Cuban Missile crisis. As with so many other aspects of the historiography of the Vietnam War, there is no academic consensus on how to interpret and judge the LBJ decisions. There is not even a consensus on exactly *when* the key decisions were made. A common interpretation sees LBJ wading into a 'quagmire' between late 1963 and the summer of 1965. Confrontational language, along with plans for bombing and covert action, appeared in LBJ's early national security memoranda. Gareth Porter (2005: 267–8) describes Johnson as being trapped by his advisers (notably Mac Bundy, Robert McNamara and General Maxwell Taylor) into making a series of decisions which plunged him ever deeper into the mud of Vietnam. Such arguments develop the familiar view that US leaders stumbled into war without seriously understanding the implications of incremental decisions and without properly reviewing options.

Such lines of interpretation have their merits. By the early 1960s, US policy-makers had become almost unconsciously wedded to policy positions which understated the obstacles to American success in Indochina. Some fine historical writing, notably Brian VanDeMark's *Into the Quagmire* (1991), has emanated from the wider 'quagmire' paradigm of US decision-making on Vietnam. For the moment, however, my principal point is that 'bureaucratic entrapment' interpretations are far from persuasive. Such interpretations severely overstate the cohesiveness of the bureaucracy, just as 'quagmire' views downplay LBJ's control, intelligence, and self-awareness. Johnson had doubts about everything, including his close advisers. He was more than capable of standing up to men who, as in the case of Robert McNamara, he actually distrusted. David Barrett (1993: 170) has it right when he argues that Johnson, far from being the prisoner of a hawkish coterie of Kennedy hold-overs, 'had a voracious appetite for information and reached widely for diverse points of view'. Armed with these thoughts, we will now consider the controversial 1964 and 1965 decisions.

For Johnson, the disorder surrounding the coup against Diem indicated the need for greater control by Washington and greater flexibility for its decision-makers. Despite all his doubts, Johnson made immediate commitments in a style which was more direct and more personal than that of Jack Kennedy. Throughout the early months of 1964, White House advisers Mac Bundy and Michael Forrestal hardened their line on the need for tough military action. The Pentagon carried out air strike feasibility assessments. LBJ's foreign policy team, meeting in Honolulu in early June, considered air strikes and also the possible introduction of a congressional resolution, designed to strengthen the presidential hand. The appointment of Maxwell Taylor to the Saigon embassy signalled a growing militarization, since Taylor remained LBJ's closest military adviser. Taylor's appointment also broke the mutually hostile stand-off in Saigon between Lodge and General Harkins, now commonly blamed for relaying over-optimistic reports to Washington. Harkins was replaced by William Westmoreland, who by the latter part of 1964 was directing US combat operations in Vietnam. However, LBJ was still tormented by doubts, some of which he was prepared to express to political associates (Ball 1982: 377). Johnson vividly remembered the Korean conflict and was unwilling to risk any direct confrontation with China. Still, by the summer of 1964, LBJ was convinced of the need for Washington to take firmer, and more militarized, charge of the destiny of South Vietnam.

The crisis came on 4 August, 1964, when Johnson announced to the American public that North Vietnamese patrol boats had launched torpedoes at two US destroyers: initially at the *Maddox* in international waters in the Gulf of Tonkin, and subsequently at both the *Maddox* and the *Turner Joy*. Johnson ordered retaliatory air strikes against North Vietnam. Three days after LBJ's public announcement, and despite considerable unease in the Senate, Congress overwhelmingly passed the Gulf of Tonkin Resolution, authorizing the President to 'take all necessary measures' in response to aggression (Stone 2007: 35–42).

Elements of the Gulf of Tonkin crisis remain murky, especially the degree to which the US might have deliberately provoked a North Vietnamese attack. However, even most revisionist historians accept that Johnson's account of the crisis – both in his statements at the time and in his memoir, *The Vantage Point* – was a gross distortion of ascertainable fact. The US National Security Agency released detailed intercept evidence in 2005 and 2006, revealing numerous errors and misunderstandings, but also clearly indicating that no naval engagement took place on 4 August. At the very least, LBJ was guilty, in his 4 August meeting with congressional leaders, and subsequent public announcements, of jumping the gun – acting without sure knowledge of what actually had occurred off the coast of North Vietnam. He later admitted, in connection with the *Turner Joy*: 'For all I know, our navy was shooting at whales out there'. The text of the congressional resolution had been prepared well in advance of the August crisis, and would, in any case, have been submitted to Congress within weeks. Senator J. William Fulbright, chairman of the Senate Foreign Relations Committee, was told by LBJ and George Ball on 26 July that an authorizing resolution could actually *prevent* irresponsible escalation, by depriving Barry Goldwater (LBJ's Republican opponent in the 1964 presidential election) of the ability to depict the Democrats as soft on communism (Goulden 1969: 160; Moise 1996: 203; Logevall 1999: 201; NSA 2005).

The attack on the *Maddox* almost certainly did take place. North Vietnamese torpedo boats chased the US ship out of their territorial waters, attacking it in international waters. The American destroyer was taking part in the 'Desoto' patrol programme, an intelligence-gathering operation which had been proceeding for two years. Despite many public denials, administration leaders accepted at the time that the Desoto patrols were connected to Operation Plan 34A commando raids on the North Vietnamese coast. The raids were conducted by South Vietnamese special units, working under American direction. Official Vietnamese communist histories suggest that the *Maddox* had been tracked for several days, and that the North Vietnamese did not necessarily see the destroyer as directly linked to the 34A raids (Moyar 2006: 310). Another 34A raid was launched on the night of 3 August, after the initial *Maddox* attack. US conduct was provocative; however, the crisis was probably deliberately provoked only in the sense that Washington was ready to exploit any of many likely opportunities to shift its ground on the war.

The Tonkin Gulf crisis fed into complex and interlinking concerns of the decision-making elite. To administration hawks, it was a godsend. James Thomson, then working for Mac Bundy at the NSC, recalled a policy planning meeting, chaired by Walt Rostow at the State Department two days after the onset of the crisis. According to

Thomson, Rostow exclaimed: 'You know, the wonderful thing is, we don't even know if this thing happened at all. Boy, it gives us the chance really to go for broke on the bombing. The evidence is unclear, but our golden opportunity is at hand' (Appy 2008: 116). Bombing of North Vietnam also, at one level, represented an American response to the various military and diplomatic pressures emanating from South Vietnam. The regime in Saigon was wobbling, and tentative openings were being made towards Hanoi. Firm action in August 1964 sent messages to General Khanh, just as it cut ground from under Barry Goldwater. McGeorge Bundy wrote in the mid-1990s, in one of the 'fragments' he composed for an uncompleted study of war decision-making, that the predominant concern was 'win, win, win the election, not the war' (Goldstein 2008: 97).

Johnson saw himself in the latter part of 1964 as holding the line against excessive escalation. He suspended the 34A raids and expressed annoyance at Pentagon leaks which were designed to enhance the case for increased American commitment. LBJ seems later to have felt that he had been deceived by the military in connection with the Tonkin Gulf attacks. Speaking to McNamara in late September, the President expressed regret that his actions the previous month had been based on unreliable intelligence. With another Gulf confrontation looming on 18 September, Johnson complained about his own naval forces: 'I don't know why in the hell, some time or other, they can't be sure they are being attacked' (Beschloss 2001: 38, 133). Johnson continued to question and agonize over the recommendations coming from the Pentagon, the White House Vietnam advisers, the Saigon Embassy, and the State Department. Much of this advice was hawkish, but not all. In October, George Ball warned that America's allies were coming to the view that the administration was being drawn into a 'fruitless struggle' in Vietnam which 'we are bound to lose' (White 2007: 289–91). LBJ let it be known that he was listening to all sides of the debate, and actually welcomed contributions from a devil's advocate. Washington discussion revolved around the options of ground troop commitment, sustained bombing of the North, targeted air raids, graduated and conditional escalation, with even the occasional call for action against China. When the US air base at Ben Hoa, north of Saigon, was attacked two days before the presidential election, LBJ resisted calls for direct retaliation against Hanoi. Military and civilian leaders differed over the question of whether nuclear weapons might ever be used in Vietnam.

McNamara told the Joint Chiefs that he and Johnson were preparing for direct action, against both North Vietnam and China, though he also told LBJ that a middle course between extreme options would be best (Lumbers 2008: 114).

By mid-December, and following the election, Johnson had tentatively approved the first phase of a course of action which committed the US to intensified action, including reprisals for communist attacks in South Vietnam. After thirty days, phase two of the plan would take effect, involving sustained air strikes and US troop deployments in South Vietnam and Thailand. LBJ's advisers had differing views about the possibility of negotiating with Hanoi, though it was accepted that some kind of negotiated solution would be sought, either sooner or later. Planning at this stage was also hostage to the fortunes of the government in Saigon. Technically, the plan depended upon Saigon making progress towards stability; it was not entirely clear whether growing weakness in Saigon would trigger a diminution or an intensification of the new American commitment. As it happened, by the end of 1964, Ambassador Maxwell Taylor was reporting the virtual disintegration of government in South Vietnam. Johnson saw Khanh's regime as simply incapable of taking effective military action against the communists; asking it to do so was like asking a 'widow woman to slap Jack Dempsey' (*FRUS* 1964–68, 1: 966; Kaiser 2000, 360–81).

The 1965 Escalation Decisions

At times, Johnson was prepared to let policy drift. His preference was to concentrate on the historic civil rights legislation that was finding its way through the Congress. Yet, by the end of 1964, Washington did have a plan for Vietnam. The plan was for graduated pressure on Hanoi, with the two clear phases of involvement decided upon in December 1964. Also, as we have seen, LBJ did have some foundational beliefs. These included the view that communism needed to be contained in Vietnam, and that the Vietnamese would eventually come to see the virtues of capitalist development. Yet, Johnson's wait-and-see, consensual leadership style left him exposed to criticism from both ends of the spectrum. Orthodox and revisionist commentators excoriate LBJ for sliding into unsustainable policy commitments without being fully alive to their consequences. For

Frank Vandiver (1997: 116), describing events in June 1965, for too long LBJ had 'pushed Vietnam ahead of him'. He 'had wished it away, tended it one-handedly', while 'all the while he knew it lurked in wait for him'. For H.R. McMaster (1997: 217), Johnson simply spent too long imagining 'that he could pursue a policy of gradual escalation without involving the United States in a major war'. Johnson *could* act decisively; the order to invade the Dominican Republic in 1965 was an example. Decisiveness for LBJ, Hamlet in the White House, had something of the quality of emotional release. Decisions half-made in 1964 came to dominate the agenda in 1965. Johnson was probably pleased when, as in the Gulf of Tonkin, events could plausibly be regarded as having forced his hand.

Air strikes on a PAVN barracks in the south of North Vietnam were launched in February 1965, following an artillery attack on the US Marine compound at Pleiku, in the Central Highlands. US reaction to the Pleiku attack, and to related action at Qui Nhan, ended debate about possible – what Robert McNamara later called 'fork in the road' – American options. The full 'Rolling Thunder' bombing campaign, which lasted, with many pauses, until the final days of the Johnson presidency, began on 2 March. The initial, post-Pleiku, assault was launched while Soviet leader Aleksei Kosygin was visiting Hanoi. The bombing was opposed in Washington by Vice President Hubert Humphrey, and by Senator Mike Mansfield, though not initially by George Ball. Mansfield told LBJ at a meeting immediately following the Pleiku attack: 'I would negotiate. I would not hit back. I would get into negotiations' (Barrett 1993: 18; McNamara 1995: 168; Hunt 1996: 102). Johnson again steered a middle way between the Joint Chiefs, supported by Westmoreland, who saw Rolling Thunder as little more than token action, and non-bombers like Mike Mansfield.

Like the Gulf of Tonkin incidents, scholarly assessment of the Pleiku attack has become surrounded by conspiracy theories – not all of them entirely implausible. Clearly, Pleiku did merely trigger action which LBJ had already approved. McNamara famously told a reporter some weeks after the attack: 'Pleikus are like streetcars.' If the Marine compound attack had not occurred, some other pretext for the launching of air strikes would have come along. To a generation, the 'streetcars' remark came to epitomize the cynicism which led the US into a disastrous war (Halberstam 1972: 533). The Pleiku attack has also stimulated conspiracy-oriented speculation unrelated to the 'streetcars' remark. It seems likely that Kosygin was in Hanoi not only to agree terms for more aid to the DRV, but also to warn Hanoi against excessive provocation of the US. Both the CIA and the State Department had such an understanding. Under some interpretations, Washington, spoiling for a fight, bombed North Vietnam during the Kosygin visit precisely to head-off Russian support for negotiations. Such a reading of the events rather ignores the severity of the Pleiku attack, which induced a spontaneous emotional reaction from Mac Bundy who was, at the time of the attack, visiting Saigon to make final assessments prior to a bombing campaign. More persuasive is the view that the attack was deliberately timed by Hanoi to put pressure on Kosygin. Retaliation for the raid would both enhance the case for Soviet aid and weaken Russian pressure to hold back from provoking Washington. Robert McNamara, after meetings in Hanoi in the 1990s, came to believe that the attack was completely unconnected to the Kosygin or Bundy presences in Vietnam. Though this seems rather unlikely, it may be that the Pleiku assault was, after all, ordered by local NLF commanders, acting on their own initiative (Halberstam 1972: 533; Kahin 1986: 277; McNamara *et al.* 1999: 173; Dumbrell 2004: 96–101; Elliott 2008).

As Rolling Thunder progressed, Moscow stepped up its military and logistical support to North Vietnam. On July 24, a US F-4 became the first American aircraft to be shot down from a Russian anti-aircraft (SAM missile) site, staffed by Soviet technicians. Far from being insulated from the wider international dynamics, the leading decision-makers in Washington constantly saw the developing situation in terms of the great-power rivalries. Johnson fretted that his decisions would lead to superpower confrontation. In July 1965, he quizzed General Earle Wheeler (chairman of the Joint Chiefs) and Harold Johnson (Army Chief of Staff) about the prospect of either China and/or the USSR entering the war: 'If we come in with hundreds of thousands of men, won't this cause them [China and Russia] to come in?' When General Johnson gave his view that Beijing and Moscow wanted to avoid direct confrontation with the United States, LBJ recalled the Korean War: '[Douglas] MacArthur didn't think they would come in either.' At the 25 July meeting at Camp David, Clark Clifford, a close friend of LBJ and opponent of the escalation, declared that 'Russia and China don't intend for us to win this war'. In general, the escalatory decision-making proceeded on the assumption that the great communist powers would step aside from direct involvement. However, LBJ's decisions ultimately were driven by the perceived need to stand up to those powers, even as fear of Moscow and Beijing led him to the doctrine of 'limited war'. In comparison to LBJ, Secretary of State Dean Rusk was the rock of certainty. One can imagine LBJ being swayed by the Georgian's declaration of 21 July 1965: 'If the communist world found out that the United States would not pursue its commitment to the end, there was no telling where they would stop their expansionisms' (*FRUS* 1964–68, 3: 215; Berman 1982: 110; Clifford 1991: 420).

In late February, LBJ, responding to a request from General Westmoreland, sent 3,500 Marines to protect the Danang air base. Westmoreland's troop requests, made against a background of a worsening military situation, drove the timing of the escalation decisions, and caused Washington to abandon the 1964 notion of committing large numbers to Thailand, rather than directly to South Vietnam. By mid-May, around 47,000 American troops were in-country (compared with 23,000 at the beginning of 1965), with the US military commitment on course to reach 87,000. The major ground troop escalation decisions were, in fact, made as late as July 1965. An exchange between LBJ, George Ball and Mac Bundy on 21 July encapsulated key administration worries and mindsets as America finally went to war. The president raised the question of credibility. Would not the US be seen as a 'paper tiger' if mass troop commitments were further delayed? Ball responded that 'the worst blow would be that the mightiest power in the world is unable to defeat guerrillas'. Bundy argued the enemy would sustain many more losses than the US, to the point where Hanoi would simply have to accept defeat (Goldstein 2008: 213).

On 28 July 1965, LBJ announced that US fighting strength in Vietnam would rise as soon as possible to 125,000. The total reached 385,000 by late 1966 and 535,000 by the end of 1967. Lyndon Johnson thus committed his country to a gradualist, but open-ended, war. He also, as is sometimes overlooked, embarked on major air operations, beginning in April and code-named 'Steel Tiger', against the Ho Chi Minh Trail in Laos, and involving naval aircraft from December 1965. Johnson's decisions transformed the various theatres and centres of war, with, for example, power flowing away from the Saigon Embassy and to the US military command in Vietnam. The judgement of posterity is that LBJ made bad decisions. The decisions were not simply the product of drift. Johnson actually had a reasonably clear purpose: to do enough to contain communist advances in Indochina without risking confrontation with the big communist powers. He was not the prisoner of the bureaucracy; neither was he trapped in a narrow, self-reinforcing never-never land. As we have seen, Johnson received a wide range of advice. Some of it, such as Ambassador Lodge's plan to turn the direction of the conflict over to the US Navy, was simply daft. George Ball and Mike Mansfield urged disengagement, while Senator Richard Russell offered a cautious, conservative analysis of American options in Vietnam. The common view of George Ball as a lonely, institutionalized devil's advocate does not pass muster. Even among the 'hawks' there was a wide variety of policy choices on display. Throughout 1964 and 1965, the Joint Chiefs offered a rococo selection of suggestions about how to progress the war; these included bombing, troop commitments and amphibious expeditionary activity. JCS recommendations were invariably reflective of inter-service rivalry and embodied an almost congenital underestimation of the enemy. The job of the Joint Chiefs, it is true, was made more difficult by LBJ's prickly attitude towards military advice, as well as the rather stifling quality of McNamara's leadership at the Pentagon. LBJ should have more assiduously pursued a clear, integrated military assessment of what was needed to win in Vietnam. LBJ was no more the prisoner of the military than he was the prisoner of the civilian bureaucracy. Nevertheless, the Joint Chiefs must shoulder their share of the blame for a decision-making process that was, indeed, yielding bad decisions (McMaster 1997; Winters 1997: 173).

Some familiar charges against Johnson are fair. As a president, LBJ was too emotion-driven to undertake much systematic and rational analysis of his own assumptions, or of the options open to him. He tended, like many other presidents, to think in terms of short-term electoral cycles. Despite the range of advice coming into the White House, incomplete analysis carried the day. What can be said in favour of Johnson is that he always had a sensible fear of a third world war. Indeed, the fear of global nuclear conflict was arguably the single biggest concern of his entire presidency. He opened and concluded his first National Security Council meeting in 1963 with the statement that 'nuclear war would be the death of all our hopes and it is our task to see that it does not happen'. The efforts of the Joint Chiefs to talk him into blockading North Vietnam and start direct bombing of Hanoi infuriated LBJ. The President berated

he military heads in November 1965, in words recalled by military
aide Charles Cooper: 'You're trying to get me to start World War III
with your idiotic bullshit ... How can you fucking assholes ignore
what China might do?' Going half-way to war in 1965 was LBJ's
way of balancing the perceived need (geopolitical and ideological, as
well as narrowly political) to hold the line in Vietnam, with this overwhelming commitment to avoid a nuclear catastrophe (Berman
1982: 146; Hatcher 1990: 185–7; Record 2002; Dumbrell 2004: 60;
Appy 2008: 122–3).

Walt Rostow: True Believer

The idea that Johnson's outlook on Vietnam was shaped by narrow,
self-reinforcing 'groupthink' is invariably linked to the personality
and influence of Walt Rostow, who served as national security
adviser from March 1966 to the end of the Johnson administration.
For Irving Janis (1982: 119), Rostow was LBJ's 'mindguard'.
Towsend Hoopes (1969: 61) described Walt Rostow as a 'fanatic in
sheep's clothing'. By the early part of 1966, Mac Bundy's relationship with the overbearing President had deteriorated, though there is
conflicting evidence about the degree to which creeping policy
doubts caused Bundy to welcome a release from office. The choice
of Rostow to succeed Bundy was a step in a hawkish direction.
Bundy himself regarded Rostow as foolishly optimistic in regard to
Vietnam. Bill Moyers, press secretary to LBJ, saw the association
between the 'true believer' Rostow and a president 'who felt inexpe-
rienced in the nuances of foreign policy' as inherently dangerous
(Bird 1998: 405; Milne 2008: 163; Blight *et al.* 2009: 185).

There is no real question about Rostow's hawkishness. What is
much more problematic, however, is the 'mindguard' accusation.
During 1966 and 1967, Johnson continued his practice of reaching
out to old friends and individuals across the administration, many of
whom had significant doubts about the war. During Rostow's time in
office, the weekly 'Tuesday lunch' meeting developed as the key
forum for Vietnam decision-making. Regular attendees at lunches
(which actually did not always meet on Tuesdays) included LBJ,
Rostow, Rusk, McNamara (with Clark Clifford eventually succeeding as Secretary of Defence), General Earle Wheeler, and CIA head
Richard Helms. However, far from contracting to an embattled core

of bellicose die-hards, the lunch meeting membership actually grew between 1966 and 1969. The attractions of the Tuesday lunches included flexibility and reliable confidentiality, and it is not difficult to understand why LBJ favoured this mechanism over the full National Security Council. Rostow organized the lunch agendas and subsequently communicated decisions to the bureaucracy. However, this was no more than his duty as special assistant. The legend of Rostow as a White House Rasputin, trapping Johnson in a Tuesday lunch capsule, is another misleading war myth. Also relevant here is LBJ's creation in 1965 of a parallel body of 'wise men' (including at various times Henry Cabot Lodge, LBJ's friend Justice Abe Fortas, UN Ambassador Arthur Goldberg, and former Secretary of State Dean Acheson) to advise on Vietnam. Rostow had no influence with this group (Mulcahy 1995).

Walt Rostow was born in Brooklyn, New York in 1916, the son of a Ukrainian Jewish refugee father and an American-born mother, herself the daughter of Russian immigrants. His story was one of immense achievement and intellectual distinction, as was that of his brother, Eugene, who worked as an Undersecretary of State under Dean Rusk. (The Rostows thus joined the brothers Dulles, Kennedy, Ngo Dinh and Bundy in claiming important roles in the saga of America and Vietnam.) The Rostow brothers rejected and rebelled against their parents' progressive/popular front socialism. Their anti-communism was intellectual, as well as profoundly emotional. After study at Yale and Oxford, Walt was appointed Professor of Economic History at the Massachusetts Institute of Technology. His great work, *The Stages of Economic Growth* (largely deriving from work in Cambridge, England, in the late 1950s) depicted communism as a malady of societies progressing from traditional to modern stages of development. Joining a group of intellectuals in the Kennedy administration, Walt Rostow sought to test and apply his views on global modernization. A combination of directed aid and sensitive coercion could cure the communist malady.

Walt Rostow (1958: 143) saw a major problem for America in the rise of big institutions and the decline of 'private adventure'. As deputy to McGeorge Bundy, Rostow set himself up as a buccaneering policy entrepreneur, offering JFK a range of hawkish advice: against the neutralization of Laos, for committing US ground forces to the Mekong Delta as early as 1961, even for invading North Vietnam after issuing a warning to stop meddling in the affairs of

South Vietnam. His October 1961 trip to Vietnam with Maxwell Taylor confirmed his view that only pressure on Hanoi could secure the future of Saigon. President Kennedy saw Rostow as bright, but extreme. Walt was moved out of the White House and into the headship of the State Department Policy Planning staff. Here, Rostow developed ideas, about the purpose of air power, which had been hatched during his Second World War service as a bombing analyst for the Office of Strategic Services. According to his developing line, the US needed to appreciate that North Vietnam had an industrial base to defend. Rostow told Dean Rusk in February 1964 that graduated pressure from the air would force Hanoi to 'call off the war principally because of its fear that it would otherwise risk loss of its politically important industrial development' (Milne 2008: 136). Rostow's views about the economic dimension of air power coercion, though not entirely accepted either by LBJ or by McNamara, still fed into the rationale for the Rolling Thunder campaign. Rightly regarded as an 'advanced hawk', Rostow was nevertheless, until the autumn of 1965, an advocate of gradualism rather than all-out war.

From 1966, Rostow combined the role of hawkish policy advocate with a degree of procedural neutrality appropriate for the role of national security adviser. His extreme scepticism about opportunities for negotiated peace was an important factor in the collapse of various negotiating initiatives based on mutual de-escalation. Where Johnson agonized, Mac Bundy wobbled and McNamara changed course, Rostow stayed firm and upbeat. When LBJ decided, in mid-1967, against massive extra troop commitments and clearly set his face against invading the DRV, Rostow told the President that the US was still 'on a winning track' if only it had 'the capacity to sweat it out' (Barrett 1993: 105). Rostow's views did not mesh with LBJ's, and the President did not have the same level of respect for Rostow as he had for the (almost) equally hard-line Dean Rusk. For Johnson, Rostow's views represented the extreme limits of acceptable policy. Thus did Rostow become one pole of the compass – arguably Mike Mansfield was the other – by which President Johnson could plot his decisional middle way.

During 1968, Rostow continued to urge wider bombing and positive responses to Westmoreland's troop requests. The White House should reject panicky and unrealistic calls for concessions and peace negotiations. Rostow argued, in February 1968, that Hanoi's Tet Offensive revealed that ordinary South Vietnamese people did not want to become slaves of Moscow or Beijing. As the dynamics of American policy developed in the wake of the Tet Offensive, Rostow found himself drawn into conflicts with Clark Clifford, McNamara's successor at the Pentagon, and with Averell Harriman, named by LBJ as chief negotiator at the Paris peace talks. From his office at the Lyndon Johnson Presidential Library in Austin, Texas, Walt Rostow spent the postwar years in academic pursuits and in defending the purpose, and even conduct, of America's war in Vietnam.

1965–67: Peace Feelers and War Developments

Even as the escalation decisions were being made, the White House retained hopes for a negotiated peace. After all, in the last analysis, the success of graduated war depended on the possibility of eventual negotiations. The US has often been accused of sabotaging peace efforts between 1964 and 1968 (Kraslow and Loory 1968: 52; Porter 1975: 55). Such accusations contain an element of truth. United Nations mediation efforts in 1964–65, for example, were not exactly rebuffed by Washington, but they were not exactly taken very seriously either. Johnson referred to his willingness to give peace feelers 'the old college try' – exploring possibilities, partly for national and international public effect, but partly also in what his wife called 'almost a little boy sort of hope ... for peace' (Dallek 1996: 153; Vandiver 1997: 264). The dominant American position, prior to the 1965 escalation, was that – given the parlous situation in Saigon – the US would be negotiating from a position of weakness. Following his Johns Hopkins University speech of 7 April 1965, with its vision of turning the Mekong Basin into the Tennessee Valley, LBJ decided on a one-week bombing pause. Hanoi responded by issuing its Four Points – essentially a restatement of the Geneva terms of 1954, with a demand for an end to 'foreign interference'. Discussions with North Vietnamese diplomats in the 1990s revealed that Hanoi wished to avoid being seen by China to respond positively to the Johns Hopkins speech, which Beijing interpreted as a straightforward attempt to sow dissension between the DRV and China (Herring 1995: 91; McNamara *et al.* 1999: 263; Carter 2008: 170).

The post-1964 peace initiatives were ferociously complex and can only be treated here in crude outline. Several lines of indirect contact with Hanoi were established by Washington during a 37 day bombing pause, beginning on 24 December 1965. Such action was taken by the Johnson administration in the teeth of opposition from the Joint Chiefs. In his 1966 State of the Union address, LBJ promised to consider the 'views of any group' – presumably including the NLF – in order to achieve a Vietnam settlement. From Saigon, however, Ambassador Lodge reported that 1,000 PAVN troops per day were moving south. Divisions in the administration were revealed in Robert McNamara's expressed view that infiltration levels from the DRV were unrelated to US bombing. By this time, McNamara was coming close to his crisis of faith in the entire war strategy. Administration doubts were reinforced by civil disorder in South Vietnam in April 1966, when the Pentagon was ordered to draw up a contingency plan for a quick American exit from the country (*FRUS 1964–68*, 4: 317). The peace initiatives of 1966–67 were undermined by these administration divisions about whether any purpose was being served by them beyond that of international public relations. There was also an inherent paradox about seeking to negotiate while fighting. As John McNaughton (chief assistant to McNamara) put it in January 1966: 'while going for victory, we have the strength for compromise, but if we go for compromise we have the strength only for defeat' (*PP* 4, 1972: 47).

Following the failure of the 1965 UN mediation, George Ball took charge of secret contacts in Paris with Mai Van Bo, a North Vietnamese representative based in France. The main focus of debate at this time was on reconvening the Geneva Conference following mutual de-escalation. Bo pulled back from serious discussion of this in September 1965. A significant channel was opened via the Hungarian government of Janos Kadar. A major Polish initiative, obliquely backed by Moscow, developed into a massively complex diplomatic operation, with Rome and London also involved. Code-named 'Marigold', the initiative centred on the possibility of linking Hanoi's agreement to recognize an independent, non-communist Saigon, along with mutual de-escalation. Further bombing pauses ensued. As part of the initiative, Arthur Goldberg (former Supreme Court Justice and now US Ambassador to the UN) publicly stated that the US was prepared to move to talks if Hanoi provided credible assurances of de-escalation and good faith. The Marigold contacts collapsed amid mutual distrust and the failure of Moscow to provide firm endorsement of the process. The episode was formally terminated by resumed

American bombing in mid-December 1966 (Herring 1994: 212, 389; Gardner 2000: 41).

Despite the collapse of the Marigold initiatives, in early 1967 Soviet sources informed Washington that Hanoi was now open to the possibility of negotiations commencing without prior US acceptance of a communist role in a future Saigon government. Contacts between US and DRV diplomats were developed via the North Vietnamese Embassy in Moscow. Alexander Zinchuk, a Soviet diplomat, reported in January 1967 that there were 'forces for moderation in Hanoi – forces who think they cannot win the war and that a compromise must be made at some point'. A series of de-escalatory initiatives, codenamed 'Sunflower', involved direct written communication between LBJ and Ho Chi Minh. There were indications from Moscow – indeed, from Aleksei Kosygin at the Glassboro (New Jersey) summit of June 1967 – that some kind of deal might be available on the basis of a new understanding of South Vietnamese 'self-determination'. Kosygin told LBJ that the US should stop dealing with Hanoi via intermediaries: direct talks were a real possibility (Dumbrell 2004: 120, 125).

Hints like these led on to what LBJ seems to have regarded as the most promising of all initiatives between 1965 and 1967: the 'Pennsylvania' contacts of July–September 1967, overseen by (Pennsylvanian) Benjamin Read in the State Department. The contacts (which involved Henry Kissinger, then a Harvard academic with links to the administration) were sufficiently promising to stimulate a significant public statement of America's public position: the 'San Antonio formula', announced by LBJ in the Texan city on 29 September. The speech was largely drafted by McNamara, who saw it as a chance to further the peace initiatives. LBJ announced that the US was 'willing to stop all aerial and naval bombardment of North Vietnam when this will lead promptly to productive discussions'. The credibility of the San Antonio position was reinforced by LBJ making it clear that Washington would not tolerate the DRV taking 'advantage of the bombing cessation or limitation'. The US position in the Pennsylvania contacts was that open negotiations could begin if Washington was convinced that Hanoi was stopping (or had stopped – this was never clear) infiltrating to the South. If Hanoi wanted secret talks, there would be no bombing halt. Washington also signalled its willingness to be reasonably flexible on the issue of South Vietnamese self-determination. By early September, Robert

McNamara was urging LBJ to signal that the NLF would be accepted into a future Saigon coalition. LBJ, heeding Dean Rusk's cautious line, never went quite so far, but does seem to have been prepared to countenance NLF involvement in a future South Vietnamese government, if the organization could somehow be prevailed upon to renounce its communist and revolutionary programme. Ellsworth Bunker (who served as Ambassador in Saigon from 1967 right through to 1973) favoured pressurizing Saigon to admit former communists – indeed, former Viet Cong – into government. Johnson preferred a more general broadening of the government to 'make it as civilian as possible' (Gardner 1995: 384, 389; Dumbrell 2004: 25–6).

The modalities of the Pennsylvania proto-dialogue proved impossible to agree, or even clearly to codify. In what sense *could* the NLF be transformed into a credibly non-communist, non-revolutionary organization? How *could* assured reciprocity in de-escalation be achieved? The problem here was similar to that faced by negotiators in Northern Ireland in the 1990s. There, resolution was assisted by the concept of all sides – London, loyalists and republicans – 'jumping together'. The 1967 Vietnam contacts failed to produce any such shared commitment. Though some North Vietnamese leaders were impressed by the San Antonio and Pennsylvania opportunities, the official Hanoi line was that Washington was simply engaging in trickery. The 1967 initiatives expired as American bombers, yet again, returned to the skies over North Vietnam (McNamara *et al.* 1999: 308; Brigham and Herring 2004).

It is too easy simply to blame the Johnson administration for squandering the opportunities for negotiations in this period. Some of the American peace activity was, as we have seen, ritualistic and unconvincing. However, the Johnson administration was genuinely hopeful that Moscow could and would push Hanoi towards a viable negotiating position – essentially, through halting infiltration and through modifying demands for communist participation in a post-settlement government in Saigon. Washington was encouraged along these lines on numerous occasions. For example, USSR Foreign Minister Andrei Gromyko told Dean Rusk in September 1965 that a peace conference between the US, the Soviet Union and the DRV was feasible, and that Beijing 'would not use force to prevent it'. Hopes for positive Soviet involvement were not unreasonable, but were consistently disappointed. Aleksei Kosygin seems to have wished for a quick end to the war, not least because of the drain on Soviet resources. Other senior figures in the Soviet capital were not necessarily of the same view. At base, the Soviet attitude was that Hanoi *should* move towards serious negotiations. However, there was sufficient doubt about the eventual success and accept-ability of such negotiations to cause Moscow to step back from doing anything approaching forthright sponsorship of a peace process. Above all, prospects were dimmed by the operation of the Sino–Soviet rivalry. The most authoritative account of the Hungarian channel concludes that the inter-communist split, rather than American bad faith, was the main reason for the failure of the Kadar initiatives. Moscow was wary of fulfilling Beijing's prophe-cies of Soviet complicity in America's imperialist agenda. Moscow and its Warsaw Pact allies supported Hanoi in order to fend off Beijing while enhancing the DRV bargaining position: 'Instead of strengthening Hanoi's desire for peace, these contradictory policies prepared the North Vietnamese for a protracted war and reinforced their conviction that they could win a war regardless of what the United States did' (Dumbrell 2004: 107–8; Gaiduk 2005; Szoke 2010: 122).

The first half of 1967 saw massive American search-and-destroy sweeps in South Vietnam: notably Cedar Falls (in the 'Iron Triangle' northwest of Saigon) and Junction City (aimed at the elim-ination of COSVN). The sweeps inflicted significant damage on both the PAVN in North Vietman and the People's Liberation Armed Forces (PLAF) in South Vietnam, causing Hanoi to switch strategy away from Thanh's 'liberated base zones' and towards reliance on border sanctuaries. By this time, LBJ saw the most likely resolution of the war as coming from stabilization in the South, followed by handing-over security responsibilities to Saigon. Some of the most famous initiatives of the Nixon years – including the CIA Phoenix programme against communist cadres in the South, as well as 'Vietnamization' – were already under way before 1968. Ellsworth Bunker, sent to Saigon in early 1967 to replace Ambassador Lodge, was told that his job was to 'wind up the war for American troops as quickly as possible', pending the handover to the South Vietnamese. A strategy conference, held in Guam in March 1967, stimulated a major debate about troop levels and bombing. Westmoreland was gloomy: he complained that too many bombing pauses and failure to meet extra troop requests could lead to the war going on 'indefinitely'. Eventually, in July 1967, LBJ announced that he was sending just over 47,000 additional troops – well under half the number requested by General Westmoreland (Palmer 1984: 48; Barrett 1993: 77, 104).

Johnson was still seeking middle ground between 'peaceniks', like Averell Harriman and Arthur Goldberg, and 'bombers', like Abe Fortas and Walt Rostow. Now firmly in the de-escalation camp, Robert McNamara considered various ways out of what he had come to see as a military impasse. He promoted plans for an anti-infiltration electronic fence across the DMZ, an idea condemned by Admiral U. S. Sharp (head of Pacific Naval Command from 1964 to 1968) as ridiculous. Some sections of 'McNamara's wall' were completed and fitted with sensors to detect major troop movements. At the Guam conference, McNamara recommended troop increases of no more than 30,000, with bombing restricted to the North Vietnamese infiltration routes. He continued to convey his doubts to LBJ, who seems to have taken the former hawk's views very seriously, despite severe strains in their personal relationship. Exhausted and very close now to Bobby Kennedy – Johnson's hated political enemy – McNamara effectively left his post by the end of 1967, though he continued to participate in high-level war debates in early 1968. Johnson rejected JCS calls to invade Laos and/or North Vietnam itself; but he also ordered bombing to continue. The day when Saigon could assume responsibility for its own security seemed stubbornly far away. A gathering of the 'wise men' in early November 1967 held unanimously that withdrawal was inconceivable 'without a satisfactory settlement with the North' (Taylor 1972: 379).

One emerges from an examination of the events of 1964 to 1967 with a degree of sympathy for Johnson. At times, he was given some extraordinary advice, such as when McGeorge Bundy argued in 1965 that a failed US intervention in Vietnam would somehow be better for American credibility than no intervention at all. However, as we have seen, LBJ was his own boss. His dissembling over the Tonkin Gulf crisis is very difficult to defend. It stretches to the point of implausibility the classic *mea culpa* argument later put by Robert McNamara: that the 1964–65 war decisions were wrong, but that they rested upon 'honest mistakes' by American national security leaders (Oliver 2004a; Goldstein 2008: 167). By 1967, much less 1968, LBJ was a man operating under almost unimaginable stress.

Yet, however much we appreciate the Texan's conflictions and dilemmas, the conclusion cannot be resisted that the balance of most 'orthodox' *and* 'revisionist' writing on the war is correct: Johnson led the US (and other affected countries) into a disaster that was in large part of his own making.

4

The Tet Offensive

The year 1968 was when everything changed. In late 1967, optimism in the US was offset by gloomy private predictions from General Westmoreland about what might happen if American troop levels failed to keep pace with military need. President Johnson was in his customary state of self-doubt, bordering on existential despair. Yet, in 1967, it was still just about possible to give a plausibly persuasive public account of anti-communist progress in the war. South Vietnam had, in 1967, at least some of the appearance of a functioning state. By the end of 1968, and despite a major military victory over the communist forces, Washington was looking for a way out of Vietnam. The main purpose of this chapter is to explore the paradoxes and multi-levelled complexities of 1968.

Much of the current chapter will be taken up with an analysis of the background to, significance of, and American reaction to, the Tet (Vietnamese New Year) Offensive, launched by Hanoi on 30 January. We first consider the context of the DRV's military initiative, especially in relation to the communist great-powers. How successful was the Offensive? Why was it launched? Why did Washington fail to see it coming? We will also take this opportunity to consider the role of the US Congress, media and public opinion, thereby addressing some of the factors conventionally seen as shifting the terms of the war. By the end of 1968, LBJ had been ousted from the presidential election campaign by a challenge led, at least in part, by Eugene McCarthy, a rather unlikely leftist hero from Minnesota. How did domestic American factors, especially but not exclusively in the context of the Tet Offensive, shape the war? We end the chapter by considering the election of Richard Nixon, inheritor of LBJ's commitment to South Vietnam.

1968: Saigon, Hanoi, and the International Context

Saigon, in the later part of 1967, showed signs of greater stability, following the suppression of the Buddhist protests which had flared up during the previous year, when the government temporarily lost control of the ancient Vietnamese capital of Hue. By early 1968, South Vietnam was formally operating under a constitution, though scarcely a democratic one. The 1967 elections were not the complete farce that Washington feared. The US applied huge pressure on the leading candidates, and Marshall Ky was persuaded against directly challenging General Thieu. The latter's victory rested on 35 per cent of the popular vote, with a 'peace' candidate, Truong Dinh Dzu – who favoured negotiations with the NLF – gaining 17 per cent. Dzu's protests against election rigging were rewarded by his arrest. Yet, from Washington's viewpoint, this was almost a credible election. By many other criteria, South Vietnam was still very unstable. War-related disruption led to a drastic decline in the percentage of land under cultivation. South Vietnam was now a net *importer* of rice. Refugee levels in South Vietnam were reaching the level of nearly 2 million at the time of the Tet Offensive (Kahin 1986: 410, 429; Bradley 2009: 118).

The Tet Offensive has sometimes been interpreted as a sign of North Vietnamese weakness. According to James Wirtz (1991: 49), by 1967 PAVN and PLAF 'units were suffering a gradual erosion of combat capability, caused by a decrease in troop morale, and the logistics system in the south was being slowly eliminated by allied search-and-destroy operations'. General Thanh's move towards big-unit warfare in 1965 and 1966 had not delivered the goods. The way was open for a new military initiative, aimed at urban targets in the South and designed to incite a general popular uprising in South Vietnam. The Offensive would be protected by diversions, deceptions (not least the keeping open of negotiating channels) and secrecy. Most revisionist writers see the planning for the Offensive as flawed and unrealistic, reflecting both Hanoi's foolish obsession with the notion of the general Southern uprising, and its panicky reaction to Thanh's failure to achieve major breakthroughs (Davidson 1988: 448). How persuasive is this analysis?

Precise and reliable understanding of the strategic debates which took place in Hanoi prior to the Tet Offensive is almost impossible, and is overlaid by a series of postwar agendas. Official Vietnamese authorities have been concerned to claim Tet as a measured and almost preordained victory. Rather unconvincing postwar efforts have also been made to downplay the military damage done by the Offensive to the Southern revolutionary forces. Interpretations of the Offensive have been affected by the desire of some antiwar American historians to stress the futility of Westmoreland's search-and-destroy tactics, as well as by the wish of some revisionists to portray Tet as a lost American victory. A couple of points may help clarify the picture. First, Hanoi's strategic debates of 1967 were not panicky; they were prolonged and deliberative, even if they produced an inherently flawed plan. Hanoi's deliberations were conducted in a kind of dialectic between pragmatic planning on the one hand, and, on the other, adherence to Maoist doctrine of revolutionary stages culminating in a general uprising. Second, political and military leaders in Hanoi were often divided. Understanding of the Vietnam War has been hugely distorted by later western inclinations to see the North Vietnamese as monolithic, united and untroubled by doubt. Most decision-makers in Hanoi were troubled by General Thanh's lack of spectacular success. However, they also recognized the failure of Saigon to extend its control over most of the territory of South Vietnam, and the lack of penetration in the US bombing campaign. The Tet Offensive was more a reaction to apparent stalemate, and to the possibility of yet more American commitment to the war, than a gesture of desperation.

The decision to undertake the Offensive was not primarily traceable to the inexorable process of applying (or misapplying) Maoist principles. It was the product of intensely personal power struggles in North Vietnam, as well as of the indirect effect of pressures associated with the Soviet–Chinese rivalry. The move to urban attacks in the South, linked to a popular uprising there, had been under consideration by the Politburo since 1963, with Le Duan (party secretary general and former NLF chief) putting the case for such action in opposition to advocates of negotiations and/or prolonged war. General Giap, who favoured protracted guerrilla assaults on enemy lines of communication, regarded the Thanh line as adventurist and premature. Some recent Vietnamese scholarship tends to downplay the differences between Giap and Thanh; yet, there were clear differences of emphasis. The Plenum of the Lao Dong (the North Vietnamese communist party) passed a resolution in April 1967, calling for a 'spontaneous uprising in order to win a decisive victory in the shortest possible time' (Ang Cheng Guan 2002; Nguyen 2006: 31; Willbanks 2007: 10).

Although later communist accounts tend to exaggerate this aspect of the Plenum's decision, the doctrine of 'spontaneous uprising' was also intended, at some level, to take advantage of LBJ's political weaknesses in an election year. The Tet Offensive was thus designed to affect US congressional and public opinion in such a way as to make further American military commitments unlikely (Elliott 1993: 80; Long 1996). General Thanh's strange death in July 1967 did not alter the decision, which was upheld and vigorously supported by Le Duan. General Tran Van Tra, a senior PLAF commander in 1968, later provided an interesting, if tendentious, account of the genesis and objectives of the Offensive. For the Viet Cong leadership, the Offensive was the product of confidence in a winning situation, not of strategic weakness, though Hanoi certainly did fail to allow the PLAF adequate preparation time. Objectives for the operation included: transferring power from the Saigon regime to 'the people'; forcing Washington into making difficult and damaging strategic choices; destroying America's military infrastructure in Vietnam; and breaking the US 'will of aggression' (Tran Van Tra 1993: 40; Currey 1999; Nguyen 2006: 32; Willbanks 2007: 11, 80; Schandler 2009: 122).

Beijing's line in the build-up to the Tet Offensive was that the DRV should follow a long war of guerrilla attrition. The April 1967 Hanoi Plenum decision, though sometimes seen as fulfilling Maoist 'revolutionary stages' doctrine, actually flew in the face of Chinese advice. As Quiang Zhai (2000b: 177) explains, the Tet Offensive 'shifted the focus of revolutionary struggle from the rural to urban areas well before the third' (general offensive) 'stage and committed the revolutionary forces to positional war prematurely'. Beijing saw a long and enervating American involvement in Vietnam as beneficial to Chinese interests, not least because only the Soviets could supply the kind of military hardware necessary to pursue a decisive positional or big-unit war. The April 1967 decision to some degree reflected the perception in Hanoi that the internal Chinese upheavals, associated with Mao's Cultural Revolution, made Beijing a less potent regional force. North Vietnamese attitudes to Beijing were traceable less to ancient geopolitical suspicion, and more to the horrors of contemporary Chinese politics. Preoccupied by its internal troubles, unenthusiastic about the post-Tet peace process and concerned about a possible US–Soviet rapprochement, Beijing began severely to cut its aid to Hanoi (Garver 1996; Zhai 2000a: 122; Stolberg 2003: 254).

Hanoi further developed its policy of playing the communist great-powers off against one another. A new Soviet aid package was agreed at the end of 1967, more or less in direct response to the Chinese package of August 1967. Both aid packages were finalized *after* the April 1967 Hanoi decision to pursue 'spontaneous uprising'. A few days before the invasion, Llewellyn Thompson, US Ambassador in Moscow, reported that 'so long as the situation does not get out of control', the Soviet leadership was prepared to go along with Hanoi (Dumbrell 2004: 126). As we will see, the post-Tet peace talks were punctuated by interventions from Moscow. The Offensive, however, was primarily the initiative of Hanoi, not that of its powerful sponsors.

The Tet Offensive and American Reactions: January to April 1968

Hanoi camouflaged its military preparations by a strategy of deception, though US intelligence did pick up signs of the strategy shift. Deception was both diplomatic and military. On 30 December 1967, North Vietnamese Foreign Minister Nguyen Duy Trinh stated publicly that the DRV would respond positively to a bombing halt. This effective revival of the Pennsylvania process put Washington on the back foot and affected American assessments of likely DRV behaviour during the holiday ceasefire. Previous ceasefires had been violated; however, Trinh's statement made it almost impossible for Washington fully to accede to Westmoreland's request that no concessions be made to the enemy during the 1968 Tet celebrations. In general, the official US line was that military progress was being achieved, and that the 'crossover point' (where enemy fatalities were greater than the number of possible replacements) either had, or would soon, be reached. American analysis was made on the basis that Hanoi was operating from a position of weakness. Westmoreland certainly had some indications of what was to come. He cabled General Earle Wheeler on 20 December 1967 about an enemy decision, designed to reverse the 'deterioration of his position over the last six months' to 'undertake an intensified countrywide effort, perhaps a maximum effort, over a relatively short period'. LBJ himself told the Australian cabinet and the Pope on December 21 and 23 that Hanoi might do something desperate, even something 'Kamikaze' to reverse its fortunes (Wirtz 1991: 131–2, 190, 209).

American Vietnam War intelligence was chronically affected by cross-agency rivalry and lack of connectedness. Relations between the National Security Agency, America's signals intelligence facility, and the US military in Vietnam were especially dysfunctional (Warner 2010; Aldrich 2011: 271–2). In 1967–68, US estimates of enemy strength on the eve of the Offensive also reflected the sheer difficulty of assessing shifting numbers of PLAF guerrilla forces and communist regular units. In general terms, CIA analyses were more reliable than those coming from the US military, whose intelligence reports tended to understate enemy numbers. Scholarly analysis of America's Tet intelligence failure has focused on questions of politicized intelligence, distorting mindsets, and the so-called 'intelligence-to-please' syndrome, where intelligence agencies – even in the absence of pressure from higher authority – seek to be rewarded by presenting information which reinforces existing assumptions. There are significant parallels here with later intelligence failures, notably in relation to the presence of weapons of mass destruction in Iraq in 2002–03. Regarding Tet, Larry Cable (1996: 178) argues that the intelligence work of the CIA and of the State Department's Bureau of Intelligence and Research (INR) was 'excellent'. The real failure 'was one of strategic conceptualization, which in turn was the product of the polluted policy process'. The CIA produced a fairly accurate analysis of the developing communist attacks, compiled by Joseph Hovey, in early December 1967. Though the CIA and INR analyses failed to shift consensual assumptions about likely enemy behaviour, there is little evidence of official pressure to skew intelligence in favour of existing policy. American intelligence officers were not so much keen to please, as unwilling to contemplate that the DRV would launch such a massively risky assault (Wirtz 1991: 259, 273; Jervis 1996: 235; NSA 2008: 11).

Like Westmoreland and the decision-makers in Washington, the Central Intelligence Agency and the National Security Agency were misled by the diversionary tactics of the DRV. On 31 January 1968, the CIA reported that the coordinated attacks of the previous day were preparations for a major attack in the region of Khe Sanh; the NSA subsequently claimed credit for predicting the entire Offensive, but now seems also merely to have picked up information about the Khe Sanh attack. The siege at Khe Sanh, a remote outpost near the 17th parallel, was the culmination of a battle for control of the surrounding high ground which had begun in mid-1967. Westmoreland saw the Marine base at Khe Sanh as an ideal launching point for an invasion of Laos. By January 1968, however, US Marines there were defending themselves, as Michael Herr (1979: 89) memorably put it 'like antichrists at vespers'. Westmoreland's view, that this would be the crucial battle of the war, was accepted in Washington and communicated to the press, who covered the story as a possible re-run of Dien Bien Phu. The degree to which Khe Sanh actually was intended as a deception is still disputed. The diversions were intended to be large; however, if Khe Sanh was intended as a diversion, it was an extraordinarily costly one. The siege was lifted in April, though the Marines abandoned the base in June 1968. US losses were about 200 and enemy fatalities possibly as many as 10,000. Khe Sanh may have been seen by General Giap as a test of American will. It was too big an operation to be regarded *merely* as a diversion, even though it functioned as such – for example, in causing US intelligence resources to be switched away from the cities of South Vietnam. The very over-commitment of Hanoi to the putative 'diversion' made it more difficult for US intelligence, whose understanding of communist motivation tended to assume goal-oriented rationality, to interpret enemy behaviour (Davidson 1988: 495; Wirtz 1991: 198, 234; Ford 1995: 111; Willbanks 2007: 64).

Like Khe Sanh, the North Korean seizing of the US intelligence ship, *Pueblo*, on 23 January 1968 has sometimes been regarded as intentionally diversionary. The degree to which official Washington was preoccupied with the *Pueblo* crisis unquestionably damaged its ability to process information relating to the Tet attacks. Lyndon Johnson and Walt Rostow maintained for the rest of their lives that there had been inter-communist collusion, extending to Moscow, with regard to the *Pueblo*. Recent scholarship tends to oppose such an interpretation. The Tet attacks were preceded by a series of – in retrospect, fairly obvious – smaller diversionary operations, designed to concentrate US attention along the DMZ. Hanoi also fostered rumours, intended to unsettle Saigon, that the US was about to call a truce for captured Viet Cong prisoners. When the non-diversionary Tet attacks came, they were initially devastating. Near-simultaneous assaults were mounted on over 100 South Vietnamese cities and military bases. Some of these assaults were not properly coordinated, and some (like the partial occupation of the US Embassy compound in Saigon) were effectively suicide missions. Around 84,000 communist forces were involved, though more from the South than from the North. Le Duan later commented: 'We are not so dumb as to use our main force units' (Oberdorfer 1971: 62; Duiker 1995: 212; DeGroot 2000: 164–6; Lerner 2003; Dumbrell 2004: 52).

There were some local risings in the South, but the mass 'spontaneous uprising' did not occur. The extreme secrecy surrounding the operation backfired to the extent that some local commanders were not properly attuned to the revolutionary schedule. The mobility of American forces also left little time for local cadres to organize. Hints of what was to come had caused Westmoreland to concentrate some important forces nearer urban centres in the south of the country in mid-January. He also managed to persuade ARVN commanders to keep large parts of their forces battle-ready over the holiday. In the urban centres, only cadres in Hue managed to set up a revolutionary organization, slaughtering thousands of South Vietnamese military and civilian personnel in the process. The 25-day siege of Hue lay at the centre of the post-invasion conflict. Between 29 January and 31 March, the combined communist forces lost around 58,000 personnel, with the ARVN and the Americans having about 3,400 killed or seriously wounded. The assault was a military failure, based on the illusion that the NLF had as much strength and popularity in the towns as it had in the villages. In purely military terms, Hanoi would have done better to heed Chinese advice and to keep to the maxim that revolution would come slowly from the countryside.

General Westmoreland proclaimed a great victory, actually so doing as he spoke to press reporters in the damaged American Embassy compound in Saigon. The MACV chief compared the Tet outcome to the enemy situation at the Battle of the Bulge in December 1944, following desperate German efforts to regain the initiative following the allied invasions. Especially when he insisted that the real battle was still for Khe Sanh, Westmoreland appeared out of touch with American domestic reaction to the Tet assaults. General Westmoreland now endorsed an expanded strategy, involving commando assaults on North Vietnam, attacks on communist supply lines in Laos and Cambodia, and unrestricted bombing. He also formally requested the eye-watering figure of 206,000 additional troops. Johnson immediately balked at this figure, which seemed simply undeliverable in an election year and in conditions where press, public, and congressional opinion had been shocked by the Tet attacks. The 206,000 request was cynical in the sense that it represented a negotiating bid, rather than a realistic assessment of need. The request came via MACV, but originated with General Earle Wheeler. The JCS chairman saw Tet as an opportunity to move away from limited warfare, or at least to shift blame in the likely event of the full request being rejected (Buzzanco 1996a: 312–4; Record 1998: 167).

The Tet Offensive signalled a shift in LBJ's decision-making apparatus in the direction of fluidity – even further removed from the 'groupthink' model which some analysts saw as characterizing procedures in 1965. Clark Clifford, recently confirmed as successor to McNamara at the Pentagon, was ordered to review the Westmoreland requests; he rapidly assembled a task force effectively to assess the entire Vietnam commitment. Clifford consciously used his 'relative ignorance' and quasi-outsider status to raise fundamental questions about the American military purpose in Vietnam. Clifford's report concluded, in effect, that the US Army had no coherent plan for victory. The new Defence Secretary recommended sending 'only' 22,000 extra troops, though he did suggest that reservists be alerted. Clifford's task force saw the solution to America's dilemmas as lying in a shifting of responsibilities to South Vietnam and the ARVN. It concluded: 'Perhaps the country we are trying to save is relying on the United States too much'. LBJ approved Clifford's recommendation for 22,000 troops, though not for reserve activation. The President seemed to be moving clearly away from the strategy of attrition, and further towards the Vietnamization policy that he had favoured since the middle of the previous year (Clifford 1991: 475, 492; Barrett 1997: 644; Haney 1997: 71–2; Willbanks 2007: 73, 121; Acacia 2009: 163–74).

As battles raged in South Vietnam, Johnson was being buffeted by critics of the war: by antiwar protestors; by journalists; by the Eugene McCarthy candidacy in the 1968 Democratic primary elections; even by his Treasury Secretary Joe Fowler, who warned about the war's impact on confidence in the dollar. With Eugene McCarthy running LBJ close in the New Hampshire primary election in early March, there ensued a battle for the soul of Lyndon Johnson. The declaration on 16 March of Robert Kennedy's ('Bobby', or 'RFK') candidacy in the 1968 election was a further arrow in the presidential heart. In the debates over the war's future, Westmoreland, the Joint Chiefs, Ambassador Bunker and Abe Fortas stood on the side of further escalation, designed to force home the gains made during the Offensive. According to Fortas, 'unless we "win" in Vietnam, our total national personality will ... change'. America would succumb to 'self-doubt and timidity'. Opposing them were the disengagers and proponents of rapid Vietnamization. A proposal from Arthur Goldberg on 16 March for a new bombing halt was taken seriously by LBJ. Goldberg, the US Ambassador to the UN, wrote: 'No foreseeable time will be better for negotiations than the present and never has a serious move toward a political settlement been more necessary' (Berman 1989: 185; Barrett 1993: 141).

Vice President Hubert Humphrey, whose advocacy of de-escalation tended to be pursued with Johnson in private, regarded the President in the immediate post-Tet period as 'desperate for peace'. LBJ convened a meeting of the 'wise men' on 26 March. Ground had clearly shifted since the previous year. McGeorge Bundy now declared that he had come to agree with George Ball. Douglas Dillon, a Republican who had worked for JFK as treasury secretary, gave his view that bombing should stop and that there should be no new troop deployments. He cited recent intelligence briefings, on lack of progress in the countryside, as the basis for his position. Several members of the group protested at the drift of advice coming from the likes of Bundy, Ball and Dillon. Maxwell Taylor saw the group as in danger of capitulating to panic on the home front. Dean Acheson expressed the view which seemed to capture the mood of the majority, and which formed the basis for LBJ's eventual decision: 'The issue is can we do what we are trying to do in Vietnam. I do not think we can.' On 27 March, LBJ heard the intelligence briefings which had already been considered by the 'wise men'. The President was told that the situation in rural South Vietnam was deteriorating and that Hanoi was convinced that the US had no real, lasting commitment to the fight. Johnson was not entirely persuaded by the pessimistic intelligence. The Tet attacks, after all, had been beaten back and Hue had been retaken, albeit after some of the bloodiest combat yet seen. Johnson, however, was now sure that something dramatic was required (Humphrey 1984b: 357; Barrett 1993: 151; 1997: 713–15; Spector 1993: 21).

On 31 March 1968, LBJ appeared on television to announce that bombing would be restricted to the area immediately north of the

DMZ as a first step towards de-escalation of the conflict. The US was now prepared to move immediately to negotiations. Johnson, one of the most ambitious and driven men ever to occupy the White House, also announced that he was no longer seeking the presidential nomination of the Democratic Party. LBJ gave his address some two weeks after mass killings of Vietnamese villagers in Son My district, south of Danang. The name of one of the affected villages, My Lai, would later become an abiding symbol of the madness of war.

Eugene McCarthy: Clean for Gene in '68

Eugene McCarthy, one of the most enigmatic political figures to be associated with the Vietnam conflict, was first elected to the House of Representatives in 1948 (at the age of 32) to represent Minnesota. He was elected to the Senate 10 years later. McCarthy wore his Roman Catholic intellectual background rather prominently, filling his Senate bookshelves with volumes by St Thomas Aquinas and frequently invoking Catholic social teaching. McCarthy made no secret of his desire to be America's first Catholic president, and was not a supporter of John Kennedy, whom he considered his intellectual inferior. In 1968, author Norman Mailer declared that McCarthy looked less like a president, 'more like the dean of the finest English department in the land'. McCarthy also had a difficult relationship with the senior Senator for Minnesota, Hubert Humphrey. The two were rivals for the vice presidential nomination under LBJ in 1964, with Humphrey – in contrast to the labels of 1968 – standing well to McCarthy's left. During 1965, only two other senators were more loyal than McCarthy to the presidential line on foreign policy votes. McCarthy supported the Gulf of Tonkin Resolution in 1964, declaring on television that it 'was a matter of responding to a direct attack on our ships' (Schlesinger 1978: 892; Sandbrook 2004: 126, 131).

McCarthy's emergence as an antiwar liberal derived from his experience on the Senate Foreign Relations Committee, to which he was assigned in April 1965. He came strongly under the influence of Committee chairman J. William Fulbright and antiwar committee staffers Pat Holt and Carl Marcy. McCarthy told the *Minnesota Tribune* in February 1966 that there was 'a much stronger element of a South Vietnamese civil war' to the conflict than the White House, obsessed by containment of communism, was prepared to admit. In 1967, McCarthy published *The Limits of Power,* ostensibly a critique of American imperialist internationalism. In practical terms, the book did little more than urge LBJ against becoming internationally isolated over Vietnam. McCarthy argued that military strategy should concentrate on consolidating control in chosen areas of South Vietnam, rather than attempting to dominate more widely. Eugene McCarthy denounced CIA interference in Vietnam and recommended UN mediation. During 1967, McCarthy also developed what was to become a major 1968 campaign theme, and a strong feature of late 1960s antiwar thinking: deep suspicion of executive power *per se*. McCarthy indicated that he would, if elected, be a one-term president. He viewed the presidency as a 'kind of channel' rather than as a platform of personal power. Following Senate testimony given by Undersecretary of State Nicholas Katzenbach in August 1967, McCarthy accused the Johnson administration of proposing a 'kind of dictatorship in foreign policy'. Asked in 1967 if he believed that the US should act to stop communism, McCarthy replied: 'Yes, I do. And South Vietnam is the worst possible place to try' (McCarthy 1967: 95, 191–5; Rinzler 1969: 24; Sandbrook 2004: 137, 167, 194).

By early 1968, Eugene McCarthy was the candidate of the 'dump Johnson' tendency in the Democratic Party, organized by Allard Lowenstein and attracting antiwar student leftists. The McCarthy candidacy was treated initially as a joke. Lowenstein would have preferred a Bobby Kennedy challenge to LBJ; *Newsweek* described McCarthy in October 1967 as 'a scholarly, witty, somewhat lazy man who writes books, reads poetry and laces his lectures with dollops of theology'. Yet, the Tet Offensive transformed the campaign, igniting Democratic Party 'new politics'. By the time of the New Hampshire vote, Johnson saw McCarthy as a viable protest candidate. According to the President, 'Every son-of-a-bitch in New Hampshire who's mad at his wife or the postman or anybody is going to vote for Gene McCarthy'. Johnson had a point. Political researchers found that significant numbers of McCarthy voters in New Hampshire in March 1968 actually supported the southern, prowar Democratic breakaway candidate George Wallace in the November election. First reports from New Hampshire indicated that LBJ had beaten McCarthy 49 to 42 per cent, though, when Republican write-ins were counted, the margin narrowed to less than 1 per cent (Converse *et al.* 1969; Barrett 1993: 137; Dallek 1998: 525; Woods 2006: 813).

During the ensuing primary races, with LBJ no longer a candidate, McCarthy scored many clear rhetorical hits in respect of the war. Responding to the argument that the Tet Offensive had been a defeat for the communists, McCarthy argued that 'by this logic ... if the Vietcong captured the entire country, the Administration would be claiming their total collapse'. McCarthy did, however, agree with LBJ on one point: that Bobby Kennedy was a shameless opportunist. Soon RFK was outdoing McCarthy's antiwar rhetoric, becoming one of the first people to invoke parallels between Vietnam and the American Civil War. Kennedy told an audience at Kansas State University that the war in Vietnam had 'divided Americans as they have not been divided since your state was called Bloody Kansas'. In fact, Robert Kennedy was able fairly easily to overtake McCarthy's momentum, through a combination of money, Kennedy fame and the ability to transcend the single antiwar issue, especially in his appeal to minorities. Yet, the campaign was hard fought, with McCarthy coming back in the Oregon primary and the two leftist candidates coming face to face in a debate for the California primary in early June. The difference between the candidates on the war was not easy to discern. Neither proposed immediate US withdrawal from Vietnam. Kennedy accused McCarthy of wanting to 'force' a coalition government on Saigon even before the beginning of negotiations. 'Clean for Gene' supporters made much of RFK's links with Robert McNamara, still regarded by many antiwar radicals as an unreconstructed hawk. McCarthy insisted that the NLF would take its place as part of a new South Vietnamese government (Heymann 1999: 456; Sandbrook 2004: 177–8).

Robert Kennedy's assassination on 4 June 1968 set in train the events which culminated in the tempestuous Chicago Democratic Party convention and the nomination of Hubert Humphrey. In retrospect, it can be seen that McCarthy had little realistic chance of the nomination. He lacked both the charisma of RFK and the party establishment support of Humphrey. McCarthy's conduct after the convention bordered on the bizarre, as he dithered about whether or not to endorse Humphrey. Hubert Humphrey, defeated in the 1968 presidential election, took over McCarthy's Senate seat in 1970, as the hero of New Hampshire from 1968 tried another presidential bid. The 1968 McCarthy campaign is now remembered as a species of idealistic but doomed children's crusade. There can be no question about McCarthy's historical significance: in contributing to LBJ's decision to quit, in sparking Robert Kennedy's campaign, and in channelling antiwar frustration and emotion. Introspective and sometimes arrogant, McCarthy was a rather unworthy leftist hero. Hubert Humphrey, with uncharacteristic bitterness, recalled his fellow senator from Minnesota as cynical and 'extremely superficial' (Carter 2010: 141). Yet, McCarthy somehow retained a degree of perceived 'authenticity' – a key, if sometimes counter-productive, concept in the political self-image of 1960s and 1970s American leftism.

Media War Coverage and Public Opinion

Both President Johnson and President Nixon blamed irresponsible media coverage for making their jobs as war leaders more difficult – even to the point of blaming the media for failures in Vietnam. The theme of the irresponsible, even unpatriotic, media remains prominent in revisionist analysis. LBJ told the National Association of Broadcasters, on the day following the announcement of his withdrawal from the 1968 nomination race, that he had been the victim of 'punk kid reporters' and vivid television filming of combat. Earlier war presidents, he argued, had not had to contend with emotive visual imagery of combat being relayed into the living rooms of ordinary voters (Halberstam 1979: 429; Hallin 1986: 103). US servicemen, especially in the war's later stages, tended to assume that the domestic media coverage of the war was balanced against them, especially in relation to the reporting of war atrocities. A veteran quoted by Kyle Longley (2008: 151) recalled finding the mutilated corpses of *montagnard* women, murdered by the Viet Cong, and reflecting that only the forces' newspaper, the *Stars and Stripes*, was ever likely to report it.

LBJ began seriously to worry about the effects of television coverage of the war in August 1965 when CBS correspondent Murray Safer filed a report which showed US Marines burning thatched peasant homes in the village of Cam Ne. The Pentagon insisted that the village huts, or 'hooches', had somehow caught fire by accident. By 1967, the administration was consciously operating to contest the media image of stalemate in Vietnam. Westmoreland was brought back to Washington in November to announce evidence of progress, along with the need for patience and persistence. Media coverage of the Tet Offensive tended to portray the US military as shaken, demoralized, and even in retreat. The Offensive produced what was probably the most famous statement made by a US military figure about the war, and one of its most shocking photographic images. The post-Tet battle for Ben Tre provoked the notorious US military pronouncement: 'We had to destroy the town to save it'. Near the beginning of the Offensive, NBC carried footage of a South Vietnamese general shooting a captured Viet Cong commander in the head. The still photograph of this incident became an iconic emblem of the war, along with the later, equally familiar, photo of the nine-year-old naked Vietnamese girl, Kim Phuc, a victim of napalm bombing. Reacting to television and photographic reporting of the Offensive aftermath, LBJ aide Harry McPherson recalled: 'I put aside the confidential cables. I was more persuaded by the tube and the newspapers.' On 27 February 1968, NBC anchorman Walter Cronkite hosted a Vietnam TV 'special' in which he portrayed the military situation as one of stalemate, and proclaimed the need for negotiated disengagement. Johnson reportedly told his press secretary George Christian, 'If I've lost Cronkite, I've lost middle America' (Braestrup 1983; Karnow 1983: 548; Kolko 1987: 309; Kinney 2000: 187; Willbanks 2007: 69; OH 2010c: 3; Pach 2010).

Media coverage of the Vietnam War was facilitated by technological change – primarily the development of lightweight sound cameras and jet transportation of film – and by the relative absence of censorship. Edith Lederer of Associated Press later recalled: 'You could go down to one of the helicopter bases, get on a helicopter – if there was an empty seat – go out to one of the battle zones, stay for as long as you wanted, and then get a ride back' (OH 2010c: 6). This, after all, was not an all-out conflict, attracting the full weight of US government control. An accreditation system for reporters involved the acceptance of voluntary guidelines about the communication of military sensitive information. US journalists in Vietnam frequently complained about lack of cooperation from the military authorities. However, there was considerable freedom for reporters to travel and to file stories which were potentially damaging in terms of domestic US support for the war. It would also be wrong to imagine that most reports (or even most reporters) were automatically 'antiwar'. It is also wrong to imagine that the American public was saturated with real life/real time coverage of combat. Television companies were very conscious of the danger of offending the families of American war casualties. Daniel Hallin (1986: 103) noted that the 'visceral grimness and a sense of psychological damage done by the war' was much more evident in novels and memoirs of the war, rather than in TV coverage. Certainly before 1968, US war reporting was overwhelmingly supportive of the American cause. Even figures such as David Halberstam and Neil Sheehan were not initially so much opposed to the war as to the way it was being conducted. Critical in-country journalism had to run the gauntlet of more conservative editors in the United States. Nevertheless, and particularly after February 1968, many journalists tended to adopt a directly adversarial stance, which complicated the task of the war managers. Yet, post-Tet negotiating initiatives by Johnson and Nixon were given favourable coverage, while large questions about anti-communist containment, the strategic importance of Vietnam and the wider morality of the war were raised surprisingly rarely.

Whatever the conventional wisdom may be, wars are not won or lost on television screens. What Vietnam War scholarship has so far failed to achieve is a persuasive analysis of the interconnections between media coverage, public opinion and war decisions. Let us put forward a few relevant considerations.

First, although they had some successes, neither the Johnson nor the Nixon administration found a viable way of selling the war. LBJ never developed a persuasive public rationale for limited war. It was not easy to convince either press or public that half-leading the country into war would produce victory rather than stalemate. Nixon had public relations successes, notably in connection with the policy of Vietnamization and invocation of the 'Silent Majority', but was unable to sustain widespread backing for military action whose underlying purpose had become blurred. Both presidents saw media coverage as moulding public opinion, rather than press and TV reporting as reflecting public concerns and anxieties. LBJ paid attention to polls, and was increasingly troubled by them. He also tended to read public opinion through the lens of activity in Congress. By contrast, Nixon tended to see public opinion as mutable and more of an obstacle to 'right' policy. Both presidents saw public opinion as a 'problem', rather than as a resource or a democratic strength. War decisions were not made as a direct reflection of public opinion, not least because unambiguous statements of public preference were very rare. Political science literature tells us that presidents will take account of clear and stable expressions of public preference. It also suggests that public opinion operates on decision-making in a negative sense: typically setting barriers to action, rather than driving specific decisions. Presidential freedom of action is enhanced by the ambiguity and incoherence of aggregated public opinion (Nixon 1982: 324; Turner 1985; Dumbrell 1997a: 151–3; Foyle 1999: 185).

Second, what *was* the relationship between war reporting and public opinion? Since the war ended, argument and counter-argument have been distorted by the search for excuses for military failure on the one hand, and by the cult of the crusading, heroic journalist on the other. In his memoirs, Walter Cronkite (1996: 264, 383) tried to refute the Pentagon's 'belief that the media lost the war', *and* to claim credit for the 'daily coverage of the Vietnamese battlefield' having 'helped convince the American public that the carnage was not worth the candle'. Some journalists did later accept that media coverage directly damaged the American cause. According to Robert Elegant, an experienced Vietnam journalist, media distortions of the Tet Offensive inflamed public opinion and gravely harmed the US war effort. During the 1973–75 period, moreover, 'the political pressures built up by the media made it quite impossible for Washington to maintain even the minimal and moral support that would have enabled the Saigon regime to continue effective resistance'. This point about the very end of the war is an important one, but even Elegant tended almost instinctively to *assume* that the media were central to the war's outcome. Even in the case of clearly negative media coverage, observable and measurable empirical links between such coverage and public opinion shifts are almost impossible to establish (Elegant 1981: 79; Wyatt 1993: 146; Hammond 1998: 122).

Lastly, what were the main characteristics of US public opinion towards the war during the long years of American involvement in Vietnam? In broad terms, the Vietnam War demonstrated the unwillingness of the American public indefinitely to tolerate a conflict which appeared to lack clear objectives and which was producing high casualty rates. Until 1967, the public mood was hawkish. In June 1965, the weight of polling evidence indicated a public preference for sending in more troops. With the exception of Nixon's 1972 Christmas bombing of the DRV (opposed 51 to 37 per cent), the major escalatory decisions of the war did achieve public endorsement in the polls. By the end of 1967, however, there were signs of a change in the general structure and inclination of opinion. October 1967 polls indicated real anxiety about the apparent stalemate; for the first time in Gallup polling, a plurality of respondents (46 to 44 per cent) recorded their view that the war was a mistake. Only about 23 per cent of poll respondents appeared to accept Westmoreland's view in 1968 that Tet had been an American triumph; yet, only about 5 per cent of Americans seemed to favour anything like an immediate withdrawal. The Offensive reinforced the trends that had surfaced in the late 1967 polling. Contrary to the view that the irresponsible media mugged public opinion in early 1968, there was no dramatic change in support for the war. Rather, there was a proliferation of anxiety about the conflict, and an endorsement of the strategy announced by LBJ on 31 March. There is some evidence in the polling to suggest that self-identified 'hawkishness' actually increased in the immediate wake of the Tet Offensive, though 'dove' identification increased significantly between late 1967 and early 1969. Gallup polling in March 1968 showed 49 per cent of respondents describing the war as a mistake. By September 1968, however, half of respondents saw the US as making progress in Vietnam. President Nixon appreciated the complex structure of public opinion, in which a 'Silent Majority' was still prepared to support presidential initiatives. The invasion of Cambodia in 1970 was supported by narrow majorities in the polls. Nixon had, however, particularly after 1970, to contend with a high degree of generalized public opposition to the war. Sections of the organized working class, notably the auto worker unions, came to oppose the war by 1970. There seems to have been a further shift of opinion in May 1971, when polls began to indicate a substantial majority favouring complete US withdrawal, even if that meant the end of an independent South Vietnam. Rather startlingly, however, a December 1971 poll revealed only 15 per cent of respondents identifying Vietnam as the most important issue facing America (Harris 1973: 69–71, 75; Mueller 1973: 107; 1984; DeBenedetti 1990: 298, 322; VanDeMark 1991: 163; Appy 1993: 41; Walton 2002: 35; Schmitz 2005: 53, 112; Lawrence 2008b: 151–2).

The Role of the US Congress

During the later years of the Vietnam War, the executive branch of government was forced to operate within a framework of extreme congressional (or, more accurately, US Senate) hostility to the war, and particularly to any widening of the conflict. However, if we look at the entire history of the war, the picture that emerges is one of considerable legislative acquiescence in executive direction of American policy in Vietnam. By the mid-1960s, Congress had developed a tradition of deferring to the executive in Cold War decision-making. To some extent this deference had broken down during the Korean conflict, when Republican Senators attacked President Truman's handling of that war. However, the general thrust of congressional action between 1945 and the mid-1960s was to support anti-communist 'preponderant power' strategies, either from a conservative internationalist position (geared to the wide projection of US military power), or from a liberal internationalist stance, committed to exporting American political and economic practice to the developing world. Both types of legislative internationalism, conservative and liberal, accepted the need for strong executive discretion. The bipartisan tradition of legislative support for executive foreign policy discretion, especially associated with the memory of Republican Senator Arthur Vandenberg (Senate Foreign Relations Committee chairman in the early Cold War years) was slow to expire. Even Senator Wayne Morse, the Democrat from Oregon who had switched from the Republican Party in 1952, positively invoked the memory of Vandenberg when he rose to oppose the Tonkin Gulf Resolution in 1964 (*Congressional Record* 1 August 1964, 17762; Woods 2003).

During the Johnson years, Democratic congressional opposition to the war was held in check by a range of factors, including LBJ's sensitivity to legislative concerns, the fact that taxes were not noticeably raised to pay for the war, and the sheer reluctance to undercut the flow of money to troops fighting in Vietnam. Several Members of Congress regularly made antiwar speeches only to go ahead and vote for Vietnam War military appropriations. A range of antiwar opinions were voiced in Congress during the 1960s. Members questioned the morality of the war, but more often the practical wisdom of LBJ's handling of war decisions. Occasionally a quasi-isolationist note was struck, as in Republican Congressman Tim Lee Carter's remark of 1967: 'Our sons' lives are too precious to lose on foreign soil' (*Congressional Record* 28 August 1967, 24279). However, Members were reluctant to move far away from the Vandenberg rule on trusting the executive. While Senators were freer to develop anti-war stances, Representatives tended to be especially anxious not to be seen as straying far from constituency opinion. Roll call analysis of House votes on the war shows a correlation between voting patterns and regional public opinion, with Representatives from north-eastern states being most likely to register antiwar stances. Representatives also seem to have been aware of the visibility of antiwar votes. Only 17 war-related measures came to a House vote before 1969, with 94 being taken after Nixon's inauguration (Frye and Sullivan 1976: 199; Sinclair 1982: 119–25).

Conspicuous House doves in the Johnson years included Philip Burton, John Conyers and William Ryan – all Democrat. The Republican leadership in Congress – figures such as Charles Halleck in the House and Everett Dirksen of Illinois in the Senate – generally upheld bipartisan norms. However, the Senate Grand Old Party had a considerable number of war sceptics, including Jacob Javits of New York and John Sherman Cooper of Kentucky. The most cele-brated 'peacenik' of the period was J. William Fulbright, Democrat from Arkansas, chairman of the Senate Foreign Relations Committee. Fulbright's 1966 war hearings provided a platform for a range of antiwar positions: not least for George Kennan, the father of anti-communist containment, who argued that his doctrine had been torn out of its European context and inappropriately applied to Asia. A rather unlikely antiwar radical, Fulbright had sponsored the Gulf of Tonkin Resolution on the Senate floor. By the mid-1960s, he had come to the view that American international power was dangerously arrogant and over-extended. White House aide Jack Valenti told LBJ that Fulbright's new antiwar allies 'forget that he has consistently … obstructed measures aimed at extending the civil rights of Negroes'. Fulbright's journey to hostility to the war was linked to the general disillusionment with executive foreign policy discretion, beginning with his response to the invasion of the Dominican Republic in 1965. It was also connected to a feeling that his loyalty to LBJ had been abused at the time of the Tonkin Gulf crisis. In a closed committee session in 1968, Fulbright argued that, unless the Senate acted to reverse the kind of power abuse inherent in the 1964 Resolution, the institution would become 'just a useless appendix on the governmen-tal structure'. Fulbright's conversion was mirrored by that of Senator Stuart Symington of Missouri, whose enthusiasm for the war began to wane in 1967 as he became disillusioned with executive secrecy and misdirection of Congress. In 1969, Symington led a Senate subcommittee investigation into America's overseas commitments, establishing for the first time in public the extent of the 'secret war' being fought by the US in Laos (Fulbright 1966; Stennis and Fulbright 1971: 46; Dietz 1986; Dumbrell 1989a: 106; Johns 2006; 2010; Stone 2007).

The Fulbright hearings of 1966 and 1971 – and, to a lesser degree, the Symington investigations – are well-known and frequently cited as examples of Congressional checking of the president. Less often discussed, but just as consequential for policy direction, were the hearings held by Senator John Stennis (Democrat of Mississippi) under the aegis of the Senate Armed Services Preparedness Investigating Subcommittee. Directly reflecting the views of the Joint Chiefs, Stennis developed a full-scale, right-wing critique of LBJ's middle-way in Vietnam. Stennis argued that war should be declared in Vietnam, that taxes should be raised for the war effort, and (in November 1966) that 'other less important matters, such as Great Society-type welfare programs' should be cut to make funds available for the war. Pressure from the Joint Chiefs, as articulated via the Senate Armed Services Committee, can plausibly be interpreted as leading to LBJ's decision to widen Rolling Thunder bombing targets in February 1967. Senator Howard Cannon of Nevada, a prominent member of the Preparedness Subcommittee, metaphorically pinned McNamara to the Senate floor in April 1967. Responding to the Defence Secretary's pleas that mining of North Vietnamese harbours was impractical, and that enhanced bombing could not stop DRV troop infiltration, Cannon ridiculed McNamara as effectively arguing: 'Let us get out ... because we cannot handle the problem.' On the House side, the Armed Services Committee leadership also urged escalation. At least in the Johnson years, legislative 'bombniks' had just as much influence on Vietnam policy as the 'peaceniks' (Fry 2006: 97–8, 127).

In June 1970, the Senate voted to repeal the Gulf of Tonkin Resolution and to accept the Cooper–Church amendment prohibiting further US military action in Laos and Cambodia. President Nixon's discretionary authority over the war was seriously impeded by Congress, with legislative power directly affecting the timing and conduct of the peace negotiations. The theme of Congress distorting the necessary scope of executive authority has become a major theme in revisionist interpretation (Kissinger 1979: 513). However, it is still worth emphasizing that, even in the Nixon years, Congress as a whole was less than keen to deny wartime discretion to the White House. The repeal of the Tonkin Gulf Resolution was not as drastic as such action might appear. LBJ had, in August 1967, already effectively discarded the Resolution, basing his handling of the war on his constitutional Commander-in-Chief authority rather than the controversial 1964 measure. The six months of debate surrounding the Cooper–Church amendment was an occasion of huge significance in the history of congressional reassertion of authority in the Vietnam War era. However, the measure, which had passed the Senate (58 to 37), failed in the House of Representatives (237 to 153). In December 1970, Congress did pass a measure to prohibit US ground operations in Laos and Thailand. From early 1971, Senate efforts to end the war centred on the Case–Church amendment, designed to terminate US military involvement and assistance in Indochina. Even as late as May 1972, Richard Nixon was able to secure a major victory in the shape of an amendment to Case–Church, offered by Senator Harry Byrd of Virginia. The Byrd amendment linked US withdrawal from the region to the setting up of an internationally enforced ceasefire, and US prisoner-of-war releases. As we will see in Chapter 9, it was not until July 1973 that Nixon was, in effect, compelled to accept an inter-chamber measure which prohibited direct US military involvement.

War Developments and Peace Talks: April to December 1968

In early April 1968, the largest combined US/ARVN operation to date, Operation Thoan Tang, was launched, to eliminate PAVN and PLAF forces threatening Saigon. The initiative involved 42 American and 37 South Vietnamese battalions. Post-Tet assaults were driven back, with huge communist losses, though street fighting in Saigon indicated again the permeability of security approaches to the capital. The official North Vietnamese military history admitted that 'we did not fully appreciate the new enemy schemes', and 'underestimated the enemy's capabilities and the strength of his counterattack' (*VV* 2002: 237). The 'new enemy schemes' included a greater American commitment to pacification and more direct assistance to the ARVN. Westmoreland became Army Chief of Staff and was replaced as MACV head by General Creighton Abrams. PLAF force fighting strength may have been depleted by as much as 80 per cent during 1968, through deaths, desertion, and the failure to find new recruits. By 1970, US reports estimated that around 25 per cent of enemy forces in South Vietnam were from the South, compared with about 75 per cent in the mid-1960s. North Vietnamese regular forces suffered lower fatality rates in 1968 than the Southerners, though the PAVN lost significant numbers at Khe Sanh, Hue, and in the second-wave Tet Offensive attacks (Spector 1993; Long 1998: 80; Van Atta 2008: 257; Bradley 2009: 152).

Hanoi's relations with Beijing deteriorated during 1968, not least because of Chinese disapproval of the adventurism of the January Offensive. Beijing began to strengthen its influence in Laos, partly to counter Soviet influence in Hanoi (Zhai 2000b: 180). By April 1968, Washington's hope for Soviet mediation had strengthened to the extent that the military disaster had weakened the DRV's negotiating leverage with Moscow. LBJ's 31 March speech was discussed in advance of its actual delivery with Soviet Ambassador Anatoly Dobrynin, with Johnson insisting that the US was not about to pull out of Vietnam. Johnson's main hope of keeping Moscow in line with his new peace strategy was to convince the Soviets that they had a shared interest in checking Chinese aggression. Dobrynin was informed that a wider regional war, serving Chinese interests, would ensue if there were no lasting settlement for Vietnam. The new Chinese commitment to the Pathet Lao was a straw in the wind. Averell Harriman detected distinct signs of hope from the Soviets. However, Moscow was also aware of the political impact of the Tet Offensive within the United States. Ambassador Dobrynin later described an 'obvious' – maybe slightly desperate – 'appeal to the Soviet government to help end the military conflict in Vietnam', and to do so 'essentially on the President's terms'. As so often during the Vietnam War, the Russian road to peace offered hard travelling, rather than a secure arrival (Dobrynin 1995: 171; Zhai 2000b: 180; Dumbrell 2004: 127).

Both Hanoi and Moscow were prepared at least to start talks. Beijing harangued Le Duc Tho, the leading DRV negotiator, against accepting 'the compromising and capitulationist proposals put forward by the Soviet revisionists'. However, North Vietnamese diplomat Luu Doan Huynh later recalled Mao Zedong as telling him in November 1968 that China approved of Hanoi's policy of talking while fighting. The DRV position was that they would enter negoti-ations 'in the position of a winner, not as a loser' (Duiker 1995: 216;

Westad *et al.* 1998: 136; Luu Doan Huynh 2007b). Such an attitude reflected, to some degree, the kind of unrealism which had led to the Tet Offensive. Yet, it also reflected the DRV's understanding of Johnson's political weakness, as well as the fact that the majority of North Vietnamese main military units had survived the Offensive. Hanoi's confidence stemmed also from the determination of its main backer, the Soviet Union, to secure a good deal in peace talks. After a period of wrangling, dominated as much by Saigon's concern to be properly represented in the talks, preliminary negotiations between Washington and Hanoi began at the Paris Majestic Hotel on 10 May 1968.

The talks exposed deep divisions among LBJ's advisers. Averell Harriman was assigned as chief negotiator in Paris, with Cyrus Vance and Philip Habib as deputies. General Andrew Goodpaster, a close associate of Dwight Eisenhower (now in his last year of life), accompanied the delegation to represent the Joint Chiefs. Harriman was concerned to end his career with a diplomatic *coup de théâtre*, and (in the words of Goodpaster) from 'the outset ... tried to get approval for offering a "scaling back" of our military operations in Vietnam as a negotiating gambit with the North Vietnamese' (Sorley 1999: 90). Johnson was, yet again, torn between opposing positions. The President was continually pressed against making concessions by the Joint Chiefs, who reported the ways in which the DRV was using the new bombing limitations to regroup and resupply. William Jorden, from Walt Rostow's staff, recalled how the President agreed to send him to Paris to monitor the behaviour of Harriman and Vance – 'to keep an eye on those bastards and make sure that they don't give away the family jewels' (Milne 2008: 225). For its part, Hanoi showed no willingness to move towards the American position, certainly not in the absence of a complete halt to the bombing of North Vietnam.

Hanoi's position on bombing was endorsed by the Kremlin in a letter of 5 June, wherein Aleksei Kosygin urged LBJ to order 'a full cessation' before meaningful talks could commence. The Soviet interventions exposed still further the splits in Washington. Clark Clifford argued that Moscow was promising to coerce Hanoi to make concessions, if bombing halted. Walt Rostow held, in effect, that bombing was the only way to peace. The CIA advised that there was a real danger of overestimating the degree of leverage which Moscow had over Hanoi. A report handed to LBJ in mid-July by CIA head Richard Helms insisted that 'the outcome Moscow will be working for' would have to be 'one satisfactory to Hanoi'. As Clark Clifford later recollected, Johnson sought desperately to reconcile competing advice, behaving even more like a consensus-seeking legislative leader, rather than an executive head (Clifford 1991: 527; Milne 2008: 227).

The White House, under pressure from Ambassador Bunker and the Thieu government, insisted that Hanoi accept South Vietnamese representation in the Paris talks prior to a bombing halt. Rocket attacks on Saigon should also stop, as should the ever more frequent DRV incursions into the demilitarized zone. On 31 October, on the basis of ambiguous undertakings from Hanoi, Johnson finally decided to order the bombing halt – in effect, terminating the Rolling Thunder coercive bombing of the North. The decision was the product of intense US–Soviet interaction, with Moscow promising a speedy DRV response in the event of a bombing cessation (Gardner 2000: 56). At this time, there seemed to be the possibility of an opening, with Hanoi and the NLF negotiating on one side, and Washington and Saigon on the other. If leaders in Saigon accepted the presence of the NLF (and actually turned up in Paris to sit opposite its representatives), Hanoi *might* accept the Thieu regime as a legitimate negotiating entity. Whatever the negotiating formulae, whatever the shape of the negotiating table, the immediate concern now was American democratic politics: the imminent transfer of power in Washington.

The Election of Richard Nixon

Hubert Humphrey's agonies during the 1968 presidential campaign replicated in microcosm those of his former boss. A private critic of the escalation in American commitments to South Vietnam, Humphrey had publicly to defend the record of the administration of which he had been a leading member. Humphrey appreciated that LBJ's actions during the election period would, to a large degree, determine the outcome of the contest with Nixon. Humphrey finally broke with the Johnson line, in a speech made in Salt Lake City on 30 September, when he declared that, as president, he would call an immediate bombing halt. LBJ was assured by Humphrey that such a halt must be preceded by evidence that

Hanoi intended to restore respect for the DMZ. By this time, Johnson was, as we have seen, also coming to the view that a more or less unconditional bombing halt was inevitable. Yet Johnson, who had long despised Humphrey, was also being increasingly attracted to the promise of the Republican candidate in 1968. In one of the most extraordinary episodes in the history of American politics, Johnson was increasingly making common cause with, of all people, Richard Nixon.

Iwan Morgan (2002: 124) writes: 'When it came to foreign policy, Richard Nixon was like the school thug who happened to be the smartest kid in the class'. During the election campaign of 1968, the Republican presidential candidate avoided specific commitments on Vietnam, bolstering vague policy statements with oblique references to new negotiating strategies, designed to extricate the US from war. Nixon's campaign language reflected the new realism of 1968. America was now seeking an honourable peace, rather (so it seemed) than an outright victory. The concept of the 'new diplomacy', launched in a Nebraska address during the Republican primary campaign in May, drew on a widely-read *Foreign Affairs* piece which Nixon had authored in 1967. Elements of a Vietnam exit strategy, based around new 'balance of power' approaches to American relations with Moscow and Beijing, were unveiled at the Republican nominating convention in Miami. Nixon also promised to progress towards an all-volunteer army (Nixon 1967; Berman 2001: 45; Bailey 2009: 2).

Behind the scenes, Nixon was seeking to court the good opinion of LBJ as a way of undermining Humphrey, with the Reverend Billy Graham acting as something of an LBJ–Nixon intermediary. Evidence of progress in the Paris talks on delegate seating raised the temperature in mid-October. Nixon encouraged General Thieu to undermine the 31 October bombing halt by refusing to attend the Paris talks. Saigon was assured, via Taiwanese businesswoman Anna Chennault, that a better deal would be available from a President Nixon. LBJ became aware of the intrigue before the election and discussed it with Senate Republican Leader Everett Dirksen, as well as Nixon himself. On 4 November, the day prior to the election, LBJ's top advisers discussed whether to make the knowledge public. Credible indications from the White House that Nixon had been involved in illegal, possibly treasonable, activity could hardly have failed to help the Democratic candidate in a close election. Clark

Clifford argued that the story was 'so shocking in nature' that its disclosure would harm the national interest, especially if Nixon *were* to be elected. LBJ agreed. Humphrey also considered making the rumours of the Nixon–Chennault–Thieu link public, but decided that such a move might backfire, especially since he (unlike LBJ) was uncertain of the degree of Nixon's personal culpability. Johnson was angry at Nixon's electorally motivated efforts to destroy the 31 October peace initiative. However, it is also likely that LBJ saw Nixon as more likely than Humphrey to secure a Vietnamese settlement which did not amount to an American capitulation (Bundy 1998: 20–48; Dallek 1998: 578, 592; Woods 2006: 875).

The election of Richard Nixon, the old anti-communist red-baiter, like the victory for the Right in the June legislative elections in France, appeared to signal the end of hope for international leftism in 1968, the year of global revolutionary upheaval. For the US, 1968 had seen the assassinations of Martin Luther King and Bobby Kennedy, urban rioting, the violent shambles of the Democratic nominating convention, and the destruction of a presidency. American public opinion had not suddenly been converted from hawk to dove. However, something dramatic had changed. Probably by late 1967, even before the Tet Offensive, the difficulty of mounting a new escalation of American military commitment to South Vietnam had become extreme. Any real will – among the public, in Congress, and in the executive branch of government – to recommit and redirect massive new force levels had now disappeared. Johnson persevered with his middle way throughout 1968. However, *contra* some revisionist understandings, his post-Tet decisions were neither panicky, nor based on a false analysis of the implications of the Offensive. They were rooted in close understanding of the limits to a purely military solution in Vietnam, along with consideration of the damage that the war was doing to the United States. All this did not mean that the anti-communist cause in Vietnam was entirely lost. Elements of a new, superior American military strategy were evident by the end of the year. The US made military progress during 1968, though North Vietnam was nowhere near the point of surrender – or, indeed, of withdrawing its military presence from South Vietnam. The war that Nixon inherited was one that would be dominated by regular North Vietnamese forces. It was a conflict which would require incisive strategic understanding, a willingness to compromise, a stepping away from the pull of immediate political advantage, and the ability effectively to mobilize the entire American political system. The idea of a 'new diplomacy' for Asia was interesting. However, Nixon's near-treasonable conduct during the election campaign against Humphrey did not bode well.

5

Richard Nixon's War

The opening of peace negotiations in 1968 led to a qualitative shift in the internationalization of the Vietnam War. Even more than Lyndon Johnson, President Nixon was convinced that the solution to his Indochinese dilemma lay in the realm of international balances of power. The Nixon administration's 'grand design' for international order was at the driving centre of post-1968 internationalization of the war. We begin this chapter with an assessment of the transformed international context of the war after 1968, moving on to an assessment of US foreign policy in this period. Again, we find global factors constantly bumping up against intrastate developments, especially in the context of American electoral and legislative politics. The chapter offers a brief account of the significant influence of Senator Frank Church, organizer of legislative constraints on Nixon's war leadership. The chapter ends with an analysis of Hanoi's 1972 Easter Offensive and of the eventual Paris Agreement of January 1973. It raises a range of questions relating to the internationalization of the war, and to its handling by Richard Nixon and his national security adviser, Henry Kissinger. Why did it take so long to reach a peace agreement? Did the road to peace lead via the politics of international détente? How responsible and defensible was the Nixon–Kissinger handling of the war? How did the Sino–Soviet rivalry affect the war after 1968? Was the 1973 Agreement anything other than an international recognition that the state of South Vietnam would, sooner or later, be incorporated into a Vietnam reunified under communist leadership?

Saigon, Hanoi, and the Transformed International Context

Between 1968 and 1972, the Vietnam War negotiations showed little sign of movement. Hanoi's position was that America must withdraw all troops; that a settlement should be based on an 'in-place' cease-fire (that is, one that left PAVN forces in parts of South Vietnam); and that the NLF (or the Provisional Revolutionary Government (PRG), as the NLF's political/organizational wing was called from 1969) must take at least partial substantive power in Saigon, with the removal of the Thieu regime. Until May 1971, Washington was formally committed to complete mutual withdrawal and to the Thieu government in Saigon. Negotiations in the Nixon era began in January 1969, with Henry Cabot Lodge replacing Averell Harriman. The NLF/PRG and Thieu's government tended to concentrate on the political; the US and DRV on the military issues. Henry Kissinger (1979: 260) later wrote that, to the communists, 'the Paris talks were not a device for settlement but an instrument of political warfare'. Nixon and Kissinger favoured secret contacts over public negotia-tion, while the American 'carrot and stick' approach to conciliation was not all that far removed from the North Vietnamese strategy of talking while fighting. However, there was precious little sign of movement in the DRV position. Hanoi was concerned to regroup after the setbacks of 1968, but was not keen to make concessions, especially in view of the apparent American domestic disarray. The DRV leaders also saw new opportunities as well as dangers emerg-ing from the deepening of the Sino–Soviet split. In early 1969, Sino–Soviet border clashes along the Ussuri River almost led to a more general war between the two major communist powers. Such tension, of course, interested the Nixon administration and encour-aged Washington's plans for a new stance on the communist split.

Intensified rivalry between China and the USSR directly affected Indochina in the context of developments in Cambodia. Between 1969 and 1971, the DRV and Beijing found themselves pursuing clearly divergent geopolitical strategies. American bombing led to the deposing of the neutralist Cambodian ruler, Norodom Sihanouk, in March 1970, and his replacement by the US-backed government of General Lon Nol. The Cambodian authority in Phnom Penh faced a force of radical communists, the Khmer Rouge, as well as DRV forces occupying eastern provinces. Beijing's line was initially to back Sihanouk, as a lever against both Soviet and DRV influence.

The objective of Chinese policy was the creation of independent buffers against the enhancement of Soviet and DRV power in the region. Hanoi wanted to facilitate its use of bases in Cambodia in relation to the American war, as well as to enhance its prospects for postwar security, by minimizing Chinese influence in neighbouring countries. These strategies led Hanoi and Beijing to adopt competing approaches to the increasingly difficult-to-control Khmer Rouge, as well as to the Lon Nol regime. Despite all this, relations between Hanoi and Beijing actually warmed at the time of Ho Chi Minh's death in September 1969, especially with the publication of Ho's 'testament' – effectively a posthumous appeal for communist unity. The rifts between Hanoi and Beijing, over the Paris talks and the future of Cambodia, were unprecedented in the history of Vietnamese communism. However, neither Hanoi nor Beijing wished to sever their relationship. The Chinese saw themselves as attempting to strengthen the hand of the DRV hardliners, who were pushing for an outright military victory over the US, rather than as in any way opposing North Vietnam. From Hanoi's point of view, an outright break with China would not only be intrinsically dangerous, it would threaten the precarious balance achieved between the communist great-powers. For these complex reasons, Chinese pressure may be identified as a factor in hardening the DRV stance in Paris between 1969 and 1971 (Zhai 2000b: 184; Nguyen 2008a: 230).

Moscow was an even more important influence. LBJ's idea of achieving progress in Vietnam by going via Moscow had always involved a degree of misunderstanding of power distribution in the communist world. For one thing, Vietnamese communism was a disciplined, but by no means factionless, movement. Pressure from one great-power sponsor, especially if it seemed to threaten Vietnamese independence, would always be resisted by one or more factions. By the late 1960s, Moscow was Hanoi's main sponsor, but the DRV was never the creature of the USSR. The emotional, patriotic underpinning of Vietnamese communism depended on some plausible narrative of self-determination. American hopes of exploiting the Sino–Soviet split to achieve an acceptable Vietnamese peace also tended to betray a problem in understanding the dynamics of the rift. By the time Nixon came to office, Vietnam had become the outstanding international cause for left-wing movements across the globe. Moscow was acutely sensitive to the accusation from Beijing that it was somehow betraying the cause of the Vietnamese, and trying to force the NLF/PRG into a premature and doomed compromise. Soviet aid to Hanoi actually increased even as the DRV hardened its stance in Paris. Moscow's view (or at least the view of influential forces within the Soviet leadership) in the early 1970s seems to have been that the DRV would emerge from the war with greatly enhanced regional prestige and power, even if South Vietnam survived in some form in the short to medium term. Vietnamese communism would thus become increasingly central to Soviet geopolitical ambitions in the context of the split with China. A report from the Soviet embassy in Hanoi in May 1971 argued that 'when the DRV has become the leading force in the struggle of the peoples of Indochina, we will possess comparatively more possibilities for establishing our policy in this region'. Contrary to Nixon's hopes, Moscow did not press Hanoi all that hard (Gaiduk 1998: 148; Geyer and Selvage 2007; Lawrence 2008b: 142).

Both sides at the Paris talks, communist and capitalist, had their internal tensions. The NLF/PRG surely harboured resentment at the extent to which it, rather than the North Vietnamese, had borne the brunt of the 1968 losses. However, any such resentment was held in check by the increased dependence of the Southern wing of the revolutionary movement upon the North. On the capitalist side, tensions were far more evident. The year 1968 was almost a point of no return for US–South Vietnamese relations. From 1968, President Thieu concentrated on eliciting as much material support from Washington as possible, while stalling on political reform which would backfire in the event of an American abandonment of Vietnam. Thieu combined a residual loyalty to Washington with a rational awareness that powerful forces in the US were seeking to ditch him. His negotiating stance offered no role for NLF/PRG involvement in government. In June 1969, at a meeting with Nixon on Midway Island, Thieu was forced to accept the reality of major US troop withdrawals. Direct, secret talks between Kissinger and DRV negotiators were deliberately designed to exclude Thieu. As noted in Chapter 1, in 1970, Thieu did, at the price of yet more financial assistance from Washington, proclaim meaningful land reform. The authority of the Saigon government was growing, but Thieu's worries about the direction of American policy increased, especially with Hanoi still insisting that his removal from office was a condition for peace. According to Kissinger, Le Duc Tho in mid-1971 raised parallels

with 1963. If the US could not get rid of Thieu in the upcoming presidential elections in South Vietnam, 'an assassination would do
admirably'. In October, Thieu, backed by Ambassador Ellsworth
Bunker, won an uncontested, fraudulent election. Washington had
decided, for the time being at least, not – as Kissinger put it – 'to toss
Thieu to the wolves' (Kissinger 1979: 1024, 1035; Hung and
Schecter 1986: 47–9; Truong Nhu Tang 1986: 137; Bui Diem 1987:
276; Berman 2001: 68–70; Hanhimaki 2004: 149; Nguyen 2008a:
246).

Nixon, Kissinger, and 'Madman' Foreign Policy: 1969–70

Nixon and Kissinger's understanding of effective foreign policy-
making was elitist to the point of being anti-democratic.
Nevertheless, the coherence of their attack on decentralized modes of
policy-making has probably been exaggerated, as has the eclipse in
these years of the State and Defence departments in favour of White
House policy direction. William Rogers, Nixon's first Secretary of
State, was certainly a very unhappy figure. Nixon remarked in
February 1971 that Kissinger was 'psychopathetic about trying to
screw Rogers'. Rogers was consistently attacked by Kissinger; for
example, over the Secretary's relative caution about extending the
war to Cambodia and Laos. Nixon certainly considered sacking
Rogers, but he also periodically pondered the firing of Kissinger, the
possessor of what even Nixon could recognize as an 'unbelievable
ego'. Even by the standards of American presidential politics, this
was an administration distinguished by an extraordinary level of
intrigue and personal rivalry (Kimball 1998: 309; Dallek 2008: 250,
437–8).

Melvin Laird, Secretary of Defence in the first Nixon term, was a
substantial figure, and the main bureaucratic proponent of handing
over as much responsibility as possible to the South Vietnamese – a
policy commitment about which Kissinger was later keen to record
his doubts. Laird was able to follow the Kissinger–Nixon intrigues
via his access to intelligence taps on White House telephone conversations. At one stage in late 1969, following the leaking of information about the 'secret' bombing of Cambodia to the *New York Times*,
Kissinger and Laird began wire-tapping one another, just as Nixon
tried to intercept Kissinger's calls to journalist Joe Kraft. Laird, and

to a lesser degree Rogers, were significant figures in the rejection of the 1969 escalation plan, code-named 'Duck Hook'; though Laird only found out about the plan when it was leaked to the press. Both Rogers and Laird were subsequently blamed by Nixon and Kissinger for temporizing and diluting rational strategy (Kimball 1998: 371; Kissinger 2003: 93; Perlstein 2008: 374).

The Nixon–Kissinger approach to the making of foreign policy involved quite sophisticated evaluations of the weaknesses of the 'Tuesday lunch' system inherited from LBJ. Crisis decision-making was structured very formally, with members of the inter-agency Washington Special Actions Group reporting to the national security adviser, and Kissinger reporting to Nixon. However, despite efforts to impose rationality through formal process, high-profile, crisis-oriented decision-making was determined primarily by complex interaction between the two men at the top. The thrust of the Nixon–Kissinger system was towards exclusion of democratic controls, particularly as exercised by Capitol Hill. One of the main White House criticisms of Laird was that the Defence Secretary was much too bothered about Congress. To a dangerous degree, Vietnam policy became an expression of elite personality (Hoff 1994: 213; Haney 1997: 76; Bundy 1998; Siniver 2008: 57).

The most alarming expression of elite, personality-driven foreign policy in this period was the 'madman' theory. Bob Haldeman, White House chief of staff in the early Nixon years, later described the theory – conceived by Richard Nixon and 'perfected' by Henry Kissinger – as a 'threat of military action by an unpredictable US President who hated Communism'. According to Haldeman, Kissinger communicated the image of presidential unpredictability – random 'madman' escalations, but also the possibility of surprising flexibility – to North Vietnam in 1969, 'fully expecting the plan to be successful'. Haldeman quoted Nixon himself as referring to the 'Madman Theory' and as explaining: 'I want the North Vietnamese to believe I've reached the point where I might do *anything* to stop the war' (Haldeman 1978: 97–8, 121–2; Garthoff 1994: 251; Kimball 2004: 53–61).

Nixon and Kissinger saw their strategy as super-rational: a kind of enhanced and elevated version of 'carrot and stick' diplomacy, based on sure knowledge and logical analysis of international political moti-vation. Upon assuming power in January 1969, Nixon and Kissinger felt they could thereby end the war on terms which unambiguously preserved American international credibility. Richard Nixon told David Frost (2007: 291) in 1977 that he had seriously considered the advice of 'some of my friends' who urged him in 1969 to 'just get out of Vietnam', and to 'put the blame on Johnson and Kennedy, who got us in'. Such a course of action, according to Nixon, 'made political sense', but it ignored the need to retain American international credibility: 'It didn't make sense for the country ... It didn't make sense for the world'. By early 1969, notions of 'credibility' had taken over from the domino theory as the foundational elite belief for why America was in Vietnam. Nixon told Kissinger and British counter-insurgency expert Robert Thompson in October 1969 that 'the survival of the US as a world power with the will to use this power' was at stake in Vietnam (Kimball 2004: 45). Henry Kissinger (2003: 37) later argued that 'the last moment' when the US could have withdrawn with 'tolerable' credibility costs was 'either just before or just after Diem was overthrown'. On assuming power in January 1969, Nixon and Kissinger felt they could achieve a successful American exit from Vietnam, not immediately, but within six to twelve months. How exactly did they propose to do this?

An important part of the Nixon–Kissinger approach involved development of the military programmes, including enhanced pacification and the Phoenix initiatives, which had experienced some degree of success in 1968. The battle of 'Hamburger Hill' (Ap Bia) in May 1969 helped further trigger this switch towards counter-insurgency. The engagement was designed to keep PAVN forces from making attacks in the northern coastal provinces of South Vietnam; it culminated in a fight for 'hill 937' and major American casualties. *Life* magazine published photographs of some 241 US soldiers killed in one week in defence of a hill which, following the PAVN retreat, was abandoned. The new White House sought also to move forward with another Johnson policy, that of Vietnamization. Vietnamization under Nixon involved substantial investment in the South Vietnamese economy, but its prime objective was military: the transformation of the ARVN into a self-sufficient force. Laird, the leader of military Vietnamization, found himself opposed not only by the Joint Chiefs, but also by a sceptical Kissinger, who advised that 'the Communists cannot be fooled by the rate of progress' in transforming the ARVN. Laird found important allies for Vietnamization in the persons of William Colby, who headed civil operations in South Vietnam between 1968 and 1971, and Ambassador Ellsworth

Bunker. However, excessively enthusiastic reports from Colby and Bunker tended somewhat to detract from accurate evaluation of what the programme actually was achieving on the ground (Kimball 1998: 88; Schaffer 2003: 224; Van Atta 2008: 237).

From the very start of his presidency, Nixon saw the war as unwinnable through purely military means. He told Kissinger in May 1969 that 'in Saigon the tendency is fight the war to victory. But you and I know it won't happen – it is impossible'. The President added that General Creighton Abrams agreed with this analysis. The signalling and demonstration of 'madman' intentions were designed precisely to push Hanoi in the direction of negotiated concessions. The 1969 'secret' bombing of Cambodia (code-named 'Menu') was thus intended to demonstrate to the enemy, and to Moscow, that the new administration would not recognize constraints that had been respected by LBJ. As we have seen, bombing of the Laotian Ho Chi Minh Trail was begun in 1965; it was extended in 1968, when fixed-wing American gunships attacked the Cambodian Trail. However, the 1969 'secret' bombing was intended as a major escalation from the bombing levels inherited from LBJ. Of course, Nixon and Kissinger were not completely unrestrained. The Menu bombing, which lasted over a year from March 1969, involved over 3,500 B-52 bomber sorties. It had military objectives – interrupting the Cambodian Trail, elimination of communist 'sanctuaries' and forward headquarters (COSVN) – as well as psychological ones. 'Secrecy' was pursued in a strange system of dual reporting, involving interference with auto-mated aircraft control records. The Nixon initiatives failed not only in Cambodia, but also in early 1970 in Laos, when Nixon stepped up air support for the Souvanna Phouma regime. Following leaks to the press, and a congressional investigation, the White House acknowl-edged the 'secret' Laotian bombing in February 1970. Secrecy, opposed by Laird, was rather an extraordinary policy, especially given the vulnerability of all Nixon decisions to press leakage. It illus-trated the limits imposed on executive freedom of action by the Nixon–Kissinger perceptions of what domestic and international opinion would tolerate. It also exemplified the White House's contempt for the normal patterns of congressional oversight (Nixon 1985: 102; Hoff 1994: 215–6; Kimball 1998: 194; Dallek 2008: 126).

By the middle of 1969, the Menu bombing was far from achiev-ing a breakthrough. Nixon decided to force the pace by sending (via a French intermediary) a stark ultimatum to Ho Chi Minh: to move on negotiating concessions by 1 November, or face further 'measures of great consequence and force'. The reference here was deliberately vague, but would have been understood to have involved a resumption of direct bombing of North Vietnam. A resumed Rolling Thunder campaign, minus the Johnsonian constraints, had been considered by the White House earlier in the year; but it had been rejected, in the face of opposition by Melvin Laird, in favour of the somewhat less drastic Menu programme. Kissinger conveyed various threats to DRV negotiator Xuan Thuy in their private meetings. In late August, Hanoi gave what Kissinger strangely called an 'almost insolent' response to the ultimatum (Nixon 1978: 397; Prados 2009a: 307).

In the wake of the failed ultimatum, the White House returned to various plans for military escalation which had been considered earlier in 1969. The shooting-down of a US spy-plane by North Korea in April stimulated a major debate about whether to respond in a consciously 'irrational' manner, designed to intimidate the DRV as much as the North Koreans. Rogers, Laird, and General Earle Wheeler at that time successfully counselled against such 'madman' action. The revised escalation plan was considered at the highest level in September and October 1969. Indications of Nixon's 'madman' reactions to DRV intransigence were communicated to Moscow. Kissinger (1979: 305) later recorded his own decision not to convey some of Nixon's more extreme signalling of willingness to use nuclear weapons. However, on 6 October the national security adviser set in motion a nuclear alert schedule which was designed to be visible to Moscow. This version of the Duck Hook plan included proposals for resumed bombing of the DRV, the mining of North Vietnamese ports, destruction of the dike system in the DRV, as well as possible use of tactical nuclear weapons – something that President Johnson had always explicitly ruled out. Nixon told Republican senators in late September that he was considering an invasion of North Vietnam. A graduated programme of intensifying escalation geared to produce the maximum psychological impact on Hanoi and Moscow, Duck Hook represented the high point of 'madman' thinking. Soviet Ambassador Dobrynin was told in late September that the escalation 'train had just left the station' (Garment 1997: 174; Suri 2008: 76).

Duck Hook was the dog that did not bark in the Vietnamese night. Nixon's eventual rejection of the plan was (as we shall see in Chapter

6) linked to the likely domestic disorder which would follow. The October nuclear alert was abandoned following advice from Laird's deputy Robert Pursley that it would be seen by the Soviets as an empty bluff. The rejection of Duck Hook escalation was also linked to advice from the Joint Chiefs that the escalation faced major logistical obstacles, not least from the worsening weather. Laird advised that 'anything done in North Vietnam will take at least a year' to impact on the peace negotiations. The prospect of handling increased domestic dissent for over a year, with no obvious concessions coming from Hanoi, was a prospect too far. Nixon altered the speech that had been drafted to announce the escalation, turning it into the relatively emollient 'Silent Majority' address of 3 November 1969. Duck Hook escalation may also have been seen as inconsistent with the emerging 'grand design' for exploiting further the Sino–Soviet split. The rift between Moscow and Beijing had already experienced a modest coming-together in response to Ho Chi Minh's dying 'testament'. The unprecedented escalation planned by Kissinger's staff in September 1969 could only have served to alleviate the communist split (Berman 2001: 54; Sagan and Suri 2003; Hanhimaki 2004: 498; Burr 2005; Prados 2009a: 311).

The order to invade Cambodia in April 1970 represented a partial resumption of 'madman' thinking. Warned by Melvin Laird about the possible reactions in Congress if the President failed to consult Capitol Hill in advance, and by William Rogers about campus reactions, Nixon responded: 'If I decide to do it, it will be because I have decided to pay the price.' There would no repeat of the failure of nerve over Duck Hook. The Cambodian incursion was less drastic than earlier escalation proposals. Though it had 'madman' aspects, it was also a response to the specific problem of COSVN, the communist sanctuaries in Cambodia, and the perceived need to protect the regime of Lon Nol – described by Nixon on April 22 as 'the only government in Cambodia in the last 25 years that had the guts to take a pro-Western and pro-American stand'. To a large extent, at least among the political advisers, Nixon was now isolated. Kissinger had real doubts about whether the DRV really intended to occupy Phom Penh following the coup against Prince Sihanouk. He also shared some of worries of Laird and Rogers about the domestic reaction to invasion of a legally neutral country. On the other hand, the Joint Chiefs had been pushing for direct action against the communist sanctuaries since the mid-1960s. Alexander Haig (deputy to

Kissinger) strongly upheld the view that Phnom Penh would fall to communist forces unless an intervention, legitimated by Lon Nol's request for help, was mounted (Bundy 1998: 83; Reeves 2001: 201; Appy 2008: 400; Dallek 2008: 195).

Nixon's personal distress and emotional exhaustion were evident to all. His accelerated alcohol consumption and repeated viewing of the film, *Patton: Lust for Glory*, hardly eased the worries of his associates. Roger Morris and Tony Lake (later President Bill Clinton's national security adviser) resigned from the NSC staff in protest at widening of the war. The incursion into Cambodia involved over 29,000 ARVN forces, and about 19,300 US troops; many more were committed to border areas in South Vietnam in search of COSVN, which proved typically elusive. Reviewing progress at the beginning of May, General Abrams felt that progress had been made, but saw domestic pressures as likely to prevent the achievement of major objectives. Under intense pressure from Congress and on American streets, Nixon declared an end to the incursion by the end of June and also imposed strict limits on the geographical dispersal of allied forces across eastern Cambodia. The invasion interrupted communist military planning, making possible further progress on Vietnamization, and significantly lengthened communist supply lines. The action also prevented a North Vietnamese conquest of Phnom Penh, though it set in motion the series of events which culminated in the taking of control in Cambodia by the mass-murderous Khmer Rouge in 1975. The Cambodian invasion brought no communist diplomatic concessions. Indeed, in September 1970, it was Kissinger who broached with the DRV delegation in Paris the possibility of an 'in-place' ceasefire, linked to the holding of elections. Such a suggestion, of course, represented a move away from what was still the official US line on not accepting PAVN forces in South Vietnam after a negotiated peace (Kissinger 1979: 514; Shawcross 1979; Sorley 1999: 203–4; Willbanks 2004: 84; Shaw 2005; Perlstein 2008: 478; Hunt 2010: 110–11).

Enhanced domestic disquiet was the most obvious product of the 'madman' policies, and especially of the decision to invade Cambodia. Nixon's most potent way of managing domestic discontent lay in US troop reductions. A graduated programme of reductions was begun in June 1969, with the announcement of cuts of approximately 100,000 being made during the year. US military personnel levels in South Vietnam fell to 475,000 by the close of 1969, compared with 534,700 in June 1968, and to 334,600 at the end of 1970. The draft system was reformed, with a change to a lottery process. In Guam in July 1969, Nixon developed the line, begun during the 1968 campaign, that the US would stand by its treaty obligations, but in the future would not fight wars on behalf of Asian allies. The remarks were consciously trailed by the administration as the 'Nixon Doctrine'. The promise of 'no more Vietnams', was designed to reassure the US public, as well – after all, this was Nixon speaking – as to send messages to Moscow, Beijing, and allied Asian capitals.

Throughout this period, Nixon sought to calm public protest by seeking to marginalize the demonstrators not only by troop cuts, but also by implying that there was no middle ground between the Nixon–Kissinger policies and a humiliating, and credibility-destroying, immediate withdrawal. The White House struggled to fire-fight the various war-related public relations crises that erupted, notably the public emergence of information, in November 1969, about the 1968 My Lai massacre. Nixon's own incomprehension regarding domestic antiwar positions became evident in the extraordinary encounter between the President and demonstrators at the Lincoln Memorial in the early hours of 9 May 1970. A student who met Nixon reported to the press that the presidential comments were rambling: 'Here we had come from a university that's completely uptight – on strike – and ... he talked about the football team. And surfing.' The administration's responses to domestic disquiet often lapsed, especially in the speeches of Vice President Spiro Agnew, into ugly populism. However, Nixon's mobilization of the 'Silent Majority' – patriotic Americans who rejected the arguments of the antiwar movement – was accomplished with a degree of skill. Yet, Nixon's public defence of US Vietnam strategy was often inherently contradictory. Journalist Eric Sevareid summarized the central contradiction very clearly in his comments on Nixon's television address of November 1969: 'If this war ... was of this cosmic and universal importance, then the war should be won, but he has said that ... a military victory is not to be sought' (Dallek 2008: 203; Perlstein 2008: 437). Such inconsistencies were taken up by the growing antiwar lobby in the US Senate.

Frank Church: Dove or Isolationist?

As we saw in Chapter 4, President Nixon was forced to take serious account of the potential setting of limits on the Vietnamese commitment by Congress. By the early 1970s, the legislator with the best case for being seen as leader of the 'Senate doves' was the Democratic Senator from Idaho, Frank Church. Born in Boise, Idaho in 1924 and a graduate of Stanford University Law School, Church viewed the war through western Progressive lenses. As his understanding of the war developed, however, Church brought together and catalyzed a range of antiwar positions.

Those revisionist historians who see Church as an isolationist are able to cite his oft-stated respect for his Republican Idohan predecessor, Senator William Borah. Yet, for Church, Borah's inter-war isolationism had run aground with the Second World War and the need for collective security enshrined in the creation of the United Nations. In arguing for a 'negotiated settlement' in Vietnam in 1964, Church advocated a central role for the UN. In June 1965, he again urged Washington to take the UN seriously, to 'deal with representatives of the Vietcong' and to make 'South Vietnamese self-determination the basis of any settlement'. Borah's uncompromising rejection of 'entangling alliances' was not replicated by Church. However, other aspects of Borah's philosophy of foreign policy – notably anti-imperialism and the need for Congress to check executive discretion – were constantly emphasized by his younger disciple. Church was also acutely aware of the weaknesses, as well as of the strengths, of the western-state individualist tradition. He was, for example, frequently attacked by the paranoid anti-communists of the Idaho John Birch Society (Ashby and Gramer 1994: 163; Schmitz and Fousekis 1994: 566).

Central to Church's thinking was the idea that careless interventions in the affairs of other countries simply breeds anti-Americanism and fans nationalist resentment. The US should recognize its own revolutionary past, and tread very carefully when trying to impose political solutions on others. As early as March 1964, Church was arguing that if 'Ho Chi Minh ... is regarded by the Vietnamese people, North and South, as the George Washington of Vietnam ... it will be hard for us.' A year later he declared: 'Unless we come to accept the fact that it is neither within the power nor within the interest of the United States to preserve the status quo everywhere, our policy is doomed to failure.' Here, Church was refashioning for the developed Cold War era the anti-imperialist strand in American foreign policy debate which Senator Borah had applied in the years before the Pearl Harbor attacks. Church's critique of the war also developed a strong left-leaning 'America First' orientation. In mid-1967, he chided LBJ's schemes for extending big government American liberalism to the Mekong Delta: 'We want to take the Great Society to Southeast Asia' but 'we don't even have the Great Society here' (Ashby and Gramer 1994: 248; Schmitz and Fousekis 1994: 566, 569).

During the Johnson years, Church's antiwar stances were held in check by his desire to retain some influence with the President, who had, as Senate Majority Leader, helped Church attain assignment to the Senate Foreign Relations Committee. On the committee, Church pushed Senator Fulbright in the direction of holding public hearings on the war. In the earlier 1960s, however, Frank Church was also restrained by his generalized support for anti-communist containment. During 1963, Church worked with the State Department to pressure Diem with threats to cut off aid if the South Vietnamese leader failed to liberalize. A Church-sponsored resolution of September 1963, warning Diem of the consequences of continued anti-Buddhist repression, was drafted in the State Department. Church supported the Gulf of Tonkin Resolution and continued to vote for military appropriations until the Nixon years. In July 1965, he wrote that Wayne Morse and Ernest Gruening (the two Senators who had opposed the Tonkin Gulf Resolution) 'may be right, but they have been "written off", and so exercise no influence on the future course of events' (Schmitz and Fousekis 1994: 577).

By 1970, Church had abandoned any residual loyalty either to containment policy or to the good faith of the executive branch. The true purpose of Vietnamization, declared Church in May 1970, was American imperialist power-projection: 'preserving an American bridgehead on the mainland of Asia'. His opposition to Nixon's conduct of the war combined absolutist condemnation of executive discretion with a belief that American imperialism had provoked the Vietnamese to the point where they would never be content with anything less than national reunification. Responding to the Linebacker I bombing campaign in May 1972, Church delivered the following oration: 'Darken their skies with clouds of bombers, rain down destruction upon them, spread the carnage far and wide, and they may scurry for cover but they (the Vietnamese people) will not yield' (Ashby and Gramer 1994: 308, 382). Church remained sensitive to the argument that his campaign to end the war was proceeding without due regard to the fate of the US prisoners of war. Prisoner issues reverberated significantly in Idaho. Unsurprisingly, Church found it difficult both to argue that Nixon was using the prisoner issue to extend the war, *and* publicly to recognize that a satisfactory peace had to involve some credible assurance of prisoner releases.

Church's Senate career – he died in 1984, having represented Idaho in the US Senate between 1957 and 1981 – is most remembered for his leading of major investigations into the Cold War conduct of the CIA and FBI. In the later 1970s, Church saw the constitutional problem of executive discretion in Vietnam as relating primarily to the extent to which presidents, however implausibly in constitutional terms, were able to invoke 'emergency powers'. He recalled how Defence Secretary Laird had argued in the early 1970s that, even if Congress did vote to cut off Vietnam funding, Nixon would continue paying the troops. Laird mentioned as authority for this the Feed and Forage Act of 1861, under which the Union cavalry in the Civil War was able to buy feed for its horses even when Congress was not in session. Church devoted much of his energy in the later 1970s to attempting to reverse some 470 such 'emergency' statutes (Church 1977). Church was perhaps the most prominent leader of post-Vietnam War efforts to reassert congressional authority in foreign policy. However, Church was actually rather ambivalent about what is sometimes seen as the central legislative feature of his reassertion, the War Powers Resolution of 1973. Designed to inhibit future presidential discretion over troop commitment, the campaign for the Resolution was led, not by Church, but by Republican Senator Jacob Javits of New York. Church supported Javits, but felt that the Resolution was poorly drafted and perhaps unworkable. Subsequent failures to limit executive discretion over military action proved Church right (Franck and Weisband 1979: 71, 15–34).

Frank Church ran as a fringe western candidate in the 1976 presidential primary elections, securing victory in Nebraska, Montana and Oregon, as well as Idaho. Along with greater legislative control of foreign policy, Church argued for a fundamental reorientation of the assumptions of globalized anti-communist containment (Schmitz

1996). Frank Church's thought and policy stances did contain many internal tensions. His opposition to gun control legislation, for example, reflected both western individualism and public opinion in the generally conservative state of Idaho. His journey – from cautious critic of the war, basing his objections on realist calculation of American interests in Vietnam and on the need for more congressional assertion, to outright opponent of what he had come by 1970 to see as murderous American imperialism – was replicated elsewhere in Congress and in the nation. Dove and occasional neo-isolationist, Church reapplied the Borah tradition of anti-imperialism in the context of the Vietnam War. In so doing, Church found an original and efficacious political voice.

Nixon and Kissinger: Grand Designers

The Nixon–Kissinger foreign policy was complex and holistic. A timely, credibility-preserving exit from Vietnam was its main early priority, but the policy quickly developed its own globally integrationist dynamic. The 'grand design' grew from the pre-White House thinking of the two principals, as well as the progress achieved towards superpower détente by LBJ. Intimations of a 'grand design', involving a new understanding with Moscow linked to a settlement in Vietnam, emerged in Kissinger's 1969 contacts with Soviet Ambassador Anatoly Dobryinin. The dialogue with Dobrynin was predicated on the assumption of 'linkage' – or, as Nixon put it, the understanding that 'progress in one area is bound to have an influence on progress in other areas'. If Moscow could persuade Hanoi to move the Paris talks 'off dead-center', the USSR could expect American cooperation in other areas, notably in arms control agreements designed to relieve the spending pressures on the superpowers. The early overtures to Dobrynin thus combined offers of *quid pro quo* diplomacy with elements of 'madman' signalling. As we have already noted, the pressures on Moscow to influence Hanoi achieved little at this stage. Moscow did not accept the terms of 'linkage', preferring to treat issues separately and also to avoid any appearance of being, in Dobrynin's words, 'bribed or intimidated' by the United States. The Soviet Ambassador also repeatedly protested that Washington was drastically exaggerating the degree of influence possessed by Moscow over North Vietnam (Hanhimaki 2004: 49; 2008: 35; Dallek 2008: 110).

The grand design dominated White House foreign policy after 1970, though 'madman' policies, including the use of nuclear signalling, were not thereby abandoned. The most egregious such instance occurred in October 1973, when US nuclear forces went on high alert during the Yom Kippur War in the Middle East. Nevertheless, after 1970, the Nixon–Kissinger policy was transformed by what was to become the centre of Washington's hopes for an acceptable Vietnamese settlement: the opening to China. Diplomacy in 1970, particularly via Pakistan, paved the way. Mao Zedong met DRV leader Pham Van Dong in September 1970. A few hints were dropped about possible grounds for a new relationship with the US, though Kissinger was dismissed by Mao as a 'stinking scholar, a university professor who does not know anything about diplomacy' (Westad *et al.* 1998: 176–7). The dynamic of US–China reconciliation seemed to be picking up from the interruption triggered by the Cambodian invasion. In early 1971, however, conditions in Laos seemed likely to derail them once more.

In late 1970 and early 1971, Nixon and Kissinger were preoccupied with fixing a timetable for further US troop withdrawals, with continuing efforts to induce Moscow to pressure Hanoi, and with plans for possible escalation – all in the context of the upcoming 1972 presidential election. In December 1970, Nixon rejected a scheme to match major troop cuts with resumed bombing of the North and mining of DRV harbours. Kissinger feared domestic protest and worried about an enemy offensive timed to coincide with the election. Bob Haldeman recorded Kissinger's preference to have all US troops home by the end of 1972 rather than 1971, 'so that we won't have to deliver finally until after the elections and therefore can keep our flanks protected'. In the event, US troop levels were reduced to about 200,000 by December 1971, and to under 50,000 by the middle of the 1972 election season. Ambassador Dobrynin was told in January 1971 that Washington needed Hanoi 'to respect a cease-fire during the US withdrawal plus a certain period of time, not too long, after the US withdrawal'. The White House was also concerned about intelligence reporting a major communist offensive in early 1971, and began plans for a major incursion into the Laotian communist sanctuaries (Kimball 1998: 239; Sorley 1999: 230; Dallek 2008: 257).

The administration regarded the 1970 Cambodian invasion as a military success, and looked again to interrupt PAVN military preparation, apparently being coordinated at a command centre near the communist stronghold of Tchepone. The assault would be by South Vietnamese forces, with US air support, thus signalling the progress being made by Vietnamization. Objectives included the seizing of military equipment, especially tanks, and the severing of the Ho Chi Minh Trail. The domestic reaction to the Cambodian invasion effectively ruled out US ground troop participation. The operation took place in February 1971, with South Vietnamese forces moving west into Laos from Khe Sanh (now reoccupied by US Marines). The South Vietnamese lost approximately 9,000 men, about half of the invading force. Though Tchepone was initially seized, the South Vietnamese retreated under intense PAVN attack. North Vietnamese fatalities may have reached nearly 20,000, with large numbers of tanks and weapons lost. Ambassador Bunker concluded that the enemy had understood that 'we were after his jugular' and threw everything into its response to the invasion. Nixon claimed a victory for Lam Son 719, as the ARVN invasion was code-named, though he privately acknowledged the disastrous nature of the televised retreat. Postwar communist accounts indicated that Hanoi had taken the lesson that ARVN leadership was incompetent, and that Vietnamization was *not* working (Van Tien Dung 1977: 124; Turley 1986: 138; Haldeman 1994: 259; Kimball 1998: 248; Sorley 1999: 261, 265).

The attention of Nixon and Kissinger was constantly shifting between the conflict in Vietnam, the onrush of global détente, and the threat of disorder on the streets of America. The grand designers sought to integrate the three levels. The complexity of US public attitudes to the war was illustrated in reactions to the conviction in March 1971 of Lieutenant Willam Calley, platoon leader at My Lai. Nixon saw the public as receptive to the idea that Calley was some kind of scapegoat. Vietnam Veterans Against the War declared that Calley simply illustrated 'the moral agony of America's Vietnam war generation' (Zaroulis and Sullivan 1984: 355). Nixon intervened to remove Calley from imprisonment, confining him to barracks, pending appeal. Originally sentenced to a life term, Calley was released on parole in 1974. In June 1971, Nixon fought the publication by the *New York Times* of the leaked *Pentagon Papers*, the history of the US commitment to Vietnam which had been commissioned by Bob McNamara towards the end of his tenure at the Defence Department. Failing to achieve Supreme Court backing for a publication ban, Nixon took the opportunity to condemn the irresponsibility of both the press and of his Democratic presidential predecessors.

Key differences between Nixon and Kissinger in terms of general outlook on the war became evident during 1971. Both President and national security adviser saw the problem as one of prolonging the survival of the anti-communist Saigon regime – certainly until after a complete US withdrawal, and *possibly* into the indefinite future. Kissinger was fully committed to the strategy of resolving the problem of America's commitment to Saigon by enfolding it in the emerging grand design. Nixon tended to be more impatient, wanting to achieve a clear settlement before the 1972 elections, and favouring 'madman' tactics. The President began to refer to the unrestrained bombing of the DRV as his 'hole card' – to be played in the event of stalled negotiations. Such bombing would force a settlement, blunt DRV military capabilities, and serve notice of American intentions if Hanoi were to break any future agreement. Nixon would not, as he told Bob Haldeman, 'go out of Vietnam whimpering' (Kissinger 1979: 1018; Kimball 1998: 263–4). Diplomacy, however, was to come first. The presidential announcement, on 15 July 1971, that Kissinger had made a secret trip to China, and that Nixon himself would visit the country the following February, appeared to transform the negotiating environment.

By the time Nixon made his announcement about his visit to China, movement had resumed in the talks with the DRV. Kissinger made good the hints made in Paris the previous September when, in May 1971, he conceded that a date could be set for complete US troop withdrawal simply on the condition that Hanoi ceased infiltrating forces into South Vietnam, Laos and Cambodia. The previous insistence that the PAVN must itself withdraw from South Vietnam was dropped; an in-place ceasefire peace seemed closer. The huge concession was not discussed in advance with President Thieu, whose 'four no's' – 'no coalition, no neutralization, no territorial concessions, and never let Communist forces operate openly in South Vietnam' – were being whittled away. The May 1971 concession reflected White House assessments of the military situation in South Vietnam, following the exposure of ARVN weaknesses during the Laotian invasion. Policy now seemed to be moving towards the unequivocal American acceptance of a 'decent interval' between the US exit and the communist takeover. Nixon was looking for a pre-election breakthrough, with the final pressure on Hanoi being applied within the framework of the quickly emerging grand design (Hung and Schecter 1986: 16; Asselin 2002: 28; Kimball 2004: 187).

In his later writing on the war, Henry Kissinger tended to stress the limits of Soviet influence over Hanoi. 'Least of all', according to Kissinger (2003: 77–8), North Vietnam 'wanted a negotiation in Moscow which implied Soviet tutelage and would strain their relationship with China'. Describing the 1969 plan to send Cyrus Vance to Moscow directly to solicit Soviet intervention in the negotiations, Kissinger wrote that 'Moscow would not risk its relation with Hanoi – and the leadership of global Communism – to engage itself in ending the war.' To some extent, the escalations, and aborted escalation plans, of 1969 and 1970 were responses to the failure of Soviet pressure on the DRV. Kissinger's later account of Soviet failure was also linked to his desire to justify the 1972 bombing of North Vietnam – bombing which, in Kissinger's view, succeeded in turning the errant North Vietnamese back to the possibility of negotiated peace. By 1971, White House hopes of a game-changing Soviet intervention in the negotiations had indeed decreased, although they were certainly not abandoned. The centre of attention now was Chinese détente. In April 1971, Kissinger reported to Nixon on progress with Beijing: 'Mr President, I have not said this before but I think if we get this thing working, we will end Vietnam this year.' Following his secret visits to China, Kissinger told Nixon in February 1972 that there could be a trade-off, linking US support for the Chinese nationalist regime in Taiwan with Beijing's attitude to Hanoi: 'Only we can help them concerning Taiwan, and they can help in Indochina. Accordingly, I have indirectly but consistently linked these two in my talks' (MacMillan 2007: 264). Nixon and Kissinger also hoped that the opening to China would shift the dynamics of the Sino–Soviet rivalry. Moscow and Beijing, each appreciating the value of global détente, might now compete to lure and cajole Hanoi towards negotiated peace.

As of early 1972, there was still little evidence of progress. Nixon's trip to Beijing in February produced more mood music than concrete undertakings of Chinese cooperation regarding Vietnam. Still, China no longer opposed negotiations over the future of Vietnam and, indeed, urged an obdurate Hanoi to consider dropping its insistence that the Thieu government be removed before any deal with the US could be reached. Chinese premier Chou En-lai briefed the DRV leadership in March 1972 in terms which left no doubt that China's stance towards the Paris negotiations had shifted. 'If the problem of Indochina is not solved', declared Chou, 'it will be impossible to realize the normalization of China–US relations.' Yet, Beijing's attitude towards the peace remained complex and cautious. Chou En-Lai assured Hanoi that he had no intention of terminating aid. Beijing was not about to deliver Hanoi into the arms of Moscow. Soviet behaviour towards the war similarly failed to reflect any newly-invigorated will to impose a change of behaviour on Hanoi. Like Beijing, Moscow supported Hanoi's efforts to strengthen its hand in the peace negotiations. Each communist great-power favoured a measured peace agreement, leading to eventual reunification of Vietnam, rather than precipitate US withdrawal and the creation of a regional power vacuum which might be filled by its geopolitical rival. As the USSR moved towards an arms control deal with Washington, new generations of tanks were being supplied by Moscow to North Vietnam (Randolph 2007: 25; Goh 2005: 182; MacMillan 2007: 271; Luthi 2009).

Nixon and Kissinger trusted to the logic of the emergent Moscow–Beijing–Washington 'strategic triangle' to bring some kind of acceptable peace in Vietnam. They were disappointed. The most obvious effects of the unveiled grand design were a sense of panic in Saigon, and a decision in Hanoi that only success on the battlefield would pre-empt possible betrayal by the communist great-powers. As Thieu made increasingly desperate efforts to dissuade Washington from trying to link negotiating terms in Paris to support for his regime, Hanoi launched a new military offensive.

Towards the End: From the 1972 Easter Offensive to the Peace Agreement

The new attack came in late March 1972, between the Nixon trip to Beijing and the Moscow Summit of May 1972. Though influenced by the need to avoid the monsoon season, the timing seemed almost to constitute a North Vietnamese declaration of independence – independence from its major communist sponsors, from the international politics of détente, and from the grand design. From Hanoi's point of view, a military initiative would shift the terms of any negotiating peace. It would also provide a response to recent US air attacks. The main focus of US airstrikes before the Easter Offensive was southern Laos. Between November 1971 and March 1972, around 2,500 attack sorties were launched against targets, usually linked to the Ho

Chi Minh Trail, in Laos. However, although a major sustained renewal of American bombing of North Vietnam did not occur until May 1972, there were also significant earlier US air strikes on the DRV during the Nixon years, usually in response to major PAVN troop infiltrations. In late December 1971, US aircraft undertook over 1,000 sorties against strategic military and supply targets north of the DMZ. General J. D. Lavelle, commander of the Seventh Air Force, oversaw major 'protective reaction' strikes, designed to weaken DRV capabilities and to pre-empt a new offensive. Following a congressional investigation, Lavelle, who appeared to have broken the rules of engagement, was recalled in disgrace in mid-1972. The release of White House tape recordings later showed that Nixon had approved the 'protective reaction' bombings, subsequently admitting: 'I don't feel right about our pushing [Lavelle] into this thing and then, and then giving him a bad rap.' In August 2010, President Barack Obama recommended to the US Senate that Lavelle be posthumously exonerated (Whitlock 2010).

The new PAVN offensive sought, as the Plenum of the DRV Communist Party put it, to 'defeat the policy of "pacification" and crush the enemy's plan to "Vietnamize" the war'. The attacks occurred at a time when approximately 95,000 US military personnel remained in Vietnam, and swift on the heels of Nixon's announcement of more reductions by May. The decision to attack followed a debate between General Giap, who favoured a major offensive, and voices in Hanoi who called for consolidation of the home front. The timing of the attacks was certainly influenced by the grand design developments, but also reflected Hanoi's understanding of the domestic and electoral pressures on Nixon. Giap and Le Duan saw Nixon as unable to send reinforcements, and forced to rely on a still under-prepared ARVN. Some later Vietnamese accounts described the Easter Offensive as a deliberate effort to stimulate anti-war opinion in the US (Truong Nhu Tang 1986: 210; Asselin 2002: 29, 31; Willbanks 2004: 125; Randolph 2007: 26).

The PAVN was better equipped with heavy weaponry, supplied by both China and the USSR, in the 1972 Easter Offensive than at Tet, 1968. The two northern provinces of South Vietnam were taken by communist forces by early April. Two other fronts were opened, in the Central Highlands and at An Loc (northwest of Saigon), with major assaults being launched from Cambodia and Laos. MACV had been aware of an impending assault and, indeed, was accused of alarmism when no attacks appeared during the 1972 Tet holiday. When the attacks came, Nixon saw the crisis as not just a test for Vietnamization, but as a threat to the grand design, (inevitably) to American credibility – and, equally importantly, as a threat to re-election. Saigon must not fall – especially in election year, and especially not just before the Moscow Summit. In a sentence which has come to be seen as encapsulating his attitude to the war, Nixon exclaimed on 25 April that North Vietnam must not be allowed to emerge victorious from the Offensive. He raised with Kissinger the possibility of using nuclear weapons – 'I just want you to think big, Henry, for Christ's sake! ... for once we've got to use the maximum power of this country against a shit-asshole country to win the war' (Hunt 2010: 113). Nixon was aware that the Easter Offensive had been made possible by the supply of Soviet-made tanks, but was still somehow hopeful that Moscow could be induced to pressure Hanoi to desist. He considered action which he hoped would stem the Offensive, without destroying the prospects for the Moscow summit.

Nixon's military response came to a head in May, with major escalation. Action included the mining of Haiphong harbour, which contained many Soviet ships, as part of a naval blockade of the North. Nixon also began to bring into play his 'hole card', with the launch, first, of the 'Freedom Train' bombing of North Vietnam in April 1972, followed by the Linebacker I campaign. Nixon felt a sense of emotional release, composing a memo to Kissinger after announcing the escalation on television: 'I cannot emphasise too strongly that I have determined that we go for broke' (Reeves 2001: 474). According to Nixon Library tape recordings, transcribed by Rick Perlstein (2008: 656), John Connally (senior adviser and Treasury Secretary in the early 1970s) urged the President: 'Don't worry about civilians. Go ahead and kill 'em. People think you are now. So go ahead and give 'em some.' Nixon responded: 'That's right.'

Washington signalled to Moscow that the military response to the Easter Offensive was proportionate: for example, in initially relaying the view that the US would not engage in sustained, indiscriminate bombing. Reflecting a different perspective to that contained in Nixon's memos to him, Kissinger (1979: 1116) wrote: 'If we wanted to force a diplomatic solution, we had to create an impression of implacable determination to prevail.' Linebacker activity intensified after the Moscow Summit, with over 2,000 B-52 aircraft bombing missions in September alone, with a wider range of targets than had been approved under the Rolling Thunder campaigns of the Johnson years. Against the advice of Defence Secretary Laird, Linebacker involved more than simple and direct support for the ARVN. Nixon urged the CIA to use 'black propaganda' including the dissemination of reports that 'madman' options, such as the invasion of North Vietnam by two US Marine divisions, were being considered (Dallek 2008: 388; Van Atta 2008: 403).

At the May Summit in Moscow, Soviet Communist Party leader Leonid Brezhnev offered nothing substantial on Vietnam, beyond referring to earlier undertakings by Kissinger on the possibility of supporting an interval between the US exit and the fall of Saigon. Brezhnev recorded Kissinger's view that 'if there was a peaceful settlement in Vietnam you would be agreeable to the Vietnamese doing what they want, having whatever they want after a period of time, say 18 months'. Kissinger told Soviet Foreign Minister Andrei Gromyko that 'we want a political settlement which does not guarantee a Communist victory, but also, we emphasize, that does not exclude it'. Neither China nor the USSR wished the US response to the Easter Offensive to derail détente. In a strange echo of the Pleiku attack of 1965, Aleksei Kosygin was actually in Hanoi as it was being bombed by American B-52s in the summer of 1972. Moscow and Beijing did urge Hanoi to resume negotiations in the months after the Offensive. What neither great-power ally could or would do was to *compel* Hanoi to come to agreeable terms (Hanhimaki and Westad 2004: 231; Bradley 2009: 167).

Linebacker I bombing is generally credited with repelling the PAVN assault, which in any case was spread too thinly. However, as with so many other aspects of the military history of the war, evaluations of the ARVN's response to the Easter Offensive vary hugely. PAVN losses probably exceeded 100,000 in the long months of conflict which followed the attacks of late March. North Vietnamese forces became tied down in long, destructive engagements (notably at An Loc and around Kontum in the Central Highlands) with limited strategic significance. Tactical mistakes were made on the communist side, with the invading forces appearing on occasion to lose direction, allowing the ARVN to regroup. The Easter Offensive reversals triggered a transfer of DRV military authority from General Giap to General Van Tien Dung, who was to command the final phase of North Vietnamese military strategy (Willbanks 2004: 154; Randolph 2007: 25).

Despite Giap's failures, the Easter Offensive was not an unmitigated disaster for Hanoi. The fighting exposed the degree to which the South Vietnamese military depended on US air support. South Vietnamese General Ngo Quang Truong (1980: 156), one of the ablest of the South Vietnamese commanders, later wrote that the 'staunch resolve of the US to stand behind its ally stunned the enemy'. One wonders how deliberately Ngo Quang Truong chose the word 'behind' in preference to 'alongside'. Anti-communist losses were considerable, though probably exaggerated by Hanoi in later claims to have 'annihilated about 200,000 of the enemy' and 'liberated and gained control of more than one million people' in the South. South Vietnamese refugee numbers were swelled by about 1 million in this period. The PAVN in 1972 failed to take and hold any provincial capital. However, by July 1972, a swathe of rural South Vietnam – from the DMZ, along the Laotian and Cambodian borders, into the northern Mekong Delta – had effectively been abandoned to the communists. North Vietnam began referring to this region as 'Third Vietnam' (Sorley 1999: 339–41).

Domestic American opposition to Nixon's response to the Easter Offensive was intense. However, the recent US troop withdrawals ensured that the critical temperature did not reach the levels of 1970. The Senate Democratic caucus committed itself to cutting off war funding, a move which was endorsed by the *New York Times* as a way 'to save the President from himself'. By this time, the domestic political debate on the war was becoming structured around the 1972 presidential election. One interesting development involved the articulation, in the 1972 campaign, of right-wing criticisms of the Nixon foreign policy. The conservative *National Review* applauded the Linebacker bombing, but noted the paradox of Nixon simultaneously pursuing what significant numbers of conservatives saw as appeasement of Moscow. George Wallace of Alabama, breaking away from the Democrats, offered Nixon advice which chimed with a recognizable section of domestic opinion: 'Get it over with, and if you can't get it over with, get out now' (Perlstein 2008: 657; Scanlon 2009).

On the mainstream Democratic side, Senator George McGovern of South Dakota, drawing on opportunities provided by party rule changes designed to avoid the calamities of 1968, emerged as presidential candidate. McGovern was co-sponsor, with Mark Hatfield of Oregon, of the 1970 Senate 'Amendment to End the War' (technically a military procurement bill amendment). During the 1972 campaign, the South Dakotan offered a blend of peace and progressivism. Vulnerable to Republican charges of irresponsibility, McGovern lost electoral ground due to the declining public saliency of the war following Vietnamization. However, the White House took the McGovern candidacy very seriously; indeed, the whole Watergate scandal erupted in the context of illegal efforts to undermine the 1972 Democratic campaign. Nixon saw his best chance of winning as being seen to be tough towards Hanoi. Bob Haldeman (1994: 500) recorded in his diary of 30 August that Nixon 'wants to be sure' not to 'let Henry [Kissinger]'s desire for a settlement prevail; that's the one way we can lose the election'.

On both sides of the negotiations, the turning back of the Easter Offensive and the election campaign fed into developing positions on the emerging settlement. Secret contacts between Washington and Hanoi resumed in July 1972. The Americans rejected DRV plans for a coalition government in the South; while Hanoi – still under military pressure from the Linebacker I bombing – at long last dropped its insistence on the removal of the Thieu regime in Saigon. Hanoi seems to have become unnerved by McGovern's poor performance in the election campaign. The US also moved. On 15 September, Kissinger accepted that prisoner releases would not commence until a settlement was agreed. This concession involved an acceptance of the efficacy of Hanoi's use of American prisoners of war as a bargaining chip. Nixon is often seen as using the prisoner issue as a way to buy time for Vietnamization; the US–DRV exchanges of September 1972 indicated the double-edged nature of the issue, which also became bound up with Hanoi's demands for war reparations (Allen 2009: 90–2). As Pierre Asselin (2002: 70) explains, Hanoi was by this time seeking assurances that 'there would be no Korea-style armistice and no American forces in Vietnam after the settlement'. By early October, Kissinger felt he had a deal on the table. A settlement would be based on an in-place ceasefire, which effectively recognized DRV control of 'Third Vietnam'. A complete US troop withdrawal would take place under the supervision of a new Council of National Concord.

The apparent US acceptance that there would be no 'Korea-style armistice' was seen in Saigon as a straightforward betrayal. American military presence in the South would disappear and, given the state of public and congressional attitudes in the US, seemed unlikely to reappear when Saigon faced future threats. Despite

Hanoi's earlier acceptance that Thieu's government might remain in power, Kissinger's stance looked very much like outright pursuance of the 'decent interval' strategy – a face-saving gambit to cover the eventual abandonment of the South Vietnamese ally. Kissinger informed Beijing in June 1972 that the US was 'putting a time interval between the military outcome and the political outcome'. Though Nixon had his own doubts, the early October deal was torpedoed by Thieu, who simply refused to give it his support. The puppet proclaimed his independence from the puppeteer. The South Vietnamese leader announced directly that he was no 'lackey of the US'. Kissinger was livid with anger and threatened to make a separate, direct peace with Hanoi, cutting out Saigon. Alexander Haig patiently explained to Kissinger that Thieu was 'being asked to relinquish sovereignty over a large and indescript portion of South Vietnamese territory. He has never agreed to such a concession and given his paranoia about what has brought us to this point, it is understandable that he would now accept an open break' (Asselin 2002: 98; Hanhimaki 2004: 242; Hanhimaki and Westad 2004: 232).

Nixon's landslide victory over McGovern in early November enabled Washington to regain the initiative. Nixon rejected Kissinger's idea of a separate peace with Hanoi, preferring to open a dialogue with Thieu and, once more, to use military action to force through a settlement. Despite the McGovern rout, Hanoi was not prepared to make more concessions regarding a deal (the October draft agreement) that had, in its view, already been made. The North Vietnamese simply launched yet another military offensive, aimed at expanding the area of 'Third Vietnam'. The final, and perhaps most controversial, American military action of the war followed as Nixon once more turned over the 'hole card'. Beginning on 18 December, US aircraft launched 36,000 tons of bombs on North Vietnam in a period of 11 days. The bombing was intended to demonstrate American power to the DRV and to other regional enemies; to signal the possible consequences of violating a future peace treaty; to weaken Hanoi, at least in the short term; to shift the terms of a restarted negotiation; and to bolster chronically failing confidence in Saigon. The bombing inaugurated yet another round of international and domestic American condemnation. The *Washington Post*, now beginning its hunt for Nixon's scalp over the Watergate burglary, described the bombing as 'the most savage and senseless act of war ever visited, over a scant ten days, by one sovereign people over another'. The conventional view of the Christmas bombing is that it did contribute to the achievement of a settlement in January 1973, but that the eventual peace deal was no more than the kind of 'decent interval' abandonment of Saigon which had been sabotaged by Thieu in October 1972. Hanoi was still being pressured by Beijing and Moscow, while DRV officials were beginning privately – before the Linebacker II campaign – to acknowledge that the people of North Vietnam were 'tired of war'. The 'decent interval' solution would have been available without the Christmas air assault. Former White House aide John Negroponte put the case very succinctly: 'We bombed them into accepting our concessions' (Herring 2001: 318; Dallek 2008: 446; Luthi 2009: 95).

By January 1973, 60 per cent of American Gallup poll respondents were of the view that it had been a mistake to send US troops into Vietnam. Nixon might have humiliated McGovern, but renewing commitments to the Vietnam battlefield was not an option. The final meetings for US–DRV negotiation were bizarre occasions, with Kissinger telling the DRV negotiators that he was not to blame for the bombing. The Paris Peace Agreement, signed on 9 January 1973, allowed over 160,000 North Vietnamese military personnel to remain in South Vietnam, effectively conceding 'Third Vietnam' to communist control. Hanoi returned to the negotiating table after the Linebacker II assaults, in line with the preferences of Moscow and Beijing, and with regard to the war-weariness of its population. However, Hanoi returned to Paris to negotiate the terms of triumph, not of retreat. Washington's suggestion – that PAVN troops in the South would somehow be abandoned by Hanoi under the terms of the Agreement – was simply absurd.

Any eventual reunification of Vietnam would, according to the Paris terms, be subject to 'discussions' between North and South. A three-party National Council would oversee elections in the South. Prisoner releases were to follow the ceasefire, which was to be enforced by a Joint Military Commission, working on a somewhat unrealistic principle of unanimity. The Agreement was a reworking of the failed October deal, with Thieu now being successfully pressured to accept it by Washington through a mixture of threats and promises. The deal was accompanied by a range of secret presidential undertakings, including the provision of reconstruction aid to the DRV provided treaty terms were not violated. Nixon assured Thieu that, if Saigon supported the peace, the US would respond with 'full force' to violation of the settlement by Hanoi. From Saigon's perspective, the Agreement was 'like a policeman interrupting a robber holding up a candy store', with the robber left 'pointing his weapon at the frightened store owner instead of hauling him off to jail in handcuffs' (Tran Van Don 1978: 195).

Motivated by concern for US credibility and for their place in history, Nixon and Kissinger tried to rescue something positive from the difficult Vietnam inheritance from LBJ. They prolonged the misery and followed a policy which involved placing the lives of many people hostage to the quirks of erratic personality. Self-styled rationalists in politics, Nixon and Kissinger embraced irrational wishful thinking quite as enthusiastically as their predecessors in office. They seem to have veered between hopeful and cynical interpretations of the 1973 Agreement. Kissinger told Singapore leader Lee Quan Yew in August 1973 that he 'came away from the January negotiations with the feeling that we would have to bomb the North Vietnamese again in early April or May' (Berman 2001: 261). Both American credibility and the reputation of Nixon's presidency were damaged, rather than enhanced, by the President's 1969 decision to ignore the advice of those who urged a swift exit from Vietnam.

6

The Antiwar Movement

Before moving directly to discussion of the fall of Saigon in 1975, Chapters 6, 7, and 8 offer thematic perspectives on the war up until the Paris Agreement of 1973. The current chapter focuses on the nature and significance of the antiwar movement. Here, we consider the movement, as such – direct protest against American policy in Vietnam, rather than the mainstream electoral and congressional initiatives discussed at points in Chapters 4 and 5. Following a brief invocative picture of the movement, we will discuss the role of Tom Hayden, central figure in the student-led American New Left and in the protests surrounding the 1968 Democratic Party national convention in Chicago. We proceed then to consideration of the chronological development and structure of the antiwar movement, emphasizing its internal divisions and conflicting positions over strategy and purpose. Our main concern is with the American movement, which led global antiwar protest and which plausibly had a major, substantive impact on the course of the war. Both orthodox and revisionist writing tends to give considerable prominence to US antiwar protest, seeing it as having influence over policy-makers, as shutting off war options, and even as affecting the conduct of the war on the ground. Various questions present themselves. Did the American antiwar movement shorten or lengthen the war? To what extent did the movement represent a morally, intellectually, and organizationally coherent response to the American military presence in Vietnam? We also consider the movement as a global phenomenon. Was there anything approaching an integrated international anti-Vietnam protest movement? How did international protest affect war decisions and conduct? The concluding section offers a route between polarized judgements on the effectiveness and integrity of protest against the American-led war in Vietnam.

Both internationally and in the United States, the antiwar movement had a strong 'fun' element. It conformed at various times to the Leninist concept of 'festive energy', leading to revolutionary change. The movement also embraced profound tragedy and seriousness. On up to eight occasions, US activists protested the war by burning themselves to death in imitation of the Buddhist self-immolations in Vietnam itself. Hillary Clinton (2003: 32) later expressed her reasonable annoyance with those 'who have tried to dismiss the anguish of those years as an embodiment of 1960s self-indulgence'. Describing the combination of self-indulgent frivolity and high moral seriousness in the American movement, Todd Gitlin (1989: 263) wrote that that 'only true believers in the promise of America could have felt so anti-American'. The 'fun' aspect of the antiwar movement was implicated in one of its most strikingly impressive features: the sheer imaginative brio of its activities. Protest ran the gamut from university 'teach-ins' in the mid-1960s, to the marches and demonstrations of the 1970s. The March against Death, in November 1969, saw 45,000 people marching past the White House for a period of nearly forty hours. Protesters pronounced the name of a particular deceased US soldier as they passed the residence of President Richard Nixon. The Moratorium demonstration in Melbourne, Australia, in May 1970 was a very lively yet dignified expression of legitimate dissent; around 70,000 demonstrators marched 60-abreast. In the summer of 1971, a local referendum in San Diego, California, was organized as part of the antiwar Stop Our Ship (SOS) campaign against the departure of the aircraft carrier USS *Constellation* for war service. Antiwar sailors on the USS *Coral Sea* deactivated bombs and applied notices to them reading, 'repaired by SOS'. In June 1972, around 2,500 women and children linked hands around the Capitol building in Washington, DC in protest against legislative failure to end the war (MacPherson 1984: 33; Gitlin 1989: 263; Wells 1994: 391, 526, 550; Ham 2008: 525;).

Tom Hayden: Antiwarrior

The protest career of Tom Hayden between the early 1960s and the close of the Vietnam War typified some important features of the wider antiwar movement: the early political awakening associated with the civil rights movement in the American South; the developing political consciousness of a new, university-educated generation,

self-consciously at odds with its predecessor generation; reform liberalism giving way to intense radicalism; the re-discovery in the 1970s
of the virtues of electoral politics. Coming from an Irish-American
Catholic background, Hayden graduated from the University of
Michigan in 1961. By the end of 1961, he had become involved in
student political campaigns in California, spent seven months working with the Student Nonviolent Coordinating Committee in the
South, and had authored his 'Letter to the New (Young) Left'.
Published in *Activist* magazine, the letter appealed to the ideas of radical sociologist C. Wright Mills and deplored the 'drift of decision-
making power away from directly representative, legislative or
executive institutions into corporate and military hands'. In 1962,
Hayden became principal author of the Port Huron statement – in
effect, a manifesto for the newly-organized Students for a Democratic
Society (SDS) and promulgated at its Michigan convention. The Port
Huron statement represented a rejection of Old Leftism, especially in
its Stalinist and bureaucratized guises, but also a repudiation of the
insistent anticommunism of Cold War liberalism. Hayden drew on
Wright Mills' notion of 'the young and the intellectuals as the new
vanguard', arguing for 'participatory democracy', community organization and personal commitment to practical, progressive change.
Hayden allied the New Left with 'the colonial revolution' in developing countries and deplored a foreign policy based on 'pugnacious
anticommunism and protection of interests' (Mills 1956; Hayden
1988: 80; 2008: 20, 50).

While attending graduate school in Michigan, Hayden became
president of SDS and, in effect, a full-time political organizer. His
goal was to organize pressure on the Johnson administration to 'turn
away from Cold War militarism and toward domestic priorities'. His
outlook on the war reflected his impatience with his parents' generation: 'they failed to see Vietnam as a popular and nationalist struggle,
with elements of civil war, against the new foreigners, who happened
to be Americans' (Hayden 1988: 115, 179). Hayden travelled to
Hanoi, partly to attempt to negotiate the release of US prisoners, and
conversed with North Vietnamese and NLF leaders at a conference in
Czechoslovakia in late 1967. In North Vietnam, he was impressed by
the optimism of the people and particularly shocked by the new
American fragmentation bombs.

The assassination of Robert Kennedy in June 1968 was a turning
point in Hayden's disillusion with the politics of reform, and set the

scene for the violent confrontations in Chicago in August. Hayden was by now engaged in exchanges with the radical pacifist David Dellinger, with Hayden pointing out the limits of non-violent protest. Hayden was apprehended by the police twice in Chicago. He donned a false beard, giving at least one television interview in disguise. Doug Dowd (who, with Hayden, Dellinger and Rennie Davis, had been prominent in organizing the Democratic national convention protests) recalled of Hayden in Chicago: 'He was doing all kinds of crazy things. He was just having the time of his goddam life.' Summing up his own mood in Chicago, Hayden later wrote: 'reform seemed bankrupt, revolution far away'. Pro-Johnson Democrats had been taught 'the lesson that business as usual was a formula for polit- ical defeat and moral self-destruction'. In March 1969, Tom Hayden became one of the leading defendants in the 'Chicago conspiracy' trial, connected to the events of the previous August, and lasting from September 1969 to February 1970. The extraordinary trial, at one stage involving the gagging and binding of Black Panther leader Bobby Seale, became a pivotal event in the history of counter-cultural politics. By now, SDS was radicalizing to the point of disintegration. In October 1970, Tom Hayden offered his encouragement to the Days of Rage protest, organized by the 'Weathermen' (an SDS radical splinter, named after a line in Bob Dylan's song, 'Subterranean Homesick Blues'). The protest involved the blowing up of the police monument in Chicago's Haymarket Square. Hayden and the other defendants were found guilty of conspiracy charges, only to have their appeals against conviction upheld in November 1972, primarily due to the eccentric and overbearing conduct of the trial by Judge Julius Hoffman. Despite some expressed sympathy for the Weathermen and for revolutionary violence, Hayden now mourned the effective eclipse of SDS. Debating the radical Terry Robins, Hayden argued that the Weathermen 'were not the conscience of a generation, but its *id*, finally surfacing' (Dellinger 1975: 121; Hayden 1988: 321, 360; Miller 1994: 78–90; Horn 2007: 146–8).

Remembering 1968, Staughton Lynd (a Christian pacifist and Yale historian who accompanied Hayden on his 1965 trip to Hanoi) recalled that 'on Monday, Wednesday and Friday', Tom 'was a National Liberation Front guerrilla, and on Tuesday, Thursday and Saturday, he was ... on the left wing of the Democratic Party'. Following the conspiracy trial, Hayden moved firmly in the direction of electoral politics. In the later stages of US engagement in Vietnam,

he – along with actress Jane Fonda, whom he married in 1973 – led the
Indochina Peace Campaign, designed to pressure Congress to end the
war. The IPC opposed aid to South Vietnam following the Paris
Agreement of 1973. Hayden became involved in Californian state
politics, serving in both the State Assembly and the State Senate. His
later writing combined a continuing commitment to the efficacy of his
early political stances with a degree of mature reflection about the
excessive certainties of youth. In 2000, he argued that the authoritarian record of the post-1975 Vietnamese should not blind following
generations to the wilful and tragic ignorance that the US displayed
towards its Vietnamese adversary during the war. The Vietnam War,
according to Hayden, should be viewed not in the context of a world-
historical struggle against communism, but as an aspect of America's
messianic impulse to Manifest Destiny: 'Ho Chi Minh should be
viewed less like Joseph Stalin and more like Sitting Bull' (Hayden
1988: 174, 415; Wells 1994: 236).

The Movement Develops: 1964–73

The antiwar movement drew from the heritage of disarmament
groups (notably SANE, the National Committee for a Sane Nuclear
Policy) of the earlier years of the Cold War, and especially from the
activist traditions which, in the later 1950s, had pushed for a ban on
atmospheric testing of nuclear weapons. Important strands in this
earlier peace tradition included radical pacifists, concerned scientists,
Women Strike for Peace (a group, founded in 1961, who had achieved
the tacit support of President Kennedy regarding its campaign to ban
atmospheric nuclear testing), and various Christian groupings. By the
time of the Gulf of Tonkin Resolution, however, there was, to quote
Charles DeBenedetti (1990: 99) 'for all practical purposes no independent left and no alternative for Johnson's dovish critics'. With at
least a degree of justification, the New Left saw itself as starting anew,
following the social conformism of the 1950s and the McCarthyite
attacks on American leftism. The Gulf of Tonkin Resolution did stimulate some acts of protest – again, mainly from the ranks of the older
peace movement. In August 1964, pacifists associated with the
Catholic Worker Movement, the War Resisters League (the internationally organized antiwar group, whose American branch had been
founded in 1923) and the Committee for Non-Violent Action (an anti-

nuclear organization dating from the late 1950s) organized protest events at the Democratic Party national convention in Atlantic City.

By the early part of 1965, student leftists had clearly established themselves as leaders of the war protests. The teach-in movement, inaugurated at the University of Michigan in March 1965, spread to hundreds of other campuses. The Vietnam Day Committee, formed at Berkeley, organized various activities, including the blockade of troop trains and the setting-up in Washington, DC in August 1965 of a 'Congress of Unrepresented People'. The National Coordinating Committee to End the War in Vietnam, the first of many efforts to bring war protest under one umbrella, was also the initiative of Berkeley radicals, led by Jerry Rubin. Following the October 1965 'International Days of Protest' (yet another Berkeley initiative), former president Dwight Eisenhower condemned the 'moral deterioration' of American youth. Defying the radicalizing New Left orientation of the movement, SANE and Quaker groups also organized Washington events in late 1965 and early 1966. Student protest became increasingly directed at the draft process, with SDS effectively kick-starting the draft resistance movement in May 1966. Students at the University of Chicago disrupted efforts to produce class rankings following a Selective Service System move to induct lower-ranking students into the military. Non-student oriented protest included the campaign by women in San Jose, California, to disrupt the transportation of napalm bombs. In November 1966, Defence Secretary McNamara faced protests during a visit to Harvard University. The experience contributed to his worries about the war and to the commissioning of the *Pentagon Papers* (McNamara 1995: 253).

By the early part of 1967, the movement was operating along a number of paths whose direction only sometimes intersected. Efforts to coordinate activity were continued, largely under student leadership, in the form of various national mobilization committees, including the 'Spring Mobe' which organized demonstrations in New York and San Francisco in March 1967. By this time, the SDS was preoccupied with draft resistance activity, with various other anti-draft organizations quickly emerging. Various wings of protest activity were designed to bring anger at the war to the direct attention of policy-makers, and to move towards concerted civil disobedience. In March 1967, two young protesters threw themselves in front of President Johnson's car following an address given by LBJ in Tennessee. Lady Bird Johnson's diary recorded the unmediated and lasting impression made by the incident: 'I looked back and saw the young girl's naked legs – her dress around her hips, her feet held by one officer, her shoulders by another – being lifted from the road' (Johnson 1970: 501–2). In early 1967, Clergy and Laymen Concerned about Vietnam (CALCAV), which had launched itself on a national basis in 1966, mounted peace vigils and fasts. In June 1967, Jan Barry, a West Point drop-out, founded Vietnam Veterans against the War (VVAW). The 'Vietnam Summer' protest organization of 1967 saw a coming-together (at least, at its top) of CALCAV and the SDS, along with nationally-known figures such as Martin Luther King and child psychologist Benjamin Spock. The movement's National Mobilization Committee organized, amid huge disagreements over the effectiveness and desirability of civil disobedience, a mass demonstration at the Pentagon on 21 October 1967. The event led to nearly 700 arrests, as well as to one of the major, and most influential, literary productions of movement history, Norman Mailer's *The Armies of the Night* (1968).

The year 1968 was marked by the disorder in Chicago, a new anti-movement campaign on the part of the Federal Bureau of Investigation, and by the disintegration of the 'Mobe'. In May, two radical Roman Catholic priests, Philip and Daniel Berrigan applied home-made napalm to draft board files in Catonsville, Maryland, following an incident the previous October where they led a Catholic group which poured blood on files in Baltimore. The brothers disappeared from custody before starting prison sentences, only to be apprehended again in 1970. The Berrigans were also named by the FBI in 1970 as conspirators in a plot to kidnap Henry Kissinger and to sabotage federal buildings in Washington; the conspiracy charge collapsed in 1971. In movement terms, the Berrigans represented the ultimate in conscience-driven extreme civil disobedience. The election of Richard Nixon in 1968 produced a flurry of dialogue between movement leaders and the new administration. At one level, the movement regarded the exit of the 'war Democrats' as their achievement. CALCAV leaders met Henry Kissinger in February 1969, while student leaders met Kissinger and White House counsel John Ehrlichman in April. Draft resistance leader David Hawk recalled the general impression made by the meeting: 'These guys are going to be worse than the last bunch' (Wells 1994: 295).

The 1968 disorder in Chicago and the Nixon election stimulated a sense of powerlessness and failure among many activists. The SDS disintegrated in June 1969, with the Weathermen emerging from the wreckage. However, 1969 eventually witnessed major, peaceful campus protests. A fresh umbrella protest body – 'New Mobe' – was launched from a national antiwar conference held in Cleveland, Ohio. 'New Mobe' generally represented the more radical face of protest, yet it did manage to work more or less effectively with the more liberal Vietnam Moratorium Committee to organize unprecedented and coordinated protest on 14–15 October. In the event, some 2 million citizens participated in these protests. The success of the October 1969 protests was attributed later by Adam Garfinkle (1997: 173) to the Moratorium Committee's ability to allow ordinary citizens to protest silently against the war 'without having to travel anywhere, without having to break the law, and without having to be seen in the company of others who were breaking the law, waving Vietcong banners, or shouting obscenities at police'. The October protests were succeeded by a mass march of around 250,000 people in Washington on 15 November 1969 (two days after the dignified March against Death). The White House predicted that the November march would be violent, and refused to grant a permit for 'New Mobe' gatherings. Much of the march on November 15 was peaceful; though, when David Dellinger led protesters towards the Justice Department, the police responded with tear gas.

The momentum achieved by the October protests was undermined by Nixon's 'Silent Majority' speech; by the November disorder in Washington; and, to some degree, by the signing (on 26 November 1969) of the new draft lottery bill. The Moratorium Committee disbanded in April 1970 amid massive debt. David Hawk recalled many protesters concluding that, if the war were to be ended soon, 'Congress has to do it'. 'New Mobe' was still being challenged by the Trotskyist Student Mobilization Committee (SMC), which actually revived in early 1970. The SMC's Cleveland conference in February attracted large numbers and was characterized by the display of red, blue and gold National Liberation Front flags, brandished by an SDS splinter group called the Revolutionary Youth Movement II. The Cambodian invasion and the subsequent killing by National Guardsmen of four students at Kent State University, Ohio, on 4 May 1970, transformed the situation. Following further killings at Ohio State and Jackson State University in Mississippi, massive campus protest ensued: 536 colleges and universities were closed, at least temporarily. The protests were echoed across the mainstream political spectrum. Over 250 State Department employees signed a statement criticizing administration war and anti-protester policy. On 9 May, Nixon had his extraordinary exchanges with demonstrators at the Lincoln Memorial. Alongside the student protests, 1970 witnessed a host of other antiwar activity, including fasting organized by CALCAV and theatrical war 're-enactments' by antiwar veterans. A new effort to launch a coordinating organization was mounted in September 1970 with the formation of the National Coalition against War, Racism and Repression – rapidly dubbed by detractors 'the coalition against everything' (Banks and Banks 1989; Gordon 1990; Wells 1994: 461).

Antiwar protest in 1971 and 1972 was, even more so than in 1969–70, hostage to declining US troop levels in Vietnam and the perception that America's war in Vietnam was coming to an end. Much of the movement's impetus now came from the veterans. Reflecting widespread worries about declining force morale in Vietnam, VVAW spokesman John Kerry addressed the Senate Foreign Relations Committee in April 1971: 'How do you ask a man to be the last man to die in Vietnam?' Kerry, Democratic presidential candidate in 2004, was later to chair the committee. Over 100 veterans testified in the February–March 1971 'Winter Soldier' investigation into Vietnam War crimes. The investigation was coordinated by the antiwar veterans, with assistance from Jane Fonda and rock group Crosby, Stills and Nash. The VVAW's Operation Dewey Canyon III formed a major part of the movement's 'spring offensive' in 1971. The name echoed the American codename – Dewey Canyon II – for US support within Vietnam for the 1971 ARVN invasion of Laos. Featuring 'guerrilla theater', Dewey Canyon III involved medal returns and incursions into the Capitol buildings. Beyond the general desire to 'bring the war home', the operation had various more specific aims, including the setting up of drug rehabilitation facilities for veterans. Coordinated Washington demonstrations in late April and May 1971 saw large numbers of arrests. Over 150 Quakers, part of the 'People's Lobby' in the capital, were detained for praying on the pavement outside the White House. May Day protests saw major disorder and fragmentation between radicals – such as the 'May Day Tribe', and more peaceful protesters – such as the Quakers. Attorney General John Mitchell compared the demonstrators to 'Hitler's brownshirts'. Demonstrations later in the year were coordinated by yet another pair of mutually distrustful organizations: the People's

Coalition for Peace and Justice (the New Left successor of the National Coalition against War, Racism and Repression, involving activists such as Sidney Peck), and the Trotskyist National Peace Action Coalition. The movement remained fissiparous to the very end. Antiwar protest became largely subsumed under the McGovern presidential campaign in 1972, and revived at street level in response to the Christmas bombing of North Vietnam (Wells 1994: 514, 556; Isserman and Kazin 2008: 281).

A Variegated Movement

It will be evident from the foregoing narrative that there were many American antiwar movements, despite complex overlaps and efforts (some successful, most not) to bring the factions together. The various wings of the movement were divided by arguments over both means and ends. Should the movement follow the line of the civil rights activists and respect the principle of non-violence? Like the civil rights movement, the movement had to address the problem of self-defensive 'violence'. Should protesters always obey the law? What if permission for peaceful demonstration was withheld by the authorities? Should aims be calibrated, or should all protest demand nothing less than immediate American withdrawal? Should activity be geared to war-related issues, or to wider programmes for political and social change? How far should protesters take into account the need to bring along an as wide as possible spectrum of American public opinion? When exactly did legitimate protest slide over into giving comfort and encouragement to the enemy?

These were real and important debates, not merely self-indulgent and enervating self-interrogation. Fractious controversy about the means and ends of antiwar protest were evident across the protest movement, not just in its student wing. A 1967 Central Intelligence Agency analysis concluded that there were, 'not one, but many movements'; antiwar protest embraced 'pacifists and fighters, idealists and materialists, internationalists and isolationists, democrats and totalitarians, conservatives and revolutionaries' (DeBenedetti 1983: 35). Conservative protesters were hardly thick on the ground, though some libertarian conservatives opposed aspects of the war, notably the draft; some movement radicals – notably Carl Oglesby – tried to make common cause with them (Andrew 2001). For purposes of analysis, the following elements of the American antiwar movement present themselves: the New Left and the student movement; the older, pacifist and church-oriented peace movement; the draft resistance movement; African-American activists; and the veterans' movement. Let us look at each in turn, making specific reference to this issue of destructive intra-factionalism.

The factionalism within the student left was endemic. The SDS experienced constant internal strife: for example, between advocates of local, community organization and supporters of national mobilization. Feminists began increasingly to question the dominant male culture of the student organizations. The most obvious split was that between 'within-the-system' and 'revolutionary' leftism. For the moderate wing, the point of protest was to win over public and congressional opinion to the policy of withdrawal from Vietnam: students should work with the grain of patriotic public opinion, and also alongside the kind of liberal antiwar activism advocated by organizations such as Americans for Democratic Action, and leaders such as Walter Reuther of the United Auto Workers. Sam Brown (effectively the founder and leader of the Vietnam Moratorium Committee in 1969) later recalled his impatience with those radicals who delighted in boasting about the number of times they had been arrested in the cause of transforming the world: 'I wanted the killing to stop ... We're not dealing here with the entryway to heaven – we're dealing with how do you end the war. And that frequently got confused' (Wells 1994: 371).

The radical, revolutionary analysis was put most famously by Trotskyist Peter Camejo in his address to the 1969 Vietnam Moratorium demonstration on Boston Common: 'Vietnam ... isn't a mistake, but an absolute inevitability of the system'. Carl Oglesby, speaking as president of the SDS, told demonstrators in Washington, DC in November 1965 that Vietnam was the war of liberals like Harry Truman and, indeed, like the 'flaming liberal' John Kennedy. The way out of the conflict required something more than 'liberal half-ass ideas'. The case for direct action was well put by antiwar leaders like Oglesby; indeed, Vietnam *was* the liberals' war. The problem with direct action was that it tended to upset mainstream public opinion. The question which advocacy of direct action immediately involved was the relationship between direct action within-the-law and action which challenged, or even deliberately flouted, the law. Peaceful protest often, though by no means always, degenerated into disorder.

Such degeneration was usually traceable to a combination of deliberate provocation, heavy-handed police responses, and even (especially in the later stages of movement history) *agents provocateurs*. Almost as damaging as the mainstream public response to disorder was the sheer energy wasted in constant intra-movement wrangling over confrontation *versus* pragmatic moderation. Student meetings focused almost obsessively on the Marcusian theme of co-optation by the liberal, pro-capitalist mainstream. Student radicals, like J. D. Salinger's hero in *Catcher in the Rye*, prized 'authenticity'; above all considerations of pragmatism, the chief sin was to be a 'phoney'. Madeline Duckles exclaimed: 'Now I'm at the point where I'll do anything for my country but go to another meeting' (Marcuse 1964; Halstead 1978: 490; Wells 1994: 62, 160; Mattson 2002: 253; Oglesby 2008).

The major structural fracture within the student movement was that between Old and New Left. New Leftists saw themselves as responding to C. Wright Mills' 1960 call to 'forget Victorian Marxism' by offering a more libertarian, anti-bureaucratic leftism (Isserman and Kazin 2008: 177). Yet, the Communist Party was involved in, especially, the early stages of antiwar student radicalism; as was Progressive Labor, the Maoist group. The most significant organized revolutionary faction within student leftism was the Trotkyist Socialist Workers' Party, which tended to favour mass demonstrations and to condemn multi-issue approaches as playing into the hands of would-be Democratic Party co-opters. 'Victorian Marxists', of course, not only clashed with New Leftists, they also fought each other – sometimes literally, as at the 1965 convention of the National Coordinating Committee to End the War in Vietnam

Moving on to the older tradition of peace activism, groups such as SANE tended to look with a degree of horror at the antics of the radical students. Yet, SANE had constant internal debates about whether to accept a pragmatic alliance with the student-led organizations. Benjamin Spock, who stood as candidate for the antiwar People's Party in the 1972 presidential election, urged SANE and similar, liberally inclined groups to be 'less self-righteous' in their attitude towards leftist antiwarriors. Some members of the non-student peace groups favoured immediate US exit from Vietnam; others looked to ally their part of the movement with mainstream liberal demands for a negotiated settlement which did not involve abandoning South Vietnam to communism. Older peace activists recalled the damaging left factionalism of the 1930s, and were also much more aware than their younger associates of the dangers of becoming associated with domestic communism. In January 1968, 87-year-old Jeanette Rankin led a march of 5,000 black-clad women on Capitol Hill to protest the war. (Rankin, former member of the House of Representatives, had been the only member of Congress to cast a vote against both world wars.) Congress was the preferred point of pressure for Women Strike for Peace, who ran the campaigns of feminist Democratic Congresswoman Bella Abzug in the early 1970s. Yet, especially if we look towards American pacifism, it is clear that even these older movements had their own internal tensions. Frequent divisions attended the editorial board of *Liberation*, the radical pacifist journal founded in 1955–56 by David Dellinger on the model of William Lloyd Garrison's pre-Civil War anti-slavery paper, *The Liberator*. In 1967, David McReynolds and Charles Bloomstein left the board in protest at Dellinger's perceived move away from pacifism. Dellinger, who stood trial as part of the 1968 'Chicago conspiracy' with Tom Hayden, became increasingly radical. Within the wider movement, Dellinger argued the case for privileging civil disobedience over peaceful marching. His 1970 book, *Revolutionary Nonviolence*, ridiculed the 'superstitious belief in the underlying decency of American institutions'. Within strictly religious groupings, one has only to recall the actions led by the Berrigans to appreciate the limits of the pacifist stereotype (Dellinger 1970: 101; DeBenedetti 1990: 24, 189; Jeffreys-Jones 1999: 158, 161; Lieberman 2000: 185; Small 2004: 163–4).

Draft resistance was, second only to violent revolutionism, the most problematic aspect of the movement from the point of view of mainstream public opinion. To many mainstream observers and commentators, student activism could be explained simply by reference to the draft. In fact, students were – because of the college deferment system, which ended only in December 1971 – the least likely members of their age-group to serve in Vietnam. In his war memoir, *The Pawns of Dishonor*, Micheal Clodfelter (1976: 307) recalled the serving soldier's perception of 'spoiled, gutless and middle class kids who cowered in college classrooms to escape the battlefield'. The number of draft offenders during the Vietnam War era may have been as high as 570,000; only 209,517 seem to have been actually accused of draft evasion by the government. Organized draft card burning began in 1965. David Harris, draft resistance organizer, regarded his part of the antiwar movement as its 'shock troops'. Though enforcement of the law against draft-dodging was sporadic, significant numbers of resistance leaders, including Harris, did serve prison terms. The impact of the draft resisters was lessened by the understandable disinclination of many of the potential 'shock troops' to take action in public. A quiet exit to Canada was a preferred option for many. One of the ironies of draft resistance history – again, in line with our theme of the movement's splitting tendencies – was the apparent contempt held by some student radicals for those whose opposition to the war sprang 'merely' from a desire to avoid service. According to the Harvard University branch of Progressive Labor, draft 'noncooperators' were just 'bourgeois moralists' (Baskir and Strauss 1978: 23; Clifton 1989; Wells 1994: 270, 371).

Martin Luther King's speech on the Vietnam War, delivered at the Riverside Church in New York on 4 April 1967, was a turning point in the movement's history. To quote Rhodri Jeffreys-Jones (1999: 111): 'For the first time, the leading advocate of nonviolence as a civil rights tactic systematically criticized the international violence used by his former allies in the Democratic Party'. King's speech was interpreted by some members of the Johnson administration as a slightly desperate attempt to retrieve the leadership of organized civil rights politics, following the historic legislative achievements of 1964–65 and the rise of black radicalism. In fact, King mounted a lucid and powerful assault on LBJ and the war managers. For King, the war was a denial of Great Society values: taking resources away from domestic reform, and causing black soldiers to risk their lives in defence of the freedom which was denied to them at home. Dr King also raised the issue of racism in the military and the discriminatory nature, largely through the operation of the college deferment provision, of the draft.

By the time of Martin Luther King's antiwar address, several leading organizers of civil rights protest, including James Forman and Bob Moses from the Student Nonviolent Coordinating Committee, had publicly criticized the war. Stokely Carmichael declared the war to be a case of 'white people sending black people to make war on yellow people to defend land they stole from red people'. Boxing champion Muhammad Ali refused the draft in 1966 on the grounds of his membership of the Nation of Islam: 'I am a member of the Black Muslims and we don't go to no wars unless they're declared by Allah himself. I don't have no personal quarrel with those Vietcongs.' Carmichael, Ali, and black radicals such as Bobby Seale actually offered a rather similar analysis of the Vietnam conflict to that presented by Martin Luther King. The main opposition to this radical antiwar line within African-American politics came from the non-violent, moderate wing of the civil rights movement, whose natural leader was Dr King himself. Whitney Young, leader of the National Urban League, told King that 'Johnson needs a consensus ... If we are not with him, then he is not going to be with us on civil rights.' By 1970, both the Urban League and the National Association for the Advancement of Colored People had formally adopted antiwar positions, though they remained opposed to positive integration into the white-dominated antiwar movement (Hall 2003: 678; Gibson 2009: 27; Tuck 2010: 339).

Despite some chaotic episodes, Vietnam Veterans against the War organized some of the most imaginative and effective of the movement protests. The organization, especially in the 1960s, deliberately aspired to a maturity and a dignity which set it apart from the student left. It achieved important successes in linking antiwar protest to patriotic values. A 1971 VVAW pamphlet declared: 'we grew up in a violent society with John Wayne movies ... and in the Nam we saw many of our brothers die because they thought they were John Wayne ... Freedom includes freedom from the role we were trained for – the role of violence' (Rossinow 1998: 232–3). The peculiar status attaching to the veterans was recognized by the Johnson and Nixon administrations, who took every opportunity to harass the organization, not least by insisting that many members were not genuine veterans at all. FBI infiltration was a major problem for the veterans; following a 1972 planning meeting to organize protest at the upcoming Republican Party convention in Miami, one regional VVAW coordinator revealed himself to his colleagues as an FBI agent. Dissension within VVAW centred on familiar rifts between 'confrontational' and 'orderly reform' wings. On the confrontational wing, in 1971 Al Hubbard, a black Air Force veteran, organized the 'chickenshit' brigade, which pelted the Pentagon with excrement. The movement broadened out in the early 1970s, though in the process it brought in radical elements from the Maoist Revolutionary Union. Re-organized in early 1972 as the VVAW-Winter Soldier Organization, the veterans' movement became, as Air Force veteran Joe Urgo later recalled, squeezed between extreme radicals and 'police agents'. At its best, however, as in much of the Dewey Canyon III initiative, the veterans' movement staked a claim to a uniquely dignified and effective position within the wider movement (Moser 1996; Nicosia 2001: 150, 122, 226; Prados 2002: 410; Hall 2011: 16).

Interpreting the War: The Impact of the American Antiwar Movement

[handwritten: Historical debate → anti-war protests]

In February 1973, Tom Hayden acclaimed the Paris Agreement as a victory for the antiwar movement: 'It is our victory, ours and Vietnam's, and not Richard Nixon's.' The victory, for Hayden, was made possible by the growth of antiwar sentiment in every walk of American life, 'perhaps most dramatically within the armed forces where tens of thousands have deserted'. The movement had caused Johnson to retire and Nixon to try 'to make the unpopular war invisible and, that failing, formally terminate it'. The economic cost of the war was aggravated, according to Hayden, by the movement 'making it impossible for the Executive to ask the Congress for war taxes'. Antiwar protest also demonstrated to 'the Vietnamese and Third World people that an aggressive war will be met with broad resistance inside America' (Hayden 2008: 115).

The notion of the antiwar movement as a credible and potent agent of precipitate American withdrawal from Vietnam has found its way into many accounts of the conflict. In various forms, approving and disapproving, this view of the antiwar movement informs both orthodox and revisionist interpretations of the war. George Christian, White House aide in the later 1960s, felt that Lyndon Johnson's 'inability to move about the country freely without having demonstrations' definitely did affect Vietnam policy, and contributed to LBJ's 31 March 1968 turnaround. Tom Wells specifically enumerated instances where protest activity appeared to have a clear impact on war-related decisions, such as LBJ's determination in 1965 not to call up American reserve forces. Plans for a 1971 antiwar movement 'spring offensive' were seen by Wells as influencing President Nixon's decision to announce the withdrawal of 100,000 troops on 7 April. Wells quoted Sidney Peck, a protest organizer, as concluding that the 'offensive' had succeeded also in having 'really a major impact on Congress' (Wells 1994: 37, 105, 153, 513).

Assessments of the impact of the antiwar movement on actual policy are often couched in terms which recognize the counter-productive effect of movement excesses. George McGovern (1992: xii), for example, later saw public opposition to movement extremism as contributing to his own electoral defeat in 1972. Yet, George McGovern felt in 1992 that the movement had set the stage for America's exit from Vietnam. Even for Tom Wells (1994: 6), the movement's impact was damaged by 'internal strife', as well as the 'unrealistic expectations and political impatience of many activists'. However, without the movement, 'the domestic political constraints on the war would have been considerably weaker': there would have been more bombing, more troop deployments, a wider Indochinese ground war and more deaths. Without antiwar protest, the US, wrote Wells, 'might well eventually have pummelled Hanoi into submission – if not, as protestors feared, sparked World War III'. Todd Gitlin acknowledged in the late 1980s that 'unpopular as the war had become, the antiwar movement was detested even more'. However, the antiwar protest movement was also, for Gitlin, 'probably the largest and most effective anti-war movement in history' (Gitlin 1989: 335, 435; 1994: xiv)

Melvin Small saw the policy impact of the antiwar movement as evident in at least two White House decisions, both of which had an important effect on the course of the war. According to Small, the Pentagon protest of 21 October 1967 'compelled' Lyndon Johnson to launch his ill-fated public relations campaign in defence of General Westmoreland and American progress in Vietnam. With the Tet Offensive exposing the shallowness of the campaign, Small argues that the Pentagon protest was an indirect cause of the American public and media reaction in early 1968, and a contributory factor in LBJ's war-limitation decisions at the end of March. Such arguments are more than a little speculative, especially in view of some of the complexities of public and elite responses to the Tet Offensive discussed in Chapter 4. Nevertheless, it is reasonable to argue that awareness of antiwar protest did shape the elite – Johnson adminis-tration and congressional – perceptions of how to respond to the situ-ation in early 1968. Small also argued that the Moratorium protests of 15 October 1969 effectively closed off Nixon's options in Vietnam. Antiwar protest contributed to Nixon's decision to shelve the escalation planned by Kissinger's staff in April and September 1969. Nixon set Ho Chi Minh a date – 1 November 1969 – by which to show positive movement in the Paris peace talks, or face severe military action. The intercession of the October Moratorium, in which around 2 million Americans participated, arguably inclined Nixon to drop the ultimatum, and effectively to abandon the Duck Hook plans (Small 1996: 124–5). Nixon (1978: 400) himself recorded: 'Although publicly I continued to ignore the raging antiwar movement, I had to face the fact that it had probably destroyed the credibility of my ultimatum to Hanoi'. Acceptance of a role for the movement in affecting policy in 1968–69, however, is not tantamount to demonstrating that antiwar protest actually shortened the war. Bob Haldeman's later opinion was that the 1969 Moratorium protests 'eliminated the possibility of a negotiated settlement' at that time, extending the war by three years (Small 1988: 186–7). Such a view is rather extreme, but no easier to refute than Tom Hayden's view that protest brought the war to a premature conclusion.

The antiwar movement influenced war policy in at least three ways: by moulding the decision-making environment; in terms of the complex interaction between the movement, the US Congress, and public opinion; and through affecting the morale of fighting forces – both American forces in Vietnam, and communist fighters and leaders. Let us briefly explore each of these avenues.

From at least 1965, elite war managers operated in a decisional environment which was influenced by the antiwar movement. Antiwar protest touched decision-makers directly; examples would include McNamara's Harvard visit of November 1966, LBJ's exposure to the protesters who flung themselves in front of his car in Tennessee in 1967, and Nixon's meeting with demonstrators at the Lincoln Memorial. In line with the declared movement objective of 'child stealing', many war managers found themselves having to defend the war against their rebellious children. Elite doubts about the war were strengthened by personal exposure to antiwar sentiment, especially in family and academic settings. Universities provided much of the context for elite transmission of antiwar thinking, especially between the generations. John Kenneth Galbraith in 1971 held that America's universities were 'forcing the pace of our present withdrawal from Vietnam'. One of the most poignant instances of intergenerational conflict occurred at the 1972 funeral of Colonel John Paul Vann. Vann's son, Jesse, tore up his draft card, placing half on his father's coffin; he was persuaded by his family and by Brent Scowcroft (then a military assistant to the President) from presenting the other half to Richard Nixon at the post-funeral White House reception (Lipset and Dobson 1972: 146; Sheehan 1990: 32; Aldrich 2011: 243).

There is no doubt that decision-makers paid serious attention to movement activity, responding to it in both rational and paranoid ways. Sometimes, the war managers were able to turn movement activity to their advantage. Nixon speech writer William Safire recalled the movement's utility as 'a villain, the object against which all our supporters could be rallied'. In June 1970, President Nixon told Republican candidates in the upcoming congressional elections to 'tie their opponents into hippies, kids, demos' (Small 2005: 160). Nixon's entire 'Silent Majority' strategy represented an effort to turn the antiwar protests to positive partisan advantage. Henry Kissinger (1979: 1013) described 'the uneasily dormant beast of public protest' as 'our spur': yet, it was also 'our nightmare'. If executive leaders sought to benefit by demonizing protesters, they were also frightened by the prospect of sporadic, marginalized activity becoming mainstream; or, alternatively, by the prospect of being seen to fail in their duty of ensuring domestic peace. Despite their condemnation of 'extremists', Washington policy-makers seemed not to make much private distinction between different aspects of antiwar opinion and activity. Richard Helms, CIA Director under President Johnson, told Tom Wells that the real pressure was 'the *totality*' of pressure on officials: 'I don't think that President Johnson or Nixon tried to sort out which groups this was coming from. Just the fact that there was a lot of it' (Wells 1994: 255–6).

Lyndon Johnson in private seems, indeed, to have made little distinction between different aspects of antiwar opinion. He saw antiwar senators as 'crackpots' who had 'just been plain taken in'; it was 'the Russians who are behind the whole thing'. Johnson told journalist Robert Spivack in 1965: 'So the kids are running up and down parading, and most of them are led by Communist groups.' Ludicrously, LBJ was recorded as worrying about the offspring of antiwar senators dating staff at the Soviet Embassy. Nixon evidenced a similar mixture of paranoia and contempt for the movement, as well as a disinclination to distinguish between different aspects of it. In March 1969, he commented on student antiwar demonstrations: 'this is the way civilizations begin to die'. He told national security staff in 1970 that campus protesters 'are reaching out for the support – ideological and otherwise – of foreign powers and they are developing their own brand of indigenous revolutionary activism'. Intelligence chiefs were told to use 'every resource' to 'halt these illegal activities'. The campaign against radicalism coordinated by Tom Huston (White House domestic intelligence chief) linked directly into the Watergate scandals. Like LBJ, Nixon effectively refused to accept intelligence reports which indicated (as the CIA informed Huston in June 1969) that there was no evidence of 'foreign communist support to revolutionary protest movements in the United States' (Dumbrell 2004: 116; Dallek 2008: 133, 134, 208).

Presidential paranoia about antiwar protest arguably undermined rational decision-making. Presidents responded to the 'totality' of antiwar opinion by trying harder to 'sell' the war, sometimes with counter-productive effects; by ruling out across-the-board escalations; and by moving as rapidly as they felt possible towards Vietnamization. They were also keen to avoid being seen (not least by their adversaries in Hanoi) to compromise with a movement they regarded as treasonable and contemptuous. The matching of particular decisions to particular protests is not completely convincing. Decisions, and the timing of decisions, are complex processes, rarely reducible to a clear action/reaction process. Antiwar movement activity (at least insofar as decision-makers did manage to abstract such activity from more mainstream antiwar politics) was just as likely to stimulate stubborn persistence with failed policy as to promote policy reversal. From a revisionist perspective, antiwar activity – in effect, a spectrum stretching from liberal senators to street demonstrators – operated to rule out decisive actions which might actually have shortened the war. In response, it can be argued that such actions – including the invasion of North Vietnam, comprehensive war mobilization, and even the use of nuclear weapons – would certainly not have guaranteed swift American success. Indeed, it is not unreasonable to hold that, insofar as antiwar protest fended off such courses of action, the movement did the world a good service. The downside of all this, however, is that the movement also contributed to policy drift.

Empirical studies of the relationship between the antiwar movement and public opinion tend to tell against any simple developmental relationship between protest and declining public support for the war (Lunch and Sperlich 1979). A study by Doug McAdam and Yang Su (2002) suggested only tentative positive linkages between protest, public opinion, and congressional voting. Media portrayal of the antiwar movement was generally negative, and probably had a negative effect on public perceptions of the protests. The shift in the early 1970s to less obviously student-centred protest triggered changes in media coverage, as did the emergence of veteran protests. However, it is not easy to find evidence, even at the time of the Cambodian invasion, of positive public reactions to protest. Polling in early June 1970, a few weeks after the killing of students by National Guardsmen in Ohio and by state police in Mississippi, showed majority disapproval of antiwar demonstrations and a 59 per cent approval rating for the President. Occasionally, peaceful protesters were congratulated by press and television reporters for 'daring to be different', but much coverage focused on the movement's violent and radical fringes, as well as on prowar counter-demonstrations. Counter-antiwar demonstrations in New York City by 'hard hat' construction workers in May 1970 were widely reported, while a related narrative about pampered 'doves' facing working class 'hawks' found its way into many subsequent press reports (Appy 1993: 40; Small 1994: 166–8; Lawrence 2008b: 148; Sandbrook 2008: 92).

Hostility between 'middle America' and antiwar radicals was not entirely a creation of war propaganda. Working-class Americans, even if they opposed the war, were more likely than their middle-class counterparts to disapprove of antiwar demonstrations (Appy 1993: 41). Adam Garfinkle (1997: 13) has even suggested that 'the war would have been even more unpopular than it was, sooner than it was, among a broader and more politically salient segment of the American people had radical-led protests *not* occurred'. Data does not really exist to support such an argument, and Garfinkle has been reasonably criticized for erecting his case on a scaffolding of shaky counterfactuals (Young 2002). At the very least, the US public was kept aware of the case against the war – from realist notions of US overextension to evidence of war crimes – by the sheer visibility of the antiwar movement. The fact remains, however, that Nixon's 'Silent Majority' did exist. A majority of the public, until the very last months of US involvement, did not favour the kind of immediate and total military withdrawal advocated from the mid-1960s by the antiwar movement. Even on the campuses, antiwar protest was never the norm. At universities where major demonstrations did occur (around 10 per cent), only about 10 per cent of students seem to have participated in such activity. Protest was not entirely absent even in the country's more conservative regions; nevertheless, there were large regional disparities in antiwar activism (Wheeler 2001).

Antiwar protest intermingled in complex ways with mainstream antiwar electoral and congressional activity. During the course of the war, much of what I. M. Destler *et al.* (1984: 19) called 'the liberal-moderate elite' defected from the Cold War consensus and reconstituted itself as the antiwar wing of the Democratic Party. Again, it can be argued that such defection was as much delayed by antiwar movement excesses as accelerated by the example of protest in the streets. What can reasonably be asserted, however, is that key elite figures were impressed by youthful protest, and came to appreciate the force even of its more extreme incarnations. With the opening-out of the movement during the Nixon years, liberal elite figures came to constitute one wing of the movement, no longer rather disengaged figures embarrassed by association with direct action. For example, Ernest Gruening, as an ex-senator, argued for sentence mitigation in relation to the convicted bomber of a war-related Wisconsin research centre in 1970. He recalled the tale of presidential deception which stretched back to the Tonkin Gulf Resolution (which, of course, he had opposed), describing it as 'something we must bring home to the American people and which so fully justifies all acts of resistance to this war in whatever form it takes' (Bates 1992: 413). Senator George McGovern reacted to the bombing of Capitol Hill itself in March 1971 as follows: 'It is not possible to teach an entire generation to bomb and destroy others in an undeclared war abroad and not pay a terrible price in the derangement of our own society' (*Congressional Quarterly Almanac* 1971: 625).

It is impossible to be precise about the effect of the antiwar protests on the morale of the US military and in hardening resolve in Hanoi. The antiwar movement had, in effect, a wing inside the American military. By the early 1970s, there was a system of institutionalized contact with servicemen; for example, through the antiwar coffee-shops set up near training bases. Antiwar GI newspapers circulated both in America and in South Vietnam. The relationship between sceptical American military officers, offering a realist assessment of American over-commitment in Vietnam, and the antiwar grunts mirrored the relationship between elite antiwar senators and street demonstrators at home. Many recruits into the military would have had friends in the US who participated in demonstrations; by the early 1970s, many recruits would have participated in demonstrations themselves. From the viewpoint of servicemen in Vietnam also, the wavering of the home front could hardly have been anything other than dispiriting. Like LBJ and Nixon, the many serving soldiers who still broadly believed in the war were unlikely to make much distinction between different wings of the antiwar movement. Bob Hope's famous greeting to forces in 1967 exemplified the kind of black humour which characterized their experience: 'I have good news. The country is behind you – 50 per cent.' Veterans testified to the bitterness felt towards the American war protesters. Tom Corey, who served in Vietnam with the First Cavalry Division, recalled: 'I think they had a right to protest, but I don't think they knew what they were doing to the morale of our soldiers' (Appy 1993: 220; 2008: 519).

The notion of domestic war protesters giving aid and comfort to America's enemy was a common theme for the war managers. Dean Rusk declared as early as March 1964 that 'insofar as anybody here or abroad pays attention to the quitters, they are lending aid and comfort to our enemies'. He told the Fulbright hearings in 1966 that the North Vietnamese might (wrongly) conclude that '20,000 demonstrators circling around the White House' meant the 'war is over so far as we are concerned'. The simple truth is that Rusk was probably correct. We have noted above that Hanoi did orchestrate actions in order to influence American domestic politics. The North Vietnamese population and the Southern insurrectionists were human beings, not unblinking patriotic automatons. They needed boosts to their morale. Truong My Hoa, a Southern communist who was imprisoned by the Saigon regime for 11 years, recorded the gratitude felt for 'the support of peace-loving people throughout the world, and especially from the American people'. Xuan Vu, a transplanted Southerner working as a writer in North Vietnam, later recorded the encouragement given by visiting antiwar Americans, as well as by letters and tapes from high-profile European opponents of the war such as philosophers Bertrand Russell and Jean-Paul Sartre. It defies belief that the antiwar movement did not give comfort to America's enemy (Rusk 1990: 472, 493; Chanoff and Doan 1996: 81; Johnson 2003: 72; Fry 2006: 69; Appy 2008: 230–1).

International Antiwar Protest

Public action against the war was most intense in the United States, and the American antiwar movement provided much of the inspiration for protest elsewhere. From abroad, the American movement

tended to be perceived as more of a direct heir to the civil rights movement than it arguably was; it gained in prestige as a consequence.
American policy-makers were necessarily particularly attuned to
antiwar activity at home. Nevertheless, the emergence of international
protest certainly increased Washington's sense of isolation, while also
presenting very significant morale and propaganda gifts to Hanoi.

The closest non-American parallel to the US antiwar movement
was related to the Australian troop presence in Vietnam. Significant
protests greeted Lyndon Johnson when he visited Australia in 1966.
The movement grew alongside the cause of opposition to conscription, with a few high-profile draft resisters (such as Simon Townsend)
achieving national notoriety. Student radicalization followed a similar
trajectory to that of the American movement; parallel tensions also
emerged between Christian pacifist, Maoist pro-NLF, and labour
union wings of the wider movement. A limit to the Australian commitment was announced by Prime Minister John Gorton in early 1968, as
public opinion adjusted to the Tet Offensive. The tardiness of disengagement stimulated wide protest. The Vietnam Moratorium of May
1970 has a claim to be regarded as the largest public protest in
Australian history, with around 200,000 people participating in
demonstrations over a three-day period. Australia experienced a
degree of 'silent majority' backlash. However, the public protests can
certainly be seen as stimulating the early 1971 decision to begin
significant withdrawals. This protest-related exit from Vietnam was
dramatically accelerated when the US opening to China apparently
removed much of the strategic rationale for Canberra's original military commitment. Virtually the first act of the incoming Labor Party
government of Gough Whitlam in December 1972 was to abolish
conscription (Ham 2008: 261, 272, 523–5, 558; Edwards 2003:
231–3).

Antiwar protest in non-combatant countries usually took the form
of activity directed against American military or diplomatic presence
in those countries. In 1968, Japanese students blockaded Sasebo naval
base to coincide with the docking of the US aircraft carrier *Enterprise*
on its way to South Vietnam. Later, Japanese protests included battles
at a Tokyo hospital which was treating US Marines injured in
Vietnam. Mexican student protests combined demands for university
reform with a wider political analysis which linked US imperialism in
Vietnam and in Latin America. In some European countries, protest
was also aimed at home governments which were seen as taking a

mealy-mouthed stand on the war, even if they were not actually sending troops. The Free University in West Berlin became a hub for
European student radicalism. The Vietnam War seemed to call into
question the very model of liberal democracy for which the Free
University stood as a symbol. Radical European students saw home
governments as complicit in the capitalist structures which produced
imperialist war. French students in 1968 were acting against a regime
which was itself highly critical of US policy in Vietnam. However,
they viewed themselves as opposing a French ruling class, which was
implicated in colonialist outrages in Indochina and North Africa. The
British antiwar movement, largely organized by the Trotskyist-led
Vietnam Solidarity Campaign, aimed to prevent any UK commitment
of troops to Vietnam by threatening disorder on the streets. The 27
October 1968 London demonstration, starting at Hyde Park and passing the US Embassy in Grosvenor Square, attracted around 100,000
marchers. Prior press commentary drew parallels with the mass
French student-worker action of the previous May. In fact, the British
student movement remained far more focused on the Vietnam War
than did its French equivalent. By French, Japanese, or Mexican standards, the 1968 London event was peaceful. Home Secretary James
Callaghan unnerved some of the demonstrators by turning up in Hyde
Park and observing loudly: 'Nice day for a march'. *The Guardian*
newspaper editorialized on 28 October that 'the sincerity' of the antiwar protest was 'real', even if the 'shouts of "Ho, Ho, Ho Chi Minh"
echo without meaning' (Birchall 1987; Ellis 1998; Boren 2001: 166,
171; Williams 2009: 185; Kraushaar 2010: 81).

The European leftist upsurges of the late 1960s and early 1970s
had a strong internationalist ethos. America's SDS and the radical
West Berlin students, led by Rudi Dutschke, developed quite strong
links. International socialists – often Trotskyists opposed to 'national
communism' – took a central organizing role in many countries.
Radical philosopher Herbert Marcuse, invited to the Free University
in May 1966, called for individuals across the globe to achieve self-
realization through mass action against the 'repressive technological
rationality' which underpinned the war (Cornils 1998: 106). Key
events, such as the February 1968 antiwar demonstrations in Berlin,
were conceived as part of a consciously global campaign against
imperialist war. The War Crimes Tribunal, organized in 1967 by the
Bertrand Russell Peace Foundation and convening in Sweden, played
an important role in internationalizing the antiwar effort. The Russell

Tribunal brought together a range of antiwar figures, including Americans David Dellinger and Stokely Carmichael, Filipino poet Amado Hernandes, and former Mexican President Lazaro Cardenas. Jean-Paul Sartre testified to the tribunal that the war emanated from American racism. The tribunal accused the US of genocide. For 1960s youth, the Vietnam War became the equivalent of the Spanish Civil War for an earlier leftist generation: a conflict which structured political attitudes, radicalizing political outlooks within a new awareness of global possibilities. American policy in Central America in the 1980s and the US invasion of Iraq in 2003 performed parallel functions for later generations.

Despite its international character and ethos, the global antiwar movement was still made up of various national movements, with distinctive identities and preoccupations. After all, this was an era of, at least by later standards, relatively primitive international communications: no internet, no cheap air travel. Ambitious efforts to set up internationalist student revolutionary/antiwar umbrella organizations generally fell flat. Europe – and, indeed, much of the world – was radically divided into communist and non-communist blocs. Herbert Marcuse's 1966 call for people across Eastern and Western Europe to use the war as the occasion to rise up against capitalist and Stalinist oppression became lost in the air of a divided Berlin. Nevertheless, antiwar organizers such as British student leader Tariq Ali continually sought to put the movement on a truly global footing. In February 1967, during a visit to Hanoi, Ali suggested to Politburo member Pham Van Dong that the DRV should emulate the example of the Spanish Civil War and invite 'international brigades' to fight alongside the PAVN and Viet Cong. Tariq Ali was told that international brigades 'are no good against B52 bombers' and that, in any case, Moscow and Beijing would be opposed to the idea. Pham Van Dong nevertheless congratulated Tariq Ali on UK antiwar protest, especially the work of Bertrand Russell, and predicted that antiwar sentiment in the US would lead to America's defeat (Ali 1987: 107–9; Klimke 2010: 102–6).

A Qualified Success

It is difficult to argue convincingly that the antiwar movement shortened a long war. In the US, with a few exceptions, such as the 1969 Moratorium, the movement failed to seize the initiative from the war managers. For most of the war's duration, the White House retained the ability to reframe and refocus the domestic war debate, most notably with Nixon's 'Silent Majority' and Vietnamization initiatives. In America, as in Europe, the student movement seemed to stimulate rightist political reaction, rather than decisive leftward change. Drawing on arguments such as these, and reacting against the kind of simple triumphalism expressed by Tom Hayden in 1973, David Steigerwald (1995: 112) concluded that the American antiwar movement was a 'qualified failure'.

Judgements on the American antiwar movement should take account of the vindictive and illegal harassment visited on it by the Johnson and Nixon administrations, including the various covert and often mendacious White House efforts to 'try to make the innocents see they are being used' – as Bob Haldeman later described the policy. At the local level, vigilante attacks (such as the firebombing of a student cooperative in Buffalo, New York, in early 1971) represented another layer of repression, as did police hostility and the emergence of semi-official state-level 'red squads'. The straightforward – and, indeed, correct – verdict is that the movement had a right to protest, and that it deserves praise for asserting that right in the face of often illegal repressive action. Yet, it is also worth remembering that the extent of public protest in the Vietnam War era was a function of two other conditions: the American free speech tradition, and the failure of the federal government to move towards full war mobilization. Federal agencies attacked the free speech rights of the protesters; they did not destroy the deeper legal framework which protected them. Presidents Johnson and Nixon presided over a kind of 'relaxed repression' – a mirror image of Herbert Marcuse's notion of 'repressive toleration' – of the antiwar movement. Full war mobilization, including a formal declaration of war, would have had the effect of making 'comfort to the enemy' protest far more difficult. In this sense, as in so many others, LBJ's 'limited war' strategy had unintended consequences (Jensen 1991: 240–7; Heineman 1993: 262; Haldeman 1994: 110; Jeffreys-Jones 2007: 162, 238).

The weaknesses and confusions of the antiwar movement are manifest. Despite the excesses of the New Left and the many intra-movement divisions, impressive mass marches and demonstrations were organized. The movement's impact on public opinion was complex and, to some extent, counter-productive. Yet, marches, petitions, occupations and teach-ins did shake complacency and slowly altered the decisional climate. Antiwar arguments were kept in the public consciousness. By the later 1960s, American war managers were confronted by a US public whose unquestioning acceptance of official versions of the war could no longer automatically be accepted. The war managers also witnessed widespread, if patchy and sometimes unfocused, international public action against the war. In contributing to this situation, the antiwar movement may be judged a qualified success.

7
The Military Dimension

A running theme in General William Westmoreland's memoir, *A Soldier Reports*, was the simple incomprehension, shown by many opponents of the Vietnam conflict, towards rational debate concerning the application of force in conditions of war. Describing the domestic reaction to the 1970 invasion of Cambodia, Westmoreland (1980: 240) commented: 'Denying what your adversary is doing to you and turning the other cheek may make sense in social intercourse, but it can hardly be justified as a principle of war.' Many orthodox histories of the war have, indeed, been written by authors who seem unwilling or unable to take seriously the views and perspectives of military actors. Like most other studies, *Rethinking the Vietnam War* has concentrated on high-level political decision-making, rather than the experiences and decisions of direct combatants. Political leaders made the key decisions. The current chapter, however, offers an assessment of various *military* arguments and counter-arguments concerning the reasons for American failure. It discusses the role of ground forces: communist, American, and American-allied combatants in South Vietnam. We then consider the problems of America's air war. The final sections of the chapter raise questions which have become central to revisionist understandings of the war. We assess Westmoreland's leadership. Is it conceivable (as one strand in revisionist scholarship would argue) that Westy was the King Lear of the Vietnam War, a man more sinned against than sinning? Could alternative military strategies have produced different results? Was the 'one-war' strategy of General Creighton Abrams actually winning the war when America withdrew? Could some kind of enhanced counter-insurgency approach have produced different results for MACV?

While the possibility of American/South Vietnamese victory will be raised, most of the chapter inevitably dwells on US tactical and strategic shortcomings. At the outset, however, it is worth emphasizing that the communist side also made serious mistakes. Both major communist offensives, Tet and Easter 1972, were, to varying degrees, flawed in their conception and execution. Hanoi's broad strategic concept was appropriate to the elongated geography of South Vietnam, with pressure consistently applied to the approaches to Saigon, to the Central Highlands, and to the northern provinces. However, the simple story of linear communist strategic success – based on self-reliance and the juggling of political struggle, armed struggle and a people's war – is one of the Vietnam War myths.

Poor Bloody Infantry

Three, intertwined military forces waged the war on the anti-American side: the People's Army of Vietnam (PAVN, the North Vietnamese army); the People's Liberation Armed Forces (PLAF, the South Vietnamese, communist-led military, which included main units and dedicated guerrilla fighters); and large numbers of 'irregular' Southern-based guerrillas, supporting the militarized communist-led forces, and intersecting with both the PAVN and the PLAF. In general terms, as we have seen, Southern fighters dominated the conflict until the disasters of Tet, with regular PAVN forces predominating after 1968. By the time Saigon fell in 1975, there were around 220,000 PAVN troops in the South, supported by about 50,000 PLAF troops. At the numerical peak of US troop commitment in 1968–69, combined numbers of American and Saigon government forces probably outnumbered 'regular' communist-led troops in the territory of South Vietnam by a ratio of about 3:1. Such figures do not, however, include the irregular activity by many South Vietnamese peasants. Supplied directly from the South Vietnamese countryside and via infiltration from the North, communist fighters in the South also had a logistical efficiency denied to the Americans – or, indeed, to the ARVN. The anti-communist forces in the South relied on massive logistical, 'rear echelon' operations, maybe as much as 5:1 in terms of support/combat ratio (Appy 1993: 121–5; DeGroot 2000: 243).

It has become conventional wisdom that the main cause of the communist victory in Vietnam was the DRV's superior will and commitment. General Giap declared in 1989 that the secret of success was 'involvement of all the elements' – not just weaponry – 'and patience' (Wintle 1992: 406). The crucial expression of Hanoi's will to prevail was the discipline and patriotic ethos of DRV society and of the PAVN. Between 1964 and 1974, the PAVN grew from a force of about 250,000 to one of about 570,000 regular forces, organized into 18 infantry divisions. During this time, Soviet and Chinese aid had transformed its equipment base, which by the later 1960s included hundreds of heavy and light tanks, and heavy artillery. By July 1966, virtually all adult males in the DRV were being recruited into the military. The demography of North Vietnam aided the revolution, as over 100,000 males reached maturity during the later 1960s. The supply of men, however, was not limitless. By the end of 1967, draft eligibility was extended to all males aged between 16 and 45, with women starting to join the PAVN in 1969 (Appy 1993: 121–5; Duiker 1995: 18–25; Record 2002: 133; Bradley 2009: 135).

There were tensions in the communist military between minorities and ethnic Vietnamese, as well as between southern and northern soldiers. PAVN personnel were regularly assigned to PLAF units, to facilitate coordination and to enhance cross-organizational understanding. As we have already seen, coordination was also achieved through the mechanism of the Central Office for Vietnam (COSVN), whose head in the mid-1960s was PAVN General Thanh, who (like Le Duan) had Southern origins. Until the period after the Tet Offensive, the PLAF undertook the bulk of the ground fighting. Here, it should be emphasized that, even before 1968, the war was not entirely dominated by irregular operations. By 1965, it is estimated that the PLAF had about 45 main force battalions, with 35,000 guerrilla fighters and 80,000 irregulars (Bradley 2009: 108).

Despite the overwhelming ethos of common national purpose, the revolutionary forces did have some problems of morale and discipline. Main force PLAF fighters were not always keen to operate far away from their home territory. Desertions from the North Vietnamese military may have reached a figure of nearly 30,000 in the early 1970s. The lot of the *bo doi*, the regular soldier in the PAVN, was often a grim one, preoccupied with the search for food. The journey via the Ho Chi Minh Trail was arduous, long – it could take as many as six months to travel from North Vietnam through Laos and Cambodia to the south – and dangerous. Probably over 1 million PAVN and PLAF military and guerrilla personnel were killed during the conflict – the equivalent in terms of population to around 7 million American deaths (Summers 1985: 91; Duiker 1995: 24; DeGroot 2000: 120; Bradley 2009: 131, 144).

As on the American side, the revolutionary Vietnamese military experience is greatly illuminated by works of memoir and literary imagination, including *Novel without a Name*, by the female Vietnamese dissident author Duong Thu Huong. The book was written through the voice of a North Vietnamese fighter in the South. After 10 years of fighting, the narrator considers the gap between party ideology and the terrors of war. The fragmented structure of the book echoed the work of American war writers, notably Tim O'Brien, as well as providing a framework for the expression of feelings of alienation and futility. *The Sorrow of War*, by Bao Ninh, also had an unconventional narrative structure, with the protagonist (Kien) looking back on his war experiences from the perspective of his current position as postwar collector of human battlefield remains. Kien recalls party propaganda from his youth, including the depiction of love affairs between communist youth as 'a disgrace, unpatriotic'. The diary of Dang Thuy Tram recorded the experiences of a young, Hanoi-trained female doctor, working in the Central Highlands of South Vietnam to treat PAVN and PLAF casualties. The diary reflected a characteristic amalgam of patriotic service and deep concern at the insouciance displayed by Hanoi towards the sacrifice of young lives (Bao Ninh 1994: 121; Huong 1995; Pham 2007: 128).

The lore and experiences of the American 'grunt' – the ordinary soldier and equivalent to the Vietnamese *bo doi* – are familiar to us from Hollywood depictions of the war, and from many big-selling novels. Karl Marlantes' *Matterhorn,* a novel of Marine combat, includes a detailed glossary of technical war terms and Vietnam War slang. Memorable entries include 'short-timer's stick' (a wooden staff gradually whittled away by its owner as days of service in Vietnam were fulfilled) and 'splib' ('a non-derogatory term for a black Marine'). American infantrymen trudged through jungle, paddy-fields and over mountains. 'Humping the boonies' in search of the enemy brought exhaustion and frustration, and sometimes encouraged an inability to conceive of the elusive enemy as human. 'Those dead Cong', wrote Louis Willett from the Fourth Infantry Division in 1966, 'didn't seem like people ... They felt like a pile of rags or something, can't really explain it' (Edelman 1985: 36, 53; Marlantes 2010: 592–3).

The operation of the draft system in the later 1960s ensured that up to 80 per cent of US ground forces in Vietnam were from poor or working-class backgrounds. Junior officers – often blamed by their seniors for military failures – also tended to come disproportionately from working-class backgrounds. The US Army offered a professional career for many African-Americans. However, the operation of the draft and the failure of the US military to adapt to social changes associated with the civil rights movement led to instances of severe racial tension. With an average age of 19, American soldiers in Vietnam were younger than their equivalents in previous conflicts. College deferments offered a way of at least postponing service for more advantaged Americans, as did family connections. As seen in the phenomenon of the 'short-timer' with his stick, the overriding concern of many draftees became that of somehow simply to survive the one year of service in-country. The constant turnover of both 'grunts' and officers was a problem freely acknowledged in the later US military memoirs (Westmoreland 1980: 388; Milam 2009:15).

American Vietnam War imaginative war literature, memoirs and letters-home were marked by some recurring themes: the horror, intense discomfort, and boredom of war, occasionally balanced by feelings of authenticity and excitement; the common realization that the enemy were setting the terms and pace of combat engagement; the cultural dislocations and misunderstandings as West met East; the sense of alienation, not only from the Vietnamese, but also from people living at peace in the United States. Sergeant Michael Kelly wrote home in September 1970 about his efforts 'to visualize the enemy living from day to day here by this beautiful little gorge, cooking his rice, laughing and splashing in the creek ... it's hard to believe that there really is someone out there trying to kill you. And it's even harder to understand why.' Memoirists frequently referred to the impossibility of distinguishing ally from adversary. Chasms of incomprehension divided American forces even from those South Vietnamese who were allies. In *Going After Cacciato*, Tim O'Brien, in a chapter entitled 'The Things They Did Not Know', explored the issue of cultural dislocation. 'Not knowing the language', the US forces 'did not know the (Vietnamese) people. They did not know what the people loved or respected or hated.' In her memoir, *Daughter Gone to War*, Winnie Smith, who served as a nurse in Saigon, recorded her stuttering efforts to understand the motivations and behaviour of the Vietnamese: 'No one has explained to me that for the Vietnamese not meeting someone's eyes is a sign of respect'. A visit to an Army hospital in the Central Highlands was followed 'by a trip to downtown Pleiku – a typical GI town with bars, bars, and more bars'. Returning to the US, Smith found America 'in an uproar over secret bombing raids in Cambodia'. Her response was one of impatience: 'It was no secret that we were bombing the Ho Chi Minh Trail and no secret that the trail goes through Cambodia. What did people expect?' (Smith 1992: 59, 165, 290; Edelman 1985: 260; O'Brien 1978: 309).

Letters home from Vietnam recorded, especially earlier in the war, a common sense of purpose. Richard Marks of the Third Marine Division wrote in 1965: 'I don't like being over here, but I am doing a job that must be done – I am fighting an *inevitable* enemy that must be fought – now or later' (Edelman 1985: 113, 219). Following the Tet Offensive, the prospect of some imminent negotiated settlement affected combat attitudes. David Hackworth, a battalion commander, later described the situation in 1969, with the vast majority of his unit being draftees who 'just wanted to stay alive and get the hell out'. Hackworth's job was 'to keep them alive, not win an unwinnable war' (Longley 2008: 154; Prados 2009a: 277). Famously, Vietnam was a war with no fronts. Mines were every bit as terrifying as the physical sight of the enemy. For the vast majority of American military personnel, who were not involved in regular combat, the priority was to survive the danger of illness and accidental death (over 1,000 died in vehicle crashes) – as well as continuing to stay out of direct combat.

Desertion from the American military often took the pre-emptive form of draft-dodging. Fleeing in-country was scarcely a viable option, though significant numbers of military personnel did desert while in the United States. By the early 1970s, the demoralization of the Army officer class was evident in large numbers of resignations. Of the West Point class of 1965, 25 per cent resigned during 1970. Demoralization is often linked to drug use by US forces, though the point can be made that soldiers over the centuries have used whatever intoxicants are locally available. Veterans such as Engineer Officer William Badger, interviewed at Texas Tech University in 2000, saw the deliberate provision of drugs by the Viet Cong to American soldiers as a significant factor in the American defeat (TTU 2000a). However, like the plight of the traumatized veteran, the addicted state of the American soldier in Vietnam can be overstated. Drug use was far more common in rear areas than in combat zones. Mandatory tests of homecoming draftees in June 1971 found 3.6 per cent with traces of heroin in their urine. Bob Hope received his biggest cheer in a December 1970 concert in Vietnam by linking drug use to draftee exasperation with politicians: 'Instead of taking away marijuana from the soldiers – we ought to be giving it to the negotiators in Paris'. As we saw in Chapter 6, indiscipline was also evidenced by the inroads made into the US military by the antiwar movement. Small-scale 'combat refusals' occasionally developed into actual mutinies. There were apparently 36 combat refusals within the elite First Cavalry Division in 1970 alone. The US Navy saw some of the most severe cases of racial tension. By the early 1970s, as US ground troops withdrew, the Navy became more central to the war and a major African American recruitment drive was launched under the slogan, 'You can be Black, and Navy too'. The aircraft carriers *Kitty Hawk* and *Constellation* experienced extreme instances of racial violence in October 1972 (Dean 1997; Sorley 1999: 292; Longley 2008: 134; Westheider 2008: 90–2; Kuzmarov 2009: 15, 19; Prados 2009a: 277).

Most spectacularly, 'fragging' – the murder of officers by their own men – became a recognized Vietnam War phenomenon. The *threat* of murder by fragmentation grenade became a major influence on commissioned and non-commissioned officer behaviour. Tacit, and sometimes actual, agreements were made between officers and men about the acceptable degrees of danger to which reluctant soldiers could be exposed. Reported 'fragging' incidents reached their annual peak in 1971, a year of major US troop *withdrawals*, at an estimated figure of 333. General Creighton Abrams exclaimed in typically effusive fashion in 1971: 'I've got white shirts all over the place – psychologists, drug counsellors, detox specialists, rehab people ... Is this a god-damned army or a mental hospital? Officers are afraid to lead their men into battle, and the men won't follow. Jesus Christ!' 'Fragging', of course, has taken its place in the mythology of the war. In fact, most incidents seem to have occurred in base areas, rather than in combat zones. 'Fragging' also probably reflected the peculiar difficulties of Vietnam-era recruitment more than any generalized soldiers' revolt against the war. The madness of the war will certainly endure in literary form. In *Going After Cacciato*, Tim O'Brien described each squad member touching the grenade in turn, before murdering an officer who had ordered them to reconnoitre dangerous enemy tunnels (O'Brien 1978: 252–3; Appy 1993: 246; 2008: 395; Sorley 1999: 203; Longley 2008: 141; Lepre 2011: 115).

The war without fronts had a kind of intrinsic wildness, with atrocities being committed by every side in the war. We noted in Chapter 4 the perception among the US military that communist atrocities would not make global news, while (at least, after 1967) American behaviour was constantly scrutinized. However, there is no question that American abuse of civilians in Vietnam reached chronic proportions. An internal Pentagon document of December 1967 acknowledged serious problems of casual civilian abuse by US military personnel. Tiger Force, originally organized by David Hackworth as a 101st Airborne special group designed to 'outguerrilla the guerrillas', was involved in major war crimes in the Central Highlands during 1967. Hackworth was supposedly the model for Colonel Kilgore in Francis Ford Coppola's 1979 film, *Apocalypse Now* – leading a chopper raid on a South Vietnamese village to the strains of Wagner. A severe critic of General Westmoreland and of American over-reliance on orthodox firepower, Colonel Hackworth well-represented the irregular side of in-country US military leadership. Hackworth was accused in an anonymous complaint to Westmoreland of specifically giving the order to murder civilians during Operation Speedy Express in the Mekong Delta during March 1969. In the region southwest of Saigon (IV Corps Tactical Zone), US ground troops were accused of conducting 10 civilian massacres between December 1968 and July 1970, with the ARVN allegedly committing 17 massacres between May 1968 and August 1970 (Bergerud 1994: 256; Sallah and Weiss 2006: 13; Greiner 2010: 125, 256, 266).

As in many conflicts with a strong irregular, guerrilla dimension, the entire indigenous population, regardless of age or gender, tended to be seen by US soldiers as potential 'enemy'. David Martin, who served with the 2/17th Cavalry, recalled being 'probably more scared of children and women than men': 'I'd have blown a guy away in a New York minute, I didn't know if I could do that with a woman or a child.' John Gary Morris, a Marine squad commander, later recalled that it was rare to take 'disciplinary action against anybody. What are you going to do, send them to Nam?' (TTU 2000b; 2005). Demoralization was patchy, and certainly did not disable all sections of the American military. Nevertheless, by the early 1970s, official Washington was concerned to extricate from Vietnam an American military force whose levels of indiscipline were approaching uncontrollable levels.

Combatant Allies: The Army of the Republic of Vietnam

By 1969, the 500,000 American military personnel in Vietnam were complemented by 850,000 or so South Vietnamese forces (primarily the Army of the Republic of Vietnam) and by nearly 69,000 other allied forces. Apart from the ARVN, America's main combatant ally was the Republic of Korea, whose 'Tiger' and Marine forces undertook major roles of security support in the central coastal region. Jack Valenti, aide to LBJ, commented in January 1966 that Koreans were 'cheap' and 'ready to fight' (Colman 2010: 51). The South Koreans lost nearly 4,500 men in Vietnam. Though American assessments of the Korean effort were often critical of inflated support requests and long planning phases, General Westmoreland appreciated particularly the role played by the Koreans in smoothing cultural sensitivities in Vietnamese villages. The Korean troops, recalled Westmoreland (1980: 338), were 'good at persuading Vietnamese women or elders to convince their VC sons and husbands to return to the government under the *chieu hoi* ("open arms" or amnesty) program'. The MACV regarded Asian forces generally as especially suited to mount controversial cross-border operations. Thailand, which sent over 11,000 troops and an air contingent, was involved in action in Laos, as well as in the *chieu hoi* programme (Larsen and Collins 1975: 47).

At a peak in 1969, Australia had 7,600 men in Vietnam – suffering 521 fatalities, while New Zealand supplied artillery and commando units. American assessments of the Australian effort in Vietnam were especially positive, stressing their expertise in jungle warfare, participation in major search-and-destroy sweeps, and their role in training the South Vietnamese paramilitary regional and popular forces. From 1965, Australian forces were accorded special responsibility for, and practical tactical independence in, Phuoc Tuy province, the coastal region south-east of Saigon which included the deepwater port of Vung Tau. By 1970, US Generals Fred Weyand and Michael Davison concluded that Phuoc Tuy was close to 'full pacification'. Australian veterans often subsequently recalled the American Army as using little camouflage and (in the words of Private Terry Burstall) 'crashing through the bush' with scant concern for the caution appropriate for jungle warfare. The Australians (of course, lacking the US firepower capability) developed an ethos of 'smart' jungle fighting and village-oriented counter-insurgency. Australian forces and personnel were not unaffected by the wildness of the war. Cathy Wayne, a singer from Australia, was shot dead, apparently by accident, by a drugged US soldier during a performance. There were three confirmed Australian 'fraggings' (Ham 2008: 138, 282, 338, 530, 662; Doyle *et al.* 2002).

By far the most important combatant ally of the United States was South Vietnam itself. By January 1973, the South Vietnamese military had been built up into a major force with over 1 million men under arms. The ARVN had three tank, 105 light infantry, and nine airborne battalions. There were several thousand paramilitary regional and popular forces, of various gradations of regularity, supported by the South Vietnamese police. The Air Force had 2,000 aircraft – the fourth largest air force in the world. The Navy had 1,500 vessels, while a South Vietnamese Marine Corps had been organized in the late 1960s. South Vietnamese military war casualties were far in excess of American totals, with over 220,000 killed in action prior to the 1975 Final Offensive.

The record of the ARVN in particular is conventionally seen as abysmal. To many American soldiers, the force was partly a joke, partly a dangerous impediment to their own safety. Ignoring the high ARVN fatality rate, many US veterans remembered a South Vietnamese force which avoided contact with the enemy and even warned the communists about impending action. There were occasional reports of ARVN effectiveness. By late 1967, Ambassador Ellsworth Bunker was informing Washington that the ARVN was becoming a more reliable ally. General Westmoreland, not often seen as a friend of the ARVN, noted the successful role played by South Vietnamese forces in pushing back the Tet Offensive. Yet, John Sylvester, Binh Long province senior adviser to the US Army, painted a more familiar picture of the ARVN in September 1969: they were 'lazy and gutless ... content to let the Americans do the fighting' (Summers 1982: 327–8; Bergerud 1994: 246; Brigham 2006: xi, 92, 97).

Several factors need to be considered when judging the ARVN performance. One is simply the reluctance of many in the American military to take them seriously at all. We also need to take into account the peculiarities of ARVN history and organization. A relevant line of argument here relates to the putative development of the ARVN as a mirror image of the American forces – a 'hollow likeness', replicating and duplicating Uncle Sam (Willbanks 2004: 285). Andrew Wiest (2007; OH 2010d) has argued that the ARVN should have been organized as a specialist counter-insurgency force, rather than a duplicative conventional army. There is some weight to this proposition, especially in view of the general neglect of counter-insurgency in the entire anti-communist war effort. However, a pure counter-insurgency force would hardly have had much prospect of fending off DRV assaults once the Americans had quit Vietnam. The South Vietnamese military shifted in composition during the course of the war, thus making definitive judgement about the appropriateness of its capabilities rather problematic. The argument about duplication is also linked to Westmoreland's decision not to seek full operational control of allied forces in Vietnam. General Westmoreland foresaw both operational and morale drawbacks in failing to treat allied forces as independent, professional units of command. However, at least as far as the ARVN is concerned, there is doubt that the parallel command structure, oiled by full-time US advisers at various levels within the South Vietnamese military, became very disjointed. It did not deal well with problems of poor, cynical, or ill-motivated ARVN leadership. Too often, as Bui Diem (1993: 234) put it, the Americans and the South Vietnamese seemed to be fighting 'two separate wars'.

By 1970, all South Vietnamese males aged between 16 and 50 were subject to the draft, with many serving seven or more continuous years in uniform. With massive levels of draft calling in the later war years, the young male population was not legally available to work the farms of South Vietnam except during their 15 days of annual leave. Commitments to family and to bringing in the harvest contributed to high desertion rates. An enlisted ARVN soldier from Tay Ninh province told Robert Brigham (2006: 51): 'We thought of life in terms of generations and centuries. We saw the French and the Americans as temporary, but our family stretched out in front of us and stood solidly behind us.' Many deserters managed, usually through money and influence, to avoid the severe official punishments for desertion. Corruption, including pay for fictitious ghost-soldiers, was as common in the military as it was in wider South Vietnamese society. Corruption combined with inflation to make nonsense of American efforts to boost ARVN pay. The US aimed to promote a West Point ethos at military academies at Dalat and Thu Doc, but could not overcome the malaise engendered by cultural confusion and the weakness of the South Vietnamese identity. It would also not have gone unnoticed by the South Vietnamese that the American military, the model being held before them, was having its own problems of leadership, cohesion and morale.

Prior to American withdrawal, the great tests for the ARVN related to the Cambodian invasion of 1970, the Laotian incursion (Lam Son 719) of 1971, and the response to the 1972 Easter Offensive. As we saw in Chapter 5, all three episodes involved claims of success and reasonably encouraging comments from Washington. In Cambodia and in Lam Son 719, the ARVN relied heavily on US tactical air support. In Cambodia, there were major problems in ARVN handling of new weapons supplied by the Americans. The objective of Lam Son 719 was essentially defensive: to set back preparations for an attack on South Vietnam's Quang Tri province. Some objectives were met, yet the performance of the ARVN leadership under General Hoang Xuan Lam bordered on the shambolic. The ARVN withdrawal was undertaken against the wishes of General Abrams. President Thieu had apparently told General Lam to go into Laos 'just long enough to take a piss and then leave quickly' (Prados 2009a: 415). Washington proceeded with its support for the ARVN invasion of Laos on the assumption that the communists had spies in the South Vietnamese high command. Lam Son 719 stimulated a major effort to improve the ARVN's coordination of operations and ability to use its own air power. The South Vietnamese Navy made progress in its maritime interdiction programme. The ARVN – now, of course, far outnumbering US forces – did manage to repel the 1972 Easter Offensive. Yet, familiar problems were still on view in 1972, including the indecision of General Lam and the indiscipline of the ARVN leadership. American advisers took direct control of ARVN units which appeared to be on the verge of disintegration. John Paul Vann, now acting (just before his death) as adviser to ARVN General Ngo Dzu, reported in late April 1972 on the outlook of the ARVN rank-and-file: 'Soldiers, witnessing the timidity and incompetence of their leaders developed an irrational fear of the enemy' (Willbanks 2004: 88, 114; Brigham 2006: 101; Randolph 2007: 139).

The Nixon–Laird programme of military Vietnamization failed to transform the ARVN into a completely reliable and efficient force. From some viewpoints, military Vietnamization during the Nixon years appeared slow. It was held in check by the scepticism of the Joint Chiefs as reflected in the attitudes of more junior US military commanders. However, on the ground, military Vietnamization often seemed helter-skelter. Reviewing the experience of the US Green Berets, Shelby Stanton (1985a: 293) found a 'headlong rush to rapidly turn over our Special Forces to the Vietnamese government, regardless of their readiness or the consequences'. The rapid expansion of the ARVN involved entry into its ranks of more inadequately trained and poorly-motivated South Vietnamese. The ARVN was unable efficiently to absorb the massive and technologically complex grants of American military equipment. The creation of a 1 million-man military in South Vietnam looked impressive. In practice, it exemplified what became a standard military verdict on Vietnamization – and, indeed, on America's wider relationship with South Vietnam: 'Everything worked, but nothing worked enough' (Sorley 1999: 200).

The Air War

Precise statistics on American bombing during the Vietnam War are still difficult to cite with complete confidence. Harry Summers (1985: 100) estimated that, across Southeast Asia, US Air Force bombers and fighter-bombers dropped over 6 million tons of explosives. This was in addition to the significant amount of bombing undertaken by US Navy and Marine Corps fighter-bombers and by the South Vietnamese Air Force. The US Air Force bombing total was three times the figure for American bombing in the Second World War, and far more than the Korean War total of less than 500,000. Other sources suggest that the total US bombing figure for Laos, Cambodia and Vietnam was 8 million tons. A range of aircraft were used: from the B-52 Stratofortresses, capable of delivering a 27-bomb tonnage from a height of 22,000 feet, to the propeller-driven 'spad' or A-1 Skyraider, and the Air Force 'thud' F-105, which flew the majority of Rolling Thunder missions. Most Navy and Marine Corps bombing was delivered via the A-4 Skyhawk, with a potential 5,000-pound bomb load. If shelling is added to the bombing totals, a figure of 14 million tons seems likely. The US flew around 1.25 million fixed wing and 37 million propeller-driven sorties during the war. During the Rolling Thunder years, North Vietnamese civilian fatalities figures were about 52,000 (less than 0.05 per cent of the DRV population). This compared to 2.2 million in Japan (3 per cent of population) and 1.1 million in Germany (1.6 per cent of population) during the Second World War. In the five months between November 1971 and March 1972, the equivalent of 10 Hiroshima-strength atomic bombs was dropped on Laos. The Christmas bombing of 1972, according to DRV statistics, cost between 1,300 and 1,700 civilian lives within 12 days. Air attacks in 1972 caused around 13,000 North Vietnamese civilian deaths in all. The US lost over 8,500 aircraft in the war. US helicopter crews were especially vulnerable – not only to being shot down by the enemy, but also to weather-related crashes and mechanical failure. One of the most startling facts about Vietnam War bombing is the amount of air attacks which took place across the entire battlefield, not just over North Vietnam. In 1971, nearly 2,000 B-52 sorties attacked Cambodia, with the figure *rising* to over 8,000 as the US provided cover for the South Vietnamese in 1973, when American ground involvement had ceased. Perhaps most startling of all is the realization that over 70 per cent of US high explosives unleashed during the war fell in the territory of *South* Vietnam, where around 4 million tons of bombs were dropped. We will consider the various dimensions of the bombing, beginning with the various campaigns against the DRV (Pape 1996: 190, 351; Walton 2002: 112; Frankum 2005: 145; Prados 2009a: 461).

It is frequently argued that US war managers operated on the erro-neous assumption that North Vietnam had significant industrial targets to be hit. According to Robert Pape (1996: 192), the only DRV factory of any importance was a small explosives plant, which was easily destroyed: 'North Vietnam was primarily a funnel for military-related equipment produced in the USSR and the People's Republic of China.' Mark Clodfelter (1989) saw the undeveloped nature of the DRV economy as a major limitation on America's use of air power. Several revisionist writers have taken issue with this view, reflecting Walt Rostow's argument that the DRV *did* have an industrial base to protect. For example, in the view of C. Dale Walton, gradualism, rather than reliance on a bombing campaign *per se*, was the root of failure. There were significant military targets in the North, and the need to transport military supplies made the DRV particularly vulner-able: 'North Vietnam's ability to receive supplies through its oceanic ports could have been (and, indeed, briefly was) terminated easily, and railheads are always attractive targets' (Walton 2002: 114). This critique of airpower gradualism tends, in several military memoirs, to morph into a 'stab-in-the-back' attack on civilian-led micromanage-ment of the bombing. According to Admiral Ulysses Sharp (1978: xvii), US Pacific Commander between 1964 and 1968: 'Gradualism enabled North Vietnam to mount the most formidable air-defense system that has ever been used in combat history.' By 1967, the DRV did, indeed, have substantial air defences, including around 200 surface-to-air missile (SAM) sites and over 100 Soviet-supplied MIG fighters. Anti-aircraft guns forced incoming aircraft to fly high, where (unless they could achieve the huge potential height available under ideal weather conditions by the B-52s) they were vulnerable to the SAM sites. Gradualism, in the 'stab-in-the-back' interpretation of Rolling Thunder, projected not a terrifying vision of (to use a later air power term) 'shock-and-awe' but, rather, an impression of hesitancy and over-sensitivity to international – and, indeed, American – anti-war opinion.

In order to evaluate these claims, it is important to understand the purposes of American bombing of North Vietnam between 1965 and 1972; and, indeed, to appreciate the general objectives of coercive bombing. At one level, the intention in Vietnam was simply to inflict enough pain to cause the enemy to quit. General William DePuy, First Infantry Division Commander, declared in 1966: 'The solution in Vietnam is more bombs, more shells, more napalm ... until the other side cracks and gives up'. Contrary to the wishes of the Joint Chiefs, LBJ decided on a 'slow squeeze', allowing maximum flexibility, including, as Assistant Defence Secretary John McNaughton put it at the inception of Rolling Thunder, 'the option to proceed or not, and to quicken the pace or not'. The US sought to coordinate diplomacy and air attack, communicating to Hanoi the fact that the US meant business, while also lifting morale in South Vietnam. Stephen Ambrose called this 'ouch warfare': a war of communication with the enemy and of constant second-guessing of enemy reactions (Palmer 1978: 75–6; Ambrose 1988: 214; Appy 2008: 200).

In following this line, the US drew on various ways of understanding the purpose of coercive bombing. One obvious purpose was that of interdiction. In regard to North Vietnam, this principally took the form of efforts to interrupt the flow of personnel and supplies to the South – mainly by bombing in what was designated 'route package one', an area immediately to the north of the DMZ. General Earle Wheeler and Admiral Ulysses Sharp argued that this 'denial by inter-diction' strategy should be the principal purpose of American bomb-ing of the North. Another possible purpose of the bombing derived from the theories of Thomas Schelling, whose ideas were explicated in *Arms and Influence* (1966). The purpose of bombing here is precisely to communicate risk, primarily to enemy leaders, with indicative bombing concentrated on civilian and economic targets, and gradualism the preferred course. In contrast, air power theorist Giulio Douhet (1942) argued for the efficacy of high levels of damage on civilian populations. Anti-civilian bombing was seen by Douhet as leading to irresistible mass demands to end the war. Various versions and combinations of these approaches were defended by American civilian and military leaders during the Johnson years. In the analysis offered by Robert Pape, Robert McNamara and John McNaughton favoured a 'lenient' Schelling approach: essentially, a graduated assault on economic targets as a way of inducing the DRV leadership to abandon its support for the Southern insurgency. The US Air Force preference was for a 'genteel' Douhet strategy. This was not to be an all-out assault on North Vietnamese civilians but, rather, intense, ungraduated bombardment of economic targets. General Curtis Le May, Air Force Chief of Staff, wrote in 1965: 'The military task confronting us is to make it so expensive for the North Vietnamese that they will stop their aggression against South Vietnam and Laos. If we make it too expensive for them, they *will* stop.' The Joint Chiefs in June 1967 looked to 'a gradual degradation of the will and morale of the populace' (Schelling 1966: 3; Pape 1996: 178–9).

Evolving phases of Rolling Thunder reflected all these preferred approaches, with the result that the campaign lacked coherence. Rolling Thunder seemed to exemplify the argument made by Earl Tilford (1993: 192) that the disparity in all aspects of power between the US and North Vietnam 'led to the illusion that applied firepower, even in lesser doses, could substitute for strategy'. There were at least four distinct phases to the campaign. McNaughton's 'lenient' Schelling approach dominated from the inception of bombing until the summer of 1965. The second phase, from mid-1965 to early 1967, concentrated on interdiction. The most intense bombing, during the remainder of 1967, saw a significant widening of targeting, with the adoption of the Air Force 'genteel' Douhet strategy. The final phase came in the wake of the Tet Offensive, and involved an erratic de-escalation of the campaign, until Rolling Thunder was finally cancelled prior to the 1968 presidential election. The failure of the campaign was acknowledged by General Wheeler in April 1965: 'I think it is fair to state that our strikes to date, while damaging, have not curtailed DRV military capabilities in any major way' – a view which was clearly endorsed by Robert McNamara in 1967 (Berman 1982: 52; Karnow 1983: 454; Pape 1996: 182–400). Why did it fail?

There were problems of confusion, lack of coordination and the sheer difficulty of successfully orchestrating 'ouch warfare'. Political leaders in Washington controlled the air operations far more closely than they did ground operations. General Dave Palmer in *Summons of the Trumpet* (1978: 79) complained that 'the policy-makers did everything but fly the aircraft'. Nevertheless, the extent and impact of civilian 'interference' in military operational discretion has been exaggerated. In 1966 and 1967, for example, the Air Force was free to choose targets that related to interdiction (Pape 1996: 186). Beyond doubt, this was not 'saturation' bombing without limits. The main focus was on interdiction, with large-scale population centres and targets near the Chinese border largely being avoided. The various strategies on offer were nonetheless pursued conscientiously by the US military, who were given scope to make at least 'lenient' or 'genteel' versions of the strategies work. In general terms, the North Vietnamese were able to devise ways, largely through evacuation of urban populations, to minimize civilian fatalities. The Air Force/Walt Rostow focus on economic targets overstated the importance of nascent industrial development in the DRV, both to the communist war effort and in the scale of priorities as identified by the Hanoi Politburo. The uneven development and application of Rolling Thunder, rooted in the philosophy of gradualism, did result in some major economic and military targets (such as the dike system) escaping the attention of the US Air Force. However, as Robert McNamara painfully explained to the Stennis Subcommittee in 1967, DRV troop infiltration along the complex trails was inherently difficult to halt from the air. Moreover, until 1968 at least, the strong insurgency in the South could withstand long interruptions to the flow of men and material from the DRV.

Any case for the efficacy of air power over North Vietnam rests not on Rolling Thunder, but on Nixon's air campaigns, primarily Linebacker I and II. By this time, after the disasters of 1968, the DRV was fighting a conventional war, and was much more vulnerable to air attack. The Freedom Train bombing campaign of April 1972 was a short-lived attempt to frighten Hanoi along Schelling lines. Linebacker I, however, depositing some 150,000 tons of explosive on North Vietnam between May and October 1972, involved highly effective interdiction action, extending to the elimination of power and oil storage facilities as well as to severe damage to the DRV's anti-aircraft defences. North Vietnamese tanks were increasingly observed to be running short of petrol. The bombing unquestionably contributed to Hanoi's decision to revise its negotiating position. As with so many aspects of Nixon's policy in Vietnam, every silver lining had a cloud. Linebacker I proceeded without immediate disruption to the détente agenda. Yet, détente did not deliver the goods in terms of a viable peace. The flawed peace of October 1972 was undermined by the South Vietnamese leadership, who seem to have interpreted Linebacker's blunting of the Easter Offensive as a reason for hoping that America would continue the war (Clodfelter 1989: 150–60; Pape 1996: 200; Willbanks 2004: 172).

The 1972 Christmas bombing (Linebacker II) has sometimes been interpreted as successful 'Douhet' action, designed to incite mass civilian opposition to the Hanoi regime's policies. In fact, neither Linebacker campaign involved anything approaching utterly indiscriminate ('carpet') bombing, nor did either campaign seriously target the irrigation system of North Vietnam. The Christmas bombing, according to Earl Tilford (1993: 189) 'served very little tactical military purpose other than rearranging the rubble that Linebacker One had caused'. The bombing arguably did bring the North Vietnamese back to the conference table, but only to agree to a peace which they realistically saw as just a staging post towards eventual reunification. Linebacker II was certainly designed as a warning shot to Hanoi. In the event, as we shall see in Chapter 9, the credibility of any resumption of bombing by the US rapidly diminished. The bombing did help box Saigon into accepting the peace, but held out no prospect of lasting American guarantees to Saigon. The last gasp of Nixon's 'madman' strategy, Linebacker II incited massive domestic and international criticism, entirely undercutting any generalized enhancement of American global 'credibility'.

The American bombing in South Vietnam is generally agreed by orthodox and by revisionist commentators to have been almost entirely counter-productive. C. Dale Walton (2002: 113) offers the following 'hard' revisionist analysis: 'In essence, the United States restricted the wrong part of the air war: the air campaign in the South should have been more carefully circumscribed while the campaign in the North should have been nearly unrestricted.' So-called 'harassment and interdiction' shelling by US and ARVN artillery, usually undertaken at night and directed far into rural zones putatively controlled by the Viet Cong, was overwhelmingly indiscriminate (Laurence 2002: 173). Particular attention has been directed in the postwar years to the Southern defoliation programme, notably the Ranch Hand operations between 1962 and 1971, when over 19 million gallons of herbicides were sprayed in an effort to deny cover and food to PLAF and PAVN forces in the South. Herbicide attacks were sometimes used as preparation for firestorm attacks on enemy strongholds. The most frequently used herbicide, Agent Orange, subsequently became identified with severe health legacies among both US veterans and Vietnamese civilians.

The air campaigns in Laos and Cambodia, aimed at the interdiction of the communist supply routes, had more strategic coherence than the air activity over South Vietnam. However, they manifestly failed in their objective, while simultaneously upsetting important sections of US and international opinion. The revisionist response to this, again, is to state that LBJ and Nixon should have followed a more coherent 'war of logistical control' – using air power more purposefully to destroy the Ho Chi Minh Trail. International criticism could have been ignored, and domestic opposition dealt with by more effective mobilization of opinion. It might be noted here that the MACV was actually quite successful in severing sea connections between North and South Vietnam in its Market Time operation: a joint US–South Vietnamese naval and air campaign, launched in March 1965 (Frankum 2005: 133; Westmoreland 1980: 240). The success of Market Time increased the communist reliance on the Ho Chi Minh Trail, and strengthened the military case for concerted air action against the Laotian/Cambodian route. On the other hand, we have already noted both the difficulty of destroying the Trail by air power alone, as well as the extent to which the pre-1969 communist effort was sustained by *South* Vietnamese resources.

William Westmoreland: Scapegoat?

Born in South Carolina in 1914, William Westmoreland graduated from West Point as first captain in 1936. He commanded battalions in the Second World War, participating in the D Day landings and going on to lead the 82nd Airborne Division in the Korean War. Westmoreland subsequently worked under Maxwell Taylor at the Pentagon, becoming, in 1956, the youngest Major General in US Army history. He became formal commander of the MACV shortly before the Tonkin Gulf incidents of 1964. In 1965, *Time* magazine named him as its Man of the Year.

Westmoreland carried the can for the reversals of 1968, despite his insistence that the Tet Offensive had been an American victory. Arthur Schlesinger Jr called Westmoreland 'our most disastrous general since Custer' (Sullivan: 2005). For Bruce Palmer (1984: 133), Vice Chief of Staff of the Army from 1968 to 1973, Westmoreland 'became a national scapegoat, blamed for everything that went wrong in Vietnam, large or small, regardless of whether he had even a remote connection with the matter'. Westy is still remembered as the military leader who sent US soldiers on pointlessly dangerous 'boonie humping' missions; the commander whose obsession with 'body counts', 'crossover points' and 'attriting' the enemy encouraged indiscriminate killing, even as it misjudged the resolution and resources of the enemy; the general whose facile optimism misled politicians and public. He was the leader who organized massive search-and-destroy sweeps which destroyed villages, failed to lure the enemy into direct engagements, and simply drove the communists into Cambodia.

In *A Soldier Reports*, Westmoreland directly confronted these criticisms. He objected to familiar phrases such a 'Westmoreland's big-unit war'; and, indeed, the terms, 'search-and-destroy' and 'body count'. 'Search-and-destroy' was a 'misnomer': 'in reality the operations were aimed at finding the enemy and eliminating his military installations', such as 'bunkers, tunnels, rice and ammunition caches'. Westmoreland declared that he 'abhorred' the term, 'body count', a concept he inherited from General Paul Harkins. The US military did not, according to *A Soldier Reports,* neglect or oppose pacification and counter-insurgency. 'In reality, despite my policy of using American units to oppose the enemy's main-forces, more American troops were usually engaged on a day-to-day basis, helping weed out local opposition and supporting the pacification process, than were engaged in the big fights'. Westmoreland did acknowledge the existence of tensions between the military leadership and pacification coordinator, Robert Komer, who was sent to Vietnam in May 1967 to organize the Civil Operations and Rural Development (CORDS) programme. Komer, civilian deputy to Westmoreland, was 'like a grain of sand in an oyster', but he was 'the man for the job'. Westmoreland disavowed any personal lack of enthusiasm for pacification, but also expressed the view that such activities were best left to the South Vietnamese themselves. 'The fewer Americans in close contact with the people ... meant that much less provocation of the xenophobia of the Vietnamese.' Ultimately, for Westmoreland, South

Vietnamese 'irregulars' could not be defeated 'until the threat of the [North Vietnamese] bully boys with their crowbars was substantially eliminated'. Responding to accusations that he had been indifferent to local sensitivities, Westmoreland reasserted that 'it was necessary on some occasions intentionally to raze evacuated villages'. Blame, for Westmoreland, lay at the door of defeatist politicians. Instead of exploiting the military gains of 1968, 'our political leadership in effect became captive to the enemy' (Westmoreland 1980: 189, 197, 282, 358, 546).

Westmoreland also discussed issues of war intelligence, notably the so-called 'Order of Battle controversy' of 1967–68, which originated in disagreements between the CIA and MACV over calculations of enemy strength. Captured documents, analysed by Sam Adams at the CIA, seemed to reveal greater enemy numbers than those indicated by US military estimates. The dispute drew in the Vietnam Information Group, organized by Walt Rostow to project positive evaluations of the war to the US public. It raised issues of flawed, wishful thinking and over-optimistic estimates, along with the 'body count' and Westmoreland's reluctance to include South Vietnamese communist irregulars in the official calculation of enemy strength. The controversy was the subject of a libel action taken out by Westmoreland, and eventually settled out-of-court in respect of the CBS television documentary, 'The Uncounted Enemy: A Vietnam Deception'. Robert McNamara, in his first public statement on the war since 1968, testified in the ensuing 1984 libel trial that Westmoreland was 'a person of great integrity who could never have lied to his superiors' (Westmoreland 1980: 188; Adams 1994; Prados 1995: 120–8; Zaffiri 1994: 410; Hiam 2006).

Westmoreland has not been completely without defenders. Harry Summers, a strong critic of US ground strategy in Vietnam, argued that Westmoreland was a tactical rather than a strategic commander. The MACV chief not only had to defer to political direction; he also had to contend with a military command structure involving Earle Wheeler (chair of the Joint Chiefs) and Admiral Sharp, head of Pacific Command. For Summers (1985: 358–9), Westmoreland's historic role was to act as an absorber of postwar blame, softening the kind of 'stab-in-the-back' military backlash which developed in Germany after 1918. Several commentators have sought to defend Westmoreland essentially by reiterating the case made in *A Soldier Reports*: that any winning American strategy had first to deal with the

Northern, or Northern-supported, main units. Counter-insurgency had to take second place. This argument rests on the extremely contentious view that the Southern resistance had few local resources – a view which, as we have already seen, underpinned the failure of the Rolling Thunder bombing campaign.

The wider case for seeing Westmoreland as a leader more sinned against than sinning rests upon a series of interlinked assertions. Westy, it might be argued, had no choice but to fight in Vietnam with the military tools developed to fight the Soviet Union. The military under his command was conservative in many ways, but also managed to fight flexibly and to exploit a series of technological innovations, such as ground-based sensors to track enemy movements (Deitchman 2008; Mahnken 2008: 117). Westmoreland's hostility to counter-insurgency has (in this line of revisionist argument) been exaggerated. Robert Komer himself later acknowledged that, in the mid-1960s, 'thwarting the VC/NVA "main forces" had become indispensable to creating a climate in which pacification could get started again' after the murder of Diem (Moyar 1997: 42; Andrade 2008). The March 1966 Army Staff report, 'A Program for the Pacification and Long-Term Development of South Vietnam', is often cited as a critique of 'big-unit' strategy, but – read carefully – actually accepted much of Westmoreland's case for using America's firepower advantage against the enemy main forces (Birtle 2008). John Carland (2004b: 569) has argued that Westmoreland did appreciate the importance of counter-insurgency and actually did not see it as merely a matter for the South Vietnamese. The MACV commander wrote in September 1965 that the US military must have 'an awareness of the political and psychological factors involved' in fighting in foreign territory amid a population of ambiguous loyalty.

Westmoreland's strategic options were foreclosed by political decisions. For Jonathan Caverley (2009/10: 121), the lack of American commitment to counter-insurgency was primarily a function of Washington's political desire to spend 'treasure rather than blood' – expensive firepower rather than military manpower – in search of victory. The marginalization of counter-insurgency, according to Caverley, was not *primarily* due to Westmoreland. It may also reasonably be argued that facile optimism was more a characteristic of Westmoreland's predecessor, General Harkins, than of Westmoreland himself. After presenting his battle plan at the February 1966 Honolulu Conference, Westmoreland offered a public vision of a military long-haul. The enemy 'would have to be ferreted out over a period of time, which will involve many campaigns'. Defenders of Westmoreland also argue that the contrast between the two heads of the MACV between 1964 and 1972 has been exaggerated. Thus, it has been argued that spending priorities in the MACV budget under General Creighton Abrams did not alter all that much from the Westmoreland years, with continued reliance on artillery (Malkasian 2004: 937; Birtle 2008: 1234–5).

However, even with the best will in the world, Westmoreland cannot plausibly be pictured as a friend of effective counter-insurgency. Westmoreland and his operational deputy, General William DePuy, consistently argued for the prioritization of firepower. The MACV command was unsympathetic to Marine Corps efforts to bring US forces into counter-insurgency operations through their Combined Action Patrol and 'enclave' strategies. Disputes over pacification were exacerbated by rifts between Westmoreland and the Marine Corps in other areas, notably during the 1968 siege of Hue citadel and especially over issues of air support. Even when Westmoreland occasionally acknowledged the need for a more concerted pacification approach, he did not push his case very strongly (Krepinevich 1986: 175; Gilbert 2002a: 167; Caverley 2010: 132; McAllister 2010/11: 101). Despite the misgivings expressed in *A Soldier Reports* over the 'body count', the MACV presided over a statistically-based evaluation process which was fundamentally flawed. According to Shelby Stanton (1985b: 272), the MACV issued guidelines on 'factoring additional dead based on standard percentages by type of encounter and terrain' into the daily 'body count'; 'individual canteens were accepted as authorized substitutes if bodies were too dismembered to estimate properly'.

Amid such madness, Westmoreland often seemed profoundly out of touch. His lack of political understanding was displayed in a failed bid to become Republican governor of South Carolina in 1974. Westmoreland was an honourable soldier, but assuredly not a successful political general.

Alternative Strategies

The most obvious alternative American strategy in Vietnam was, of course, not to go there in the first place. This view – that (to quote

Mike Mansfield) the war 'was misadventure in a part of the world we should have kept our nose out of' – was not simply that of antiwar radicals. Several experienced military leaders – notably James Gavin, Matthew Ridgway and David Shoup – saw the war of attrition as essentially unwinnable and as irrelevant to core American global interests (Duffy 1992; Buzzanco 1996b; Record 1998: 184). On the whole, it would have been better for all concerned if no such involvement had occurred. Our present concern, however, is with possible winning strategies once the commitments to Saigon had been made.

Numerous alternative strategies for American victory were advanced in the postwar years. The most common argument from the revisionist side involved the attack on gradualism. If the war was worth fighting, it was worth winning (Palmer 1978; Davidson 1988). Competing versions of the attack on gradualism recommended an American declaration of war against North Vietnam with attendant domestic censorship and mobilization; possibly an actual invasion of North Vietnam, backed by massive use of airpower; and the sealing off of North Vietnam in order to deny support to the Southern insurgents. Bruce Palmer (1984: 182–4) offered a two-part alternative strategy. First, US and allied ground forces would be concentrated in defensible positions south of the DMZ, with the defensive line extending across Laos. Second, the US Navy would maintain a 'constantly visible and credible amphibious presence off the coast of North Vietnam, threatening possible invasion from the sea of various important areas of North Vietnam'. Although writers in this tradition disagree about the requisite degree of Americanization of the conflict – Bruce Palmer saw the optimum US role as providing a shield for Southern military development – most such commentators deplore LBJ's decision to rule out an invasion of North Vietnam. The best-known statement of alternative strategy is that advanced by Harry Summers (1982), who argued that the US should have seen the war for what it was – a conventional attack from the North – and taken such action as was needed to defeat the assault. As it was, the US became sidelined into pursuing essentially defensive measures to deal with guerrillas and irregulars. Summers supported the idea of an allied (US, ARVN and South Korean) push across Laos in order to prevent infiltration, as well as a credible commitment to invasion of North Vietnam. Such a strategy would have been similar to that envisaged in Westmoreland's abortive El Paso plan, originally advanced in 1966. Most versions of a 'winning' American strategy implicitly or explicitly criticize 1960s Washington for excessive timidity in advancing an Indochinese, rather than a more narrowly Vietnamese, conceptualization of the conflict.

Several variations on the 'enclave' strategy, originally promoted by General Maxwell Taylor, have also been put forward. An enclave approach would have recognized the need to secure key areas before attempting to engage enemy forces in remote regions of South Vietnam. After 1968, General Abrams recognized the force of the 'enclave' case by adopting the doctrine of 'take and hold'. Attempting to protect the whole of South Vietnam, American ground forces became desperately overextended in the mid-1960s, almost aimlessly deployed over huge swathes of the country. The battles for Khe Sanh and Hue, at the very least, could have been avoided. 'Enclave' strategies, according to their proponents, did not necessarily involve a 'defeatist' ceding of territory to the enemy. Such strategies could have been combined with assertive efforts to shield the South – or, indeed, to invade North Vietnam, thus isolating and exposing Southern-based communist forces. One version of the 'enclave' approach is the advocacy of the concentration of US forces along the entire populated coastal zone stretching from the DMZ to Saigon (Krepinevich 1986: 266; Joes 1989: 113).

What effect would a full-blown, declared war, even one based around an 'enclave' strategy, have had? More precisely, would China have intervened directly? Unsurprisingly, the answer of revisionist writers such as Summers is a loud 'no'. For the more 'gung ho' revisionists, Johnson was foolish to allow his administration to become paralysed by memories of the Chinese intervention in the Korean conflict. By the mid-1960s, Beijing was as much preoccupied by the rivalry with Moscow as with the contest with capitalism. For C. Dale Walton, Chinese intervention was not only unlikely, especially after 1965, when Beijing became increasingly concerned with the convulsions associated with the Cultural Revolution. The US would, in Walton's view, have been able to resist any actual Chinese intervention which Beijing might have been able to mount. Walton quotes a 1964 memorandum from the Joint Chiefs to Robert McNamara, downplaying the Chinese ability to commit decisive force in defence of Vietnam. According to Walton, offensive US military action in Vietnam would have been unlikely to involve repetition of 'gross errors' made in Korea, such as failing to take note of Chinese troop movements. If an invasion of North Vietnam had occurred, the US would also have had the sense to leave a buffer zone in the northern part of the country (Walton 2002: 102).

Against the view that China would not have intervened, even in the case of actual US invasion of North Vietnam, numerous expressions of Chinese commitment to the DRV, sometimes in the context of explicit warnings to Washington, may be cited. The dynamics of Sino–Soviet rivalry ran in unpredictable directions, and it would have been exceedingly rash of Washington to presume that Beijing would allow that rivalry to inhibit direct action against the Americans. As for the chaos of the Cultural Revolution, Mao would not have been the first leader to use foreign intervention as a means to mobilize domestic opinion. Walton is correct to argue that early guarantees to Saigon should more carefully have considered the implications for China. However, such guarantees were always hostage to future events and pressures. The US probably could have turned back a Chinese intervention, but only at the cost of further prioritizing the conflict in Vietnam way beyond its intrinsic importance to American interests. Even though it reflected massive self-doubts, Johnson's caution had a rational basis. Michael Lind, whose revisionist perspective was very different from that of Dale Walton, praised LBJ for ignoring wilder military advice, notably from former head of Strategic Air Command Curtis LeMay, and for appreciating the real dangers of Chinese intervention (Garver 1996; Lind 1999: 85, 104).

If America was to remain committed to the protection of South Vietnam, some kind of 'shielding the South' strategy would have made sense. However, not only would it have raised the stakes on Chinese intervention, it would also have been difficult in logistical terms. Westmoreland's El Paso plan was rejected, at least in formal terms, because of the associated support costs, which included some 18,000 engineer troops. Additionally, at least insofar as a Laotian ground incursion would have drawn attention away from the guerrilla war, it tended again to downplay the Southern roots of the insurgency. The efforts of Harry Summers effectively to write out the pre-1969 Southern guerrilla war bordered on the bizarre. A 'winning' American strategy, however, would have had to embrace the need to shield the South at some stage, and in tandem with effective Southern pacification. Similarly, an invasion of the North – in any possible 'winning' strategy – had to remain an option for Washington. What was essential, however, was for American decision-makers seriously to appreciate the dangers of such strategies. These involved not only possible direct confrontation with China, but also becoming exposed to a long and potentially debilitating (and domestically unpopular) occupation of the North. It is very unlikely that, in the event of an invasion, the communist forces would have allowed themselves to be trapped into any set-piece battle from which the US would have been likely to emerge victorious. The communists would have reconceptualized the conflict, even without Chinese intervention, as a new, long guerrilla struggle (Krepinevich 1986: 263; Record 1998: 181).

Better Wars, Other Wars

Much commentary on alternative American strategy in Vietnam relates to the role of counter-insurgency warfare. Such commentary, often developed in the context of debates about later conflicts (notably in twenty-first-century Iraq and Afghanistan), is often rather vague about what constitutes counter-insurgency warfare. Counter-insurgency in the context of Vietnam has come to stand for almost anything that was not a big-unit war, a war dominated by firepower and a war of attrition. 'Counter-insurgency' is a very broad concept, merging into 'nation-building' (the central concern of the Diem years) and into 'pacification' (the term used by Washington and the MACV for security-provision and other civilian-oriented South Vietnam development activity after 1968). Important, here, is the distinction between 'hard' or 'enemy-centric' counter-insurgency (geared towards the physical elimination of communist cadres at grass-roots level) on the one hand; and 'soft' or 'population-centric' counter-insurgency (designed to win peasant 'hearts and minds') on the other. A successful counter-insurgency strategy may be presumed as achieving an optimum balance of 'hard' and 'soft' elements. Counter-insurgency advocates also tend to espouse an 'enclave' approach to developing a viable alternative to Westmoreland's war. Thus, for Andrew Krepinevich, 'enclave strategy offered the advantage of buying time for South Vietnam at costs substantially less than those borne by the strategy of attrition' (Krepinevich 1986: 266; Nagl 2005; Dumbrell and Ryan 2007; Kilcullen 2010). We will now consider the role of counter-insurgency in the Vietnam War: especially the argument that, after 1968, a new American strategy – one linked to the embrace of counter-insurgency – actually was winning the war.

Building on initiatives undertaken under President Johnson, General Creighton Abrams advanced a 'one-war' strategy which was formally approved by the incoming Nixon administration in early 1969. The plan represented a coming together of big-unit war and elements of 'hard' and 'soft' counter-insurgency, with a particular emphasis on the provision of security for the South Vietnamese peasantry. 'One war' was a direct response to the shifting US domestic context and to the expectation of declining American troop numbers. Abrams appreciated the absurdities of the 'body count' and questioned the Army's tendency to rely on 'artillery, gunships ... and all that kind of stuff'. The new approach consciously sought to build on the post-1967 counter-insurgency initiatives, with the pacification of Quang Dia district (north-west of Hue) in 1968 providing a model. The idea was to target the cadre grass roots (or Viet Cong infrastructure (VCI), estimated at about 70,000 personnel), following the rout of enemy main forces after the Tet Offensive. The infrastructure was to be attacked via intelligence-led action, facilitated by locally recruited paramilitary regional and popular forces. 'Take and hold' ('hard' eradication of the VCI followed by 'hearts and minds' action) was to replace 'search-and-destroy' (Stanton 1985b: 283; Sorley 1999: 195, 219; Nagl 2005: 169, 171).

The 'one-war' approach sought to spread to the US Army the lessons learned in earlier US Marine operations, notably the Marine Combined Action Platoons (CAPs). By 1967, there were 75 CAP units in operation, each consisting of 15 Marines plus 35 or so village-level paramilitaries (the South Vietnamese regional and popular forces). The CAPs were intended to establish 'ink spot' development, with secure areas slowly expanding into one another. Efforts to win peasant loyalty included Marine support for farmers in coastal areas who wished to sell crops without paying tax to the local Viet Cong. Under the 'one-war' strategy, the Army would complement and extend, rather than undermine, the progress being made by the Marine CAPs. The Army began to develop its 'mobile training team' operations to extend CAP-type operations. The 'one-war' advances also built on LBJ's decision of 1967 to bring counter-insurgency operations under the umbrella of CORDS. Coordinated civil-military CORDS operations – working across military service, State Department, CIA, and Agency for International Development bureaucratic boundaries – were instituted with a clear mandate to lead the regional and popular forces towards supplanting the cadre infrastructure. CORDS initiatives also began to remove some of the more obviously corrupt and unpopular local South Vietnamese officials (Walt 1969; Krulak 1984; Hunt 1995: 276; Coram 2010; Kilcullen 2010: 208–9).

The putative success of the post-1968 pacification of South Vietnam lies at the heart of the 'lost victory' thesis, argued by William Colby, who succeeded Komer as head of CORDS in November 1968. For Colby, gains at the village level were achieved through a new spirit of US–South Vietnamese cooperation. Local CORDS assessments indicated that basic security for the majority of the South Vietnamese population had been achieved by late 1969. A plethora of organizations, built around the paramilitary regional and popular forces, had now emerged. By 1971, progress had even been achieved in integrating *montagnard* fighters (regular and irregular) with South Vietnamese units. Agencies of pacification included the Provincial Reconnaissance Units (small CIA-run bands of South Vietnamese irregulars, often made up of ethnic minority groups) and the Kit Carson Scouts (elite groups of communist defectors). Rural development teams exemplified the 'soft' approach to counter-insurgency, while the Phoenix Program represented its 'enemy-centric' face. Widely regarded as an assassination programme, Phoenix has been defended as an intelligence-led operation, geared as much to the capture and interrogation of communist cadres, as to their physical elimination (Colby 1989: 270, 277–8; Moyar 1997: 159, 224–5; Nagl 2005: 170).

There is little question that, from the point of view of Washington and Saigon, progress was being made after 1968 in terms of security-provision, VCI elimination, and even to some extent regarding peasant loyalties. We will discuss the nature of such progress further in Chapter 8. However, it is a big jump between acknowledging such developments on the South Vietnamese ground and accepting the 'better war' or 'lost victory' thesis: the view that an American 'victory' had actually been achieved in the 1970s, only to be squandered in the years 1973–75. One important *caveat* here involves the rather excessive claims made by some sympathetic commentators for the Marine CAPs. The Marine Corps in Vietnam took substantial losses, making up 28 per cent of US fatalities, a figure far greater than the percentage of Marines in the total US military commitment. The frequently repeated notion that only one CAP operation was ever overrun by the enemy is not really credible. The Army in the 1960s had little sympathy for counter-insurgency; but the characteristic Army view – that the CAPs exposed pacifiers to attack, and that the Army had to come to the rescue – was not entirely inaccurate. Moreover, the Marine Corps itself was by no means always averse to replicating the Army's attraction to firepower. CAPs were only part of the Marine operation in Vietnam; indeed, Michael Peterson (1989: 123) portrayed even the Marine commitment to counter-insurgency as 'tokenism'.

Whatever the objective success of CAPs before 1970, much of the point of the 'one-war' approach was precisely to bring Marines and the Army together, and to end Westmoreland's policy of simply leaving counter-insurgency to the South Vietnamese. Thus, it may reasonably be argued that loss of faith in the attritional war belatedly opened the door to the new concern for security-provision, and the mobilization of the regional and popular forces. However, it is going too far to argue that post-Tet Offensive counter-insurgency moved to the centre of US operational priorities. We have already noted the argument that the contrast between the approach of Generals Westmoreland and Abrams can easily be exaggerated. Between fiscal years 1969 and 1971, only 2 per cent of US funding went to the South Vietnamese regional and popular forces. Indeed, what is remarkable is the degree to which post-1968 pacification succeeded *despite* neglect of the regional and popular forces. CORDS funding did increase after 1968, though William Colby's account of the impact of its programmes should be treated with caution. CORDS brought together a range of civilian-oriented programmes in a newly efficient way. Yet, it always ran the risk of attempting to impose one-size-fits-all pacification techniques onto a very diverse population (Issacs 1983: 108; Hunt 1995: 243, 277–8; Prados 2009a: 327–8).

If 'soft' counter-insurgency continued to have its problems, the post-Tet Offensive 'enemy-centric' initiatives could be extremely harsh, abusive and counter-productive; action taken in the Hue region following the 1972 Easter Offensive was a case in point. The Phoenix Program was certainly feared by the communists, but its success in 'neutralizing' high-level cadres can be questioned. Its operations were undermined by corruption and problems of combining flexibility with a necessary degree of central control. Contrary to the view that Phoenix was unhampered by a distorting obsession with target statistics, there is evidence that the programme suffered the defects of so many other American-led initiatives: the drive to produce quantifiable goals by questionable means. 'One-war' thinking was a massive improvement on Westmoreland's war. Creighton Abrams did recognize some of the lunacies of the way the war had been conducted. He condemned 'the worship of charts', declaring that it 'finally gets to the point where that's really the whole war – fucking *charts* ... instead of thinking ... what really has to be done' (Sorley 1999: 195). Important improvements were made in both American military and civilian operations after 1967; there was far better coordination of effort, and an appreciation of the central importance of obtaining some loyalty from the South Vietnamese peasantry. Yet, inter-service rivalry did not disappear. The US Army did not suddenly become enthusiastically committed to counter-insurgency. Operational defects and misunderstandings were mitigated rather than eliminated. Most fundamentally, all the post-1967 military and civilian initiatives in South Vietnam were hostage to the success of Vietnamization, defined in terms of the creation of a viable, self-confident South Vietnamese state, able to subsist economically and to provide its own security. As we saw in relation to the ARVN and shall discuss further in Chapter 8, successful Vietnamization (political as well as military) proved elusive.

A winning alternative anti-communist strategy is not inconceivable. Such a strategy would certainly have had counter-insurgency ('hard' and 'soft') at its heart. However, an eventual communist victory in Vietnam was always a strong possibility: due to Hanoi's nationalist credentials, to the support of Moscow and Beijing, to the opposition of so many South Vietnamese to foreign occupation, and to the related difficulties in establishing a credible non-communist government in Saigon. An important conclusion of this chapter is that this likelihood of communist victory was compounded by the way that Washington *and* the MACV understood and waged the war.

8
Understanding the Vietnamese Revolution

Vietnam's revolution was proclaimed in 1945 and consolidated in 1975. Focusing on 'the American War', *Rethinking the Vietnam War* is primarily concerned with the later stages of this part-nationalist, part-communist revolution. As with so many other dimensions of the war, western discussion of the role played by the Vietnamese people in their own revolution has been plagued by rather unhelpful stereotypes: notably those relating to the communist sureness of purpose and to the virtual non-existence of South Vietnam as a viable political entity. The purpose of this chapter is to question these stereotypes – not necessarily entirely rejecting them, but subjecting them to scholarly interrogation and questioning the absolute inevitability of the communist victory. The chapter offers an account of the later stages of the Vietnamese revolution, focusing on the interpenetration of communism and nationalism. It opens with discussion of Ho Chi Minh himself – personification of the marriage of Vietnamese communism and Vietnamese nationalism. To what extent did the communist leadership in Hanoi, including Ho Chi Minh, really possess a penetrating understanding of their dimensions of advantage over the Americans, enabling them to provide clear and purposeful direction to the revolution? How can official communist histories, written by the victor of 1975, contribute to our understanding of the revolution in Vietnam? We also draw particular attention to the role played by Le Duan, a major political figure in Hanoi and (despite his relative obscurity) effective successor to Ho Chi Minh. The second part of the chapter considers South Vietnam. Who exactly were the Viet Cong? What was the National Liberation Front? We conclude the chapter by examining the putative 'non-state' of South Vietnam. What kind of state *was* South Vietnam? Did it have any indigenous support beyond that of a narrow elite, dependent upon the American presence? By way of further introduction to this chapter, we will briefly consider the nature of received views of the Vietnamese at war, contrasting these stereotypes with the recent body of scholarship on the revolution in Vietnam.

Central to received views of the Vietnamese in 'the American war' is the grudging respect paid by US participants in the war to their communist enemy. Chester Cooper, who worked for the CIA for Kennedy and in LBJ's White House, recalled: 'People thought we were going to war with this stinking little country and it would be a shoo-in, a piece of cake. But they knew how to do it and we didn't.' To Oliver Stone, who taught and served in Vietnam before becoming a film director, the Viet Cong were 'like fucking warrior ants' (Appy 2008: 85, 254). The communist leadership in Hanoi is often accredited with almost superhuman powers of prescience and determination, successfully second-guessing Washington and guiding the inevitable revolutionary progress in South Vietnam. During the war, numerous commentators attempted to explain the apparently peculiar determination and resolution of the Vietnamese communists in cultural terms. Such commentary tended to stress the degree to which communist practice was set within Vietnamese traditions of disciplined consensus-seeking (Fitzgerald 1972: 440). If western opinion, more or less across the political spectrum, was frequently prepared to acknowledge the positive qualities of Vietnam's communists, American judgements on the political elite in South Vietnam tended to veer between impatience and simple contempt. A National Security Staff study of 1964 concluded that the communist side had, in comparison with America's non-communist allies, 'far more than its fair share of talent'. William Bundy described the dual leadership of Air Vice-Marshall Ky and General Thieu which came to power in 1965 as the 'bottom of the barrel, absolutely the bottom of the barrel' (Herring 1990: 1; Woods 2006: 60).

Recent years have seen the emergence of new scholarship on the Vietnamese side of the war, drawing on a range of documentation, including official DRV histories, NLF documents captured during the war years, memoir, imaginative literature, and verbal testimony from surviving war combatants. The new scholarship tends to reject not only the familiar stereotypes of grudging respect and 'warrior ants', but also generalizations about Vietnamese culture which downplay its diverse, transnational and multi-ethnic dimensions (Bradley 2009: 5). Central to the agenda of scholars working along these lines is what Edward Miller and Tuong Vu (2009: 5) call 'the Vietnamization of Vietnam War Studies'. Such an approach seeks to transcend the 'orthodox' versus 'revisionist' dichotomies of American-centred scholarship. It involves not merely according space to Vietnamese people in accounts of their war, but also recognizing the importance of independent Vietnamese agency. The Hanoi leadership is thus seen as having an independent role in moulding the development of the Cold War, in ways which affected policy outcomes in Beijing, Moscow, and Washington. Contemporary Vietnamese scholarship also engages with wider debates about the peasantry: notably with the need to see the rural Vietnamese population – North and South – more as makers of history, less as inert and passive reactors to outside pressures (Kerkvliet 2005; Race 2010; Montesano 2011).

Ho Chi Minh and the Rise of Vietnamese Nationalism

Otherwise known as Nguyen Tat Thanh, Nguyen Sinh Cung and Nguyen Ai Quoc ('Nguyen the Patriot'), Ho Chi Minh was born in Annam in (or around) 1890, about seven years after the achievement of comprehensive French imperial control of Vietnam. Ho was born into a nationalist family; his father had rejected the bureaucratic mandarin tradition in favour of anti-imperialism. Ho Chi Minh developed a consistent adherence to nationalism, retaining always a strong element of Confucian dutiful patriotism, but also nurturing a degree of contempt for the passivity of the mandarin elite (Quinn-Judge 2003: 42).

After a brief period of study in Saigon, Ho left his country in 1912, embarking upon what was sometimes a literal voyage – he worked for a time as a steward on transatlantic liners; more often a metaphorical voyage of nationalist intellectual development. At various times, he lived in the United States, Britain, and France. Particularly after moving to Paris in 1917, Ho emerged as a leader of exiled Vietnamese nationalism; in 1920, he became a founder-member of the French Communist Party. Ho lobbied the leaders of the victorious powers in the First World War, as they met at Versailles in 1919, to advance the cause of Vietnamese self-determination. He unsuccessfully petitioned

US President Woodrow Wilson for a personal meeting. Perhaps the first of the innumerable 'what-ifs' of the Vietnam War is: what if Woodrow Wilson had met Ho Chi Minh in 1919? Ho's programme for Vietnam at this time was essentially reformist and parliamentarist; it included demands for free speech and for Vietnamese representation in the French assembly.

Given the history of French colonialism, Ho cannot have entertained much hope of the programme being accepted in Paris, but he may genuinely have looked to Wilson for support. Ho's political trajectory now veered dramatically and swiftly leftwards. The writings of Lenin seemed to hold out the prospect of integrating anti-colonial struggles in peasant societies into Karl Marx's doctrine of proletarian revolution. In ideological disputes over the revolutionary role of the peasantry, Ho tended to side with pragmatic nationalism, and against ideological proletarian internationalism. By the standards of twentieth-century communism, Ho was not an ideologue. He is conventionally regarded as a nationalist first, a communist second (Logevall 2001: 12). Such a view embodies a certain truth, but tends to downplay the degree to which Ho Chi Minh actually did see anti-colonial alliances as stepping stones to world proletarian revolution, coordinated from Moscow. Recalling his early development, Ho later wrote: 'At first patriotism, not yet Communism, led me to have confidence in Lenin ... I gradually came upon the fact that only Socialism and Communism can liberate the oppressed nations and the working people throughout the world from slavery' (Duiker 1996: 17).

In practice, the young Ho Chi Minh's relationship with Moscow and the Comintern, the body founded to foster international proletarian revolution, was difficult. Ho worked on behalf of the Comintern in China and Hong Kong. He founded the Vietnamese Revolutionary Youth League in 1925 as a forerunner to the Indochina Communist Party (organized by Ho, still in exile, as a fusion of nationalist and communist elements in 1930). Appealing to 'the great unity under heaven', Ho saw the exit of the French as coming about from progressive alliances in Vietnam, rather than as a result of actual Soviet intervention. Ho's thinking embraced a commitment to tactical pragmatism with an ultimate allegiance to the cause of international proletarian revolution (Ho Tai 1992: 180).

Ho's efforts to 'unite all oppressed people' in Vietnam were indirectly assisted by the Japanese occupation of his country during the Second World War. The occupation eased some elements of colonial repression and weakened internal Vietnamese divisions. Ho returned to his homeland in 1941 as founder-leader of the Independence League of Vietnam, or 'Viet Minh'. His programme now embraced guerrilla warfare, all-class allegiances, and cooperation with enemies of Japan. Ho actually became an agent of the US Office of Strategic Services, reporting on Japanese military activity. Soviet leader Josef Stalin's ambivalent attitude towards Ho in subsequent years may have been connected to the perception that the Vietnamese leader had stretched the limits of wartime cooperation with Britain and the United States. As outlined in Chapter 1, Ho led the Viet Minh to its August Revolution, with Bao Dai abdicating the throne on 30 August 1945. Ho's Declaration of Vietnamese Independence famously, and mischievously, invoked not only America's own Declaration of 1776, but also the 1791 Declaration of the French Revolution on the Rights of Man. Here appear more 'what-ifs'. Not only, what if Washington had responded to Ho's 1945 Declaration by opposing the French return to Vietnam? But also, what if *France* had taken the opportunity to negotiate peace with the Viet Minh, thus preventing the outbreak of war in late 1946? (Tonnesson 2010: 235).

Ho Chi Minh led North Vietnam until his death in 1969. He oversaw, though not necessarily directed, the various shifts in the DRV during the years of the 'American war'. Ho's style was pragmatic and consensual. He was certainly not the Vietnamese Stalin. Within the Politburo, the leading organ of authority in the DRV, Ho had to accommodate himself to political opponents who often took a harder, less pragmatic line than he. Ho was intelligent, charismatic, and flexible; he was not a benevolent leftist democrat. Sophie Quinn-Judge points out that the post-1975 Vietnamese leadership was content to allow Ho to 'stand as the iconic representation of communist power'; DRV historiography omits mention of challenges to Ho's authority. The false familiarization of 'Uncle Ho' – or even of 'Old Ho' (as Lyndon Johnson called him) – has distorted understanding of DRV policy-making. Ho Chi Minh presided over a political entity, the Democratic Republic of Vietnam, but often had only tenuous control over its policy-making core. Ho was also absent from Vietnam for long periods, including almost the whole of 1967, when he was in China for medical treatment (Duiker 2000: 574; Quinn-Judge 2004; 2008: 111, 130–1).

Ho set important precedents for managing relations with the communist great-powers. His relationship with the Soviet Union under Stalin was problematic, but Ho was aware of the dangers of antagonizing Moscow. Nationalist China tended to support the anti-communist Vietnam Nationalist Party, which to some extent was modelled on the Chinese Guomindang. In 1946, Ho Chi Minh famously invoked historic Sino–Vietnamese rivalry when he moved to sell to the Viet Minh the agreement allowing French return: 'I prefer to smell French shit for five years, rather than Chinese shit for the rest of my life' (*PP*, I, 1971: 19). Ho was suspicious of Chinese power (as he was of Soviet), but it is worth emphasizing that in 1946, when Ho made this famous remark about 'Chinese shit', the Guomindang was in power in Beijing. With Mao Zedong's revolutionary victory in 1949, Ho acquired a potent great-power sponsor. Bui Tin, a military officer in the DRV – later a journalist and exile – recalled: 'We were dazzled by the new light of the Chinese Revolution, which was acclaimed as our role model' (Bui Tin 1995: 4–5; LaFeber 2007: 37). Mao's success seemed to demonstrate that communist revolution could occur in peasant societies. China supplied a model of politico-military strategy. The radical and brutally administered land collectivization undertaken by the Viet Minh in the early 1950s was modelled on the Chinese experience. As Keith Taylor (1983: 297) has written, a strong China was a 'historical problem' for Vietnam, just as China tended to see a 'strong, united Vietnam as a special, almost domestic problem'. Even in the early years, Ho had to adjust to the framework imposed by great-power *Realpolitik* – as when China shifted its regional strategy in the later stages of the 1950–53 Korean War. For Ho, Vietnamese national destiny would always be played out between the limits imposed by externally led international communism. Skilled leadership resided in recognizing these limits, as well as identifying opportunities opened up by Sino–Soviet competition. Ho's ultimate 'answer' to the problem of retaining independence in the face of potential external domination was the achievement of military success. Though Ho was not primarily a military figure, his thinking was increasingly couched in military terms: in terms of 'people's war' and the Maoist model of revolution: construction of local revolutionary bases, followed by expansion and re-education of new revolutionary regions, succeeded by mass popular uprising. The three-stage Maoist programme, as we have seen, did not provide the undisputed road map for revolution in Vietnam. Nevertheless, Ho was certainly heavily influenced by Maoist revolutionary and military models, and presided over a movement which was extremely militarized. The PAVN evolved directly from the Viet Minh, with both forces effectively representing a nation in arms (Lockhart 1989: 264; Chen Jian 2001: 129; Nguyen Duy 2004).

Finally in this section, we should consider Ho's reputation as the authentic, even the only, voice of Vietnamese nationalism. Here, it is worth emphasizing that Ho's was not the only version of Vietnamese anti-colonialism on offer, certainly in the first half of the twentieth century and, indeed, beyond. Ho's movement managed to suppress various movements on the Vietnamese left, notably those who looked to radical Trotskyist internationalism. Among nationalists, the urban-based Vietnam Nationalist Party was one alternative to the Viet Minh, at least before 1949 (Dunn 1989: 143). The Buddhist tradition offered another possibility, as did the elite nationalism represented in South Vietnam by Ngo Dinh Diem after partition. The triumph of Ho's movement was not inevitable. It rested on political skill and on the pragmatic use of trans-class alliances as stepping stones to power. Perhaps above all it relied on the communists' ability, unrivalled by other nationalist groupings, to exploit (and to some degree to contain) the revolutionary explosions in China.

The Hanoi Politburo

Leadership structures on both sides of partitioned Vietnam were shaped by the constant experience of war. In North Vietnam, the leading force was the Vietnam Workers' Party or Lao Dong, the name attached to the Indochina Communist Party from 1951. (The change in name was primarily tactical; Ho continued to support Indochinese communist coordination.) The communist organization in North Vietnam presented itself as the embodiment of Vietnamese socialist aspiration, the lead-agent of the proletariat, and the engine of national reunification. It embraced a course between 'leftist deviation' (adventurist and impractical utopianism) and 'rightist deviation' (cynical and inactive pragmatism). Until 1960, when Ho's new constitution was adopted, North Vietnam presented itself as a state representing broad national interests. From 1960, the dominant purpose of government was established as the promotion of communism. As president, Ho Chi Minh had great power, but was not omnipotent. The principal site of authority was the Politburo, which represented the major party power sources: notably, the governmental apparatus and the military. The power of the Politburo was augmented by the existence of a National Assembly, which until 1971 had representatives from South Vietnam. The Politburo placed great emphasis upon consensus and unanimity. Ho's death in 1969 was not accompanied by obvious struggles for the succession. Ton Duc Thang, Ho's official successor as president, operated primarily as a ceremonial leader. Ho's position as head of the Party's Central Committee remained vacant. Leading Politburo figures included Le Duan (Party First Secretary and effective 'first among equals' in the Politburo), Pham Van Dong (head of the governmental apparatus), Vo Nguyen Giap (military chief) and Truong Chinh (head of the National Assembly) (Yong Mun Cheong 1999: 63–4).

Party rule was authoritarian, and explicit dissent was not tolerated. As in other authoritarian systems, the absence of obvious dissent should not be confused with universal support. During the war, the paintings of Bui Xuan Phai – often dismal street scenes in Hanoi – represented one, partially suppressed, indication of dissent from official thinking on the glory of war. Ho Chi Minh provided a slogan for collectivized agricultural production: 'everyone to work as hard as two'. This apparently gave rise to a popular verse of the 1960s and 1970s: 'Everyone work as hard as two/ so that the chairperson can buy a radio/ Everyone work as hard as three/ so that the cadre can buy a house and courtyard' (Kerkvliet 2005: 111; Bradley 2009: 136).

The DRV leadership embraced the rhetoric of progress, patriotism, shared purpose and common threat. With South Vietnam under the thrall of atavistic 'imperialism and feudalism', History (decidedly with a capital 'H') was on the side of communism and the DRV (*Seventy-Five Years* 2005: 164). Duong Van Mai Elliott's family memoir, *The Sacred Willow*, offers some insight into the extent to which the communist leaders in the North were able to achieve a degree of nationalist authenticity and respect, even in the eyes of ideological opponents. Recalling her anti-communist upbringing in Hanoi, Haiphong, and Saigon, Elliott recollected that 'it was the communists' perceived lack of respect for our two most cherished ideals, the family and the nation, that seemed to my parents and me the most egregious fault'. Elliott's reference to the sacrifice of 'nation' to Marxist ideology is especially interesting in view of the common assumption that the Hanoi Politburo managed successfully to fuse nationalism and communism. However, the young Duong Van

Mai 'also admired' the communist leaders, 'as did my parents, for their success in ending colonial rule, and thought of them as *gioi*, or talented and efficient' (Elliott 1999: 278).

The story of the war can be told at one level through various resolutions and other statements promulgated by the periodic party congresses, and by the plenary sessions of the Lao Dong Central Committee. Such policy statements (regularly issued in secret) sometimes represented a defeat for Ho Chi Minh. An example here is the outcome of the Second Congress in 1951, which – following the line taken by Truong Chinh – reflected a more clearly pro-Chinese policy than that preferred by Ho. Key early decisions included the 1960 move to restart the military campaign in South Vietnam, following the post-partition consolidation of communist power in the North: the 1963 decision, taken during what official communist histories call the pre-1965 'era of special war', to mount a 'bigger war', in anticipation of direct US military intervention; and the 1967 decision to launch the Tet Offensive. Later turning-point decisions included the April 1968 decision to negotiate with the Johnson administration; various post-1968 decisions linked to the general commitment to 'talking while fighting'; the decision to launch the 1972 Easter ('Nguyen Hue') Offensive; the move to a 'strategy of peace' in June 1972; the acceptance of peace terms in January 1973; and the July 1974 decision to launch the Final Offensive, with the goal of achieving victory in 1975 or 1976 (Van Tien Dung 1977: 11; Duiker 2000: 440; Ang Cheng Guan 2002: 6–10; 2004: 5–8; Nguyen 2006: 5).

The general steadfastness and sureness of purpose of the Hanoi Politburo is not seriously in question. Central to Hanoi's understanding of the war was the perceived need to marry politics and military combat. In time, this evolved into a marriage of politics, military combat, and diplomacy. Communist sources also speak eloquently of the Politburo's sensitivity both to the asymmetrical nature of the war, and to the possibility of compensating for the Hanoi–Washington power imbalance by influencing American domestic opinion. Between 1960 and 1968, the Politburo accepted Mao's dictum about resistance to imperialism: 'one should oppose them, but with care'. The enemy would quit Vietnam when the costs of remaining began to appear excessive. If Washington consistently underestimated the adaptability and perseverance of the Vietnamese, the reverse – apart from the special case of the Tet Offensive – does not seem to have been true. Official Hanoi respected American technological and economic strength. The communist approach was to deny victory to Washington, working to isolate the US in terms of international opinion, and to undermine the American home front. In some respects, the sentiment expressed by Party Secretary Truong Chinh in July 1954, during the Geneva talks, remained a guiding principle for the Politburo in the later American war: 'The more we fight, the stronger we become, and the more the enemy fights, the weaker he becomes' (Chen 1975; Ang Cheng Guan 2002: 39, 65–6; Asselin 2010: 221).

The DRV leadership consciously embraced the politics of *dich van* – making policy with one eye on American domestic opinion, and aiming propaganda at the American voter. By 1970, Le Duan was reporting that the US antiwar movement had 'taken on a new quality': 'Not only has it involved students and other young people who do not want to enlist and get killed in Vietnam but it has also spread to part of the American GIs and officers' corps. More seriously still, it has drawn in even people of business and financial circles since the war has brought about irreparable inflation in the US and reduced the profits of US monopoly capital' (Hunt 2010: 108). In 1972, the North Vietnamese negotiators in Paris were told by the Politburo to use the presidential candidacy of George McGovern 'to expose and pressure Nixon'. The tactic in October 1972 was to make President Nixon think that he could not beat McGovern without having secured an agreement on Vietnam (Luu Van Loi and Nguyen 1996: 255, 281).

The communist leaders combined sophistication, inventiveness, and cynicism. That is not to say that all their decisions were wise. The Tet Offensive turned into a military disaster. Tran Van Tra's 1982 military history was suppressed by the Vietnamese authorities for daring to state the obvious regarding the 1968 military losses. (Tran Van Tra, former deputy chief of COSVN, also challenged official attempts to ignore the Southern guerrilla support for the Final Offensive of 1974–75.) Vietnamese diplomat Tran Van Tung acknowledged in 2010 that the DRV leadership in 1968 had been 'too eager to win the decisive victory' (OH 2010a: 8). The draft peace agreement of October 1972 unravelled in ways that the Hanoi Politburo did not foresee. The internal American divisions over the war were obvious to all, and it is scarcely surprising that the Politburo sought consciously to exploit them. Highly elitist and self-reinforcing, the Politburo was always prone to serious errors of 'groupthink' – the tendency of decisional actors to become defensive in their attitudes, and unwilling to accept evidence of policy failure. The decision to sustain the Tet

Offensive during 1968 thus involved massive unnecessary costs, even as the antiwar cause in the US was being strengthened. It would also be a mistake to imagine that the internal politics of the Politburo were unaffected by personal rivalries, such as that between Generals Vo Nguyen Giap and Nguyen Chi Thanh. The Politburo was not gifted with second sight. There was, for example, a tendency to see the Americans as somehow seamlessly and simply taking over from the French; this led to reluctance to recognize Franco–American differences in the early years, and arguably to a rather one-dimensional later understanding of *American* 'imperialism'. The Politburo's means of communicating decisions, especially to Southern cadres, was usually very effective, but it certainly was not faultless. Politburo communication failures were acknowledged during former US Defence Secretary Robert McNamara's conversations with DRV personnel in the mid-1990s. Above all, it should be recognized that democratic centralism – the key working principle of the Politburo – almost inevitably degenerated into ossified and enervating authoritarianism (McNamara *et al.* 1999: 125, 379–80; Luu Doan Huynh 2007a: 86).

We have already seen how it was possible for Ho Chi Minh to be outflanked within the Politburo in 1951. Another instance occurred in the period following the assassinations of John Kennedy and Ngo Dinh Diem, with the decision for a 'bigger war' to pre-empt possible direct intervention from Washington. To quote Lien Hang T. Nguyen (2006: 17), in 1963 'the hardliners effectively silenced the more moderate Politburo members, most strikingly in the sidelining of Ho Chi Minh at the plenum'. The most common way of understanding intra-Politburo splits is, indeed, in terms of 'moderates' and 'hardliners'. The latter were able to draw on the rhetoric of embattled nationalism, tarring their opponents as willing to compromise with the forces of imperialism. The 'moderate' versus 'hardliner' split in the early years was overlaid by the rival positions of 'North-first' and 'South-first'. Until 1960, the consensus view among communist leaders was that the building of socialism in the DRV was the best way to ensure the eventual triumph of revolution throughout the country. However, the language of nationalism – involving accusations of abandoning the Southern revolution – proved a potent weapon for the cause of relative militancy. As the war developed, opposing camps developed in relation to particular decisions, often embracing policy stances which persisted over long periods. For example, responding to post-1968 American success in pacifying the countryside, one

Politburo faction wished to disperse communist military forces in the South, precisely to challenge 'imperialist' infiltration of the villages. Another faction argued that only a decisive military victory could shift the dynamics of the rural war in South Vietnam; such arguments eventually bore fruit in the form of the 1972 Nguyen Hue Offensive (Ang Cheng Guan 2004: 22).

Underpinning the internal Politburo splits were contrasting positions towards Beijing and Moscow. By the early 1960s, ostensibly 'pro-Moscow' and 'pro-Beijing' factions had emerged within the Politburo. The former, led by General Giap and Hoang Minh Chinh, tended to argue against 'hawkish' positions and to take seriously Soviet doctrines of coexistence with capitalism. The 'pro-Beijing' faction, in favour of swifter moves towards reunification, was initially led by Le Duan, who subsequently became a strong supporter of Soviet sponsorship. Soviet intelligence on the strength of the 'pro-Beijing' faction alarmed the Kremlin in the early 1960s. Periodic battles within the Lao Dong led to the arrest of 'revisionists' or 'anti-party' elements. These were often Moscow-trained bureaucrats, who supported Soviet efforts to push the DRV towards negotiation. Struggles over Soviet versus Chinese influence were linked to complex debates over strategy for reunification, with key decisions (such as those preceding the Tet Offensive) often following an 'anti-party' internal purge (Ang Cheng Guan 2002: 10; Nguyen 2006: 17, 26; Pribbenow 2008: 21; Radchenko 2009: 80).

Earlier chapters have traced the developing and complex links between Hanoi, Beijing, and Moscow. A few general points about Hanoi–Beijing–Moscow relations are, however, worth reiterating at this stage. First, the search for 'fraternal socialist allies' to support the revolution in Vietnam was always a little problematic for the nationalist cause. Bui Tin (1995: 52) later wrote that 'we were quick to condemn the regime in the South' for relying on Washington; but 'we did not then realize in the North ... that the Chinese and the Soviets were also foreigners'. Official Vietnamese accounts of the 'fraternal socialist allies' also mirrored subsequent shifts in perception and in post-Vietnamese foreign policy. Thus, in 1979 the DRV leadership claimed that Chinese support for Hanoi in 1971 and 1972 was given merely to 'mask their collusion with the US' (Ang Cheng Guan 2004: 68; *The Truth*, 1979).

A second general consideration relates to the degree to which Hanoi came to appreciate and consciously to exploit the opportunities opened up by the rivalry between Beijing and Moscow. It was argued several times in earlier chapters that the Hanoi Politburo – and, indeed, particular factions within the Politburo – became rather adept at playing off the two great communist powers against one another. At one level, the launching of the NLF in 1960 was designed to embarrass Moscow in the context of Sino–Soviet competition for the mantle of world communist leadership. Such tactics drew on a long history of Vietnamese ability to identify the asymmetric opportunities offered by relations with more powerful neighbours. Here, however, it should be emphasized that Hanoi's official line during the war years was that international communists should stick together. Any possibility of refusing help from Beijing and/or Moscow was rejected not only on pragmatic, but also on internationalist ideological grounds. Hanoi appreciated both the opportunities of the Sino–Soviet split and its dangers – notably the exposure of international communism to imperialist strategies of divide-and-rule. Taking one of many possible examples to illustrate this point: in March 1971, Chinese leaders seem explicitly to have rejected Hanoi's call for a united 'anti-imperialist front', designed to bring Beijing and Moscow together. Towards the end of the 'American war', Hanoi became to some degree isolated by the dynamics of global détente. The DRV leadership no doubt felt betrayed by, especially, the Sino–US rapprochement. The diplomacy of 1972 was conducted against a background of uncertainty about the commitment either of Moscow or Beijing to the cause of Vietnam. Nevertheless, as we have seen, the Paris Agreement was hardly a defeat for Hanoi; while Moscow's interest in continuing to sponsor communist development in Vietnam hugely influenced the post-1972 trajectory of Vietnam's revolution (Westad *et al.* 1998: 179; Ang Cheng Guan 2002: 78; Stolberg 2003: 255; Womack 2006: 2–3).

Finally, there is the question of communist 'higher morality'. The Vietnamese communist record is now quite extensive (Pham Quang Minh 2010). The tone of the official documentation combines triumphalism with a strong attachment to the 'higher good' of communist reunification. The outlook enshrined in much of this official commentary is very instrumental, as in Le Duan's apparent indication that calls for elections in 1956 (as required by the Geneva Agreement) were largely formalistic and geared to efforts to portray the DRV in the best possible international light. Cynicism, of course, is hardly the sole prerogative of communist governments. Tran Van Tung recalled Hanoi's perception that the US in 1968 wished only to begin peace talks 'in pursuance of their conditions' (OH 2010a: 4). What is striking here is perhaps less the apparent cynicism of DRV behaviour, more the willingness of post-1975 Hanoi to acknowledge the all-consuming instrumentalist morality of revolutionism – 'a flexible and wise diplomatic tactic' (to quote the Lao Dong Central Committee in 1967) 'to win victory step by step'. This 'higher good' approach of the DRV raises the issue of communist 'good faith' – already discussed in Chapter 3 – in the context of peace negotiations. Willingness to engage in negotiations tended to reflect pressure from Moscow (and sometimes Beijing) more than any inherent DRV eagerness to explore the chances of a negotiated settlement. The problems of making dogmatic judgements about the lack of 'good faith' on Hanoi's part, however, were illustrated in the 1990s conversations with Robert McNamara. In 1995, Nguyen Thi Binh – known to many westerners as 'Madame Binh', a communist representative at the Paris peace talks – discussed the politics of the late 1940s. She described Ho Chi Minh's 'attempts to reach out to President Truman' and criticized Washington's decision to 'spurn' them. Vietnamese historian and former diplomat Luu Doan Huynh indicated that some of the peace initiatives of the mid-1960s might have turned out differently if various misunderstandings about American intentions had been rectified. The implication in both cases was that Hanoi was acting in at least a degree of 'good faith'. A starker line in the McNamara conversations was argued by General Giap: 'I don't believe we misunderstood you. You were the enemy; you wished to defeat us – to destroy us' (McNamara *et al.* 1999: 16, 123, 279; Luu Van Loi 2000: 137; Ang Cheng Guan 2002: 18; Oliver 2004a; OH 2010a: 5).

Perspectives on the War: *Victory in Vietnam*

The most widely used official communist source on the war is the military history issued by Hanoi in two volumes in 1988 and 1994, and published in an English translation under the title, *Victory in Vietnam* (*VV* 2002). One slightly paradoxical result of this publication was the boost it gave to revisionist American history. *Victory in Vietnam* insisted that the revolution 'grew out of the political forces of the masses', but left no doubt that the revolutionary movement in Vietnam was *one* movement – directed ultimately from Hanoi.

Describing the communist military forces in the early 1960s, *Victory in Vietnam* (*VV* 2002: 149) eulogized the record in the South: 'With our experience in force building during the period of resistance warfare against the French and relying on reinforcements from North Vietnam, especially for cadre and technical personnel, elements of our army serving on the battlefields of South Vietnam overcame many difficulties' and 'developed innovative and effective methods for defeating even the most effective tactics employed by the United States and its puppets'.

The official history also gave some support to those revisionist historians who insisted that Saigon was making progress against communist guerrillas in the late 1950s, before Hanoi's decision to launch the National Liberation Front. Thus, official Hanoi referred to the 'ever-growing network of spies and traitors' working for Saigon, while the 'US–Diem clique forcefully suppressed the population'. It was admitted that a 'number of our local areas and units underestimated the enemy plot to establish "strategic hamlets"'. *Victory in Vietnam* additionally gave weight to the view that US-led pacification was making headway in the early 1970s. By then, '[m]ost of the cadre and soldiers of the regiments and armed operations teams operating in the lowlands were natives of North Vietnam. Going out to each hamlet and village to serve as local force troops and guerrilla fighters, living in the bosoms of the people of South Vietnam, wherever they went our cadre and soldiers were supported and protected by the people. Because our armed forces had suffered severe losses, guerrilla operations had declined' (*VV* 2002: 15, 110, 249). The translation of the official history was, in fact, encouraged by revisionist historian Lewis Sorley, who saw it as strengthening his thesis that the Americans were making real progress under the command of General Creighton Abrams in the early 1970s (Sorley 1999; Pribbenow 2002: xviii).

We considered the merits of 'lost victory', revisionist interpretations of the war in previous chapters. The main point here is that *Victory in Vietnam* does indicate a need to take very seriously the views that the Southern revolution was generally directed from Hanoi; that the Saigon government was making security inroads in the late 1950s; and that post-1968 US-led pacification was seen by Hanoi as a significant threat. Some words of caution, however, have to be issued with respect to *Victory in Vietnam*, as well as to other communist sources. As one might expect, none of the sources even hint that Northern direction was being *imposed* on the Southern population.

Errors and setbacks are acknowledged to a very limited degree, but the overarching tone of the official history is one of triumph and the inevitable crumbling of the forces of imperialism and feudalism. The desire to portray the revolutionary movement as unified under the leadership of the DRV is explicable in terms of the regime's need to establish postwar legitimacy.

Commenting on *Victory in Vietnam*, William Duiker (2002) drew attention to the continuity of the North Vietnamese military (the PAVN) from its early formation during the Second World War through to 1975. The official history noted how political action (organized around appeals to Vietnamese nationalism) and guerrilla tactics were used to counter greater military strength during both the French and American phases of war. Concerted military infiltration from the North began in 1959, expanding to include main-units in 1964. Close control of Southern forces – core, regional, and guerrilla – was a priority for Hanoi. *Victory in Vietnam* omitted any explicit mention of intra-Politburo disagreements, but left the clear impression that President Johnson's handling of the 1964 Gulf of Tonkin crisis greatly strengthened the hand of Hanoi 'hawks'. In July 1966, Hanoi was apparently prepared for up to twenty more years of war. Against this background, *Victory in Vietnam* narrated the Tet Offensive decisions as emerging naturally from earlier debates and military preparations. The official history emphasized links between the struggles in Vietnam and Laos – much less so, for obvious postwar reasons, Cambodia. Tet itself was portrayed as a victory, though problems were acknowledged in connection with the siege of Khe Sanh, as well as in relation to the depletion of communist forces in the South. The US was portrayed as experiencing a reversal with its invasion of Cambodia in 1970, though not suffering quite the losses that Hanoi would have wished. Fighting in Laos in 1971, culminating in the Lam Son 719 invasion by the Saigon military, was described as a severe defeat for Nixon's strategy of 'Vietnamization'. Much of *Victory in Vietnam* is taken up with issues of logistics and PAVN modernization and 'maturation'. One of the few admissions concerning the efficacy of US air power occurred in the context of discussion of the 1972 Easter Offensive, with associated problems of keeping forces supplied in the teeth of air bombardment. One of the more vivid passages in the official history concerned the December 1972 Linebacker II bombing of North Vietnam, when civilians 'saw with their very own eyes US "Flying Fortresses" burning in the sky'. For the authors of *Victory in Vietnam*, the 1973 Paris Agreement merely created a new opportunity 'to complete the popular democratic nationalist revolution throughout our country, and to move toward the unification of our nation' (Duiker 2002: xii; *VV* 2002: 52–3,132, 206–15, 223, 256, 271, 289–98, 324, 330).

Two final points about *Victory in Vietnam*: first, the history's authors constantly emphasized the need for military flexibility and innovation. Though the DRV formally espoused the Maoist doctrine of three revolutionary stages, the 1963 Central Committee decision in favour of 'bigger war' effectively abandoned the three-stage process. Later decisions were influenced by intra-Politburo politicking, 'fraternal socialist ally' pressure, and opportunism, rather than by Maoist orthodoxy (Nguyen 2006: 21). Second, *Victory in Vietnam* is marked by the absence of reference to Chinese and Soviet backing for revolutionary operations. The priority for the authors was to portray the victory as irrevocably nationalist.

Le Duan: Hardliner

On 21 July 1986, *Time* magazine informed its readers of the death from kidney failure of Le Duan at the age of 78. 'After Ho's death', ran the obituary, 'Le Duan (pronounced Lay Zwan) became a dominant figure in the Hanoi Politburo's collective leadership'. Le Duan 'was regarded as Hanoi's chief political strategist during the Viet Nam War; his speciality was organizing civilian populations for revolutionary warfare'. The brevity of the *Time* obituary underscored how little was known in the west about this major figure of Vietnamese communism.

Le Duan was born in what would become South Vietnam, more precisely in Quang Tri province in the French province of Annam, central Vietnam. He became a founder-member of the Indochina Communist Party in 1930, having been attracted to Leninist ideas while working as a railroad clerk. There were persistent rumours that Le Duan had Chinese heritage. Such rumours may have had an effect on his subsequent position-taking within the Politburo. Le Duan served at least two long prison sentences under the French, and advocated war with the US as early as 1956. Le Duan was identified in the late 1950s as the leader of the 'southern' faction in Hanoi – promoting the line which led to the formation of the NLF in opposition to revolutionary 'consolidators' such as Truong Chinh. An NLF document intercepted by American forces in 1966 recorded that Le Duan in the late 1950s had succeeded in giving Southern revolutionaries the ability to 'oppose the revisionist thoughts of simplistic peaceful legalism' (in other words, those communists who opposed direct action against President Diem). Le Duan, in the early war years, was generally seen as 'pro-Beijing', though he also maintained contacts with Moscow. He organized rural collectivization in the North, rescuing the programme from some of its earlier disasters. By 1960, Le Duan was First Secretary of the Lao Dong, subsequently emerging as the most durable of the first generation of communist leaders. He lacked the power to remake the Politiburo in his own image, but certainly promoted personal acolytes and became implicated in numerous factional battles. In 2007, Le Duan was officially commemorated in Vietnam as the 'bright example of revolutionary virtues'. However, at least according to a cable leaked from the US Embassy in 2011, Le Duan remained a controversial figure. He was remembered in some Vietnamese government circles as having improperly sidelined Ho Chi Minh and General Giap in the 1960s. Despite his early enthusiasm for China, Le Duan was also seen by many Vietnamese foreign policy-makers as ultimately having caused revolutionary Vietnam to become excessively close to Moscow (Latimer 1967: 5; Porter 1993: 103–5; Ang Cheng Guan 2002: 19–20; *The Guardian* 2001; Wikileaks 2011).

Le Duan is sometimes seen as the hardest of hardliners: the communist leader who led the campaign for the formation of the NLF; the chief agent of Lao Dong control of the revolutionary forces in the South, thus effectively the political head of COSVN; principal proponent of tough action against the Americans; leader of post-1975 authoritarian direction of Vietnamese society and economy; the southerner who consolidated Northern domination of the revolution. Yet, Le Duan was far from unbending. He switched quite happily between pro-Chinese and pro-Russian stances. Though an early advocate of 'bigger war' in the South, he embraced the possibility of post-1962 Vietnamese neutralization as, at least, a half-way house to reunification. Le Duan variously maintained that the revolution needed to learn the lesson of restraint necessary for 'prolonged war'; yet, he also favoured urban uprisings in 1968. In 1967, Le Duan celebrated the fiftieth anniversary of the Bolshevik revolution, declaring that Lenin had led the way for Vietnam by opening the possibility of socialism becoming a 'world system'. Le Duan advanced the distinctly 'unMaoist' argument that the communist parties in advanced capitalist countries had a vital role to play in leading world revolution. In 1970, he told Mao Zedong: 'We have been able to do a good job because we have followed the three instructions Chairman Mao gave us in the past; first, no fear, we should not fear the enemy; second, we should break up the enemy one piece after another; third, we should fight a prolonged war'. Le Duan's revolutionary thinking was presented in a range of guises, most notably a series of letters to Southern cadres and various party addresses. One of his major themes was the international importance of the Vietnamese revolution as 'spearhead of the world revolutionary tide'. He told Southern cadres in 1965 that they stood at the 'focus of the struggle between two forces – revolutionary and counter-revolutionary – in the world at present'. Le Duan consistently attacked 'legalism' – the complacent view that progress could be made exclusively, or even primarily, through peaceful political organization. Revolutionaries needed constantly to exploit 'the enemy's internal contradictions', aiming to influence US domestic opinion and encouraging international capitalist criticism of American imperialism. Le Duan's economic views combined commitments to agrarian collectivization, and to technological and industrial development. A Leninist to the last, he nevertheless promoted some economic reformers to the Party Central Committee after 1975 (Le Duan 1967: 7–8; 1970: 17, 208; 1975; 1986: 157–9; Porter 1993: 103; Duiker 1996: 222–4; Hanhimaki and Westad 2004: 221, 227–8).

The Viet Cong and the National Liberation Front

The preceding account of Le Duan's career provides a convenient bridge between discussion of the Northern and Southern aspects of the revolution. For the remainder of this chapter, we turn our attention to the South – first, to communist, then to anti-communist South Vietnam. America's enemy in the South was most commonly known as the 'Viet Cong'. The name, 'communist Vietnamese', had its origins in a deliberate attempt to deny the Southern revolutionaries the nationalist authenticity associated with the label, 'Viet Minh'. Nguyen Thi Binh (known to westerners as 'Madame Binh') later recalled 'Viet Cong' as a 'pejorative term, but many foreign activists came to hold up the name as a symbol of bravery worthy of emula-tion' (Appy 2008: 466).

The Viet Cong was the military face of the National Liberation Front, the organization set up by Hanoi in late 1960 to provide the focus for the Southern revolution. The NLF was not initially intended as a base for invasion from the North. Rather, the launch of the NLF was a result of the success of Le Duan and his allies in overcoming the argument that war in the South risked provoking the Americans, and that further consolidation of Northern socialism should be given priority. By March 1964, US intelligence estimated that around 40 per cent of the land area of South Vietnam was effectively controlled by the NLF. Under the 1963 'bigger war' strategy, the cutting edge of revolution in the South would continue to be the NLF, with Hanoi directing and supplying its military arm, the People's Liberation Armed Forces (PLAF). The purpose of the NLF was to undermine the influence of the Saigon regime – especially, but not exclusively, in rural areas. The NLF developed mass organizations, including the Women's Liberation Association, with around 1 million members by the mid-1960s. Such organizations, of course, included many non-communists, notably urban professionals who actually feared the class-based programme advocated by the NLF's leadership. Meanwhile, the job of the PLAF was to engage the South Vietnamese military in regular combat, in preparation for a general South Vietnamese uprising. The PLAF would coordinate guerrilla assaults against the Americans (Duiker 1993: 30–6; Brigham 1999: 54; Bradley 2009: 95).

The guerrilla units of the Viet Cong (or PLAF) – Oliver Stone's 'warrior ants' – have become central to the received mythology of the Vietnam War. Significant numbers of Viet Cong prisoners were inter-viewed by the Rand Corporation (working under the terms of research contracts for the US government), especially in the mid- to late 1960s; the Rand interview findings have become central to understandings of the communist cause in the South. One VC prisoner described the famous female PLAF regional commander Nguyen Thi Dinh: 'she wore black pyjamas, had a Colt hanging on her hip, and a large aluminium pot on her back' (Hunt 2009: 111). PLAF fighters were, for obvious reasons, often far from regularized but many did receive some kind of payment from Hanoi. To western eyes, the PLAF – main force, guerrillas, and irregulars – was a highly confusing organization. Discipline, in fact, was deceptively strong, with strict regulation of time, including that set aside for '*kiem thao*' (self-criticism sessions). Yet, most fighters, even in main units, were able to combine part-time active service with continued attention to their farms. As we have seen, the war in the South also brought together, in a way that was confusing to their opponents, Northern and Southern fighters. Duong Van Mai Elliott, who interviewed prisoners for the Rand Corporation, recalled significant differences between Southerners and Northern infiltrators: 'Both believed in the same cause, but the North Vietnamese had come to it more easily, having been brought up in the system and constantly indoctrinated in it. The Southern Viet Cong had come to it and accepted it as part of a more conscious decision' (Elliott 1999: 322; DeGroot 2000: 119–20; Bradley 2009: 108, 140).

The notion of Southern peasants consciously making the 'jump of no return' into the NLF fits well with the priority given to Vietnamese agency in the new Vietnamese scholarship. Many Southern peasants did make rational choices to side with the NLF on the basis of perceived self-interest and disaffection with the government in Saigon. Duong Van Mai Elliott (1999: 322) recalled Saigon in the early 1960s as 'unwittingly the best ally the Viet Cong had in recruiting peasants'. South Vietnamese soldiers accompanied landlords as they visited villages to collect back rents; 'officials conscripted villagers to build strategic hamlets and then coerced them to move there'. Many peasants were attracted by the NLF's mixture of nationalist appeal and policy of expropriating farms from absentee landlords. A former NLF cadre later described communist tactics in the Diem years: 'the communists are extremely clever. They never propagandize communism, which teaches that the land must be collectivized. If they did, how would the peasantry ever listen to them? Instead, they say: the peasants are the main focus of the revolution; if they follow the Party, they will become masters of the countryside and owners of their land, and that scratches the peasants where they itch.' Such accounts stressed peasant naivety over peasant rationality. Peasant motivation was often linked to personal circumstance, including intra-family quarrels. Peasant recruits to the Viet Cong also sometimes took the opportunity to 'rationally choose' service in a particular branch of the NLF. Around 1967, for example, cadres found it easier to recruit into the PLAF main units rather than the more vulnerable guerrilla groups (Race 1972: 129; Hunt 2010: 219).

Most detailed research on peasant motivation emanates from a combination of captured documentation, the Rand interviews, and local study of the Mekong Delta. Local investigation in the war era tended to illustrate the degree to which peasant circumstances varied across the territory of South Vietnam. Especially contentious here is the question of Northern direction of Southern forces. Clearly, conditions of war necessitated at least a degree of quasi-autonomy for elements of the Viet Cong, and (as we saw in Chapter 7) there is evidence of tension between Northern and Southern elements of 'the revolution'. Ho Chi Minh warned of splits between Northern and Southern revolutionists as early as 1957 (Ang Cheng Guan 2002: 23). Few commentators now would seriously hold the view that the Viet Cong were, in any meaningful sense, independent of Hanoi. However, some local studies have found evidence of some non-directed spontaneity in Southern peasant uprisings. A related point concerns the putative continuity between 'Viet Minh' and 'Viet Cong'. David Hunt (2009: 2) argues that 'the Viet Minh legacy alone' cannot 'explain the emergence of a revolutionary consciousness among country people in the 1960s'. David Elliott (2007: 110) found that rival local organizations in the Mekong Delta during the post-partition period were contending for the 'Viet Minh' label.

In the later war years, there is evidence of the rural appeal of the NLF running out of steam. This is traceable to war weariness, to the progress of 'better war' pacification, and to differences of perspective between cadres and regular peasants. It was also connected to the dynamics of land reform and to increased peasant willingness to resist communist-imposed taxes. If the promise of land expropriation and redistribution by the communists attracted peasants, it also led to wealthier peasants leaving NLF-'liberated' areas. The NLF land distributions produced a situation where villages tended to be dominated by self-sufficient 'middle peasants', who tended to be less than enthusiastic about committing themselves to violent revolutionism. Such peasants were also resistant to post-1975 rural collectivization (Elliott 2003: 2, 1007–12).

For many peasants, of course, support for the NLF was less a matter of choice (rational or naive), more a result of intimidation and *force majeure*. NLF takeover of a village could involve the intimidatory killing of local figures of influence, such as teachers. NLF leaders sought to foster a reputation for authentic nationalism and moral purpose. The organization's leaders agonized over the introduction of forced conscription into the PLAF, and were aware that coerced peasants might simply take the first opportunity to desert from their units or guerrilla groups. There were periodic attempts to purge the organization of cadres and organizers who terrorized the peasantry. Yet, intimidation, shading into terror, remained part of the NLF's repertoire. Many peasants were no doubt simply impressed by the degree to which the Viet Cong offered a credible and forceful alternative to the regime in Saigon. With many peasants assuming that the Americans had no stomach for a prolonged fight, at various times it seemed rational to gamble on ultimate communist success (Race 1972: 83; DeGroot 2000: 113–14; Moyar 2006: 94; Hunt 2009: 183).

South Vietnam: Balloon State?

It is often presumed that 'South Vietnam' – as at least a quasi-independent political entity, to which its citizens felt at least some kind of allegiance – hardly existed. Paul Warnke, who succeeded John McNaughton as Assistant Defence Secretary in mid-1967, recalled visiting the country soon after his appointment: 'The people I talked to didn't seem to have any feeling about South Vietnam as a country. We fought the war for a separate South Vietnam, but there wasn't any South and there never was one.' Warnke was referring to the degree to which the partition of 1954 cut across national identity. However, it is worth pointing out that South Vietnam itself had important geographic, historical, and ethnic divisions. South Vietnam combined the old regions of Annam and Cochinchina; it also included less-than-integrated ethnic groups, notably the mountain tribal peoples. It should also not be forgotten that many people in South Vietnam, at various times during the war, lived in areas controlled by the NLF. Such areas symbolically followed 'Hanoi time' – with clocks set one hour behind the time set in areas held by Saigon (Appy 2008: 279; Bradley 2009: 139).

Jonathan Schell (1989: 91) described the regime in Saigon as less an American puppet, more a 'balloon government'. Puffed up by American air, the South Vietnamese balloon lacked any real substance. If the Diem government was propped up by the United States, levels of dependence between Saigon and Washington skyrocketed after the escalations of the mid-1960s. By the early 1970s, the vast majority of the Saigon governmental budget was funded by 'Uncle Sam', through direct aid and via the US Commercial Import Program. American aid was designed to underpin and popularize the authority of Saigon. Melvin Laird told President Nixon in February 1970: 'As part of the war effort, designed to win popular support for the cause, we have followed a policy of raising the standards of living of the populace rather than austerity.' Laird worried about the willingness on Capitol Hill to add to the current annual aid total of $3.6 billion (Van Atta 2008: 236). The negative effects of the war in the countryside more than balanced any 'bought' peasant loyalty to Saigon; while, even in the towns and non-combat zones, the South Vietnamese suffered other effects of war – not least chronic and galloping price inflation.

Some qualifications nevertheless do have to be made to the idea of South Vietnam as a non-government, a non-country. For one thing, the 'puppet' in Saigon could be quite assertive and troublesome to the Americans. Diem resisted intense pressure to change his ways of governing. President Thieu fought his rearguard action against the Nixon–Kissinger exit momentum, to the point of sabotaging the October 1972 agreement and extracting extravagant, if ultimately meaningless, promises from the White House in January 1973. Saigon governments, whatever their degree of abject dependence on Washington, retained the ability to embarrass and even to defy their transpacific master. The US could play the 'coup card', implicitly threatening to connive in the downfall of a particular regime. By the same token, Saigon could play the 'stability card', pointing to the debacle which followed Diem's ouster in 1963. If there was a degree of mutuality in Saigon's relationship with Washington, South Vietnam did not come close to enjoying the degree of quasi-independence which Hanoi exercised in respect of *its* great-power sponsors. Here is Nguyen Van Thieu, recounting in 1974 his miserable experiences with what he was coming to see as a faithless Washington: 'First the Americans told me at Midway (1969) to agree to the withdrawal of a few thousand troops and I would still have half a million Americans left to fight with me'. Further cuts and withdrawals were succeeded by more promises. 'Then after there was a total withdrawal and no more air support, they told me, "We will give you a substantial increase in military aid to make up for all that ..." Now you are telling me American aid is cut by sixty per cent. Where does that leave us?' (Hung and Schecter 1986: 234–5).

Still, pending the final reckoning, the Thieu government determined to make the most of its ability to block and delay policy, as well as severely to embarrass its American ally. Thieu's 'long' ascendancy – 1965 to 1975 – had apparently brought to a close the chronic elite instability of the immediate post-Diem period. Thieu's very surviv-ability gave him leverage with Washington. However, to the bitter end Thieu remained entirely infuriating to his American sponsors. He would listen to anti-corruption harangues from Ambassador Ellsworth Bunker, 'make promises, then wait to see what would happen'. Nguyen Cao Ky simply admitted to American officials that most generals and provincial governors were corrupt; but, he added, 'corruption exists everywhere, and people can live with some of it. You live with it in Chicago and New York.' Thieu remained obdu-rately oppressive of student, Buddhist, and labour opposition. Women's group leaders, who protested against repression from Saigon and against the conduct of American forces, were arrested and tortured in the early 1970s. In deciding to stick by Thieu, Washington tacitly acknowledged that simple elite stability had its virtues, and that the mistakes of 1963 should not be repeated. The extent to which the Thieu regime failed to unite non-communist South Vietnam was illustrated by a statement issued by Catholic groups, led by Father Tran Huu Thanh, in September 1974. The statement accused the 'present, rotten dictatorial regime' of involvement in a startling array of illegal activities (Isaacs 1983: 323; Bui Diem 1987: 276–7; Herring 1990: 10).

If South Vietnam was a 'non-country', it was not – as the degree of non-communist opposition to the Thieu regime indicates – a country simply yearning for the glorious day when the DRV assumed control of a reunited nation. Nguyen Cong Hoan, a Buddhist activist imprisoned under Diem, described democratic stirrings in the brief period of civilian leadership which followed the ousting of General Nguyen Khanh in February 1965: 'Different groups like the students, Buddhists, Catholics, and the labour organ-izations found out that they could organize and demonstrate.' According to Nguyen Cong Hoan, the demands of these groups were 'for more democracy, peace, and social welfare' (Chanoff and Van Toai 1996: 85). As we have seen, the NLF itself contained non-communists, and had internal tensions between die-hards and those who looked for a negotiated settlement. The Alliance of National, Democratic, and Peace Forces emerged in the later 1960s as a kind of putative 'third force' adjunct to the NLF, tending to attract urban professionals with non-communist nationalist leanings (Truong Nhu Tang 1986: 134, 216). The central problem here, however, was that, squeezed between the competing authoritarianisms of Hanoi and Saigon, South Vietnamese democracy had extremely scant space in which to develop.

The American presence produced economic changes with complex effects on the outlook of the South Vietnamese population. Massive, US-sponsored construction projects contributed to the extreme militarization of the South, rather than fostering its independent development. Many locals served the various needs of the military, primarily the relatively wealthy Americans, but to a degree also the ARVN. Australian soldiers were apparently known to Saigon bar-girls as 'cheap Charlie'. The South Vietnamese economy became very dependent on imports coming through the corrupt Commercial Import Program, while also becoming highly service- and government-oriented. Means of economic exchange were dominated by the black market. A US report in mid-1966 estimated that up to 40 per cent of American aid and exports to South Vietnam was underwriting illegal economic activity. Economic pressures, corruption and repression no doubt led many South Vietnamese people to despair of their government, though we should appreciate that the extraordinary conditions of war created huge, largely urban, vested interests (Herring 1990: 10; Carter 2008: 202; Ham 2008: 278; Bradley 2009: 122).

Many South Vietnamese were horrified by the transformation of towns which adapted to serve the foreign military. By the late 1960s, there were around 56,000 licensed prostitutes in South Vietnam, many more unregistered. In the eyes of many in the local population, the non-communist leaders of South Vietnam seemed almost to have surrendered to the United States. Even as the first US Marines landed at Danang, an ARVN general voiced his concern about the prevailing tendency of leaders to 'let the Americans do it'. Non-communist South Vietnamese views of the American military presence are difficult to recapture. Nguyen Cong Hoan 'didn't hate' the Americans, but was certainly disturbed by what their presence was doing to the country (Herring 1990: 7; Chanoff and Van Toai 1996: 86; Ham 2008: 279). For many non-communist South Vietnamese, the American bulldozer-presence was unwelcome, but perhaps just about tolerable. It offered some transient opportunities, but ultimately was possibly seen as irrelevant to the working out of Vietnam's national destiny.

As we saw in Chapter 7, the US–South Vietnamese relationship was characterized by massive doses of mutual misunderstanding, resentment, and incomprehension. To the vast majority of Americans, who never set foot in the DRV, 'Nam' was South Vietnam. Returning US veterans immediately recognized the 'smells of this tropical country – simultaneously exotic, mysterious, and at times gross beyond description'. Chester Cooper, an NSC aide to LBJ, commented on Air Marshall Ky: 'A Hollywood central casting bureau would have grabbed him for a role as a sax player in a second-rate Manila night club.' American reports consistently expressed exasperation about South Vietnamese factionalism and recalcitrant unwillingness to respond to pressure. Perhaps the best role for Saigon politicians, as John McNaughton confided to his diary in April 1966, was to act as plausible scapegoats for an American exit: the Saigon government's 'total incapacity to behave themselves should amount to at least a minimum justification for our dumping them' (Cooper 1970: 210; Moore and Galloway 2009: 59; Harrison and Mosher 2011: 521). The US is often criticized for attempting to remake other countries in the American image. In the case of South Vietnam, in-country Americans seemed to be torn between 'can-do' optimism on the one hand, and world-weary surrender to the impenetrable 'otherness' of the Vietnamese on the other. Shuffling between the two extremes, American policy-makers created the balloon state and, in the process, made their own peculiar contribution to the Vietnamese revolution.

Assessment of the viability of the South Vietnamese state rests in the last resort upon an understanding of the outlooks and loyalties of the village-level peasantry. As we have seen, that loyalty was hard to find in the 1960s, when American bombing and firepower worked counter-productively and in favour of the communists. Villagers would be forcibly cleared from areas of South Vietnam to create 'free fire zones', where everyone remaining was presumed to be Viet Cong. Possibly 25 per cent of the rural population of South Vietnam experienced dislocation and/or refugee status in the 1960s. By the early 1970s, conditions had changed. Saigon's Land-to-the-Tiller reforms had an impact, as did security-oriented pacification and the US-led commercialization of the agrarian economy. One study of a village seven miles south-west of Hue found declining evidence of communist tax collecting in the later war years (Trullinger 1980: 176). A Mekong Delta farmer declared that conditions had been transformed from the days when the local peasants had to pay one quarter of each rice harvest to the NLF, as well as normal rent to the absentee landlord. Improved peasant security reduced the number of 'mung [green] bean, red bean' hamlets, constantly shifting their allegiance. US-sponsored agricultural assistance programmes, involving increased market incentives and the introduction of new rice strains, also produced some positive results, arguably encouraging the emergence of the anti-communist 'rational peasant' (Callison 1983: 285; Elliott 2003: 1, 16).

Despite such developments, it would be quite wrong to suppose that peasant loyalties decisively switched to Saigon in the early 1970s. David Elliott's Mekong Delta research yielded *some* evidence of shifts away from the NLF/PRG in these years. However, Elliott also maintained that the communists never lost their status as legitimate leaders across the whole of Vietnam. To the presumably considerable extent that nationalism remained a potent force, the memory of Ho Chi Minh as an authentic national leader was an important boost for the communist cause. Thieu and Ky had both fought in the Vietnamese National Army (forerunner to the ARVN) against the Viet Minh during the French war. The contrast with the background of the communist leadership would hardly have been lost on mass South Vietnamese opinion. The Land-to-the-Tiller reform, according to Elliott, was 'irrelevant by the time it was implemented', because of prior NLF land distributions and the inability of absentee landlords to collect rents in war conditions (Race 1972: 231–4; Isaacs 1983: 151–3; Elliott 2003: 1, 9). A major driver of the land reform was actually Saigon's desire to win elite support by directing (ultimately US-provided) compensation payments to landlords. Studies by Jeffrey Race (1972) and Eric Bergerud (1991) tend to show that the communists retained legitimacy at the village level during the whole war era. James Trullinger (1980) did find evidence of declining rates of communist taxation after 1968, but also concluded that peasant loyalties were not dramatically shifted towards Saigon. There is actually some evidence of peasant resentment at the unequal economic impact of agrarian commercialization in the early 1970s. Peasant loyalties remained ambivalent to the very end of the American presence. As already noted, many peasants drew their own conclusions about the likely trajectory for South Vietnam when American forces left, especially with DRV forces still firmly in control of 'Third Vietnam'.

Prospects for a non-communist government in Saigon depended after 1968 on the success of Vietnamization. The main focus of the programme was military rather than political. We noted in Chapter 7 the severe limitations even of military Vietnamization. If military

Vietnamization only half-worked, political Vietnamization did not work at all. American policy-makers frequently expressed the view that Vietnamization had to be political and economic, as well as military. However, the urgency of pressures on Washington to disengage helped ensure that the need for political and economic reform in South Vietnam was neglected. The Saigon regime remained corrupt, randomly authoritarian, and apparently uninterested in democratization. It was dependent on continued funding from the US Congress and devoid of adequate popular rural support. The balloon government did not deflate immediately when American forces left, but its vulnerabilities were obvious.

9

Endings and Reverberations

This final chapter will tie up loose ends. It will also consider the wider reverberations, in both space and time, of the Vietnam War. The following account of the period from America's exit to the fall of Saigon will again address the question of inevitability. Could the regime in Saigon have survived? Was substantial and sufficient support by Washington for the anti-communist cause in Vietnam after January 1973 ever a serious possibility? We go on to discuss what the war revealed about the wider structures of the Cold War, including the war's spatial repercussions on America's allies. Subsequent sections discuss the temporal reverberations. Here, we deal with the political development of Southeast Asia after 1975; the post-Vietnam War trajectory of US foreign policy; and the later history and end of the Cold War. The final section provides answers to the many riddles and puzzles of the Vietnam War.

The Final Act

The ceasefire of 27 January 1973 was preceded by North Vietnamese attacks on over 400 South Vietnamese villages. Continuing to bene-fit from the Sino–Soviet rivalry, the DRV took delivery of huge amounts of new military equipment from their communist great-power sponsors in this period. The new equipment was designed to match the US grants to the South Vietnamese military under the Nixon/Laird 'Enhance' and 'Enhance Plus' military transfer programmes. The 160,000 or more regular PAVN forces left in the

South after the ceasefire were outnumbered by the ARVN, but were supported even more efficiently from the North. Yet, Hanoi remained wary about the possibility of renewed American air intervention. Undertakings to repatriate the US prisoners of war were honoured. For his part, Henry Kissinger sought to preserve what was called an 'equilibrium' between the parties, even keeping open the possibility of American reconstruction aid to North Vietnam (Schulzinger 2008: 207).

President Thieu received more assurances of support from President Nixon, who ordered massive bombing of Cambodia in the first half of 1973. American aid to Saigon during 1972–73 stood at over \$2 billion. Thieu's governing circle was buffeted by the psychological impact of the US withdrawal, while PAVN assaults on South Vietnamese oil facilities further exposed Saigon's economic weakness in this era of massive oil price rises. Thieu reverted to resisting all compromise. In June 1973, Kissinger – now clearly leading US foreign policy as the Watergate crisis consumed presidential energies – agreed to a new ceasefire with Le Duc Tho; but soon ARVN and PAVN forces were again in direct conflict. Effectively ignoring American appeals to try to make the peace work, Thieu ordered a new offensive in the later part of 1973. Intense fighting for territory lost to the communists in the Easter Offensive resulted neither in significant gains for Saigon, nor in any miraculous return of US air support. The ARVN's former reliance on American air cover was now cruelly exposed. Saigon's own enhanced air capabilities were undermined by new communist anti-aircraft equipment, operated from bases within 'Third Vietnam'. Nevertheless, by the end of 1973, Saigon was more or less holding its ground. Graham Martin, who had replaced Ellsworth Bunker at the US Embassy in Saigon in June 1973, remained committed to Thieu. Ambassador Martin reported in late 1973 that, if the US managed to 'remain constant in our support', Saigon 'can hold without the necessity of US armed intervention' (Hung and Schecter 1986: 160; Willbanks 2004: 197).

The revisionist interpretation of the war's final act, as presented by Nixon (1985: 182) and Kissinger (2003: 550), maintains that Graham Martin was correct. If America had held its nerve, Saigon could have survived. In this perspective, the real betrayer of South Vietnam was the US Congress, with the final agony of Saigon linked to the development of the Watergate crisis and to Nixon's resignation from office in August 1974. Such arguments plunge us once again into a morass of what-ifs. Was there any realistic chance of the Congress, after 1972, voting to do whatever was needed to save Saigon? Only the most enthusiastic revisionist could argue that a post-settlement return of US ground troops to Vietnam was a possibility. However, might air support and a continued flow of funds to Saigon, combined with continuing efforts to use triangular détente diplomacy to isolate Hanoi, perhaps have done the trick? What if the watchman in the 1972 Washington night had not disturbed the Watergate burglars, and Nixon had remained in office until 1977? Could he then have used the comparative freedom of the full second term somehow to honour his promises to Saigon? After a brief review of relevant developments, political and military, we will offer some answers.

By the end of 1973, Ambassador Martin was struggling both to prevent major cuts in aid to South Vietnam being legislated on Capitol Hill, and to keep the White House's attention on Vietnam and away from Watergate. In late July 1973, Congress voted, over Nixon's veto, to curtail all funding for US military action in Indochina. The final legislation, much to the anger of its original sponsor, Senator Thomas Eagleton (Democrat of Missouri), allowed bombing of Cambodia to continue until mid-August. However, the Eagleton Amendment not only (fairly swiftly) halted the bombing of communist sanctuaries in Cambodia, it also made it extremely unlikely that there would be any US air support for the ARVN in the foreseeable future. Nixon, battling with Congress over Watergate, was in no position to order illegal bombing as he had in 1969. Also of significance for the future was the clash between Gerald Ford of Michigan (then the House Minority Leader) and the White House. Ford, reflecting shifting positions in the Republican Party, pressured a weakened Nixon into accepting the end to bombing in Laos and Vietnam, as well as Cambodia. The War Powers Resolution, limiting presidential discretion over troop commitments, was passed in November 1973. Before Nixon resigned in August 1974, Congress had effectively rejected a White House request for $850 million in aid to Saigon. Representative Patricia Schroeder (Democrat of Colorado) listened to a Pentagon official citing optimistic assessments from Ambassador Martin and responded: 'I have a feeling you believe in the tooth fairy'. Nevertheless, shortly after the presidential resignation, Congress did approve what seemed to many commentators the surprisingly large figure of $700 million in aid to South Vietnam (Franck and Weisband 1979: 21; Schulzinger 2008: 210).

On the ground in South Vietnam, Thieu's strategy was badly out of line with the changing conditions in Washington. Encouraged by the $700 million aid vote, Thieu embarked on a policy of 'economic blockade' of communist-held areas of South Vietnam. Vietnamese deaths by starvation increased significantly. Thieu's rejection of the enclave approach, and his increasingly unrealistic claims of 'holding everywhere', had echoes of the Westmoreland years. The policy left South Vietnamese forces – as it had left American forces in the 1960s – badly stretched and exposed. Thieu seemed concerned to send messages of assurance and determination to the White House, without fully appreciating the degree to which executive authority was now inhibited by a resurgent US Congress. Thieu's government also resorted to more domestic repression of non-communist oppositionists. The ARVN's chronic problems of morale and ineffective leadership persisted. Relations between the Saigon government and the Provisional Revolutionary Government of Vietnam (effectively, the old NLF) had now broken down. Under the Paris Agreement, the Saigon government and the PRG were supposed to work together towards reconciliation and elections. Towards the end of 1974, however, the PRG announced that it would not negotiate with Saigon 'as long as Thieu and his gang remain in power' (Hung and Schecter 1986: 276–81; Schulzinger 2008: 212).

The PAVN/PLAF Final Offensive, launched from Cambodia on Phuc Long province (north-west of Saigon), began in late 1974. The final campaign was marked by severe disagreements, adjudicated by Le Duan, over the required time schedule for achieving victory, and over the battle-strength of the ARVN. The failure of Washington to offer any substantive reaction to the taking of Phuc Long seems to have convinced Le Duan that victory was at hand. Prodded by Ambassador Martin, (now President) Gerald Ford vainly requested supplemental funding for Saigon. Hanoi's plans for a three-year offensive to take the South were now telescoped into what became the decisive push. Again, the DRV used its three-pronged strategy, attacking in the far north, the centre, and the Delta. The attacks did not stretch the North Vietnamese forces in the manner of the Easter Offensive; they took place over a longer period than in 1972, while more communist forces were now already in South Vietnam. Further last-ditch efforts were made by Ambassador Martin and by General Frederick Weyand (who had succeeded General Abrams at the MACV in 1972) to secure new American assistance to Saigon.

The ultimate assault towards Saigon – the 'Ho Chi Minh Campaign' – was launched on 31 March 1975. A species of fatalism seemed to be affecting Washington, with Henry Kissinger preoccupied with American international credibility rather than with the fate of South Vietnam. Melvin Laird recalled that Kissinger failed to spend 'a single day in Congress – *not one day* – in support of the (Saigon) government in those last months' (Van Atta 2008: 481). Congress rejected President Ford's request for a new substantial aid package. On 3 April, four weeks before Saigon fell, Vice President Rockefeller was reported in the *New York Times* as saying that it was 'too late to do anything' about the fate of Saigon. Thieu resigned on 21 April, declaring his implacable opposition to the Paris Agreement and fleeing to Taiwan. His South Vietnamese successor, Vice President Tran Van Huong, desperately attempted to form a government with which Hanoi would negotiate. Secretary of State Kissinger clashed with Ambassador Martin, who complained about the lack of either support or even direction from Washington. Saigon fell on 30 April, following frenzied evacuations from the US Embassy (Jesperson 2002: 442, 466).

The fall of Saigon was not inevitable, any more than American entry into the war – or, indeed, American defeat in the war – were inevitable. A return of American air power to support the ARVN in 1974 might have turned the tide, as it did in 1972. The point, however, is that any such return was so unlikely as to be almost unimaginable. Supplemental aid appropriations would have helped Saigon, and would have sent messages to Hanoi, but would have done little more than delay communist victory. The Ford administration was less committed than its predecessor to the survival of South Vietnam. However, attempts to blame the fall of Saigon on Watergate and the Nixon resignation are unconvincing. If Nixon had continued as president until 1977, there is no likelihood whatsoever that a congressional majority would substantially have raised military funding to South Vietnam, much less allowed the White House to mount new air campaigns. Hanoi and the PRG were encouraged by the divisions between America's executive and legislature; the Vietnamese communists had always seemed more prescient than the Thieu regime in reading US domestic politics. However, to *blame* Congress for the collapse of the ARVN again misses the point. Congress acted between 1972 and 1975 in line with its long-compromised constitutional power directly to limit executive discretion over US foreign policy. In very broad terms, Congress was still willing after 1972 to vote economic, but not military, aid to Saigon. The ARVN was still in no condition indefinitely to defend South Vietnam, much less to win the war, when America left Indochina; prospects for improving its condition as it fought the final battles were dim. Also significant was the continued failure of international détente to yield much in terms of help for the anti-communist cause in Vietnam. A major new agreement on aid from Moscow to Hanoi was agreed in November 1973. Moscow, as the military situation moved against the ARVN, drew Hanoi closer. A reunified Vietnam was seen by the Soviets as an important regional ally, with significant strategic assets including deepwater naval facilities. Nevertheless, there is some evidence (against the 'backing winners' analysis of Soviet motivation) that, right up to April 1975, Moscow saw Hanoi as vulnerable to some kind of dramatic reversal (Gaiduk 1998: 150; Andrew and Mitrokhin 2005: 13). Let the final words of this section come from a US naval commander, speaking to his crew as his ship left Vietnam for the Philippines. His address, recalled by journalist John Pilger (1989: 229), stands as an ironic epitaph for the whole war: 'Well folks, that just about wraps up Vietnam. So let's have a party and get outta here, so we can mosey on back to Subic Bay and get ourselves a *genuine* Budweiser beer.'

The Wider Cold War and Alliance Structures

Discussion of the international dimensions of the Vietnam conflict in previous chapters has tended to confirm some familiar, received views of the Cold War. The Vietnam War was structured around Soviet–US (geopolitical and ideological) rivalry, which by the mid-1960s was itself becoming complicated by the Sino–Soviet split. Yet, Cold War regional conflicts were never entirely explicable in terms of pure superpower rivalry. Apparent creatures, or satellites, of the big Cold War players developed strategies to maximize their leverage. In the case of Vietnam, this potential for leverage was enhanced by North Vietnam's ability not only to play off Beijing against Moscow, but also by its success in promoting to the world its role as a heroic anti-imperialist fighting nation. By the mid-1960s, neither Beijing nor Moscow wished to be seen to be deserting or undermining its communist ally in Indochina.

Nevertheless, and despite the quasi-autonomy developed by Hanoi, the Vietnam War was at some level a proxy conflict between the major Cold War rivals. The treatment of the Vietnam War given in the preceding chapters strengthens the case made by those commentators who see the Cold War as a contest for control of the developing world, though it should be emphasized that Vietnam itself lacked the obvious economic importance of some other contested regions (LaFeber 1992; Westad 2007). What is very striking in this context, however, is the degree to which the conflict actually became insulated from the wider great-power relationships. The war in Vietnam never came close to spilling over into a direct clash between the US and the USSR. A potential direct conflict between America and China was a little closer, and was arguably fended off by President Johnson's decision to rule out an invasion of North Vietnam. Nevertheless, in general terms, the history of the Vietnam War seems to bolster the view of the Cold War as (especially following the 1962 Cuban Missile Crisis) a controlled contest, with no one wishing to push regional rivalries anywhere near the point of world war (Lynch 1992). As Mike Sewell (2002: 10) has put it, Cold War leaders 'internalised Q's advice to that archetypal fictional Cold warrior, James Bond, always try to keep an escape route open'. The most dangerous inter-superpower flashpoints of the era of the Vietnam War – the 1967 Six Day War and the October 1973 US nuclear alert – related primarily to the Middle East rather than Indochina. In the case of Vietnam, China's participation in the controlled contest was always very difficult to read. However, as we have seen, even Beijing ultimately was prepared to accept the war in Indochina as part of a wider controlled contest. In its interactions with Hanoi, the Chinese leadership was also far more preoccupied with the dynamics of rivalry with Moscow than with any ideological commitment to Maoist revolutionary strategy.

The Vietnam War can be cited in connection with a host of possible perspectives on the Cold War. Though it largely proceeded as a controlled contest without imminent nuclear dangers, the Vietnam conflict and its associated military spending thus contributed to the 'security dilemma': the situation whereby the enhancement of one state's security leads to cycles of worry, insecurity, and rearming. The war, at least initially, supported American policy-makers in their self-image as defenders of small states against external bullies, just as it reinforced the Soviet self-image of anti-imperialism. The war was also of huge significance for the coherence of the two rival international systems, capitalist and communist (Halliday 1994: 171–4). We will now consider this question of intra-systemic, intra-alliance discipline.

The war had severe implications for American-dominated alliance structures. Among America's combatant allies – principally South Korea, Australia, and Thailand – there was huge sensitivity to the accusation that their military support had somehow been 'bought'. Clark Clifford recalled a visit to Asian capitals with General Maxwell Taylor in July 1967. The two found considerable degrees of resentment in Bangkok and Seoul, despite the fact that (according to Clifford) Washington was 'in effect paying Seoul twice for each soldier that went to Vietnam' through US aid to South Korea. In Bangkok, Pote Sarasin (former Thai Ambassador to Washington) treated Clifford and Taylor to a lecture on American ethnocentrism, declaring: 'Don't you Americans know that the Chinese and the Vietnamese have hated each other for centuries?' Travelling to Australia, Clifford and Taylor found Prime Minister Harold Holt 'extremely evasive' about future commitments to Vietnam, while Clifford joked that 'more people turned out in New Zealand to demonstrate against our trip than the country had sent to Vietnam'. Clark Clifford acknowledged that perceptions of severe irresolution, even among the combatant allies, was a factor in shaping his outlook when he became Secretary of Defence in January 1968. After 1968, Asian resentment at the dilution of American commitments to regional security under the Nixon Doctrine further damaged Asian willingness to assist the US in Vietnam. Thus Thailand, a major player in Indochinese security, significantly shifted its pro-American position in 1969 (Clifford 1969; 1991: 448–50; Kislenko 2003).

Other American allies met President Johnson's call for 'more flags' in Vietnam with varying degrees of nuanced or outright refusal. Among the non-combatant allies, France occupied a place made very special not only by the imperial history of Indochina, but by the nationalism of French President Charles De Gaulle. French proposals for the neutralization of Vietnam in the mid-1960s were welcomed by the DRV and the NLF, who advanced to Paris the claim that they were 'national communists', rather than in any sense agents of Soviet or Chinese power. Washington regarded the French initiatives, with some justification, as part of a more or less concerted effort to limit America's international reach. France's 1967 exit from NATO's unified command structure represented, in the context of the Vietnam

War, a massive rupture between Washington and the old imperial power. Other European powers were less confrontational than Gaullist France, making complex calculations of the costs and benefits of asserting independence from the US line on Vietnam. The centre-left government in Italy thus sought to blur its stance on Vietnam by becoming involved in the 1966–67 peace initiatives via contacts in Poland and Romania. In the Nixon years, despite widely expressed outrage at the Linebacker bombing campaigns, European leaders (including De Gaulle's successor as French president, Georges Pompidou) generally tried to repair relations with Washington. After 1968, as US forces disengaged, Washington did not seriously expect new countries to join the war effort. In the later war years, however, US–European tensions did erupt over US foreign economic and monetary policy in a context not unrelated to the Vietnam War. European capitals tended to blame international inflation on US war spending, seeing Nixon's effective ending of the Bretton Woods financial system in 1971 as emblematic of arrogant, but war-damaged, American power (Herring 2002; Nuti 2003; Schwartz 2003: 31; Zimmerman 2003; Ellison 2007; Martin 2011; Blang 2011).

The war put strains on virtually all of America's bilateral alliances. Canada offered a series of peace initiatives, designed to head-off further American escalation in the mid-1960s. These annoyed Washington and were damaged by intentional lack of clarity from the Johnson administration about its negotiating intentions. Canadian diplomat John Holmes recalled Washington as seeing Canada as 'a tiresome and self-righteous nag'. The lack of Japanese enthusiasm for provision of direct military support for America in Vietnam particularly infuriated LBJ in view of the direct benefits to the Japanese economy which were being derived from US war-related spending. In Britain, the Labour government under Harold Wilson tried to disguise its unwillingness to provide troops by proclaiming its special status as potential 'honest broker' in Vietnam as co-chair (with the USSR) of the Geneva Conference, responsible for overseeing partition. Though Britain had supported the Kennedy policy in Vietnam via the British Advisory Mission under counter-insurgency expert Robert Thompson, Wilson saw any direct commitment of UK troops to Vietnam in the mid-1960s as impossible in domestic political terms. The Johnson administration backed away from using economic pressure effectively to force British troops into Vietnam. In February

1967, Wilson became involved in direct negotiations in London with Soviet leader Aleksei Kosygin over a possible road to peace in the context of mutual (Washington–Hanoi) de-escalation. Washington failed to give the initiative – the so-called 'Phase A/Phase B' plan – its unambiguous backing. Recriminations over the 1967 failure continued to affect British attitudes as London moved to make massive cuts to its forces committed in the Far East (Logevall 1999: 160–2; Busch 2003; Dumbrell and Ellis 2003; Schaller 2010: 167; Vucetic 2011: 93).

On the communist side, the war was the occasion of a significant worsening of the Sino–Soviet split. Indeed, to the considerable extent that the war contributed to the deepening split between Moscow and Beijing, the Vietnam conflict may be seen as having had even graver implications for communist than for capitalist cohesion. In geopolitical terms, Vietnam stood firmly 'under the dragon' of Beijing, in the way that Latin America is said to be 'under the eagle' of Washington, and Eastern Europe 'under the bear' of Russia. Yet, neither Washington nor Moscow was willing to concede Vietnam to Chinese control. Despite the DRV's stated passion for international communist solidarity, Hanoi's coquettish shifting between Beijing and Moscow exacerbated the intra-communist split. We noted in Chapter 8 that Hanoi was formally supportive of intra-communist cohesion and that the Politburo appreciated the problems of schism. Nevertheless, on occasion, Hanoi's diplomacy did work explicitly to shore up the Sino–Soviet division. In June 1964, a DRV diplomat complained to Albania (a country then leaning strongly towards Beijing) that Moscow was not prepared to back Hanoi in the way that Washington was supporting Saigon (CWIHP 1964).

Nevertheless, at least within the Soviet bloc *per se*, the war did not create huge internal divisions. East European countries took the opportunity of peace diplomacy (as in the cases of Hungary and Poland in the mid-1960s) to promote a degree of diplomatic quasi-independence; however, such initiatives and channels were credible only to the extent that they led to Moscow. In East Germany, the complex popular and elite response to the war was structured around the Moscow-backed World Peace Council, which itself rapidly began to reflect Sino–Soviet divisions (Wernicke 2003). The romantic appeal of the Vietnamese revolution extended not only to radical students in America and Europe. The struggle in Indochina, after all, could be interpreted as a David and Goliath story, with small Vietnam fighting off the overbearing American giant. The implications of such an interpretation might appeal to those East Europeans who sought to emulate Hungary in 1956 and Czechoslovakia in 1968 by acting in defiance of Soviet power. Moscow sought to resist any such implication by portraying Hanoi's defeat of the United States as an indication that communism was a form of trans-national liberation. Governments allied to Moscow repeated the message. Here is Cuban leader Fidel Castro speaking in 1976 in support of anti-imperialist intervention in Angola: 'when a people struggle for their rights and their just cause they are also struggling for the just cause of others. In their struggle against imperialism the Vietnamese also fought for us' (Hanhimaki and Westad 2004: 526).

The Domino Theory and Postwar Southeast Asia

The new communist rulers of the unified Vietnam soon distinguished themselves by dogmatism and authoritarianism, as one-party rule was imposed even on groups in the South which had worked within the NLF. The burning of books at Saigon University in May 1975 set the stage for intense levels of physical and intellectual repression. Those urban professionals, who had seen the NLF primarily as a force opposed to the corrupt and repressive governments in Saigon, fared particularly badly. The fall of Saigon exposed those North–South (DRV–NLF) tensions which, at least to some degree, had been hidden during the war years. Hundreds of thousands of 'unification refugees' – many of the most educated and skilled people in the former South Vietnam – took to the high seas, some seeking a safe haven in China. To no one's surprise, American reconstruction aid did not materialize, while Vietnam remained affected by a trade embargo. However, the disaffection of large numbers of the South Vietnamese population from their new masters cannot persuasively be laid at Washington's door. The post-1975 denials of civil liberties and a rush away from capitalism created new social tensions, and caused potentially sympathetic international opinion to turn away from Hanoi. In 1979, the United States accepted an annual quota of 168,000 Vietnamese refugees. Elsewhere in Indochina, the two neighbouring 'dominoes' of 1975 – Laos and Cambodia – experienced severe repression, extending in the case of Cambodia to the mass genocide of imagined domestic enemies of the Khmer Rouge. The Pathet Lao takeover of

Vientiane led to violent retribution against the Hmong, the tribal peoples who had been organized by the CIA since 1960 and who had supported numerous American and/or ARVN raids into Laos (Hamilton-Merritt 1993).

Intra-regional relations after 1975 were dominated by the still evolving Sino–Soviet split, as well as by economic development in countries such as Thailand and Malaysia. By the time Saigon fell in 1975, the DRV had reacted to the Sino–American rapprochement by clinging closer to Moscow. Vietnam was drawn ever more firmly into the Soviet orbit, as Moscow emerged from the era of the Vietnam War as a credible winner. The principal occasion of Sino–Vietnamese estrangement was the growing tension between Hanoi and the Beijing-backed Khmer Rouge under Pol Pot. Between December 1978 and January 1979, border skirmishes with Cambodia and persecution by the Khmer Rouge of ethnic Vietnamese led to Vietnam's invasion of its neighbour. This led, in turn, to an enervating Vietnamese occupation of Cambodia, with Vietnamese forces not finally quitting Cambodia until after 1989 and the fall of the Berlin Wall. Persecution of ethnic Chinese in Vietnam provoked a second major refugee exodus, beginning in 1978. In February 1979, China launched a brief but very damaging invasion of Vietnam's border region, preceded by artillery assaults on areas which, in the 1960s, LBJ had been concerned to spare for fear of provoking a Chinese intervention. To add to the multiple ironies, Washington now found itself tilting towards a China which began describing the Vietnamese as 'the Cubans of the Orient'. Jimmy Carter (US president, 1977–81), in 1978, called the government of Cambodia 'the worst violator of human rights in the world today'. However, in September 1979, the US supported the right of the Pol Pot regime to continue to represent Cambodia at the United Nations. For Zbigniew Brzezinski (national security adviser to President Carter), the Cambodian–Vietnamese conflict was 'the first case of a proxy war between China and the Soviet Union' (Dumbrell 1995: 186; Schulzinger 2006: 16; Kaufman 2008: 164; Glad 2009: 238).

The Sino–Vietnamese War of 1979 is sometimes cited as evidence that the DRV had always been suspicious of Chinese power; that American fears of Chinese domination of Indochina were overblown; and that the Vietnamese revolutionaries were – after all – primarily nationalist rather than communist. China invaded Vietnam in 1979, according to a statement issued from Beijing, to 'teach Vietnam a lesson', following the action against Cambodia, persecution of ethnic Chinese, and Vietnamese border incursions into China. China's action also reflected feelings of ingratitude in the face of the massive aid given to Hanoi during the 'American War'. The invasion had been gestating for some time, however, and exemplified China's desire to draw a line against Soviet power in Southeast Asia. Journalist Nayan Chanda (1986: 261) reported on a Chinese leadership meeting of July 1978, when it was decided to act against Vietnam in order 'to weaken the Soviet position in the Third World'. Chinese academic Wang Hui (2011: 43) considered the Sino–Vietnamese War of 1979 'the true beginning of China's entry into the American-led economic order'. The 1979 war certainly drew on the mutual suspicion which charac- terized Sino–Vietnamese relations before 1975. However, we should resist the temptation to over-read the events of 1979 as a guide to understanding the preceding Vietnam War. After 1975, Vietnam was no longer able to juggle its great-power sponsorships. Vietnam was no longer the cutting-edge of anti-imperialism but, rather, a country with massive internal tensions and economic problems, faced by a hostile, Beijing-backed neighbour. Vietnam became a Soviet satellite. Regional Soviet power seemed to be waxing; the ethnic Chinese population of Vietnam appeared a viable scapegoat for regime diffi- culties; and aid from Moscow was more forthcoming than from Beijing. By the early 1980s, Vietnam was almost as much in thrall to Soviet aid as South Vietnam had been to American aid in the 1960s. The Soviet military base at Cam Ranh Bay (east of Dalat in south- central Vietnam) became a major strategic asset for Moscow; the base included ice-free, deepwater port facilities. Soviet visitors to Vietnam were dubbed 'Americans without dollars'. By 1990, shortly before the collapse of the Soviet Union, the gross domestic product per capita in Vietnam had shrunk to $114. Conditions began to improve only with post-Cold War programmes of economic liberalization, or *doi moi* (Luong 2003: 1; Olson and Roberts 2004: 277; Zhang 2005: 854; Lawrence 2008b: 177).

Beyond Indochina, the air of Southeast Asia after 1975 was not filled with the sound of crashing dominoes. The economic condition of Vietnam after 1975 scarcely encouraged emulation of its Sovietized development model. Japan moved to greater independence from the US following the promulgation of the Nixon Doctrine at Guam in 1969, and also after Nixon's 1971 announcement of new economic policies, including surcharges on Japanese imports. It showed no sign of being attracted to a communist model of economic or political development. More striking still was the trajectory followed by countries making up the Association of South-East Asian Nations (ASEAN). Set up in 1967 to foster regional security and economic integration, ASEAN followed a capitalist path. To some degree it drew on themes of Southeast Asian neutralism, but had always been close to the US and relatively hostile to the Soviet Union. Two ASEAN nations (the Philippines and Thailand) not only hosted major US military bases during the war, but also sent limited troop deployments. Following the war, the five original ASEAN member nations – Thailand, the Philippines, Malaysia, Singapore, and Indonesia – developed their anti-communist regimes, participating to varying degrees in the economic rise of the 'Pacific rim', even in what would by the 1980s be known as the 'Asia-Pacific economic miracle'. The so-called 'four economic tigers' – South Korea, Hong Kong, Taiwan, and Singapore – enjoyed major capitalist growth in the 1970s and 1980s (Gibney 1998; Mackerras 1998).

Some East Asian and Southeast Asian economies, notably South Korea and Japan, were boosted by war-related American spending in the 1960s and early 1970s. The rise of the capitalist 'Pacific rim', however, was linked to a complex range of economic and social factors, including state-led strategies, which went far beyond any plausible connection to the Vietnam War. To some commentators, the lesson of Southeast Asia after 1975 was that Vietnam was a special case and the domino theory always an illusion; the Vietnamese had been propelled by a unique kind of nationalism which was not exportable (Crockatt 1995: 251; Dallek 1998: 627; McMahon 2000).

However, the stability of the Southeast Asian dominoes has also been incorporated into the case advanced by Vietnam War revisionists, most famously by Walt Rostow (1995) in the context of his postwar disagreements with Robert McNamara. Reviewing McNamara's confessional memoir, *In Retrospect*, Rostow argued that Southeast Asian economic growth was directly linked to the stand taken against communism by the US – not only in Vietnam, but also in averting a communist takeover of the Sukarno regime in Indonesia in 1965. Quoting a 1966 speech of LBJ, Rostow maintained: 'In short, we certainly lost the battle – the test of will – in Vietnam, but we won the war in Southeast Asia because South Vietnam and its allies for ten years were "holding aggression at bay".' He quoted a remark made by Singapore leader Lee Kwan Yew in 1973 to the effect that the US presence in Vietnam had 'broken the hypnotic spell on the other Southeast Asians that communism is irresistible, that it is the way of the future'. Walt Rostow also did not neglect to point out that, as part of its *doi moi* post-Cold War reorientation, Vietnam itself became a member of ASEAN in 1995 (Rostow 1996: 467–8, 469). Rostow's case may be linked to the 'hard' revisionist argument made by Michael McCann (2006). McCann argues not only that the US presence in Vietnam kept Indonesia out of the communist camp in the mid-1960s, but also that the US-sponsored ASEAN framework prevented Thailand, in particular, from moving towards communism after 1975. While Rostow was more concerned to defend LBJ than Nixon, such arguments can be extended into a defence of the Nixon Doctrine, announced in 1969. The new American policies encouraged regional self-reliance and did not amount to an abandonment of Southeast Asia. The US supported ASEAN, while – in this line of analysis – American capital continued to underpin economic development in an Asian empire of what Francis Pike (2011: 733) calls American 'apparent beneficence'.

Various arguments may be mounted in support of this revisionist view of the regional impact of the American presence in Vietnam. During the Vietnam War, Lee Kwan Yew tirelessly reiterated to Washington the case that regional security depended on staying the course in Vietnam. In October 1967, the leader of Singapore told Vice President Hubert Humphrey that, in the event of a US withdrawal from Vietnam: 'there would be fighting in Thailand within one and a half to two years, in Malaysia shortly thereafter, and within three years, I would be hanging in the public square'. Lee and other regional leaders responded to the announcement of the Nixon Doctrine by urging Washington against turning its new commitment to regional self-reliance into a retreat from Southeast Asia. In 1972 and 1973, China itself joined the regional chorus of anti-Soviet voices calling for the US to remain regionally engaged. ASEAN reacted to the fall of Saigon by developing its idiosyncratic programme of defensive coordination, the so-called 'ASEAN way' – in the process, effectively replacing SEATO as the leading regional organization. Washington remained engaged at various levels and the dominoes did not tumble. Despite all the wobbles in the US Congress, American military aid to the Philippines tripled in 1973 (Haig 1984: 202; Lind 1999: 65–8; Turnbull 1999: 296–303; Sutter 2008: 78; Ang Cheng Guan 2010: 48; Pike 2011: 479).

Important qualifications, however, do need to be made to the Rostow argument. Regional anti-communist elites may have drawn comfort from America's presence in Vietnam, but can hardly have been very reassured by the American performance there. Walt Rostow's response to Robert McNamara relied on more than a degree of 'after this, therefore because of this' argumentation. It cannot persuasively be held that the US commitment to South Vietnam, with all its associated disaster and misery, was somehow *necessary* for the cause of regional anti-communism. Lee Kwan Yew was a special pleader, albeit an eloquent one. What was also missing from Rostow's analysis was a clear acknowledgement of the extent to which revolutionary communism in Southeast Asia was contained, if not actually extinguished, by sheer authoritarianism. Most of the regional regimes were politically authoritarian to various degrees. Thailand, perhaps the most unstable 'domino' after 1975, soon succumbed to repressive government – not as intensely brutal as the Indonesian anti-communist campaigns of the mid-1960s, but many miles from anything recognizable as liberal democracy.

US Foreign Policy

By the late 1970s, America's defeat in Vietnam was frequently cited as marking the beginning of the end of the (short) 'long cycle' of US global dominance which followed the Second World War. The disaster in Indochina seemed to have been compounded by weaknesses in American economic performance; by domestic social conflicts; and by apparent Soviet advances, notably the clear achievement during the Vietnam War era by Moscow of strategic nuclear parity. In the late 1970s, particularly in relation to the revolution in Iran, the US was commonly portrayed as a Gulliver in chains, repeatedly humiliated by apparently weak countries in the developing world. During the Reagan years, the US changed from being the world's biggest creditor nation to the world's biggest debtor nation. The rise of the US deficit reflected a range of problems, but was often understood as having been triggered in the context of borrowing associated with the Vietnam War. The war was implicated in increases in US labour costs, and in the early stages of rising American and global inflation (Calleo 1987; Campagna 1991). Not until the mid-1990s did America escape the declinist shadow which had taken shape during the later stages of the war. By the time President Bill Clinton took office in 1993, the Soviet Union no longer existed. The 'liberal idea' seemed to be globally ascendant, while economic boom – associated not least with the computer revolution – was on the way to extinguishing temporarily the fires of the federal deficit. Nevertheless, it is worth emphasizing that memories of the Vietnam War contributed strongly to the persistence of perceptions of American decline, even as the Soviet Union underwent its spectacular implosion between 1989 and 1991.

The most obvious effect of Saigon's fall on subsequent international history was seen in its impact on American foreign policy. In 2010, Henry Kissinger recalled the impact of the war in the following terms: 'It was America's first experience with limits in foreign policy, and it was something painful to accept' (OH 2010e: 1). The administration of Jimmy Carter (1977–81) consciously sought to build on the 'lessons of Vietnam', as well as to heal a sundered America. No longer would the US, as Carter put it in 1977, expend blood and treasure 'in a distant place on Earth where our security is not even threatened'. The war had been driven by misguided messianic purpose and an 'inordinate fear of communism': 'We have fought fire with fire, never thinking that force is better quenched with water.' Carter also consciously rejected Kissingerian *Realpolitik*, outlining in 1976–77 a foreign policy committed to human rights and moral values, as well as to a new awareness of the limits on American power (Dumbrell 1995: 4–5).

President Carter's early foreign policy approach was blown off-course by the crises of 1979–80: notably the revolution in Iran and the Soviet invasion of Afghanistan. By 1979, the era of détente had manifestly ended, with the Carter administration moving to a more orthodox, anti-communist containment-oriented foreign policy. The desire of Washington to disengage from Indochina had been an important spur to détente in the early 1970s. The ending of the war in 1975 – and subsequent conflicts between Vietnam, Cambodia, and China – were factors in the erosion of détente in the Carter years. Jimmy Carter's successor, Ronald Reagan (US president, 1981–89) offered a positive gloss on the recent conflict in Vietnam as the Cold War revived. However, the Reagan years were also years of considerable caution in the deployment of American forces, with Reagan officials (notably Defence Secretary Caspar Weinberger) extremely wary of military action in the absence of a dependable domestic consensus for such action. Secretary of State George Shultz worried about the US becoming 'the Hamlet of nations', constantly inhibited by memories of the Indochinese disaster (Dumbrell 1997a: 11–12; Schulzinger 2006: 191).

During the 1980s, despite the conservative tone in national politics, memories of the war – as conveyed particularly in American literature and film – evoked images of violence, often sexualized violence; meaninglessness; and national failure. The debates surrounding the construction of the Vietnam Veterans Memorial in Washington, DC (designed by Maya Lin, a 21-year-old Yale University student) illustrated the extraordinarily tortured nature of the war's legacy. Speaking at the memorial in 1988, President Reagan brought the conservative theme of betrayal right to the forefront of public debate. The lesson of Vietnam for Reagan was 'that young Americans must never again be sent to fight and die unless we are prepared to let them win' (Hagopian 2009; Hunt 2010: 203).

US foreign and military policy after 1975 was affected by public and congressional prudence about repeating the errors of the 1960s. A demoralized and introspective US Army was a major legacy of the war. The Pentagon itself evidenced no appetite for any ground deployment which might conceivably replicate the experience of Vietnam. US Army doctrine developed in the 1980s towards strategies for securing early, decisive victory. Wars of attrition were rejected (Jentleson 1992; Lock-Pullan 2003; 2008: 163). Understanding of the war was also profoundly shaped by the complex issues surrounding 'MIAs': US soldiers 'missing in action' and supposedly still held in Vietnam, or even Russia. The League of Families of American Prisoners and Missing in Southeast Asia became an influential force on Capitol Hill, and contributed importantly to the shaping of American attitudes towards Vietnam. Relations with the newly-unified country of Vietnam were shaped by prisoner issues (Hurst 1996; Allen 2009). Policy-makers declared that they had learned the 'lessons of Vietnam' – but it was far from clear what those lessons were. Efforts to develop tests for the commitment of US troops abroad – clear exit strategies, overwhelming force, clear and unshakeable objectives, dependable domestic support – seemed, if taken seriously, virtually to rule out *any* major new commitments. Was it a lesson of Vietnam that clear, well-defined interventions could succeed; or that such interventions would always lead to extended immersion in distant quagmires? How could the US calibrate its interventions without being vulnerable to a repetition of LBJ's limited war? To many in the US military, the war seemed to indicate the problems of charging soldiers with the duties of nation-building. Yet, did the war also not demonstrate that success for US policy in the developing world depended on the building of effective and legitimate political regimes?

George H. W. Bush, president from 1989 to 1993, attempted to define what had come to be known as the 'Vietnam syndrome'. 'What people mean', declared Bush in 1990, 'when they say we worry about a Vietnam, is that they don't want to put this nation through a long drawn-out inconclusive experience that had military action that just ended up with a kind of totally unsatisfactory answer'. The ending of the Cold War opened the way for Bush to attempt to bring the syndrome to its close. In preparing American opinion for the 1991 Gulf War, easily the biggest US force commitment since the Vietnam War, Bush sought to establish clear conceptual distinctions from the earlier conflict. The 1991 war would have clear and achievable objectives, notably the liberation of Kuwait from the Iraqi military occupation. Bush even insisted that something tangible – access to oil – was at stake, whereas the Vietnam War seemed to have been fought on the grounds of vague abstractions (Dumbrell 1997: 129; McEvoy-Levy 2001: 81–4).

The legacy of Vietnam spilled over into the post-Cold War era. The war records of presidential candidates continued to affect presidential elections. Bill Clinton, in the 1992 presidential campaign, promised: 'If I win, it will finally close the book on Vietnam.' Yet, the disorder in the Balkans in the early 1990s stimulated a kind of revised and transposed Vietnam War debate about the dangers of intervention, the perils of non-intervention, and the dilemmas associated with American nation-building. The Clinton administration finally achieved the normalization of relations with Vietnam, with President Clinton visiting the country in November 2000. In 1996, US Vietnam War veteran Pete Peterson became the first US Ambassador to the newly unified Vietnam. Clinton's own international outlook was fundamentally structured by his memories of the Vietnam War. Looking back from 2000, Clinton recalled that LBJ 'did what he thought was right under the circumstances. These decisions are hard. And one of the things I have learned, too, is when you decide to employ force, there will always be unintended consequences.' Yet, the famous 'lessons of Vietnam' remained stubbornly ambiguous. Les Aspin, Defence Secretary in the first two years of the

Clinton administration, mused publicly that many of the much-vaunted lessons amounted simply to a prohibition on limited war. He attacked what he saw as the cripplingly restrictive military doctrine of 'all or nothing', associated with General Colin Powell (Vietnam veteran and chairman of the Joint Chiefs of Staff, 1989–93). The Vietnam era debates – including the proper role for counter-insurgency in the repertoire of the US military; the possibility of effective nation-building; and the potentially counter-productive nature of US troop commitment in culturally and geographically distant countries – persisted well into the era of the War on Terror (Osgood 1984; Haass 1994: 183; Dumbrell 1997: 154, 180; 2009: 14; Dumbrell and Ryan 2007; Schulzinger 2006: 69).

Overstretch and the End of the Cold War

In September 2010, Ambassador Richard Holbrooke offered some public thoughts on the Vietnam War. A veteran of several Democratic administrations, Holbrooke had served as a diplomat in Vietnam and was a member of the US delegation to the Paris peace talks in 1968–69. Holbrooke advanced the view that the war had always been unwinnable: 'Those who advocated escalation or something called, "staying the course", were advocating something that would have led only to a greater and more costly disaster afterwards'. To paraphrase Holbrooke, America in Vietnam was bucking the logic of history, which at the time of the war was pointing to Vietnamese reunification under a nationalist/communist government. Twenty or so years after the fall of Saigon, however, the drift of history had changed. Holbrooke visited Vietnam 'a few years ago ... to host a business development conference'. He 'looked at the new buildings rising around us – buildings with logos familiar to all of us: American Express, Citicorp, Sony – and a subversive ironic thought crept into my mind: If General Westmoreland, who had died before these dramatic changes became apparent, were to be suddenly brought back to that very spot, he'd look around and say, "By God, we won"' (Laurence 2002: 840; OH 2010f: 3).

It is not easy to fit the Vietnam War into competing explanations for the result of the Cold War, and the literature on the termination of the Cold War has surprisingly little to say about America's defeat in Indochina. Explanations for the end of the Cold War tend to focus on events after 1975. Interpretations which go back into the earlier era include positive evaluations of the generalized policy of anti-communist containment, seeing containment as a strategy which pushed back Soviet aggression, exposing structural weaknesses in the Soviet system. As we saw in Chapter 1, Michael Lind (1999: 256) defended the Vietnam War as 'a battle that could hardly be avoided', despite serious mistakes in America's conduct of the war. Other defenders of containment, such as John Lewis Gaddis (2007: 168–71), tend to see the Vietnam War as part of what went wrong with America's application of the doctrine. As we saw above, the parlous state of Vietnam after 1975 arguably contributed to communism's reputation for economic under-performance. Nevertheless, the integration of the Vietnam War into generalized explanations for the end of the Cold War remains problematic. A relevant consideration here is that the bulk of 'end of the Cold War' literature relates to Europe rather than Asia. According to Bruce Cumings (1992: 94) the East Asian Cold War – Korea excepted – ended in the mid-1970s with the fall of Saigon and the US opening to China. In this version of history, the Sino–US rapprochement and the economic reforms of Deng Xiaoping were the crucial events for the region, forming the backdrop to the kind of scene recounted by Richard Holbrooke in 2010. The rapprochement, of course, was fashioned against the background of the Vietnam conflict and was intimately linked to the circumstances of the war.

However, it is rather unconvincing either to explain Asia's Cold War entirely in terms of developments in Chinese foreign and economic policy, or, indeed, to trace those developments in an uninterrupted line back to the war. Such a Sino-centric interpretation for one thing greatly underplays Soviet regional influence in the wake of the fall of Saigon. Nevertheless, it is the case that East Asia generally, and the Vietnam War in particular, fit rather uneasily with narratives of the Cold War's end which centre on the relationship between Moscow and the administrations of Ronald Reagan and George H. W. Bush. Rather than either containment or the Europe–Asia split, we will concentrate now on another important factor in understanding the end of the Cold War: the concept of 'overstretch'.

The idea that American policy in Vietnam derived from imperial hubris – part of humanity's 'march of folly' – is familiar and, indeed, quite persuasive (Tuchman 1985). Cavalier over-confidence – along with excessive faith in American technology, rationality and exportable goodwill – defined the world of the 'best and brightest'. Here is Adam Yarmolinsky, special assistant to Robert McNamara: 'all we were going to have to do was send one of our Green Berets out into the woods to do battle with one of their crack guerrilla fighters and they would have a clean fight, and the best man would win and they would get together and start curing all the villagers of smallpox' (Charlton and Moncrieff 1989: 60–1). Loren Baritz (1985: 54) put the point well: 'our national myth showed us that we were good, our technology made us strong, and our bureaucracy gave us standard operating procedures. It was not a winning combination.' In Vietnam, America became overstretched to the point of absurdity in defence of a country of little direct relevance to American security. It lost 'credibility' precisely because of this over-extension. Thus is the way of imperial overreach and the rise and fall of great empires (Kennedy 1989; Arrighi 2010: 27).

Nevertheless, overstretch in Vietnam clearly did not lead to America's defeat in the Cold War. After 1975, as we have seen, the United States was wisely cautious about consensus-breaking military engagements. For many years after 1975 – indeed, into the twenty-first century – America's enemies, with some justification, saw Washington as hobbled by memories of Vietnam. As Fred Halliday (1983: 90) put it, the defeat in Vietnam 'left the imperial consciousness numbed and defensive'. However, far from abdicating their international responsibilities, the US foreign policy managers of the late 1970s accepted limits on American power, thereby avoiding crippling overstretch. Stepping back from the Cold War was sensible policy. As already noted, when the Cold War revived in the late 1970s, and even during the Reagan years, caution, at least about actual troop deployments, persisted. Ten years or so following the collapse of global détente, the Soviet Union, rather than the United States, seemed to be experiencing overstretch.

The fall of Saigon led to the incorporation of Vietnam into the Council of Mutual Economic Assistance (CMEA), the Soviet-led bloc which also included Cuba. Moscow saw the fall of Saigon as forcing American leaders to recognize the parity of superpower capabilities or 'correlation of forces', as the concept of parity was described by Soviet think-tanks. During the later 1970s, there developed a debate among Kremlin leaders between defenders of détente and those who wished to use Hanoi's victory as a springboard for new revolutionary waves in Asia, Africa and even Latin America. With the Soviet leader,

Leonid Brezhnev, increasingly infirm, power flowed to the intelligence community. Yuri Andropov, head of the Soviet security and intelligence service (KGB), saw Moscow as winning the struggle for the developing world over its demoralized 'main adversary' in Washington (Wohlforth 1993: 207–8; Kissinger 1994: 698; Andrew and Mitrokhin 2005: 16, 23). Andropov pressed successfully for a reinvigoration of Soviet involvement in developing world revolutionary movements. The ensuing Soviet and Cuban adventurism in the developing world provided the staple of global politics during the later phases of the Cold War. Regional conflicts in Africa and Central America had local origins and reflected severe tensions between popular movements and (often US-backed) repressive governments. In Washington in the Carter years – for example, in relation to the Nicaraguan revolution of 1979 – 'regionalist' analysis clashed with a 'globalist' focus on the Soviet role in these conflicts. Much of the Reagan administration's early foreign policy was predicated on the existence of hostile Soviet activity in Central America; yet, the Reaganites preferred covert action to anything which might be interpreted as 'another Vietnam'. Thus did the new Soviet activism feed into complex regional conditions, complicating and compromising the KGB strategy – which was, in turn, conducted against the background of a fatally weakening Soviet economic base. Meanwhile, commitments associated with the maintenance of the CMEA further drained Soviet resources (Saull 2001: 165–6).

The Soviet invasion and occupation of Afghanistan (1979–89) took overstretch to a new level. George Herring, distinguished orthodox historian of the Vietnam War, drew a direct link between post-1975 Soviet emboldening and the Afghan invasion: 'Historically as hostile to foreign invaders as Vietnam, Afghanistan became the Soviet Union's Vietnam, exhausting its money and manpower and eventually contributing to its collapse' (Herring 2004: 21). The Soviet invasion of Afghanistan, undertaken in the context of the Shah's fall in Iran and the rise of radical Islam, had complex dimensions which were unconnected to the conflict in Vietnam. The initial invasion was a response to a call from the client government in Kabul for assistance following an uprising in Herat (in the north-west of Afghanistan, towards the Iranian border) in March 1979. Direct connection with post-fall-of-Saigon Soviet emboldening is tenuous at best. However, there were other links with the earlier war. Charlie Wilson, the US congressman who organized support for the anti-Soviet *mujahedin* on

Capitol Hill, declared: 'There were 58,000 dead in Vietnam, and we owe the Russians one'. Though on a much smaller scale than America's Vietnam War, the Soviet Union's Afghanistan War showed many similarities: notably, in respect of the difficulty of conceptualizing the nature of the conflict, and the links between its military and political dimensions. The Afghanistan conflict stimulated less obvious domestic discontent, but ultimately had more profound consequences for the USSR than the Vietnam War had for America. As Moscow sought to adjust to the prospects of defeat in Afghanistan, parallels with the Vietnam War were commonly drawn within the Soviet Union itself. International history produces some fearful symmetries (Crile 2002: 411; Braithwaite 2011: 114, 331–3)

Interpreting the War

Alongside its tracing of the main events of the war, this book has tried to outline the way scholarly understanding of the war has shifted over the years. In this final section, we will review the dialectic of orthodoxy and revisionism, and try to provide some brief answers to the numerous questions raised in previous chapters. First, by way of illustrating the dynamic nature of war interpretation, we will consider the changing reputations of the four American presidents most associated with the war, along with those nine individuals (Edward Lansdale, Ngo Dinh Diem, Walt Rostow, Eugene McCarthy, Frank Church, Tom Hayden, William Westmoreland, Ho Chi Minh, and Le Duan) whose war experiences we have consciously paused to discuss and evaluate.

President Eisenhower combined neo-colonialist attitudes towards Indochina with the pragmatic good sense of a man with military command experience. Though Eisenhower persisted with a questionable commitment to the importance of a non-communist South Vietnam to American security, it would be wrong to hold Ike accountable for the slide into disaster. John Kennedy deepened and further militarized the commitment to Saigon, but probably would not have gone on fully to Americanize the war in the manner of his successor. Yet, presidential failure to save Diem in November 1963 was, as JFK himself seems vaguely to have apprehended in his taped reflections, near-catastrophic. Lyndon Johnson did do what he thought was right. He was concerned to protect the Great Society, but more importantly accepted conventional wisdom about the need to contain communism in Vietnam. Johnson was not trapped in a bubble of self-reinforcing advice. LBJ could be parochial in his attitudes, but he was constantly aware of the international, great-power context of the war. However, LBJ's whole approach to the war was confused, utterly agonized and ultimately indefensible. President Nixon's handling of the war was characterized by cynicism, personal irresponsibility, and excessive preoccupation with the preservation of American international 'credibility'.

Edward Lansdale seems, today, a more substantial figure than the naive 'quiet American' stereotype would suggest. Lansdale's ideas should have been taken more seriously by Washington, though these ideas did embody the characteristic vice of wishful thinking. President Diem was no less a nationalist and no more a democrat than the members of the Hanoi Politburo. However, the war might have developed in a very different way if he had survived into the later 1960s. Walt Rostow emerges from recent scholarship not as a cynical manipulator, but still as a dogmatic and inflexible adviser to President Johnson. Of the three antiwar figures that we have considered as individuals, today, Eugene McCarthy seems the least impressive. In retrospect, he does not seem a worthy embodiment of the hopes of 1968. Frank Church now assumes the status of an interesting and engaging figure, effective leader of the Senate doves with a real impact on the history of the war. Tom Hayden's reputation is rather compromised by his flirtations with non-democratic revolutionism. Even the writings of Hayden's maturity – witness his attempt to compare Ho Chi Minh with Sitting Bull – seem unlikely to survive as serious contributions to understanding the war. William Westmoreland emerges for twenty-first-century students of the war as a dutiful soldier. *A Soldier Reports* (like Lyndon Johnson's memoir, *The Vantage Point*) repays much closer study than it is normally given. Yet, Westmoreland's leadership must still be judged as unimaginative and inflexible. Ho Chi Minh was the father of Vietnamese communism, the father of modern Vietnamese nationalism, and, by the same token, father of modern Vietnamese authoritarianism. Le Duan, from what we know of him, was a more orthodox Leninist even than Ho. Yet, like the other DRV war leaders, Le Duan was able to think strategically and creatively, though he was also capable of severe error.

The framework of discussion in the preceding chapters has been primarily orthodox. The chapters have tended to portray the war as unnecessary, the product of American miscalculation and mismanagement. Chapter 6 offered a generally sympathetic account of the antiwar movement. *Rethinking the Vietnam War*, however, has taken some revisionist arguments seriously. In line with recent scholarship, particular emphasis has been placed on the international context, with both Vietnams being somehow suspended within the dynamics of the Cold War and the Sino–Soviet split. Such an interpretation has tended to be associated with revisionist historians, though there is no organic connection between interpretative internationalism and historiographical revisionism. My discussion has, however, embraced elements of revisionist interpretations of Diem, of the nature of Vietnamese communism, and of the post-1968 'better war'. Chapter 7 incorporated sympathetic discussion of the counter-insurgency brand of revisionist scholarship on America's waging of the ground war. The book has also tended to be rather sceptical about the orthodox shibboleth of the absolute unwinnability of the war by South Vietnam and the United States.

In general terms, both orthodoxy and revisionism have their characteristic sins. Orthodoxy tends to dismiss military argumentation as somehow unworthy of serious attention. Though far less so than in earlier times, it also tends to romanticize and stereotype America's Vietnamese enemy. Some orthodox writers are inclined to exaggerate the degree to which the war damaged American purpose and social cohesion. The war *was* very damaging to America, but not on the scale of the Civil War, with which (as we have seen) the Vietnam conflict is not infrequently compared. Orthodoxy is also sometimes unwilling even to contemplate the possibility of some 'progress' being made at any stage of the US war effort. Of the orthodox texts considered in Chapter 1, Halberstam's *The Best and the Brightest* deserves attention more as a brilliant polemic and period piece than as a persuasive analysis. Gardner's *Pay Any Price* and Kimball's *Nixon's Vietnam War* remain extremely important to any sophisticated understanding of the war, though the former tends overly to stress the economic dimension of the American commitment.

The most striking feature of recent scholarship on the war has been the upsurge of revisionism. Of the revisionist texts treated in Chapter 1, Lewy's *America in Vietnam* is now noteworthy for the relative timidity of its arguments. Lind's *Vietnam: The Necessary War* is intellectually very strong, but unconvincing in its defence of LBJ and in the framing concept of Vietnam as something other than an American war of choice. Moyar's *Triumph Forsaken* is impressive in its scholarship, but compromised by its adherence to the romantic conservative myth of betrayal. The search for betrayers of the American cause in Vietnam has led in some bizarre directions. Jane Fonda's 1972 visit to Hanoi has thus attained, within the less reflective strands of conservative revisionism, the status of transcendent myth, with biblical Judas somehow becoming bound up with the liberal versus conservative 'culture wars' (Lembcke 2010). The popular-polemic wing of contemporary Vietnam War revisionism, takes the theme of betrayal to the point of self-parody (Jennings 2010). The hope for Vietnam War scholarship must be for some creative connection between the best orthodox and the best revisionist writings, grounded also in the Vietnam-oriented scholarship discussed in Chapter 8. Given the intemperate and present-oriented nature of Vietnam War interpretative scholarship, such reconciliation still seems quite remote.

Now to our answering of questions about the Vietnam War (or Vietnam's 'American War') posed previously in this book. The dates of the war are impossible to define with certainty, but are perhaps best understood as beginning with the creation of the National Liberation Front in South Vietnam in 1960 and as ending in April 1975. The war was part revolutionary war, part a war of anti-colonial independence, part a civil conflict, part a war against communist aggression, part guerrilla war, part conventional war. Constantly shifting and changing, the war was extraordinarily difficult to understand and fix in the mind. The United States became involved in Indochina for reasons connected with what was perceived to be necessary to contain communism and to protect America's hegemonic status. The US was fighting in Vietnam a combination of nationalism and communism: a revolution guided by Hanoi, but by no means entirely reducible to the narrow interests of North Vietnamese communism. The revolution depended on the support of Beijing and Moscow, though, again, was not simply reducible to great-power interests. Washington in the 1960s should have pursued the quest for a negotiated peace more energetically and seriously than it did; though it must be admitted that Hanoi showed little appetite for compromise. The Tet Offensive was a military disaster for the communist cause, but was (as is the common view) also a political success for Hanoi. The Nixon administration presided over an unnecessary and misconceived prolongation of the conflict. The United States lost the war, even if Starbucks and American Express did eventually open up in post-Cold War Vietnam. Efforts to resurrect 1973 as the year of victory rest on unrealistic assessments both of the Paris Agreement and of the success of Vietnamization.

The antiwar movement had some impact on the course of the war, but it is difficult to argue that it shortened the conflict. International protest, though at times impressive in its seriousness and sincerity, was disjointed and often lost in vapid revolutionism. The US Congress had a belated, and constitutionally proper, role in bringing American involvement in Indochina to an end. America's most important ally, South Vietnam itself, was abandoned – not so much by the US Congress as by years of executive mismanagement of the war. The failure by Washington, especially before 1969, to tackle the problem of the political legitimacy of the regime in Saigon was crucial. The DRV leadership was steadfast – though by no means either infallible, or free of internal dissension. The war was not exactly 'unwinnable' by the United States, and better decisions and better strategy would have made a victory more likely. Better American strategy would have included an enhanced commitment to counter-insurgency, the credible threat of invading North Vietnam, better coordination of effort, and a more concerted programme of Vietnamization – economic and political, as well as military. A credible economic and military commitment to the anti-communist Vietnamese following an American exit was essential to any long-term 'victory' by Washington and Saigon. Such a credible commitment, of course, was entirely lacking. A winning American strategy would have required more national will, greater domestic mobilization, more resources, smarter political and military leadership: in other words, more commitment to a cause which was, at best, of very limited relevance to core American interests. The communists made important errors in conducting the war, but had much more commitment, and more political ability to absorb military casualties, than did the US.

We have encountered numerous 'what-ifs' in our discussion of the war's development, and have not been able to resist speculating on them. What if President Truman had responded positively to Ho Chi Minh's overtures in the mid-1940s? What if Kennedy had lived? What if America had put more energy into counter-insurgency? The truth, however, is that all the counter-factual what-ifs are unanswerable. The war evolved as it did, with each side constantly adjusting (sometimes sensibly, sometimes foolishly) to circumstances as they developed, and changing those circumstances in the process.

American involvement was morally ambivalent. US hegemony and credibility were the dominant concerns of US decision-makers. When the communists took over in 1975, they brought a tougher and more authoritarian regime than had existed even under the various US-supported governments in Saigon. Defeat in Vietnam caused America to rethink. This postwar caution was beneficial to US foreign policy, at least insofar as it alleviated the kind of chronic overstretch to which the Soviet Union succumbed in its invasion of Afghanistan. However, it is impossible to argue with any degree of certainty that the communist success in Vietnam either hastened or postponed the end of the Cold War. From the American viewpoint, the war was unnecessary – a war waged as part of a misconceived effort to force distant people to be free.

Bibliography

Abshire, David M. (1981) 'Foreign Policy Makers: President v. Congress', in D.M. Abshire and R.D. Nurnberger (eds), *The Growing Power of Congress* (Beverly Hills: Sage).

Abshire, David M. and Ralph D. Nurnberger (eds) (1981) *The Growing Power of Congress* (Beverly Hills: Sage).

Acacia, John (2009) *Clark Clifford: The Wise Man of Washington* (Lexington: University Press of Kentucky).

Adams, Sam (1994) *War of Numbers: An Intelligence Memoir* (South Royalton, VT: Steerforth).

Adler, Bill (ed.) (2003) *Letters Home from Vietnam* (New York: Norton).

Ahern, Thomas L. (2010) *Vietnam Declassified: The CIA and Counterinsurgency* (Lexington: University Press of Kentucky).

Aldrich, Richard J. (2011) *GCHQ: The Uncensored Story of Britain's Most Secret Intelligence Agency* (London: HarperCollins).

Ali, Tariq (1987) *Street Fighting Years: An Autobiography of the 1960s* (London: Collins).

Allen, Michael J. (2009) *Until the Last Man Comes Home: POWs, MIAs, and the Unending Vietnam War* (Chapel Hill: University of North Carolina Press).

Ambrose, Stephen E. (1984) *Eisenhower: Volume 2* (New York: Simon & Schuster).

Ambrose, Stephen E. (1988) *Rise to Globalism* (Harmondsworth: Penguin).

Anderson, David L. (1991) *Trapped by Success: The Eisenhower Administration and Vietnam, 1953–1961* (New York: Columbia University Press).

Anderson, David L. (2005) *The Vietnam War* (New York: Palgrave Macmillan).

Anderson, David L. (ed.) (1993) *Shadow on the White House: Presidents and the Vietnam War, 1945–1975* (Lawrence: University Press of Kansas).

Anderson, David L. and John Ernst (eds) (2007) *The War That Never Ends: New Perspectives on the Vietnam War* (Lexington: University Press of Kentucky).

Andrade, Dale (1990) *Ashes to Ashes: The Phoenix Program and the Vietnam War* (Lexington: Lexington Books).

Andrade, Dale (2008) 'Westmoreland Was Right: Learning the Wrong Lessons from the Vietnam War', *Small Wars and Insurgencies*, 19: 145–81.

Andrew, Christopher and Vasili Mitrokhin (2005) *The World Was Going Our Way: The KGB and the Battle for the Third World* (New York: Basic Books).

Andrew, John (2001) 'Pro-War and Anti-Draft: Young Americans for Freedom', in M.J. Gilbert (ed.), *The Vietnam War on Campus: Other Voices, More Distant Drums* (Westport: Praeger).

Ang Cheng Guan (2000) 'The Vietnam War, 1962–64: The Vietnamese Communist Perspective', *Journal of Contemporary History*, 34: 601–18.

Ang Cheng Guan (2002) *The Vietnam War from the Other Side: The Vietnamese Communists' Perspective* (London: RoutledgeCurzon).

Ang Cheng Guan (2004) *Ending the Vietnam War: The Vietnamese Communists' Perspective* (London: RoutledgeCurzon).

Ang Cheng Guan (2010) *Southeast Asia and the Vietnam War* (London: Routledge).

Appy, Christian (1993) *Working Class War: American Combat Soldiers and Vietnam, 1953–1961* (Chapel Hill: University of North Carolina Press).

Appy, Christian (2008) *Vietnam: The Definitive Oral History Told From All Sides* (London: Ebury Press).

Arrighi, Giovanni (2010) 'The World Economy and the Cold War, 1970–1990', in M.P. Leffler and O.A. Westad (eds), *The Cambridge History of the Cold War: Volume 3: Endings* (Cambridge: Cambridge University Press).

Ashby, LeRoy and Rod Gramer (1994) *Fighting the Odds: The Life of Senator Frank Church* (Pullman: Washington State University Press).

Ashmore, Harry and William C. Baggs (1968) *Mission to Hanoi* (New York: Putnam).

Asselin, Pierre (2002) *A Bitter Peace: Washington, Hanoi, and the Making of the Paris Peace Agreement* (Chapel Hill: University of North Carolina Press)

Asselin, Pierre (2010) 'Using the *Van Kien Dang Series* to Understand Vietnamese Revolutionary Strategy during the Vietnam War, 1954–1975', *Journal of Vietnamese Studies*, 5: 219–24.

Asselin, Pierre (2011) 'The Democratic Republic of Vietnam and the 1954 Geneva Conference', *Cold War History*, 11: 155–96.

Bailey, Beth (2009) *America's Army: Making the All-Volunteer Force* (London: Harvard University Press).

Ball, George (1982) *The Past Has Another Pattern* (New York: Norton).

Banks, James and Paula Banks (1989) 'Kent State: How the War in Vietnam Became a War at Home', in J. Dumbrell (ed.), *Vietnam and the Antiwar Movement: An International Perspective* (Aldershot: Avebury).

Bao Ninh (1994) *The Sorrow of War* (London: Secker & Warburg).

Baritz, Loren (1985) *Backfire* (New York: Morrow).

Barker, Colin (ed.) (1987) *Revolutionary Rehearsals* (London: Bookmarks).

Barrett, David M. (1993) *Uncertain Warriors: Lyndon Johnson and his Vietnam Advisers* (Lawrence: University of Kansas Press).

Barrett, David M. (ed.) (1997) *Lyndon B. Johnson's Vietnam Papers: A Documentary Collection* (College Station: Texas A and M University Press).

Baskir, Lawrence and William Strauss (1978) *Chance and Circumstance: The Draft, the War and the Vietnam Generation* (New York: Knopf).

Bassett, Lawrence J. and Stephen E. Pelz (1989) 'The Failed Search for Victory: Vietnam and the Politics of War', in T. Paterson (ed.), *Kennedy's Quest for Victory* (New York: Oxford University Press).

Bates, Tom (1992) *RADS: The Bombing of the Army Math Research Center at the University of Wisconsin and its Aftermath* (New York: HarperCollins).

Bator, Francis (2008) 'No Good Choices: LBJ and the Vietnam/Great Society Connection', *Diplomatic History*, 32: 309–40.

Bergerud, Eric M. (1991) *The Dynamics of Defeat: The Vietnam War in Hau Nghia Province* (Boulder: Westview).

Bergerud, Eric M. (1994) *Red Thunder, Tropic Lightning: The World of a Combat Division in Vietnam* (New York: Penguin).

Berman, Larry (1982) *Planning a Tragedy: The Americanization of the War in Vietnam* (New York: Norton).

Berman, Larry (1989) *Lyndon Johnson's War: The Road to Stalemate in Vietnam* (New York: Norton).

Berman, Larry (1997) 'NSAM 263 and NSAM 273: Manipulating History', in L.C. Gardner and T. Gittinger (eds), *Vietnam: The Early Decisions* (Austin: University of Texas Press).

Berman, Larry (2001) *No Peace, No Honor: Nixon, Kissinger, and Betrayal in Vietnam* (New York: Simon & Schuster).

Beschloss, Michael R. (ed.) (1997) *Taking Charge: The Johnson White House Tapes, 1963–1964* (New York: Simon & Schuster).

Beschloss, Michael R. (ed.) (2001) *Reaching for Glory: Lyndon Johnson's Secret White House Tapes* (New York: Simon & Schuster).

Billings-Yun, Melanie (1988) *Decision Against War: Eisenhower and Dien Bien Phu, 1954* (New York: Columbia University Press).

Birchall, Ian (1987) 'France, 1968' in C. Barker (ed.), *Revolutionary Rehearsals* (London: Bookmarks).

Bird, Kai (1998) *The Color of Truth: McGeorge Bundy and William Bundy: Brothers in Arms* (New York: Simon & Schuster).

Birtle, Andrew J. (2008) 'PROVN, Westmoreland, and the Historians: A Reappraisal', *Journal of Military History*, 72: 1213–48.

Blackburn, Robert M. (1994) *Mercenaries and Lyndon Johnson's "More Flags"* (Jefferson, NC: McFarland).

Blair, Anne E. (1995) *Lodge in Vietnam: A Patriot Abroad* (New Haven: Yale University Press).

Blang, Eugenie M. (2011) *Allies at Odds: America, Europe, and Vietnam, 1961–1968* (Lanham, MD: Rowman & Littlefield).

Blight, James G., Janet M. Lang and David A. Welch (eds) (2009) *Vietnam if Kennedy Had Lived: Virtual JFK* (Lanham, MD: Rowman & Littlefield).

Boren, Mark E. (2001) *Student Resistance: A History of the Unruly Subject* (New York: Routledge).

Boyle, Peter G. (2005) *Eisenhower* (Harlow: Pearson).

Bradley, Mark P. (1993) 'An Improbable Opportunity: America and the Democratic Republic of Vietnam's 1947 Initiative', in J.S. Werner and L.D. Huynh (eds), *The Vietnam War: American and Vietnamese Perspectives* (Armonk, NY: Sharpe).

Bradley, Mark P. (2000) *Imagining Vietnam and America: The Making of Postcolonial Vietnam, 1919–1950* (Chapel Hill: University of North Carolina Press).

Bradley, Mark P. (2009) *Vietnam at War* (Oxford: Oxford University Press).

Bradley, Mark P. and Marilyn B. Young (eds) (2008) *Making Sense of the Vietnam Wars: Local, National, and Transnational Perspectives* (Oxford: Oxford University Press).

Braestrup, Peter (1983) *Big Story: How the American Press and Television Reported and Interpreted the Crisis of Tet in Vietnam and Washington* (New Haven: Yale University Press).

Braestrup, Peter (ed.) (1984) *Vietnam as History* (Washington, DC: Woodrow Wilson Center).

Braithwaite, Roderic (2011) *Afgantsy: The Russians in Afghanistan, 1979–89* (London: Profile Books).

Brigham, Robert K. (1999) *Guerrilla Diplomacy: The NLF's Foreign Relations and the Vietnam War* (Ithaca: Cornell University Press).

Brigham, Robert K. (2002) 'Why the South Won the American War in Vietnam', in M.J. Gilbert (ed.), *Why the North Won the Vietnam War* (New York: Palgrave Macmillan).

Brigham, Robert K. (2006) *ARVN: Life and Death in the South Vietnamese Army* (Lawrence: University Press of Kansas).

Brigham, Robert K. and George C. Herring (2004) 'The PENNSYLVANIA Peace Initiative, June–October, 1967', in L.C. Gardner and T. Gittinger (eds), *The Search for Peace in Vietnam, 1964–1968* (College Station: Texas A and M University Press).

Brogan, Hugh (1996) *Kennedy* (London: Longman).

Bui Diem (1987) *In the Jaws of History* (Bloomington: Indiana University Press).

Bui Diem (1993) 'Reflections on the Vietnam War', in W. Head and L. Grinter (eds), *Looking Back on the Vietnam War: A 1990s Perspective on the Decisions, Combat, and Legacies* (Westport, CT: Praeger).

Bui Tin (1995) *Following Ho Chi Minh: The Memoirs of a North Vietnamese Colonel* (London: Hurst).

Bundy, William (1998) *A Tangled Web: The Making of Foreign Policy in the Nixon Presidency* (New York: Hill & Wang).

Burr, William (ed.) (1998) *The Kissinger Transcripts: The Top-Secret Talks with Beijing and Moscow* (New York: New Press).

Burr, William (2005) 'The Nixon Administration, the "Horror Strategy", and the Search for Limited Nuclear Options, 1969–1972', *Journal of Cold War Studies*, 7: 4–78.

Busch, Peter (2003) *All The Way with JFK? Britain, the US, and the Vietnam War* (Oxford: Oxford University Press).

Buzzanco, Robert (1996a) 'The Myth of Tet: American Failure and the Politics of War', in M.J. Gilbert and W. Head (eds), *The Tet Offensive* (Westport, CT: Praeger).

Buzzanco, Robert (1996b) *Masters of War: Military Dissent and Politics in the Vietnam Era* (New York: Cambridge University Press).

Cable, Larry (1986) *Conflict of Myths: The Development of American Counterinsurgency Doctrine and the Vietnam War* (New York: New York University Press).

Cable, Larry (1991) *Unholy Grail: The US and the War in Vietnam, 1965–68* (New York: Routledge).

Cable, Larry (1996) 'Don't Bother Me with Facts: I've Made Up My Mind: The Tet Offensive in the Context of US Intelligence', in M.J. Gilbert and W. Head (eds), *The Tet Offensive* (Westport, CT: Praeger).

Calleo, David (1987) *Beyond American Hegemony: The Future of the Western Alliance* (New York: Basic Books).

Callison, Charles Stuart (1983) *Land-to-the-Tiller in the Mekong Delta* (Lanham, MD: University Press of America).

Campagna, Andrew S. (1991) *The Economic Consequences of the Vietnam War* (New York: Viewpoints).

Caputo, Philip (1978) *A Rumor of War* (New York: Ballantine).

Carland, John M. (2004a) Book Review, *Journal of Military History*, 68: 655.

Carland, John M. (2004b) 'Winning the Vietnam War: Westmoreland's Approach in Two Documents', *Journal of Military History*, 68: 553–74.

Carter, James M. (2008) *Inventing Vietnam: The United States and State Building, 1954–1968* (Cambridge: Cambridge University Press).

Carter, Jimmy (2010) *White House Diary* (New York: Farrar, Straus & Giroux).

Castle, Timothy N. (1993) *At War in the Shadow of Vietnam: US Military Aid to the Royal Lao Government, 1955–1975* (New York: Columbia University Press).

Catton, Philip E. (2002) *Diem's Final Failure: Prelude to America's War in Vietnam* (Lawrence: University Press of Kansas).

Caverley, Jonathan D. (2009/10) 'The Myth of Military Myopia: Democracy, Small Wars, and Vietnam', *International Security*, 34: 119–57.

Caverley, Jonathan D. (2010) 'Explaining US Military Strategy in Vietnam', *International Security*, 35: 124–43.

Chanda, Nayan (1986) *Brother Enemy: The War After the War* (New York: Harcourt, Brace, Jovanovich).

Chanoff, David and Doan Van Tōai (1996) *'Vietnam': A Portrait of its People at War* (London: Tauris).

Charlton, Michael and Anthony Moncrieff (eds) (1989) *Many Reasons Why: The American Involvement in Vietnam* (New York: Hill & Wang).

Chen Jian (1998) 'China and the Vietnam War', in P. Lowe (ed.), *The Vietnam War* (Basingstoke: Macmillan).

Chen Jian (2001) *Mao's China and the Cold War* (Chapel Hill: University of North Carolina Press).

Chen, King C. (1975) 'Hanoi's Three Decisions and the Escalation of the Vietnam War', *Political Science Quarterly,* 90: 239–59.

Chester, Lewis, Godfrey Hodgson and Bruce Page (1969) *An American Melodrama: The Presidential Campaign of 1968* (London: Deutsch).

Church, Frank (1977) 'Ending Emergency Government', *American Bar Association Journal*, 63: 197–210.

Clarke, Jeffrey J. (1988) *Advice and Support: The Final Years, 1965–1973* (Washington, DC: Center for Military History).

Clifford, Clark (1969) 'A Viet Nam Reappraisal: The Personal History of One Man's View and How it Evolved', *Foreign Affairs*, 47: 601–22.

Clifford, Clark (1991) *Counsel to the President* (New York: Random House).

Clifton, Merritt (1989) 'Vietnam War Resistors in Quebec', in J. Dumbrell (ed.), *Vietnam and the Antiwar Movement: An International Perspective* (Aldershot: Avebury).

Clinton, Hillary R. (2003) *Living History: Memoirs* (London: Headline).

Clodfelter, Mark (1989) *The Limits of Air Power: The American Bombing of North Vietnam* (New York: Free Press).

Clodfelter, Michael (1976) *The Pawns of Dishonor* (Boston: Branden Press).

Colby, William E. (1978) *Honorable Men: My Life in the CIA* (New York: Simon & Schuster).

Colby, William E. (1989) *Lost Vietnam: A Firsthand Account of America's Sixteen-Year Involvement in Vietnam* (Chicago: Contemporary Books).

Colman, Jonathan (2010) *The Foreign Policy of Lyndon B. Johnson: The United States and the World, 1963–1969* (Edinburgh: Edinburgh University Press).

Congressional Quarterly Almanac (Washington, DC: Congressional Quarterly).

Congressional Record (Washington, DC: US Government Printing Office).

Converse, Philip E., Warren E. Miller, Jerrold G. Rusk and Arthur C. Wolfe (1969) 'Continuity and Change in American Politics: Parties and Issues in the 1968 Elections', *American Political Science Review*, 63(4), December: 1083–105.

Cooper, Chester (1970) *The Lost Crusade: America in Vietnam* (New York: Dodds Mead).

Coram, Robert (2010) *'Brute': The Life of Victor Krulak, US Marine* (Boston: Little, Brown).

Cornils, Ingo (1998) '"The Struggle Continues": Rudi Dutschke's Long March', in G.J. DeGroot (ed.), *Student Protest: The Sixties and After* (London: Longman).

Cornils, Ingo and Sarah Waters (eds) (2010) *Memories of 1968: International Perspectives* (Oxford: Lang).

Crile, George (2002) *Charlie Wilson's War* (London: Atlantic Books).

Crockatt, Richard (1995) *The Fifty Years War: The United States and the Soviet Union in World Politics, 1941–1991* (London: Routledge).

Cronkite, Walter (1996) *A Reporter's Life* (New York: Knopf).

Crossman, Richard (1975) *The Diaries of a Cabinet Minister: Volume 1* (ed.) J. Morgan) (London: Hamish Hamilton).

Cumings, Bruce (1992) 'The Wicked Witch of the West is Dead. Long Live the Wicked Witch of the East', in M.J. Hogan (ed.), *The End of the Cold War* (Cambridge: Cambridge University Press).

Currey, Cecil B. (1998) *Edward Lansdale: The Unquiet American* (Washington, DC: Brasseys).

Currey, Cecil B. (1999) *Victory at Any Cost: The Genius of Viet Nam's General Vo Nguyen Giap* (Dulles, VA: Brasseys).

CWIHP (Cold War International History Project) (1964) Woodrow Wilson Center, 'Minutes of Meeting between Tran Dinh Thu and Shpresa Fuga, 6 June 1964', Cold War in Asia Collection: digital archive (available via http://legacy.wilsoncenter.org/va2/).

Daddis, Gregory A. (2011) *No Sure Victory: Measuring US Army Effectiveness and Progress in the Vietnam War* (NY: Oxford UP).

Dallek, Robert (1991) *Lone Star Rising: Lyndon Johnson and His Times, 1908–1960* (New York: Oxford University Press).

Dallek, Robert (1996) 'Lyndon Johnson and Vietnam: The Making of a Tragedy', *Diplomatic History*, 20: 147–62.

Dallek, Robert (1998) *Flawed Giant: Lyndon Johnson and His Times, 1961–1973* (New York: Oxford University Press).

Dallek, Robert (2003) *An Unfinished Life: John F. Kennedy, 1917–1963* (Boston: Little, Brown).

Dallek, Robert (2008) *Nixon and Kissinger: Partners in Power* (London: Penguin).

Daum, Andreas W., Lloyd C. Gardner and Wilfried Mausbach (eds) (2003) *America, the Vietnam War, and the World* (Cambridge: Cambridge University Press).

Davidson, Philip B. (1988) *Vietnam at War* (Novato, CA: Presidio).

Dean, Eric T. (1997) *Shook Over Hell: Post-Traumatic Stress, Vietnam, and the Civil War* (Cambridge, MA: Harvard University Press).

DeBenedetti, Charles (1983) 'A CIA Analysis of the Anti-Vietnam War Movement: October 1967', *Peace and Change*, 9, 31–41.

DeBenedetti, Charles, with Charles Chatfield (1990) *An American Ordeal: The Anti-War Movement of the Vietnam Era* (Syracuse, NY: Syracuse University Press).

DeGroot, Gerard J. (ed.) (1998) *Student Protest: The Sixties and After* (London: Longman).

DeGroot, Gerard J. (2000) *A Noble Cause? America and the Vietnam War* (Harlow: Longman).

Deitchman, Seymour J. (2008) 'The "Electronic Battlefield" in Vietnam', *Journal of Military History*, 72: 869–88.

Dellinger, David (1970) *Revolutionary Nonviolence* (Indianapolis: Bobbs Merrill).

Dellinger, David (1975) *More Power Than We Know: The People's Movement Towards Democracy* (Garden City, NY: Doubleday).

Dellinger, David (1993) *From Yale to Jail: The Life Story of a Moral Dissenter* (New York: Pantheon).

Destler, I.M., Leslie H. Gelb and Anthony Lake (1984) *Our Own Worst Enemy: The Unmaking of American Foreign Policy* (New York: Simon & Schuster).

Dietz, Terry D. (1986) *Republicans and Vietnam, 1961–1968* (Westport, CT: Greenwood).

Divine, Robert A. (1997) 'Vietnam: An Episode in the Cold War', in L.C. Gardner and T. Gittinger (eds), *Vietnam: The Early Decisions* (Austin: University of Texas Press).

Dobrynin, Anatoly (1995) *In Confidence: Moscow's Ambassador to America's Six Cold War Presidents* (New York: Times Books).

Dommen, Arthur J. (2002) *The Indochinese Experience of the French and the Americans* (Bloomington: Indiana University Press).

Douhet, Giulio (1942) *Command of the Air* (New York: Coward-McCann).

Doyle, Jeff, Jeffrey Grey and Peter Pierce (eds) (2002) *Australia's Vietnam War* (College Station: Texas A and M University Press).

Duffy, Dan (ed.) (1992) *Informed Dissent: Three Generals and the Viet Nam War* (Westport: Vietnam Generation).

Duiker, William J. (1993) 'Waging Revolutionary War: The Evolution of Hanoi's Strategy in the South, 1959–1965', in J.S. Werner and L.D. Huynh (eds), *The Vietnam War: American and Vietnamese Perspectives* (Armonk, NY: Sharpe).

Duiker, William J. (1994) *US Containment Policy and the Conflict in Indochina* (Stanford: Stanford University Press).

Duiker, William J. (1995) *Sacred War: Nationalism and Revolution in a Divided Vietnam* (New York: McGraw Hill).

Duiker, William J. (1996) *The Communist Road to Power in Vietnam* (Boulder: Westview).

Duiker, William J. (1997) 'Hanoi's Response to American Policy, 1961–1965: Crossed Signals?', in L.C. Gardner and T. Gittinger (eds), *Vietnam: The Early Decisions* (Austin: University of Texas Press).

Duiker, William J. (2000) *Ho Chi Minh* (New York: Hyperion).

Duiker, William J. (2002) 'Foreword', in Merle L. Pribbenow (trans.), *Victory in Vietnam: The Official History of the People's Army of Vietnam* (Lawrence: University Press of Kansas).

Dumbrell, John (ed.) (1989a) *Vietnam and the Antiwar Movement: An International Perspective* (Aldershot: Avebury).

Dumbrell, John (1989b) 'Congress and the Antiwar Movement', in J. Dumbrell (ed.), *Vietnam and the Antiwar Movement: An International Perspective* (Aldershot: Avebury).

Dumbrell, John (1992) *Vietnam: American Involvement at Home and Abroad* (Keele: British Association for American Studies).

Dumbrell, John (1995) *The Carter Presidency: A Reevaluation* (Manchester: Manchester University Press).

Dumbrell, John (1996) 'The Johnson Administration and the British Labour Government: Vietnam, the Pound and East of Suez', *Journal of American Studies*, 30: 111–31.

Dumbrell, John (1997a) *American Foreign Policy: Carter to Clinton* (Basingstoke: Macmillan).

Dumbrell, John (with David Barrett) (1997b) *The Making of US Foreign Policy* (Manchester: Manchester University Press).

Dumbrell, John (2004) *President Lyndon Johnson and Soviet Communism* (Manchester: Manchester University Press).

Dumbrell, John (2009) *Clinton's Foreign Policy: Between the Bushes* (London: Routledge).

Dumbrell, John and Sylvia Ellis (2003) 'British Involvement in Vietnam Peace Initiatives, 1966–1967: Marigolds, Sunflowers and "Kosygin Week"', *Diplomatic History*, 27: 113–49.

Dumbrell, John and David Ryan (eds) (2007) *Vietnam in Iraq: Tactics, Lessons, Legacies, and Ghosts* (London: Routledge).

Dunn, John (1989) *Modern Revolutions*, 2nd edn (Cambridge: Cambridge University Press).

Dunn, Peter M. (1987) 'On Strategy Revisited', in L.E. Grinter and P.M. Dunn (eds), *The American War in Vietnam: Lessons, Legacies and Implications for Future Conflicts* (New York: Greenwood).

Edelman, Bernard (ed.) (1985) *Dear America: Letters Home from Vietnam* (New York: Pocket Books).

Edwards, Peter (2003) 'The Strategic Concerns of a Regional Power: Australia's Involvement in the Vietnam War', in A.W. Daum, L.C. Gardner and W. Mausbach (eds), *America, the Vietnam War, and the World* (Cambridge: Cambridge University Press).

Eggleston, Noel C. (1987) 'On Lessons', in L.E. Grinter and P.M. Dunn (eds), *The American War in Vietnam: Lessons, Legacies and Implications for Future Conflicts* (New York: Greenwood).

Ehrart, William D. (1995) *Busted: A Vietnam Veteran in Nixon's America* (Amherst: University of Massachusetts Press).

Eisenhower, Dwight D. (1965) *The White House Years: Volume 2* (Garden City, NY: Doubleday).

Elegant, Robert (1981) 'How to Lose a War: Reflections of a Foreign Correspondent', *Encounters*, 57: 73–90.

Elliott, David W.P. (1993) 'Hanoi's Strategy in the Second Indochina War', in J.S. Werner and L.D. Huynh (eds), *The Vietnam War: American and Vietnamese Perspectives* (Armonk, NY: Sharpe).

Elliott, David W. P. (2003) *The Vietnamese War and Social Change in the Mekong Delta, 1930–1975, Volumes 1 and 2* (Armonk, NY: Sharpe).

Elliott, David W.P. (2007) *The Vietnamese War and Social Change in the Mekong Delta, 1930–1975* (concise edn) (Armonk, NY: Sharpe).

Elliott, David W.P. (2008) 'Official History, Revisionist History, and Wild History', in M.P. Bradley and M.B. Young (eds), *Making Sense of the Vietnam Wars: Local, National, and Transnational Perspectives* (Oxford: Oxford University Press).

Elliott, Duong Van Mai (1999) *The Sacred Willow: Four Generations in the Life of a Vietnamese Family* (New York: Oxford University Press).

Ellis, Sylvia (1998) '"A Demonstration of British Good Sense?" British Student Protest during the Vietnam War', in G.J. DeGroot (ed.), *Student Protest: The Sixties and After* (London: Longman).

Ellis, Sylvia (2005) *Britain, America and the Vietnam War* (Westport: Praeger).

Ellison, James (2007) *The United States, Britain and the Transatlantic Crisis: Responding to the Gaullist Challenge* (Basingstoke: Palgrave Macmillan).

Ellsberg, Daniel (2002) *Secrets: A Memoir of Vietnam and the Pentagon Papers* (New York: Viking).

Errington, Elizabeth J. and B.J.C. McKercher (eds) (1998) *The Vietnam War as History* (Westport: Praeger).

Fisher, Ross A., John N. Moore and Robert F. Turner (eds) (2006) *To Oppose Any Foe: The Legacy of US Intervention in Vietnam* (Durham, NC: Carolina Academic Press).

Fitzgerald, Frances (1972) *Fire in the Lake: The Vietnamese and the Americans in Vietnam* (London: Macmillan).

Ford, Ronnie E. (1995) *Understanding the Surprise* (London: Cass).

Foreign Relations of the United States (FRUS) (Washington, DC: US Government Printing Office).

Foyle, Douglas C. (1999) *Counting the Public In: Presidents, Public Opinion, and Foreign Policy* (New York: Columbia University Press).

Franck, Thomas M. and Edward Weisband (1979) *Foreign Policy by Congress* (New York: Oxford University Press).

Frankum, Ronald B. (2005) *Like Rolling Thunder: The Air War in Vietnam, 1964–1975* (Lanham, MD: Rowman & Littlefield).

Frankum, Ronald B. (2007) 'Vietnam During the Rule of Ngo Dinh Diem', in D.L. Anderson and J. Ernst (eds), *The War That Never Ends: New Perspectives on the Vietnam War* (Lexington: University Press of Kentucky)

Freedman, Lawrence (2000) *Kennedy's Wars: Berlin, Cuba, Laos, and Vietnam* (New York: Oxford University Press).

Fromkin, David and James Chace (1985) 'What are the Lessons of Vietnam?', *Foreign Affairs*, 63: 722–46.

Frost, David (2007) *Frost/Nixon* (London: Pan).

Fry, Joseph A. (2006) *Debating Vietnam: Fulbright, Stennis, and their Senate Hearings* (Lanham, MD: Rowman & Littlefield).

Frye, Alton and John Sullivan (1976) 'Congress and Vietnam: The Fruits of Anguish', in Anthony Lake (ed.) (1976) *The Vietnam Legacy* (New York: New York University Press).

Fulbright, J. William (1966) *The Arrogance of Power* (NewYork: Random House).

Gaddis, John L. (2007) *The Cold War* (London: Penguin).

Gaiduk, Ilya V. (1996) *The Soviet Union and the Vietnam War* (Chicago: Dee).

Gaiduk, Ilya V. (1997) 'Turnabout? The Soviet Policy Dilemmas on the Vietnam Conflict', in L.C. Gardner and T. Gittinger (eds), *Vietnam: The Early Decisions* (Austin: University of Texas Press).

Gaiduk, Ilya V. (1998) 'Developing an Alliance: The Soviet Union and Vietnam, 1954–75', in P. Lowe (ed.), *The Vietnam War* (Basingstoke: Macmillan).

Gaiduk, Ilya V. (2000) 'Soviet Policy towards US Participation in the Vietnam War', in W.L. Hixson (ed.), *Leadership and Diplomacy in the Vietnam War* (New York: Garland).

Gaiduk, Ilya V. (2005) *Confronting Vietnam: Soviet Policy towards the Indochina Conflict* (Washington, DC: Woodrow Wilson Center).

Galbraith J. K. (1969) *Ambassador's Journal* (London: Hamish Hamilton).

Gardner, Lloyd C. (1988) *Approaching Vietnam: From World War II Through Dienbienphu* (New York: Norton).

Gardner, Lloyd C. (1995) *Pay Any Price: Lyndon Johnson and the Wars for Vietnam* (Chicago: Dee).

Gardner, Lloyd C. (2000) 'Fighting Vietnam: The Russian-American Conundrum', in L.C. Gardner and T. Gittinger (eds), *International Perspectives on Vietnam* (College Station: Texas A and M University Press).

Gardner, Lloyd C. (2003) 'Vietnam: Many Wars', in A.W. Daum, L.C. Gardner and W. Mausbach (eds), *America, the Vietnam War, and the World* (Cambridge: Cambridge University Press).

Gardner, Lloyd C. and Ted Gittinger (eds) (1997) *Vietnam: The Early Decisions* (Austin: University of Texas Press).

Gardner, Lloyd C. and Ted Gittinger (eds) (2000) *International Perspectives on Vietnam* (College Station: Texas A and M University Press).

Gardner, Lloyd C. and Ted Gittinger (eds) (2004) *The Search for Peace in Vietnam, 1964–1968* (College Station: Texas A and M University Press).

Garfinkle, Adam (1997) *Telltale Hearts: The Origins and Impact of the Vietnam Antiwar Movement* (Basingstoke: Macmillan).

Garment, Leonard (1997) *Crazy Rhythm: From Brooklyn Jazz to Nixon's White House, Watergate, and Beyond* (New York: Da Capo).

Garson, Robert A. (1997) 'Lyndon B. Johnson and the China Enigma', *Journal of Contemporary History*, 32: 63–88.

Garthoff, Raymond L. (1994) *Detente and Confrontation: American Soviet relations from Nixon to Reagan* (Washington, DC: Brookings Institution).

Garver, John (1996) 'The Tet Offensive and Sino-Vietnamese Relations', in M.J. Gilbert and W. Head (eds), *The Tet Offensive* (Westport, CT: Praeger).

Gelb, Leslie H. and Richard K. Betts (1979) *The Irony of Vietnam: The System Worked* (Washington, DC: Brookings Institution).

Geyer, David C. and Douglas E. Selvage (eds) (2007) *Soviet–American Relations: The Détente Years, 1969–1972* (Washington, DC: US Government Printing Office).

Gibbons, William Conrad (1984) *The US Government and the Vietnam War: Executive and Legislative Roles and Relationships, Parts 1 and 2* (Washington, DC: US Government Printing Office).

Gibney, Frank (1998) 'Pacific Ties: The United States of America and an Emerging "Pacific Community"?', in A. McGrew and C. Brook (eds), *The Asia-Pacific in the New World Order* (London: Routledge).

Gibson, Dawn-Marie (2009) 'Muhammad Ali and the Nation of Islam', *American Studies Today*, 18: 22–9.

Gibson, James W. (1986) *The Perfect War: Technowar in Vietnam* (Boston: Monthly Press).

Giglio, James N. (1991) *The Presidency of John F. Kennedy* (Lawrence: University Press of Kansas).

Gilbert, Marc J. (ed.) (2001) *The Vietnam War on Campus: Other Voices, More Distant Drums* (Westport: Praeger).

Gilbert, Marc J. (2002a) 'The Cost of Losing the Other War', in M.J. Gilbert (ed.), *Why the North Won the Vietnam War* (New York: Palgrave Macmillan).

Gilbert, Marc J. (ed.) (2002b) *Why the North Won the Vietnam War* (New York: Palgrave Macmillan).

Gilbert, Marc J. and William Head (eds) (1996) *The Tet Offensive* (Westport, CT: Praeger).

Gitlin, Todd (1989) *The Sixties: Years of Hope, Days of Rage* (New York: Bantam).

Gitlin, Todd (1994) 'Foreword', in T. Wells, *The War Within: America's Battle over Vietnam* (Berkeley: University of California Press).

Glad, Betty (2009) *An Outsider in the White House: Jimmy Carter, his Advisors, and the Making of American Foreign Policy* (Ithaca: Cornell University Press).

Goh, Evelyn (2005) 'Nixon, Kissinger, and the "Soviet Card" in the US Opening to China', *Diplomatic History*, 26, 475–502.

Goldstein, Gordon M. (2008) *Lessons in Disaster: McGeorge Bundy and the Path to War in Vietnam* (New York: Times Books).

Goodman, Allan E. (1986) *The Search for a Negotiated Settlement of the Vietnam War* (Berkeley: Institute of East Asian Studies).

Gordon, William A. (1990) *Four Days in May: Killings and Coverups at Kent State* (Buffalo: Prometheus).

Goulden, Joseph C. (1969) *Truth is the First Casualty: The Gulf of Tonkin Affair – Illusion and Reality* (Chicago: Rand McNally).

Grant, Zalin (1991) *Facing the Phoenix: The CIA and the Political Defeat of the United States in Vietnam* (New York: Norton).

Greene, Graham (2004) *The Quiet American* (London: Penguin).

Greiner, Bernd (2010) *War Without Fronts: The USA in Vietnam* (London: Vintage Books).

Griffith, Robert (ed.) (1984) *Ike's Letters to a Friend, 1941–1958* (Lawrence: University Press of Kansas).

Grinter, Lawrence E. and Peter M. Dunn (eds) (1987) *The American War in Vietnam: Lessons, Legacies and Implications for Future Conflicts* (New York: Greenwood).

Guardian, The (2001) 'US Embassy Cables: Vietnam Picks its New Leaders' (http://www.gurdian.co.uk/world/us-embassy-cables-documents/224371/print: accessed 6 June 2011).

Haass, Richard N. (1994) *Intervention: The Use of American Military Force in the Post-Cold War World* (Washington, DC: Carnegie Institute).

Hackworth, David H. and Julie Sherman (1989) *About Face: The Odyssey of an American Warrior* (New York: Simon & Schuster).

Hagopian, Patrick (2009) *The Vietnam War in American Memory: Veterans, Memorials, and the Politics of Healing* (Amherst: University of Massachusetts Press).

Haig, Alexander M. (1984) *Caveat* (London: Weidenfeld & Nicolson).

Halberstam, David (1965) *The Making of a Quagmire* (New York: Random House).

Halberstam, David (1972) *The Best and the Brightest* (New York: Random House).

Halberstam, David (1979) *The Powers That Be* (New York: Knopf).

Haldeman, H. R. (1978) *The Ends of Power* (New York: Times Books).

Haldeman, H. R. (1994) *The Haldeman Diaries: Inside the Nixon White House* (New York: Putnam's Sons).

Hall, Simon (2003) 'The Response of the Moderate Wing of the Civil Rights Movement to the War in Vietnam', *Historical Journal*, 46: 669–701.

Hall, Simon (2011) *American Patriotism, American Protest: Social Movements since the Sixties* (Philadelphia: University of Pennsylvania Press).

Halliday, Fred (1983) *The Making of the Second Cold War* (London: Verso).

Halliday, Fred (1994) *Rethinking International Relations* (Basingstoke, Macmillan).

Hallin, Daniel C. (1986) *The 'Uncensored War': The Media and Vietnam* (New York: Oxford University Press).

Halstead, Fred (1978) *Out Now!* (New York: Monad Press).

Ham, Paul (2008) *Vietnam: The Australian War* (Sydney: HarperCollins).

Hamilton-Merritt, Jane (1993) *Tragic Mountains: The Hmong, Americans and the Secret Wars in Laos, 1942–1992* (Bloomington: Indiana University Press).

Hammer, Ellen J. (1987) *A Death in November: America in Vietnam, 1963* (New York: Dutton).

Hammond, William (1998) *Reporting Vietnam: Media and Military at War* (Lawrence: University Press of Kansas).

Haney, Patrick J. (1997) *Organizing for Foreign Policy Crises* (Ann Arbor: University of Michigan Press).

Hanhimaki, Jussi M. (2004) *The Flawed Architect: Henry Kissinger and American Foreign Policy* (New York: Oxford University Press).

Hanhimaki, Jussi M. (2008) 'An Elusive Grand Design', in F. Logevall and A. Preston (eds), *Nixon in the World: American Foreign Relations, 1969–1977* (Oxford: Oxford University Press).

Hanhimaki, Jussi M. and Odd Arne Westad (eds) (2004) *The Cold War: A History in Documents and Eyewitness Accounts* (Oxford: Oxford University Press).

Hannah, Norman B. (1987) *The Key to Failure: Laos and the Vietnam War* (Lanham, MD: Madison Books).

Harris, Louis (1973) *The Anguish of Change* (New York: Norton).

Harrison, Benjamin T. and Christopher L. Mosher (2011) 'The Secret Diary of McNamara's Dove: The Long-Lost Story of John McNaughton's Opposition to the Vietnam War', *Diplomatic History*, 35: 505–34.

Harrison, James P. (1989) *The Endless War: Vietnam's Struggle for Independence* (New York: Columbia University Press).

Hatcher, Patrick L. (1990) *The Suicide of an Elite: American Internationalists and Vietnam* (Stanford: Stanford University Press).

Hayden, Tom (1988) *Reunion: A Memoir* (London: Hamish Hamilton).

Hayden, Tom (2008) *Writings for a Democratic Society* (San Francisco: City Lights).

Hayslip, Le Ly (with Jay Wurts) (1989) *When Heaven and Earth Changed Places* (New York: Plume).

Head, William and Lawrence Grinter (eds) (1993) *Looking Back on the Vietnam War: A 1990s Perspective on the Decisions, Combat, and Legacies* (Westport, CT: Praeger).

Hearndon, Patrick J. (ed.) (1990) *Vietnam: Four American Perspectives* (West Lafayette: Purdue University Press).

Heineman, Kenneth J. (1993) *Campus Wars: The Peace Movement at American State Universities in the Vietnam Era* (New York: New York University Press).

Heineman, Kenneth J. (2001) *Put Your Bodies Upon the Wheels: Student Revolt in the 1960s* (Chicago: Dee).

Herr, Michael (1979) *Dispatches* (London: Picador).

Herring, George C. (1990) '"Peoples Quite Apart": Americans, South Vietnamese, and the War in Vietnam', *Diplomatic History*, 14: 1–23.

Herring, George C. (ed.) (1994) *The Secret Diplomacy of the Vietnam War* (Austin: University of Texas Press).

Herring, George C. (1995) *LBJ and Vietnam: A Different Kind of War* (Austin: University of Texas Press).

Herring, George C. (1996 and 2001) *America's Longest War: The United States and Vietnam, 1950–1975* (New York: McGraw Hill).

Herring, George C. (2002) 'Fighting Without Allies', in M.J. Gilbert (ed.), *Why the North Won the Vietnam War* (New York: Palgrave Macmillan).

Herring, George C. (2004) 'The Cold War and Vietnam', *OAH Magazine of History*, 18: 18–21.

Hersh, Seymour (1997) *The Dark Side of Camelot* (Boston: Little, Brown).

Hershberg, James G. and Chen Jian (2005) 'Reading and Warning the Likely Enemy: China's Signals to the United States about Vietnam', *International History Review*, 27: 47–84.

Hess, Gary R. (1987) *The United States' Emergence as a Southeast Asian Power, 1940–1950* (New York: Columbia University Press).

Hess, Gary R. (2009) *Vietnam: Explaining America's Lost War* (Oxford: Blackwell).

Heymann, C. David (1999) *RFK: A Candid Biography of Bobby Kennedy* (London: Arrow).

Hiam, Michael C. (2006) *Who the Hell are We Fighting? The Story of Sam Adams and the Vietnam Intelligence Wars* (South Royalton, VT: Steerforth).

Hilsman, Roger (1967) *To Move a Nation: The Politics of Foreign Policy in the Administration of John F. Kennedy* (Garden City, NY: Doubleday).

Hitchens, Christopher (2010) *Hitch 22: A Memoir* (New York: Twelve).

Hixson, W. L. (ed.) (2000) *Leadership and Diplomacy in the Vietnam War* (New York: Garland).

Ho Chi Minh (1973) *Ho Chi Minh; Selected Writings* (Hanoi: Foreign Languages Publishing).

Ho Tai, Hue-Tam (1992) *Radicalism and the Origins of the Vietnamese Revolution* (Cambridge, MA: Harvard University Press).

Hoff, Joan (1994) *Nixon Reconsidered* (New York: Basic Books).

Hogan, Michael J. (ed.) (1992) *The End of the Cold War* (Cambridge: Cambridge University Press).

Hoopes, Townsend (1969) *The Limits of Intervention* (New York: McKay).

Horn, Gerd-Rainer (2007) *The Spirit of '68: Rebellion in Western Europe and North America* (Oxford: Oxford University Press).

Humphrey, David C. (1984a) 'Tuesday Lunch at the Johnson White House', *Diplomatic History*, 8: 81–101.

Humphrey, Hubert H. (1984b) *The Education of a Public Man* (Garden City, NY: Doubleday).

Hung, Nguyen Tien and Jerrold T. Schecter (1986) *The Palace File* (New York: HarperCollins).

Hunt, David (2009) *Vietnam's Southern Revolution: From Peasant Insurrection to Total War, 1958–1968* (Amherst: University of Massachusetts Press).

Hunt, Michael H. (1996) *Lyndon Johnson's War: America's Cold War Crusade in Vietnam, 1945–1968* (New York: Hill & Wang).

Hunt, Michael H. (ed.) (2010) *A Vietnam War Reader: American and Vietnamese Perspectives* (London: Penguin).

Hunt, Richard A. (1995) *Pacification: The American Struggle for Vietnam's Hearts and Minds* (Boulder: Westview).

Huong, Duong Thu (1995) *Novel Without a Name* (London: Picador).

Hurst, Steven (1996) *The Carter Administration and Vietnam* (New York: St Martin's).

Isaacs, Arnold (1983) *Without Honor: Defeat in Vietnam and Cambodia* (Baltimore: Johns Hopkins University Press).

Isserman, Maurice and Michael Kazin (2008) *America Divided: The Civil War of the 1960s* (New York: Oxford University Press).

Jacobs, Seth (2004) *America's Miracle Man in Vietnam: Ngo Dinh Diem, Religion, Race, and US Intervention in Southeast Asia, 1950–1957* (Durham, NC: Duke University Press).

Jacobs, Seth (2006) *Cold War Mandarin: Ngo Dinh Diem and the Origins of America's War in Vietnam, 1950–1963* (Lanham, MD: Rowman & Littlefield).

Jacobson, Marc A. (1996) 'President Johnson's Decision to Curtail Rolling Thunder', in M.J. Gilbert and W. Head (eds), *The Tet Offensive* (Westport, CT: Praeger).

Janis, Irving (1982) *Groupthink: Psychological Studies of Policy Decisions and Fiascoes* (Boston: Houghton Mifflin).

Jeffreys-Jones, Rhodri (1999) *Peace Now! American Society and the Ending of the War in Vietnam* (New Haven: Yale University Press).

Jeffreys-Jones, Rhodri (2007) *The FBI: A History* (New Haven: Yale University Press).

Jennings, Phillip (2010) *The Politically Incorrect Guide to the Vietnam War* (Washington, DC: Regnery).

Jensen, Joan M. (1991) *Army Surveillance in America, 1750–1980* (New Haven: Yale University Press).

Jentleson, Bruce W. (1992) 'The Pretty Prudent Public: Post-Vietnam American Opinion on the Use of Military Force', *International Studies Quarterly*, 36: 49–74.

Jervis, Robert (1996) 'Perception, Misperception, and the End of the Cold War', in W.C. Wohlforth (ed.), *Witnesses to the End of the Cold War* (Baltimore: Johns Hopkins University Press).

Jesperson, T. Christopher (2002) 'Kissinger, Ford, and Congress: The Very Bitter End in Vietnam', *Pacific Historical Review*, 71: 439–73.

Joczek, David M. (2001) *The Battle of Ap Bac, Vietnam* (Westport: Greenwood).

Joes, Anthony J. (1989) *The War for South Vietnam, 1954–1975* (New York: Praeger).

Johns, Andrew L. (2006) 'Doves Among Hawks: Republican Opposition to the Vietnam War', *Peace and Change*, 31: 585–628.

Johns, Andrew L. (2010) *Vietnam's Second Front: Domestic Politics, the Republican Party, and the Vietnam War* (Lexington: University Press of Kentucky).

Johnson, Lady Bird (1970) *A White House Diary* (New York: Holt, Rinehart & Winston).

Johnson, Lyndon B. (1971) *The Vantage Point* (New York: Holt, Rinehart & Winston).

Johnson, Robert D. (2003) 'The Progressive Dissent: Ernest Gruening and Vietnam', in R.B. Woods (ed.), *Vietnam and the American Political Tradition* (Cambridge: Cambridge University Press).

Jones, Howard (2003) *Death of a Generation: How the Assassinations of Diem and JFK Prolonged the Vietnam War* (New York: Oxford University Press).

Kahin, George M. (1986) *Intervention: How America Became Involved in Vietnam* (New York: Knopf).

Kaiser, David (2000) *Kennedy, Johnson and the Origins of the Vietnam War* (Cambridge, MA: Harvard University Press).

Karnow, Stanley (1983) *Vietnam: A History* (New York: Viking).

Kattenburg, Paul (1980) *The Vietnam Trauma in American Foreign Policy* (New Brunswick: Transaction).

Kaufman, Scott (2008) *Plans Unraveled: The Foreign Policy of the Carter Administration* (DeKalb: Northern Illinois University Press).

Kearns, Doris (1976) *Lyndon Johnson and the American Dream* (New York: Harper & Row).

Kennedy, Paul (1989) *The Rise and Fall of the Great Powers: Economic Change and Military Conflict from 1500 to 2000* (London: Fontana).

Kerkvliet, Benedict J. (2005) *The Power of Everyday Politics: How Vietnamese Peasants Transformed National Policy* (Ithaca: Cornell University Press).

Kilcullen, David J. (2010) *Counterinsurgency* (London: Hurst).

Kimball, Jeffrey (1998) *Nixon's Vietnam War* (Lawrence: University Press of Kansas).

Kimball, Jeffrey (2004) *The Vietnam War Files: Uncovering the Secret History of the Nixon-Era Strategy* (Lawrence: University Press of Kansas).

Kinney, Katherine (2000) *Friendly Fire: American Images of the Vietnam War* (New York: Oxford University Press).

Kislenko, Arne (2003) 'Bamboo in the Shadows: Relations between the United States and Thailand during the Vietnam War', in A.W. Daum, L.C. Gardner and W. Mausbach (eds), *America, the Vietnam War, and the World* (Cambridge: Cambridge University Press).

Kissinger, Henry (1979) *White House Years* (Boston: Little, Brown).

Kissinger, Henry (1983) *Years of Upheaval* (Boston: Little, Brown).

Kissinger, Henry (1994) *Diplomacy* (New York: Simon & Schuster).

Kissinger, Henry (2003) *Ending the Vietnam War: A History of America's Involvement in and Extrication from the Vietnam War* (New York: Simon & Schuster).

Klimke, Martin (2010) *The Other Alliance: Student Protest in West Germany and the United States in the Global Sixties* (Princeton: Princeton University Press).

Kolko, Gabriel (1987) *Anatomy of a War: Vietnam, the United States, and the Modern Historical Experience* (London: Unwin Hyman).

Komer, Robert W. (1986) *Bureaucracy at War* (Boulder: Westview).

Kraslow, David and Stuart H. Loory (1968) *The Secret Search for Peace in Vietnam* (New York: Random House).

Kraushaar, Wolfgang (2010) 'Hitler's Children? The German 1968 Movement in the Shadow of the Nazi Past', in I. Cornils and S. Waters (eds), *Memories of 1968: International Perspectives* (Oxford: Lang).

Krepinevich, Andrew (1986) *The Army and Vietnam* (Baltimore: Johns Hopkins University Press).

Krulak, Victor H. (1984) *First to Fight: An Inside View of the US Marine Corps* (Annapolis: US Naval Institute).

Kuzmarov, Jeremy (2009) *The Myth of the Addicted Army: Vietnam and the Modern War on Drugs* (Amherst: University of Massachusetts Press).

Ky, Nguyen Cao (2002) *Buddha's Child: My Fight to Save Vietnam* (New York: St Martin's).

LaFeber, Walter (1992) 'An End to *Which* Cold War?', in M.J. Hogan (ed.), *The End of the Cold War* (Cambridge: Cambridge University Press).

LaFeber, Walter (2007) 'The United States and Vietnam: The Enemies', in D.L. Anderson and J. Ernst (eds), *The War That Never Ends: New Perspectives on the Vietnam War* (Lexington: University Press of Kentucky).

Lake, Anthony (ed.) (1976) *The Vietnam Legacy* (New York: New York University Press).

Lansdale, Edward G. (1964) 'Viet Nam: Do We Understand Revolution?', *Foreign Affairs*, 43: 75–87.

Lansdale, Edward G. (1968) 'Viet Nam: Still the Search for Goals', *Foreign Affairs*, 68: 92–8.

Lansdale, Edward G. (1972) *In the Midst of War: America's Mission to Southeast Asia* (New York: Harper & Row).

Lansdale, Edward G. (1978) 'Thoughts about a Past War', in Allan R. Millet (ed.), *A Short History of the Vietnam War* (Bloomington: Indiana University Press).

Larres, Klaus and Kenneth Osgood (eds) (2006) *The Cold War after Stalin's Death: A Missed Opportunity for Peace?* (Lanham, MD: Rowman & Littlefield).

Larsen, Stanley R. and James L. Collins (1975) *Allied Participation in Vietnam* (Washington, DC: Department of the Army).

Latimer, Thomas K. (1967) 'Hanoi's Leaders and the Politics of War' (available via Texas Tech University Virtual Vietnam Archive, www.vietnam.ttu.edu: John Donnell collection, 07201118002).

Laurence, John (2002) *The Cat From Hue: A Vietnam War Story* (New York: PublicAffairs).

Lawrence, Mark A. (2007) *Assuming the Burden: Europe and the American Commitment to the War in Vietnam* (Berkeley: University of California Press).

Lawrence, Mark A. (2008a) 'Explaining the Early Decisions', in M.P. Bradley and M.B. Young (eds), *Making Sense of the Vietnam Wars: Local, National, and Transnational Perspectives* (Oxford: Oxford University Press).

Lawrence, Mark A. (2008b) *The Vietnam War: A Concise International History* (Oxford: Oxford University Press).

Lawrence, Mark A. and Frederik Logevall (eds) (2007) *The First Vietnam War: Colonial Conflicts and Cold War Crisis* (Cambridge, MA: Harvard University Press).

Le Duan (1967) 'The Same Historical Chain: Forward under the Glorious Banner of the October Revolution' (available via Texas Tech University Virtual Vietnam Archive, www.vietnam.ttu.edu: item 3150101008).

Le Duan (1970) *Selected Writings* (Hanoi: available via Texas Tech University Virtual Vietnam Archive, www.vietnam.ttu.edu).

Le Duan (1975) 'To Build a Large Scale Socialist Agriculture', *Journal of Contemporary Asia*, 5: 235–44.

Le Duan (1986) *Letters to the South* (Hanoi: Foreign Languages Publishing).

Lederer, William and Eugene Burdick (1957) *The Ugly American* (New York: Fawcett).

Leffler, Melvyn P. (1992) *A Preponderance of Power: National Security, the Truman Administration, and the Cold War* (Stanford: Stanford University Press).

Leffler, Melvyn P. and Odd Arne Westad (eds) (2010) *The Cambridge History of the Cold War: Volume 3: Endings* (Cambridge: Cambridge University Press).

Lembcke, Jerry (2010) *Hanoi Jane: War, Sex, and Fantasies of Betrayal* (Amherst: University of Massachusetts Press).

Lepre, George (2011) *Fragging: Why US Soldiers Assaulted their Officers in Vietnam* (Lubbock: Texas Tech University Press).

Lerner, Mitchell B. (2003) *The 'Pueblo' Incident: A Spy Ship and the Failure of American Foreign Policy* (Lawrence: University Press of Kansas).

Lewy, Guenter (1978) *America in Vietnam* (Oxford: Oxford University Press).

Lieberman, Robbie (2000) *The Strangest Dream: Communism, Anticommunism, and the US Peace Movement, 1945–1963* (Syracuse, NY: Syracuse University Press).

Lind, Michael (1999) *Vietnam: The Necessary War* (New York: Touchstone).

Lipset, Seymour M. and Richard B. Dobson (1972) 'The Intellectual as Critic and Rebel', *Daedelus,* 1: 138–51.

Lockhart, Greg (1989) *Nation in Arms: The Origins of the People's Army of Vietnam* (London: Allen & Unwin).

Lock-Pullan, Richard (2003) '"An Inward Looking Time": The US Army 1973–1976', *Journal of Military History*, 67: 483–511.

Lock-Pullan, Richard (2008) 'US Military Strategy, Strategic Culture and the "War on Terror"', in J.E. Owens and J. Dumbrell (eds), *America's "War on Terrorism": New Dimensions in US Government and National Security* (Lanham, MD: Rowman & Littlefield).

Lodge, Henry Cabot (1973) *The Storm Has Many Eyes: A Personal Narrative* (New York: Norton).

Logevall, Frederik (1998) 'Vietnam and the Question of What Might Have Been', in M.J. White (ed.), *Kennedy: The New Frontier Revisited* (New York: New York University Press).

Logevall, Frederik (1999) *Choosing War: The Lost Chance for Peace and the Escalation of the War in Vietnam* (Berkeley: University of California Press).

Logevall, Frederik (2001) *The Origins of the Vietnam War* (Harlow: Pearson).

Logevall, Frederik and Andrew Preston (eds) (2008) *Nixon in the World: American Foreign Relations, 1969–1977* (Oxford: Oxford University Press).

Lomperis, Timothy J. (1996) *From People's War to People's Rule: Insurgency, Intervention, and the Lessons of Vietnam* (London: University of North Carolina Press).

Long, Ngo Vinh (1996) 'The Tet Offensive and its Aftermath', in M.J. Gilbert and W. Head (eds), *The Tet Offensive* (Westport, CT: Praeger).

Long, Ngo Vinh (1998) 'South Vietnam', in P. Lowe (ed.), *The Vietnam War* (Basingstoke: Macmillan).

Longley, Kyle (2008) *Grunts: The American Combat Soldier in Vietnam* (Armonk, NY: Sharpe).

Lowe, Peter (ed.) (1998) *The Vietnam War* (Basingstoke: Macmillan).

Lumbers, Michael (2008) *Piercing the Bamboo Curtain: Tentative Bridge-Building to China during the Johnson Years* (Manchester: Manchester University Press).

Lunch, William and Peter Sperlich (1979) 'American Public Opinion and the War in Vietnam', *Western Political Quarterly*, 32: 221–53.

Luong, Hy V. (2003) *Postwar Vietnam: Dynamics of a Transforming Society* (Lanham, MD: Rowman & Littlefield).

Luthi, Lorenz M. (2009) 'Beyond Betrayal: Beijing, Moscow, and the Paris Negotiations, 1971–73', *Journal of Cold War Studies*, 11: 57–107.

Luu Doan Huynh (2007a) 'The Perspective of a Vietnamese Witness', in D.L. Anderson and J. Ernst (eds), *The War That Never Ends: New Perspectives on the Vietnam War* (Lexington: University Press of Kentucky).

Luu Doan Huynh (2007b) Interview: Hanoi Interview Project, Annenberg School for Communications, University of Southern California (http://vietnaminterviewsusc.org/?page_id=2).

Luu Van Loi (2000) *Fifty Years of Vietnamese Diplomacy, 1945–1995: Volume One, 1945–75* (Hanoi: Gioi Publishers).

Luu Van Loi (2007) Interview: Hanoi Interview Project, Annenberg School for Communications, University of Southern California (available via http://vietnaminterviewsusc.org/?p=33).

Luu Van Loi and Nguyen Anh Vu (1996) *Le Duc Tho-Kissinger Negotiations in Paris* (Hanoi: Foreign Languages Publishing).

Lynch, Allen (1992) *The Cold War is Over – Again* (Boulder: Westview).

Mackerras, Colin (1998) 'From Imperialism to the End of the Cold War', in A. McGrew and C. Brook (eds), *The Asia-Pacific in the New World Order* (London: Routledge).

MacMillan, Margaret (2007) *Nixon and China: The Week that Changed the World* (New York: Random House).

MacMillan, Margaret (2008) 'Nixon, Kissinger, and the Opening to China', in F. Logevall and A. Preston (eds), *Nixon in the World: American Foreign Relations, 1969–1977* (Oxford: Oxford University Press).

MacPherson, Myra (1984) *Long Time Passing: Vietnam and the Haunted Generation* (Bloomington: Indiana University Press).

Mahnken, Thomas G. (2008) *Technology and the American Way of War* (New York: Columbia University Press).

Mailer, Norman (1968) *The Armies of the Night* (New York: Signet).

Malkasian, Carter (2004) 'Toward a Better Understanding of Attrition: The Korean and Vietnam Wars', *Journal of Military History*, 68: 911–42.

Maneli, Mieczyslaw (1971) *War of the Vanquished* (New York: Harper & Row).

Marcuse, Herbert (1964) *One Dimensional Man* (New York: Beacon).

Mark, Chi-Kwan (2012) *China and the World since 1945* (London: Routledge).

Marlantes, Karl (2010) *Matterhorn* (London: Corvus).

Martin, Garret (2011) 'The 1967 Withdrawal from NATO – A Cornerstone of De Gaulle's Grand Strategy?', *Journal of Transatlantic Studies*, 9: 232–43.

Mattson, Kevin (2002) *Intellectuals in Action: The Origins of the New Left and Radical Liberalism, 1945–1970* (University Park: Pennsylvania State University Press).

McAdam, Doug (1988) *Freedom Summer* (New York: Oxford University Press).

McAdam, Doug and Yang Su (2002) 'The War at Home: Antiwar Protests and Congressional Voting, 1965 to 1973', *American Sociological Review*, 67: 696–721.

McAllister, James (2010/11) 'Who Lost Vietnam? Soldiers, Civilians, and US Military Strategy', *International Security*, 35: 95–123.

McCann, Michael A. (2006) 'A War Worth Fighting', in R.A. Fisher, J.N. Moore and R.F. Turner (eds), *To Oppose Any Foe: The Legacy of US Intervention in Vietnam* (Durham, NC: Carolina Academic Press).

McCargo, Duncan (ed.) (2004) *Rethinking Vietnam* (London: RoutledgeCurzon).

McCarthy, Eugene (1967) *The Limits of Power: America's Role in the World* (New York: Holt).

McCarthy, Eugene (1987) *Up 'Til Now* (San Diego: Harcourt, Brace, Jovanovich).

McEvoy-Levy, Siobhan (2001) *American Exceptionalism and US Foreign Policy: Public Diplomacy at the End of the Cold War* (Basingstoke: Palgrave Macmillan).

McGibbon, Ian (2010) *New Zealand's Vietnam War: A History of Combat, Commitment and Controversy* (Auckland: Exisle Publishing).

McGovern, George (1992) 'Foreword', in M. Small and W.D. Hoover (eds), *Give Peace a Chance* (Syracuse: Syracuse University Press).

McGrew, Anthony and Christopher Brook (eds) (1998) *The Asia-Pacific in the New World Order* (London: Routledge).

McMahon, Robert J. (1993) 'Truman and the Roots of US Involvement in Indochina, 1945–1953, in D.L. Anderson (ed.), *Shadow on the White House: Presidents and the Vietnam War, 1945–1975* (Lawrence: University Press of Kansas).

McMahon, Robert J. (2000) 'What Difference did it Make? Assessing the Vietnam War's Impact on Southeast Asia', in L.C. Gardner and T. Gittinger (eds), *International Perspectives on Vietnam* (College Station: Texas A and M University Press).

McMahon, Robert J. (2002) 'Contested Memory: The Vietnam War and American Society', *Diplomatic History*, 26: 159–68.

McMahon, Robert J. (2003) *Major Problems in the History of the Vietnam War* (New York: Wadsworth).

McMaster, H.R. (1997) *Dereliction of Duty: Lyndon Johnson, Robert McNamara, the Joint Chiefs of Staff and the Lies that Led to Vietnam* (New York: Harper Collins).

McNamara, Robert S. (1995) *In Retrospect: The Tragedy and Lessons of Vietnam* (New York: Times Books).

McNamara, Robert S., James Blight and Robert K. Brigham (1999) *Argument Without End: In Search of Answers to the Vietnam Tragedy* (Washington, DC: PublicAffairs Press).

McNeill, Ian (1984) *The Team: Australian Army Advisers in Vietnam, 1962–1972* (St Lucia: University of Queensland Press).

Milam, Ron (2009) *Not a Gentleman's War: An Inside View of Junior Officers in the Vietnam War* (Chapel Hill: University of North Carolina Press).

Miller, Edward and Tuong Vu (2009) 'The Vietnam War as a Vietnamese War: Agency and Society in the Study of the Second Indochinese War', *Journal of Vietnamese Studies*, 4: 1–16.

Miller, James (1994) *Democracy is in the Streets: From Port Huron to the Siege of Chicago* (Cambridge, MA: Harvard University Press).

Miller, Merle (1980) *Lyndon, An Oral Biography* (New York: Ballantine Books).

Mills, C. Wright (1956) *The Power Elite* (New York: Oxford University Press, republished 2000).

Milne, David (2008) *America's Rasputin: Walt Rostow and the Vietnam War* (New York: Hill & Wang).

Moise, Edwin E. (1996) *Tonkin Gulf and the Escalation of the Vietnam War* (Chapel Hill: University of North Carolina Press).

Moise, Edwin E. (2002) 'JFK and the Myth of Withdrawal', in Marilyn B. Young and Robert Buzzanco (eds), *A Companion to the Vietnam War* (Malden, MA: Blackwell).

Montesano, Michael J. (2011) '*War Comes to Long An*, the Classic We Hardly Know?', *Journal of Vietnamese Studies*, 6: 87–122.

Moore, Harold G. (1992) *We Were Soldiers Once ... and Young* (New York: Harper Perennial).

Moore, Harold G. and Joseph Galloway (2009) *We Are Soldiers Still: A Journey Back to the Battlefields of Vietnam* (New York: Harper Perennial).

Morgan, Iwan (2002) *Nixon* (London: Arnold).

Moser, Richard R. (1996) *New Winter Soldiers: GI and Veteran Dissent during the Vietnam War* (New Brunswick: Rutgers University Press).

Moyar, Mark (1997) *Phoenix and the Birds of Prey: The CIA's Secret Campaign to Destroy the Viet Cong* (Annapolis: Naval Institute Press).

Moyar, Mark (2006) *Triumph Forsaken: The Vietnam War, 1954–1965* (Cambridge: Cambridge University Press).

Moyar, Mark (2009) *A Question of Command: Counterinsurgency from the Civil War to Iraq* (New Haven: Yale University Press).

Mueller, John (1984) 'Reflections on the Vietnam Antiwar Movement and the Curious Calm at the War's End', in P. Braestrup (ed.), *Vietnam as History* (Washington, DC: Woodrow Wilson Center).

Mueller, John E. (1973) *War, Presidents, and Public Opinion* (New York: Wiley).

Mulcahy, Kevin V. (1995) 'Rethinking Groupthink: Walt Rostow and the National Security Advisory Process in the Johnson Administration', *Presidential Studies Quarterly*, 25: 237–50.

Nagl, John A. (2005) *Learning to Eat Soup with a Knife: Counterinsurgency Lessons from Malaya and Vietnam* (Chicago: University of Chicago Press).

Nashel, Jonathan (2005) *Edward Lansdale's Cold War* (Amherst: University of Massachusetts Press).

Neese, Harvey and John O'Donnell (2001) 'Conclusion', in H. Neese and J. O'Donnell (eds), *Prelude to Tragedy: Vietnam, 1960–1965* (Annapolis: Naval Institute Press).

Neese, Harvey and John O'Donnell (eds) (2001) *Prelude to Tragedy: Vietnam, 1960–1965* (Annapolis: Naval Institute Press).

Newman, John M. (1992) *JFK and Vietnam: Deception, Intrigue, and the Struggle for Power* (New York: Warner Books).

Newman, John M. (1997) 'The Kennedy and Johnson Transition: The Case for Policy Reversal', in L.C. Gardner and T. Gittinger (eds), *Vietnam: The Early Decisions* (Austin: University of Texas Press).

Ngo Quang Truong (1980) *The Easter Offensive of 1972* (Washington, DC: US Army Center of Military History).

Nguyen Duy Nien (2004) *Ho Chi Minh Thought on Diplomacy* (Hanoi: Gioi Publishers).

Nguyen, Lien-Hang T. (2006) 'The War Politburo: North Vietnam's Diplomatic and Political Road to the Tet Offensive', *Journal of Vietnamese Studies*, 1: 4–58.

Nguyen, Lien-Hang T. (2008a) 'Cold War Contradictions: Toward An International History of The Second Indochina War, 1969–1973', in M.P. Bradley and M.B. Young (eds), *Making Sense of the Vietnam Wars: Local, National, and Transnational Perspectives* (Oxford: Oxford University Press).

Nguyen, Lien-Hang T. (2008b) 'Waging War on All Fronts', in F. Logevall and A. Preston (eds), *Nixon in the World: American Foreign Relations, 1969–1977* (Oxford: Oxford University Press).

Nicosia, Gerald (2001) *Home to War: A History of the Vietnam Veterans' Movement* (New York: Carroll-Graf).

Nitze, Paul H. (1989) *From Hiroshima to Glasnost* (London: Weidenfeld & Nicolson).

Nixon, Richard M. (1967) 'Asia after Vietnam', *Foreign Affairs*, 67: 119–28.

Nixon, Richard M. (1978) *RN: The Memoirs of Richard Nixon* (London: Arrow).

Nixon, Richard M. (1982) *Leaders* (New York: Warner).

Nixon, Richard M. (1985) *No More Vietnams* (New York: Arbor House).

Nolting, Frederick (1988) *From Trust to Tragedy: The Political Memoirs of Frederick Nolting, Kennedy's Ambassador to Diem's Vietnam* (New York: Praeger).

NSA (National Security Archive) (2003) 'JFK and the Diem Coup' (available via http://www.gwu.edu/~nsarchiv/NSAEBB/NSAEBB101/index.htm).

NSA (National Security Archive) (2005) 'Tonkin Gulf Intelligence "Skewed" According to Official History and Intercepts' (available via http://www.gwu.edu/~nsarchiv/NSAEBB/NSAEBB132/press20051201. htm).

NSA (National Security Archive) (2008) 'The Mouse that Roared' (available via http://www.gwu.edu/~nsarchiv/NSAEBB/NSAEBB121/prados.htm).

NSA (National Security Archive) (2009a) 'Kennedy Considered Supporting Coup in South Vietnam, August 1963' (available via http://www.gwu. edu/~nsarchiv/NSAEBB/NSAEBB302/index.htm).

NSA (National Security Archive) (2009b) 'The CIA's Vietnam Histories' (available via http://www.gwu.edu/~nsarchiv/NSAEBB/ NSAEBB284 /index.htm).

Nuti, Leopoldo (2003) 'The Center-Left Government in Italy and the Escalation of the Vietnam War', in A.W. Daum, L.C. Gardner and W. Mausbach (eds), *America, the Vietnam War, and the World* (Cambridge: Cambridge University Press).

O'Brien, Tim (1978) *Going After Cacciato* (New York: Delacorte).

O'Brien, Tim (1991) *The Things They Carried* (London: Flamingo).

O'Donnell, Kenneth P. (1970) *Johnny We Hardly Knew Ye* (Boston: Little, Brown).

Oberdorfer, Dan (1971) *Tet! The Turning Point of the Vietnam War* (New York: Doubleday).

OH (Office of the Historian) (2010a) US Department of State, 'The American Experience in Southeast Asia, 1946–1975: The View from Hanoi' (available via http://history.state.gov/conferences/2010-southeast-asia).

OH (Office of the Historian) (2010b) US Department of State, 'The Battle for Hearts and Minds' (available via http://history.state.gov/conferences/2010-southeast-asia).

OH (Office of the Historian) (2010c) US Department of State, 'Media Roundtable' (available via http://history.state.gov/conferences/2010-southeast-asia).

OH (Office of the Historian) (2010d) US Department of State, 'With Friends like These' (available via http://history.state.gov/conferences/2010-southeast-asia).

OH (Office of the Historian) (2010e) US Department of State, 'Address by Henry Kissinger' (available via http://history.state.gov/conferences/2010-southeast-asia).

OH (Office of the Historian) (2010f) US Department of State, 'Keynote Address by Ambassador Richard C. Holbrooke' (available via http://history.state.gov/conferences/2010-southeast-asia).

Oglesby, Carl (2008) *Ravens in the Storm: A Personal History of the 1960s Anti-War Movement* (New York: Scribner).

Oliver, Kendrick (2004a) 'Towards a New Moral History of the Vietnam War', *Historical Journal*, 47: 757–74.

Oliver, Kendrick (2004b) *The My Lai Massacre in American History and Memory* (Manchester: Manchester University Press).

Olsen, Mari (2006) 'Forging a New Relationship: The Soviet Union and Vietnam, 1955', in P. Roberts (ed.), *Behind the Bamboo Curtain: China, Vietnam, and the World Beyond Asia* (Stanford: Stanford University Press).

Olson, James S. and Randy Roberts (2004) *Where the Domino Fell: America and Vietnam, 1945–2004* (Maplecrest, NY: Brandywine Press).

Osgood, Kenneth and Andrew K. Frank (eds) (2010) *Selling War in a Media Age: The Presidency and Public Opinion in the American Century* (Gainesville: University of Florida Press).

Osgood, Robert E. (1984) 'Vietnam: Implications and Import', in P. Braestrup (ed.), *Vietnam as History* (Washington, DC: Woodrow Wilson Center).

Owens, John E. and John Dumbrell (eds) (2008) *America's "War on Terrorism": New Dimensions in US Government and National Security* (Lanham, MD: Rowman & Littlefield).

Pach, Chester J. (2010) 'We Need to Get a Better Story to the American People: LBJ, the Progress Campaign, and the Vietnam War on Television', in K. Osgood and A.K. Frank (eds), *Selling War in a Media Age: The Presidency and Public Opinion in the American Century* (Gainesville: University of Florida Press).

Palmer, Bruce (1984) *The 25 Year War: America's Military Role in Vietnam* (Lexington: Da Capo).

Palmer, David R. (1978) *Summons of the Trumpet* (Novato, CA: Presidio).

Pape, Robert A. (1996) *Bombing to Win: Air Power and Coercion in War* (Ithaca, NY: Cornell University Press).

Paterson, Thomas (ed.) (1989) *Kennedy's Quest for Victory* (New York: Oxford University Press).

Patti, Archimedes (1980) *Why Vietnam? Prelude to America's Albatross* (Berkeley: University of California Press).

Perlstein, Rick (2008) *Nixonland: The Rise of a President and the Fracturing of America* (New York: Scribner).

Peterson, Michael E. (1989) *The Combined Action Platoons: The US Marines' Other War in Vietnam* (Westport, CT: Praeger).

Pham Quang Minh (2010) 'The Meaning of *The Complete Collection of Party Documents*', *Journal of Vietnamese Studies*, 5: 208–18.

Pham, Andrew X. (trans.) (2007) *Last Night I Dreamed of Peace: The Diary of Dang Thuy Tram* (New York: Harmony).

Phillips, Rufus (2001) 'Before We Lost in South Vietnam', in H. Neese and J. O'Donnell (eds), *Prelude to Tragedy: Vietnam, 1960–1965* (Annapolis: Naval Institute Press).

Phillips, Rufus (2008) *Why Vietnam Matters: An Eyewitness Account of Lessons Not Learned* (Annapolis: Naval Institute Press).

Pike, Francis (2011) *Empires at War: A Short History of Modern Asia since World War II* (London: I. B. Tauris).

Pilger, John (1989) *Heroes* (London: Pan).

Podhoretz, Norman (1982) *Why We Were in Vietnam* (New York: Simon & Schuster).

Ponting, Clive (1990) *Breach of Promise: Labour in Power 1964–1970* (London: Penguin).

Porter, Gareth (1975) *A Peace Denied: The United States, Vietnam, and the Paris Agreement* (Bloomington: Indiana University Press).

Porter, Gareth (1993) *Vietnam: The Politics of Bureaucratic Socialism* (Ithaca: Cornell University Press).

Porter, Gareth (2005) *Perils of Dominance: Imbalance of Power and the Road to War in Vietnam* (Berkeley: University of California Press).

Porter, Gareth (2008) 'Explaining the Vietnam War: Dominant and Contending Paradigms', in M.P. Bradley and M.B. Young (eds), *Making Sense of the Vietnam Wars: Local, National, and Transnational Perspectives* (Oxford: Oxford University Press).

PP (*Pentagon Papers*) (1971/72) *The Defense Department History of United States Decisionmaking on Vietnam,* 5 vols (Gravel edn) (Boston: Beacon Press).

PPPUS (*Public Papers of the Presidents of the United States*) (Washington, DC: US Government Printing Office).

Prados, John (1995) *The Hidden History of the Vietnam War* (Chicago: Dee).

Prados, John (1999) *The Blood Road: The Ho Chi Minh Trail and the Vietnam War* (New York: Wiley).

Prados, John (2002) 'The Veterans' Antiwar Movement in Fact and Memory', in M.B. Young and R. Buzzanco (eds), *A Companion to the Vietnam War* (Malden, MA: Blackwell).

Prados, John (2009a) *Vietnam: The History of an Unwinnable War, 1945–1975* (Lawrence: University Press of Kansas).

Prados, John (2009b) *William Colby and the CIA: The Secret Wars of a Controversial Spymaster* (Lawrence: University Press of Kansas).

Preston, Andrew (2003) 'Balancing War and Peace: Canadian Foreign Policy and the Vietnam War, 1961–1965', *Diplomatic History*, 27: 73–81.

Preston, Andrew (2006) *The War Council: McGeorge Bundy, the NSC, and Vietnam* (Cambridge, MA: Harvard University Press).

Pribbenow, Merle L. (2002) 'Translator's Preface' to *Victory in Vietnam.*

Pribbenow, Merle L. (2008) 'General Vo Nguyen Giap and the Mysterious Evolution of the Plan for the 1968 Tet Offensive', *Journal of Vietnamese Studies*, 2: 1–33.

Quinn-Judge, Sophie (2003) *Ho Chi Minh: The Missing Years, 1919–1941* (London: Hurst).

Quinn-Judge, Sophie (2004) 'Rethinking the History of the Vietnamese Communist Party', in D. McCargo (ed.), *Rethinking Vietnam* (London: RoutledgeCurzon).

Quinn-Judge, Sophie (2008) 'Through a Glass Darkly: Reading the History of the Vietnamese Communist Party, 1945–1975', in M.P. Bradley and M.B. Young (eds), *Making Sense of the Vietnam Wars: Local, National, and Transnational Perspectives* (Oxford: Oxford University Press).

Rabe, Stephen G. (2010) *John F. Kennedy: World Leader* (Washington, DC: Potomac Books).

Race, Jeffrey (1972) *War Comes to Long An: Revolutionary Conflict in a Vietnamese Province* (Berkeley: University of California Press).

Race, Jeffrey (2010) *War Comes to Long An: Revolutionary Conflict in a Vietnamese Province* (expanded edn) (Berkeley: University of California Press).

Radchenko, Sergey (2009) *Two Suns in the Heavens: The Sino-Soviet Struggle for Supremacy, 1962–1967* (Stanford: Stanford University Press).

Radosh, Ronald (2001) *Commies: A Journey Through the Old Left, the New Left, and the Leftover Left* (San Francisco: Encounter).

Randolph, Stephen P. (2007) *Powerful and Brutal Weapons: Nixon, Kissinger, and the Easter Offensive* (London: Harvard University Press).

Record, Jeffrey (1998) *The Wrong War: Why We Lost in Vietnam* (Annapolis: Naval Institute Press).

Record, Jeffrey (2002) 'How America's Own Military Performance in Vietnam Aided and Abetted the "North's" Victory', in M.J. Gilbert (ed.), *Why the North Won the Vietnam War* (New York: Palgrave Macmillan).

Reedy, George (1982) *Lyndon B. Johnson: A Memoir* (New York: Andrew & McNeel).

Reeves, Richard (2001) *President Nixon: Alone in the White House* (New York: Simon & Schuster).

Rinzler, Carole E. (1969) *Frankly McCarthy* (Washington, DC: Public Affairs Press).

Roberts, Priscilla (ed.) (2006) *Behind the Bamboo Curtain: China, Vietnam, and the World Beyond Asia* (Stanford: Stanford University Press).

Ross, Douglas A. (1984) *In the Interests of Peace: Canada and Vietnam, 1954–1973* (Toronto: University of Toronto Press).

Rossinow, Doug (1998) *The Politics of Authenticity: Liberalism, Christianity, and the New Left in America* (New York: Columbia University Press).

Rostow, Walt W. (1953) *The Dynamics of Soviet Society* (London: Secker & Warburg).

Rostow, Walt W. (1958) 'The American National Style', *Daedalus*, 87, 110–44.

Rostow, Walt W. (1995) 'The Case for the War', *Times Literary Supplement* (9 June).

Rostow, Walt W. (1996) 'Vietnam and Asia', *Diplomatic History*, 20: 467–72.

Rotter, Andrew J. (1987) *The Path to Vietnam: Origins of the American Commitment to Southeast Asia* (Ithaca, NY: Cornell University Press).

Rotter, Andrew J. (2007) 'Chronicle of a War Foretold', in M.A. Lawrence and F. Logevall (eds), *The First Vietnam War: Colonial Conflicts and Cold War Crisis* (Cambridge MA: Harvard University Press).

Ruane, Kevin (ed.) (2000) *The Vietnam Wars* (Manchester: Manchester University Press).

Rusk, Dean (1990) *As I Saw It* (New York: Norton).

Rust, William J. (1985) *Kennedy in Vietnam* (New York: Scribners).

Sagan, Scott D. and Jeremi Suri (2003) 'The Madman Nuclear Alert: Secrecy, Signaling, and Safety in October 1973', *International Security*, 27: 150–83.

Sallah, Michael and Mitch Weiss (2006) *Tiger Force* (New York: Little, Brown).

Sandbrook, Dominic (2004) *Eugene McCarthy: The Rise and Fall of Postwar American Liberalism* (New York: Knopf).

Sandbrook, Dominic (2008) 'Salesmanship and Substance: The Influence of Domestic Policy and Watergate', in F. Logevall and A. Preston (eds), *Nixon in the World: American Foreign Relations, 1969–1977* (Oxford: Oxford University Press).

Saull, Richard (2001) *Rethinking Theory and History in the Cold War* (London: Cass).

Scanlon, Sandra (2009) 'The Conservative Lobby and Nixon's "Peace with Honor" in Vietnam', *Journal of American Studies*, 43: 255–76.

Schaffer, Howard B. (2003) *Ellsworth Bunker: Global Troubleshooter, Vietnam Hawk* (Chapel Hill: University of North Carolina Press).

Schaller, Michael (2010) 'Japan and the Cold War, 1960–1991', in M.P. Leffler and O.A. Westad (eds), *The Cambridge History of the Cold War: Volume 3: Endings* (Cambridge: Cambridge University Press).

Schandler, Herbert Y. (1977) *The Unmaking of a President: Lyndon Johnson and Vietnam* (Princeton: Princeton University Press).

Schandler, Herbert Y. (2009) *America in Vietnam: The War That Couldn't Be Won* (Lanham, MD: Rowman & Littlefield).

Schell, Jonathan (1989) *Observing the Nixon Years* (New York: Vintage).

Schelling, Thomas C. (1966) *Arms and Influence* (New Haven: Yale University Press).

Schlesinger, Arthur Jr (1978) *Robert Kennedy and His Times* (London: Deutsch).

Schlesinger, Arthur Jr (2008) *Journals, 1952–2000* (London: Atlantic Books).

Schmitz, David F. (1996) 'Senator Frank Church, the Ford Administration and the Challenges of Post-Vietnam Foreign Policy', *Peace and Change*, 21: 438–63.

Schmitz, David F. (2005) *The Tet Offensive: Politics, War, and Public Opinion* (Lanham, MD: Rowman & Littlefield).

Schmitz, David F. and Natalie Fousekis (1994) 'Frank Church, the Senate, and the Emergence of Dissent on the Vietnam War', *Pacific Historical Review*, 63: 561–81.

Schulzinger, Robert D. (1997) *A Time for War: The United States and Vietnam, 1941–1975* (New York: Oxford University Press).

Schulzinger, Robert D. (2006) *A Time for Peace: The Legacy of the Vietnam War* (Oxford: Oxford University Press).

Schwartz, Thomas A. (2003) *Lyndon Johnson and Europe: In the Shadow of Vietnam* (Cambridge, MA: Harvard University Press).

Selverstone, Marc J. (2009) *Constructing the Monolith: The United States, Great Britain, and International Communism* (Cambridge, MA: Harvard University Press).

Seventy-Five Years of the Communist Party of Viet Nam, 1930–2005: A Selection of Documents from Nine Party Congresses (2005) (Hanoi: Gioi Publishers).

Sewell, Mike (2002) *The Cold War* (Cambridge: Cambridge University Press).

Shapley, Deborah (1992) *Promise and Power: The Life and Times of Robert McNamara* (Boston: Little, Brown).

Sharp, U.S.G. (1978) *Strategy for Defeat: Vietnam in Retrospect* (Novato, CA: Presidio).

Shaw, John M. (2005) *The Cambodian Campaign: The 1970 Offensive and America's Vietnam War* (Lawrence: University Press of Kansas).

Shawcross, William (1979) *Sideshow: Nixon, Kissinger, and the Destruction of Cambodia* (New York: Pocket Books).

Sheehan, Neil (1988) *A Bright Shining Lie: John Paul Vann and America in Vietnam*, 2nd edn 1990 (London: Picador).

Shesol, Jeff (1997) *Mutual Contempt* (New York: Norton).

Short, Anthony (1989) *The Origins of the Vietnam War* (London: Longman).

Short, Anthony (1998) 'Origins and Alternatives: Comments, Counter-Facts and Commitments', in P. Lowe (ed.), *The Vietnam War* (Basingstoke: Macmillan).

Shultz, Richard H. (1999) *The Secret War Against Hanoi: Kennedy's and Johnson's Use of Spies, Saboteurs, and Covert Warriors in North Vietnam* (New York: Perennial).

Shulzinger, Robert D. (2008) 'The End of the Vietnam War, 1973–1976', in F. Logevall and A. Preston (eds), *Nixon in the World: American Foreign Relations, 1969–1977* (Oxford: Oxford University Press).

Simpson, Bradley R. (2008) *Economists with Guns: Authoritarian Development and US–Indonesian Relations, 1960–1968* (Stanford: Stanford University Press).

Sinclair, Barbara (1982) *Congressional Realignment* (Austin: University of Texas Press).

Siniver, Asaf (2008) *Nixon, Kissinger, and US Foreign Policy Making: The Machinery of Crisis* (Cambridge: Cambridge University Press).

Small, Melvin (1988) *Johnson, Nixon, and the Doves* (New Brunswick: Rutgers University Press).

Small, Melvin (1994) *Covering Dissent: The Media and the Anti-Vietnam War Movement* (New Brunswick: Rutgers University Press).

Small, Melvin (1996) *Democracy and Diplomacy: The Impact of Domestic Politics on US Foreign Policy* (Baltimore: Johns Hopkins University Press).

Small, Melvin (2004) *Antiwarriors: The Vietnam War and the Battle for America's Hearts and Minds* (Lanham, MD: SR Books).

Small, Melvin (2005) *At The Water's Edge: American Politics and the Vietnam War* (Chicago: Dee).

Small, Melvin and William D. Hoover (eds) (1992) *Give Peace a Chance* (Syracuse: Syracuse University Press).

Smith, R.B. (1985) *An International History of the Vietnam War*, 2 vols (London: Macmillan).

Smith, T.O. (2007) *Britain and the Origins of the Vietnam War: UK Policy in Indo-China, 1943–50* (Basingstoke: Palgrave Macmillan).

Smith, Winnie (1992) *Daughter Goes to War* (London: Warner Books).

Snepp, Frank (1977) *Decent Interval: An Insider's Account of Saigon's Indecent End* (New York: Random House).

Sorley, Lewis (1992) *Thunderbolt: General Creighton Abrams and the Army of His Time* (New York: Simon & Schuster).

Sorley, Lewis (1999) *A Better War: The Unexamined Victories and Final Tragedy of America's Last Years in Vietnam* (New York: Harcourt Brace).

Spector, Ronald H. (1983) *Advice and Support: The Early Years, 1941–1960* (New York: Free Press).

Spector, Ronald H. (1993) *After Tet: The Bloodiest Year in Vietnam* (New York: Free Press).

Stanton, Shelby L. (1985a) *Green Berets at War: US Army Special Forces in Southeast Asia, 1956–1975* (London: Arms & Armour Press).

Stanton, Shelby L. (1985b) *The Rise and Fall of an American Army: US Ground Forces in Vietnam, 1965–1973* (New York: Dell).

Statler, Kathryn C. (2006) 'Building a Colony: South Vietnam and the Eisenhower Administration', in K.C. Statler and A.L. Johns (eds), *The Eisenhower Administration, the Third World, and the Globalization of the Cold War* (Lanham, MD: Rowman & Littlefield).

Statler, Kathryn C. (2007) *Replacing France: The Origins of American Intervention in Vietnam* (Lexington: University of Kentucky Press).

Statler, Kathryn C. (2008) Book Review, *Diplomatic History*, 32: 153.

Statler, Kathryn C. and Andrew L. Johns (eds) (2006) *The Eisenhower Administration, the Third World, and the Globalization of the Cold War* (Lanham, MD: Rowman & Littlefield).

Steigerwald, David (1995) *The Sixties and the End of Modern America* (New York: St Martin's).

Steinbrook, Gordon L. (1995) *Allies and Mates: An American Soldier with Australians and New Zealanders in Vietnam, 1966–67* (Lincoln: University of Nebraska Press).

Stennis, John C and J. William Fulbright (1971) *The Role of Congress in Foreign Policy* (Washington, DC: American Enterprise Institute).

Stolberg, Eva M. (2003) 'Peoples' Warfare versus Peaceful Coexistence: Vietnam and the Sino-Soviet Struggle for Ideological Supremacy', in A.W. Daum, L.C. Gardner and W. Mausbach (eds), *America, the Vietnam War, and the World* (Cambridge: Cambridge University Press).

Stone, Gary (2007) *Elites for Peace: The Senate and the Vietnam War, 1964–1968* (Knoxville: University of Tennessee Press).

Sullivan, Patricia (2005) 'General Commanded Troops in Vietnam', *Washington Post*, 19 July.

Summers, Harry G. (1982) *On Strategy: A Critical Analysis of the Vietnam War* (Novato, CA: Presidio).

Summers, Harry G. (1985) *The Vietnam War Almanac* (New York: Ballantine Books).

Suri, Jeremi (2008) 'Henry Kissinger and American Grand Strategy', in F. Logevall and A. Preston (eds), *Nixon in the World: American Foreign Relations, 1969–1977* (Oxford: Oxford University Press).

Sutter, Robert G. (2008) *Chinese Foreign Relations: Power and Policy since the Cold War* (Lanham, MD: Rowman & Littlefield).

Szoke, Zoltan (2010) 'Delusion or Reality? Secret Hungarian Diplomacy during the Vietnam War', *Journal of Cold War Studies*, 4: 119–80.

Tarling, Nicholas (ed.) (1999) *The Cambridge History of Southeast Asia: Volume IV* (Cambridge: Cambridge University Press).

Taylor, Keith W. (1983) *The Birth of Vietnam* (Berkeley: University of California Press).

Taylor, Mark (2003) *The Vietnam War in History, Literature and Film* (Edinburgh: Edinburgh University Press).

Taylor, Maxwell D. (1972) *Swords and Ploughshares* (New York: Norton).

Taylor, Sandra C. (1998) 'Laos: The Escalation of A Secret War', in E.J. Errington and B.J.C. McKercher (eds), *The Vietnam War as History* (Westport: Praeger).

Thayer, Carlyle A. (1989) *War by Other Means: National Liberation and Revolution in Vietnam* (Sydney: Allen & Unwin).

The Truth about Sino-Vietnamese Relations in the Past 30 Years (1979) (Hanoi: Foreign Languages Publishing House).

Thompson, Kenneth W. (ed.) (1985) *The Kennedy Presidency: Intimate Perspectives* (Lanham, MD: University Press of America).

Tilford, Earl H. (1993) *Crosswinds: The Air Force's Setup in Vietnam* (College Station: Texas A and M University Press).

Toal, Gerard (2008) 'The Hamiltonian Nationalist: A Conversation with Michael Lind', *Geopolitics*, 13: 169–80.

Toczek, David M. (2001) *The Battle of Ap Bac, Vietnam* (Westport: Greenwood Press).

Tomes, Robert F. (1998) *Apocalypse Then: American Intellectuals and the Vietnam War, 1954–1975* (New York: New York University Press).

Tonnesson, Stein (2007) 'Franklin Roosevelt, Trusteeship, and Indochina', in M.A. Lawrence and F. Logevall (eds), *The First Vietnam War: Colonial Conflicts and Cold War Crisis* (Cambridge, MA: Harvard University Press).

Tonnesson, Stein (2010) *Vietnam 1946: How the War Began* (Berkeley: University of California Press).

Tran Van Don (1978) *Our Endless War: Inside Vietnam* (Novato, CA: Presidio).

Tran Van Tra (1982) *Vietnam: History of the Bulwark B-2 Theatre* (Hanoi: National Technical Information Service).

Tran Van Tra (1993) 'Tet: The 1968 General Offensive', in J.S. Werner and L.D. Huynh (eds), *The Vietnam War: American and Vietnamese Perspectives* (Armonk, NY: Sharpe).

Trullinger, James W. (1980) *Village at War* (New York: Prentice-Hall).

Truong Nhu Tang (1986) *A Vietcong Memoir: An Inside Account of the Vietnam War and its Aftermath* (London: Cape).

TTU (Texas Tech University) (2000a) Interview with William Badger (available via www.vietnam.ttu.edu/oralhistory/interviews).

TTU (Texas Tech University) (2000b) Interview with David Martin (available via www.vietnam.ttu.edu/oralhistory/interviews).

TTU (Texas Tech University) (2005) Interview with John Gary Morris (available via www.vietnam.ttu.edu/oralhistory/interviews).

Tuchman, Barbara (1985) *The March of Folly: from Troy to Vietnam* (New York: Ballantine Books).

Tuck, Stephen (2010) *We Ain't What We Ought To Be: The Black Freedom Struggle from Emancipation to Obama* (Cambridge, MA: Harvard University Press).

Turley, William S. (1986) *The Second Indochina War* (Boulder: Westview).

Turnbull, C. M. (1999) 'Regionalism and Nationalism', in N. Tarling (ed.), *The Cambridge History of Southeast Asia: Volume IV* (Cambridge: Cambridge University Press).

Turner, Kathleen (1985) *Lyndon Johnson's Dual War* (Chicago: University of Chicago Press).

Van Atta, Dale (2008) *With Honor: Melvin Laird in War, Peace, and Politics* (Madison: University of Wisconsin Press).

Van Tien Dung (1977) *Our Great Spring Victory* (New York: Monthly Review Press).

VanDeMark, Brian (1991) *Into the Quagmire: Lyndon Johnson and the Escalation of the Vietnam War* (New York: Oxford University Press).

Vandiver, Frank E. (1997) *Shadows of Vietnam: Lyndon Johnson's Wars* (College Station: Texas A and M University Press).

Vucetic, Srdjan (2011) *The Anglosphere: A Genealogy of a Racialized Identity in International Relations* (Stanford: Stanford University Press).

VV (*Victory in Vietnam: The Official History of the People's Army of Vietnam, 1954–1975*) (2002) (trans.) Merle L. Pribbenow (Lawrence: University Press of Kansas).

Walt, Lewis W. (1969) *Strange War: A General's Report on Vietnam* (New York: Funk & Wagnalls).

Walton, C. Dale (2002) *The Myth of the Inevitable US Defeat in Vietnam* (London: Cass).

Wang Hui (2011) *The End of the Revolution: China and the Limits of Modernity* (London: Verso).

Warner, Michael (2010) 'US Intelligence and Vietnam: The Official Version(s)', *Intelligence and National Security*, 25: 611–37.

Weigley, Russell F. (1984) *History of the United States Army* (Bloomington: Indiana University Press).

Wells, Tom (1994) *The War Within: America's Battle over Vietnam* (Berkeley: University of California Press).

Werner, Jayne S. and Luu Doan Huynh (eds) (1993) *The Vietnam War: American and Vietnamese Perspectives* (Armonk, NY: Sharpe).

Wernicke, Gunter (2003) 'The World Peace Council and the Antiwar Movement in East Germany', in A.W. Daum, L.C. Gardner and W. Mausbach (eds), *America, the Vietnam War, and the World* (Cambridge: Cambridge University Press).

Westad, Odd Arne (2007) *The Global Cold War* (Cambridge: Cambridge University Press).

Westad, Odd Arne, Chen Jian, Stein Tonnesson, Nguyen Vu Tung and James G. Hershberg (eds) (1998) *77 Conversations Between Chinese and Foreign Leaders on the Wars in Indochina, 1964–1977* (Washington, DC: Woodrow Wilson Center).

Westheider, James E. (2008) *The African American Experience in Vietnam: Brothers in Arms* (Lanham, MD: Rowman & Littlefield).

Westmoreland, William C. (1980) *A Soldier Reports* (New York: Dell).

Wheeler, Stephen G. (2001) 'Hell No We Won't Go Y'all: Southern Student Opposition to the Vietnam War', in M.J. Gilbert (ed.), *The Vietnam War on Campus: Other Voices, More Distant Drums* (Westport: Praeger).

White, Mark J. (2007) *Against the President* (Chicago: Dee).

White, Mark J. (ed.) (1998) *Kennedy: The New Frontier Revisited* (New York: New York University Press).

Whitlock, Craig (2010) 'Obama Restores Rank of Disgraced General', CBS news (available via www.cbsnews: accessed 30 March 2011).

Wiest, Andrew (2007) *Vietnam's Forgotten Army: Heroism and Betrayal in the ARVN* (New York: New York University Press).

Wikileaks (2011) 'Le Duan: The Mostly Unvarnished Truth' (available via http://dazzlepond.com.cable/07HANOI110/: accessed 6 June 2011).

Willbanks, James H. (2004) *Abandoning Vietnam: How America Left and South Vietnam Lost its War* (Lawrence: University Press of Kansas).

Willbanks, James H. (2007) *The Tet Offensive* (New York: Columbia University Press).

Williams, Shirley (2009) *Climbing the Bookshelves* (London: Virago).

Windrow, Martin (2004) *The Last Valley: Dien Bien Phu and the French Defeat in Vietnam* (New York: Da Capo).

Winters, Francis X. (1997) *The Year of the Hare: America in Vietnam, January 25, 1963 – February 15, 1964* (Athens: University of Georgia Press).

Wintle, Justin (1992) *Romancing Vietnam: Inside the Boat Country* (London: Penguin).

Wirtz, James J. (1991) *The Tet Offensive: Intelligence Failure in War* (Ithaca: Cornell University Press).

Wohlforth, William C. (1993) *The Elusive Balance: Power and Perceptions During the Cold War* (Ithaca: Cornell University Press).

Wohlforth, William C. (ed.) (1996) *Witnesses to the End of the Cold War* (Baltimore: Johns Hopkins University Press).

Womack, Brantly (2006) *China and Vietnam: The Politics of Asymmetry* (Cambridge: Cambridge University Press).

Woods, Randall B. (2006) *LBJ: Architect of American Ambition* (New York: Free Press).

Woods, Randall B. (ed.) (2003) *Vietnam and the American Political Tradition* (Cambridge: Cambridge University Press).

Wyatt, Clarence R. (1993) *Paper Soldiers: The American Press and the Vietnam War* (New York: Norton).

Yong Mun Cheong (1999) 'The Political Structures of the Independent States', in Nicholas Tarling (ed.), *The Cambridge History of Southeast Asia: Volume IV* (Cambridge: Cambridge University Press).

Young, Marilyn B. (1991) *The Vietnam Wars, 1945–1990* (New York: HarperCollins).

Young, Marilyn B. (2002) 'Ho, Ho, Ho Chi Minh, Ho Chi Minh is Gonna Win', in M.J. Gilbert (ed.), *Why the North Won the Vietnam War* (New York: Palgrave Macmillan).

Young, Marilyn B. and Robert Buzzanco (eds) (2002) *A Companion to the Vietnam War* (Malden, MA: Blackwell).

Zaffiri, Samuel (1994) *Westmoreland* (New York: Morrow).

Zaroulis, Nancy and Gerald Sullivan (1984) *Who Spoke Up? The American Protest Against the War in Vietnam, 1963–1975* (New York: Holt, Rinehart & Winston).

Zhai, Quiang (2000a) 'An Unlikely Relationship: China and the DRV during the Vietnam War', in L.C. Gardner and T. Gittinger (eds), *International Perspectives on Vietnam* (College Station: Texas A and M University Press).

Zhai, Quiang (2000b) *China and the Vietnam Wars, 1950–1975* (Chapel Hill: University of North Carolina Press).

Zhang, Xiaoming (1996) 'The Vietnam War, 1964–1969: A Chinese Perspective', *Journal of Military History*, 60: 731–62.

Zhang, Xiaoming (2000) 'Communist Powers Divided: China, the Soviet Union, and the Vietnam War', in L.C. Gardner and T. Gittinger (eds), *International Perspectives on Vietnam* (College Station: Texas A and M University Press).

Zhang, Xiaoming (2005) 'China's 1979 War with Vietnam: A Reassessment', *China Quarterly*, 166: 851–74.

Zimmerman, Hubert (2003) 'Who Paid for America's War? Vietnam and the International Monetary System, 1960–1975', in A.W. Daum, L.C. Gardner and W. Mausbach (eds), *America, the Vietnam War, and the World* (Cambridge: Cambridge University Press).

Index